HEART
OF
WHITENESS

AFRIKANERS FACE BLACK RULE IN
THE NEW SOUTH AFRICA

JUNE GOODWIN & BEN SCHIFF

SCRIBNER
NEW YORK   LONDON   TORONTO   SYDNEY   TOKYO   SINGAPORE

For Melina Thandiwe Schiff

SCRIBNER
1230 Avenue of the Americas
New York, NY 10020

SCRIBNER and design are trademarks of Simon & Schuster Inc.

Set in Caledonia
DESIGNED BY ERICH HOBBING

Manufactured in the United States of America

1   3   5   7   9   10   8   6   4   2

Library of Congress Cataloging-in-Publication Data
Goodwin, June.
Heart of Whiteness : Afrikaners face Black rule in the New South Africa
/ June Goodwin & Ben Schiff.
p.   cm.
Includes bibliographical references and index.
1. Afrikaners—South Africa—Politics and government. 2. Blacks—South Africa—
Politics and government. 3. South Africa—Race relations. 4. South Africa—
Politics and government—1994– .
I. Schiff, Ben. II. Title.
DT1768.A57G66   1995
305.8'00968—dc20
95-21422
CIP

0-684-81365-3

CONTENTS

CONTENTS

IV. RELIGION

V. THE AFRIKAANS LANGUAGE

VI. POLICE STATE

VII. FACING BLACK RULE

ACKNOWLEDGMENTS

This book belongs to the 125-plus Afrikaners who talked with us in interviews that lasted anywhere from an hour to five hours. From thousands of pages of transcripts we have distilled their words for our readers. In so doing we've left out a lot. For the condensation and interpretations, of course, we are responsible.

We could write an entire chapter about Afrikaners who opened their homes and cupboards to us. Hilda Burnett would top the list, for she invited us to stay for a night in her lovely home in George next to her mountain. We fondly remember sitting on the floor of Marichen Waldner's apartment as she was moving to a new house. In addition to some meals mentioned in our book, we remember many *Lekker eet!* (enjoy eating) injunctions: smoked mackerel with chives and mustard seeds at Kobus van Rooyen's; the awesome railroad-sleeper table loaded with delicious food at Harald and Arletta Pakendorf's; the *biltong* (jerky or dried meat) at Pieter and Gerda Nel's; the star-lit meal at Louwrens and Lily Pretorius's home; a merry *braai* (barbecue) in Phalaborwa with Fritz and Germien Meyer; the lovely dinner at the Bezuidenhouts', with the joshing and jokes; a nice lunch with Jack and Myrtle Botes in Pietersburg; a homey meal at Spore and Yvonne van Rensburg's; a dinner cooked by Piet and Vivienne Botha (with Bob Dylan playing on a video); traditional Boer stew and maroela jam with Attie and Carol van Niekerk; a family meal in the elegant Steynberg home in Phalaborwa; tea served by Willem Kleynhans amid his impressive archives of posters and newspapers and analyses.

Other people have been enormously generous and helpful with their insights. We especially thank Ina and Michael Perlman for opening their home and shepherding us with advice, John and Ann Barnes for guarding our tapes and for friendship, Norah and Edmund Benjamin for lovely teas and support. Sheena Duncan guided us with her usual perspicacity. We are very grateful to John Fenix for his generous translations.

We thank Amy Bell and Kitty Duma for linguistic assistance; Maanda

7

ACKNOWLEDGMENTS

Mulaudzi for his friendship that gives us warmth and perspective; Thenjiwe Mtintso, because she's gutsy and inspiring (and besides, she caused it all in a way, because she lured us to fall in love with South Africa). Tom Karis's analysis of postelection South Africa, "A Small Miracle," which we saw in draft, was very useful; his ebullience and knowledge had a great influence on us. Marq de Villiers was wondrously generous in correcting our Afrikaans and giving us good suggestions, though he did not agree with all our assessments.

Ken and Marty Grundy, "the guys," helped enormously in the manuscript stage, with expertise, words, pasta, and restorative laughter. We also thank Tom Koelble, for astute advice that expanded our thinking and lifted our spirits. Beverly Lieberman is an incisive adviser with superb judgment, as well as a friend and cheering section. Naomi Schiff shared her acumen and flew to our aid at a crucial moment. We thank her and Randall Goodall and Seventeenth Street Studios for their map expertise and artistic advice. Bill Johnston updated us with news clippings, especially on church matters. Ray Louw's *Southern Africa Report* and his prompt assistance on queries were most valuable. Thanks to the Co-op Bookstore gang for help on various searches. Mike MacDonald assisted us from South Africa while pursuing his own research. We thank Bill Goldstein for believing in our project and Nan Graham for carrying it to completion. We thank Gaby Davis for her astute guidance.

Probably few people are visited by their literary agents while in remote parts doing research, but Ellen Levine delighted us by flying into Johannesburg one week, buoying us with her enthusiasm and advice. Her strong support and understanding saved us from craze at several crucial junctures. Without her, the book would have remained a dream.

An Ohio Arts Council grant to June helped make the trip to South Africa possible, and a second one in 1995 helped us finish. Oberlin College's sabbatical system gave Ben needed time off. Thanks to Kathy Knipper, Debbie Santiago, Jill Tvaroha, and Lisa Champe for all their steady caring. We thank our parents for their unfailing support in all our projects.

FOREWORD

Reading this work left me with a mixture of feelings ranging from respect for the courage of those who challenged and defied the upper echelons of Afrikanerdom at the height of the apartheid era to a sense of loss when considering the extent to which the closed sectors of this community had been culturally and spiritually isolated and hence impoverished.

The conflict portrayed in this book is not so much about the injustices committed by certain sectors of Afrikanerdom during the apartheid era, but about the structural violence committed against their outspoken own and the damage to the psyche and cultural cohesion of this community as a whole.

It is a thought-provoking work on the dynamics at work within the Afrikaner community that will provide new insights for the uninformed reader. The informed reader will be reminded of aspects of our past as depicted through the personal perspectives provided by members of this community and will be left with the realization of the urgent need for this community to participate actively in the country's nation-building process.

There is an unabashed directness, an almost unrehearsed, naked confessional tone about some of the interviews. It borders on a quality of embarrassing boastfulness and pride about being different. It surprises, even shocks, as it asserts the obsolete values of a past with an innocence that sometimes begs for contradiction. It provokes ambivalence. The reader wants to embrace and reprove at the same time. I was profoundly disturbed by the book, which reflected what is also an essential component of my identity as a South African.

The South African psyche is such a complex and sometimes convulsed one, and yet it is suddenly transparent and simple. This candid compilation of a broad sector of the Afrikaans community is perhaps an indicator of the enormous challenges that face all South Africans to complete the "political miracle" so beloved to commentators on and of South Africa.

BARBARA MASEKELA,
Ambassador of the Republic of South Africa to France,
Former Head of Staff to President Nelson Mandela

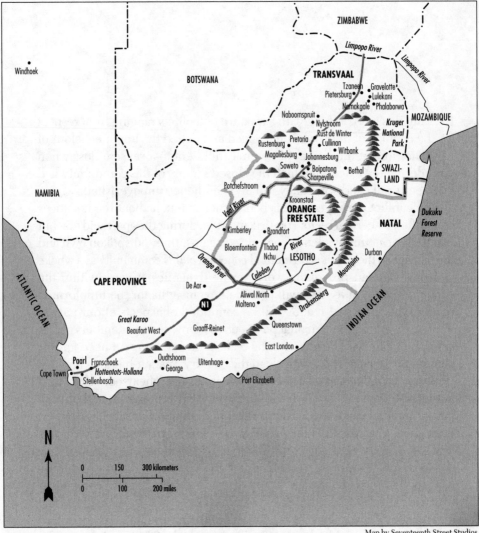

SOUTH AFRICA

INTRODUCTION

On July 15, 1992, we interviewed Johan Heyns, a leader of the Dutch Reformed Church, in his Pretoria home. On November 5, 1994, the Afrikaner churchman's head was blown off by a bullet from a high-caliber rifle as he sat in his living room playing cards with his wife and grandchildren. The bullet, modified to maximize injury, was fired through the window from six yards away. The killer deftly avoided an infrared movement detector outside Heyns's home, and left only bullet fragments as evidence.

For many years Johan Heyns had been one of the Afrikaner elite's powerful voices advocating white superiority and the notion that apartheid, apartness, or keeping nations separate, was the will of God. He helped write the Dutch Reformed Church's 1974 document, *Ras, Volk en Nasie (Race, People and Nation)*, that used the Bible to justify apartheid. By 1986, however, Heyns changed course, leading the church to declare apartheid indefensible on biblical grounds. Heyns's murder indicated that even gradualist reformers in South Africa run lethal risks. The killing pointed to the precarious state of Afrikaner politics, a condition of incipient rebellion rarely reflected in the Western press.

On February 2, 1990, President F. W. de Klerk (whose initials are pronounced "F. Veeh" in Afrikaans) reversed more than four decades of National Party (NP) apartheid policy, announcing in a speech before the South African Parliament the impending release of Nelson Mandela after twenty-seven years in prison and the legalization of the African National Congress (ANC), the South African Communist Party (SACP), and other anti-apartheid organizations. Negotiations between Mandela and de Klerk to move toward a "sharing" of governmental power had already taken place secretly, and after February 2, they continued more publicly.* After elections in April 1994, Mandela was inau-

---

*The negotiations broadened to include other political parties in 1991, broke down at the end of the year, and then restarted in 1992. An interim constitution was adopted in

gurated president of the Republic of South Africa on May 10, heading a "government of national unity" that rules South Africa under a five-year interim constitution. The new two-house Parliament, sitting as a Constitutional Assembly, is to complete a permanent constitution in 1996, and the new constitution is to go into effect with the second round of national elections in 1999.

Although in the West de Klerk is considered heroic for negotiating an end to minority rule (he shared the 1993 Nobel Peace Prize with Mandela), right-wing Afrikaners believe de Klerk completely betrayed the Afrikaner *volk*.* Johan Heyns was de Klerk's counterpart in the church—the press called him "the clerical de Klerk." Both men were leading members of the Afrikaner Broederbond (Brotherhood), the secret, all-male Afrikaner organization founded in 1918 by a few clergymen and civil service clerks to promote Afrikaner nationalism. The press speculated that Heyns was only one target on a hit list of reformers considered traitors by extreme right-wing Afrikaners.† De Klerk would likely be another.

From a distance, de Klerk's 1990 initiative appeared like hope landed on earth. Watching the events from afar, through news media and contacts with people in South Africa, we were enormously optimistic about the changes taking place and curious about why the Afrikaners were making such a radical shift. With F. W.'s 1990 speech to Parliament, the Afrikaner "white tribe" splintered and opened up dramatically. All around, there was a new willingness to air differences in public.

We arrived in Johannesburg at the beginning of February 1992, and stayed for eight months. During that time, Afrikaners were debating with new urgency the nature of the *volk*'s identity and their place in Africa. *Heart of Whiteness* is our effort to portray what we found among

---

September 1993, and South Africa's first nonracial national elections were held April 27–29, 1994. Mandela's ANC emerged victorious, with 62.7 percent of the vote. De Klerk's NP garnered second place with 20.4 percent. The white Conservative Party (CP) boycotted the election and the slightly more moderate Vryheidsfront (Freedom Front) received 572,770, or 2.2 percent, of the total votes.

Volk combines the meanings "people" and "nation" and has mystical connotations. Afrikaners use the word *volk* to invoke their collective identity.

†Because of the Conservative Party boycott of the 1994 election, there is no accurate count of how many Afrikaners oppose the government of national unity, but an indication can be found in that Afrikaners comprised the vast majority of the 875,619 (32 percent of all white voters) who in March 1992 voted against de Klerk's negotiating strategy in an all-white referendum.

the Afrikaners, a people who historically considered themselves the Christian saviors of heathen Africans. We intend our title to evoke Joseph Conrad's great 1902 novel about imperialism, *Heart of Darkness*, one of the most frequently taught works of modern fiction. His title entered the English language as a shorthand way to stereotype Africa as savage, nihilistic, violent, and mysterious. Hot debates continue over whether Conrad was a convinced British colonialist or a critic of Belgian imperialism in the Congo, a racist or an ironist.

Like Conrad's title and his novel, *Heart of Whiteness* is subject to a variety of interpretations. In his novel one of the hero's "darkest" tendencies involves his descent into the supposed degradation of mixed-race sex. Race purity was central to Afrikaner nationalism. Interracial sex not only was taboo but was made illegal. Since the *volk*'s existence as a nation was threatened by the weaknesses of the flesh that led to race mixing and intermarriage, apartheid was required to preserve the *volk* and its holy mission.

One meaning of "heart" is kindness or mercy. For us, the good heart of Afrikanerdom is to be found among those who constituted the compassionate soul of the *volk*, people who through their opposition to apartheid gave their fellow South Africans faith that the Afrikaners are capable of empathetic and moral behavior.

But the heart of a people might also be said to be their basic attitudes, their core motives. At the heart of most of Afrikanerdom, there is no moral transformation. The shift in political course is dictated by pragmatism and the intention to hold on to as much power as possible. Leaders are convinced that they can still control events. Some of them have even turned necessity into a new holy mission, claiming a unique Afrikaner Christian duty to be a "light unto the nations," showing the rest of the world how to create a truly multiracial society. Separatist messianism still beats in the hearts of other Afrikaners, those convinced that the old mission—to bring Christianity to Africa while staying apart from other "nations"—remains the *volk*'s true calling.

During our visit we were most intrigued initially by the role religion played in the change of political course. Since race separation had for decades been justified on religious grounds, we speculated that the largest of the Afrikaner churches, the Dutch Reformed Church, must have led the way in the abandonment of apartheid. We intended to determine how the Afrikaners had thus managed to "change God's will." Many of the people we interviewed are ministers (dominees) and academics, but they also include rock musicians, farmers, security police, mining experts, politicians, writers, and journalists. We decided our initial guess was wrong: the church was not leading; rather, it was a drag on change, grudgingly following the lead of the National Party.

Before de Klerk's February 1990 speech, we thought we would never see Mandela emerge from prison, let alone become South Africa's president. And we never thought June would be able to return to South Africa. In 1980 she had been denied a visa to reenter South Africa, presumably because the government hadn't liked her reporting as Africa correspondent for *The Christian Science Monitor* from 1976 to 1979. June arrived in South Africa for the first time a few weeks before the Soweto riots began on June 16, 1976. Over the next two and a half years she interviewed young blacks who had been tortured and were on the run, sat in on rigged trials, reported on South African involvement in the wars in Angola, Rhodesia, Mozambique, and Namibia, and covered the celebrations of Botswana's tenth anniversary of independence, where she interviewed the ANC's president, Oliver Tambo. She interviewed the Black Consciousness leader Steve Biko two weeks before he was detained for the last time—six weeks before he was killed by police. The ecumenical Christian Institute, especially its officials Cedric Mayson, Beyers Naudé, and Theo Kotze, helped guide her into the black community. Ina Perlman, with the Institute of Race Relations in the late seventies, also was an invaluable explicator of events.

June interviewed a security policeman who had tortured some of her friends, and who justified his actions on the basis of the Bible. After she reported on the court proceedings in Port Elizabeth—where a fourteen-year-old boy was sentenced, without evidence, to the maximum security prison on Robben Island—the South African government threatened to sue the *Monitor*. The paper's editor stood behind her and her story and the threat proved hollow.

June became friends with Biko's friend Thenjiwe Mtintso, and through Thenjie—who suffered detention, torture, and banning, then fled into exile and joined the ANC guerrilla underground—she grew to love the courage and humanity of apartheid's opponents. Thenjie picked us up at the airport when we flew into Johannesburg in 1992. In 1994 she was elected to Parliament.

In her reporting and in her 1984 book, *Cry Amandla!*, which was banned by the South African government, June also tried to probe the Afrikaner culture that had instituted apartheid. In the late 1970s the Afrikaners seemed to be members of a closed society, reluctant to deviate from the official line, monolithic in their views, xenophobic, paranoid, narcissistic. Reporters were suspect, along with all those who questioned the National Party government and condemned apartheid.

Ten years later, de Klerk's reforms marked a tectonic slippage in South Africa's political geology. Everyone began jostling for power, and the tongues of the Afrikaners were loosed. Willem Saayman, professor of missiology at the University of South Africa (UNISA), explained the previous insularity: "We didn't think it was necessary to talk to English-speaking people or to anybody else. We were conversing in Afrikaans among ourselves. People coming to ask about Afrikaner thinking, it's a bit of a nuisance. Now and then you must tell them a few things, but actually the real debate is in Afrikaner circles."

We went to South Africa with a long list of Afrikaners to interview, names we had gotten from newspaper clippings and friends. We did interview a few of those people, but many more immediately came to our attention. We found people by personal recommendation, from newspaper and magazine stories, and one from the phone book. Our objective was to cover the political spectrum until we felt we could convey the most vital elements of Afrikaner thinking.

It was a wonderful time to talk with Afrikaners. People felt free to fulminate, explain, and cajole. One woman was positively bilious about how journalists had depicted the Afrikaners as racists, and assumed we would do the same. Most felt that if they could put their case, they would be understood.

Some sophisticated academics, wise to the ways of research and writing, were more suspicious. At a gracious dinner in Louwrens and Lily Pretorius's Pretoria home, their four-year-old son, Daniel, darted in and out of the living room modeling his Superman, Batman, and knight outfits and displaying his Ninja coloring book. In their courtyard dining area with stars for a ceiling and nighttime noises as background music, little Daniel's elders politely grilled us about our intentions and purpose. Louwrens Pretorius, a sociologist, and his political scientist colleague Pierre Hugo knew about interviewing, about interpreting. We agreed that Afrikaner academics were undoubtedly more steeped in the subject than we were. But we were seeking to explain Afrikaners to a nonacademic, mainstream American audience.

Hugo and Pretorius had a complaint about the American anthropologist Vincent Crapanzano and his acclaimed 1985 book called *Waiting: The Whites of South Africa*. Hugo, in a 1985 article in a South African sociology journal, attacked Crapanzano's methodology, claiming that the study was unrepresentative of whites and that Crapanzano had betrayed the confidences of his interview subjects. In the course of the evening "Crapanzano" became a verb: "Please, don't crapanzano us in your book." The evening grew more relaxed, but their fears were clear and their warning explicit. We promised to do our best to let the Afrikaners do the talking in our book.

In the course of our eight months in South Africa, we sometimes felt the topic of Afrikaners was so vast, so imponderable, so elusive, that we were immobilized. Then someone would come along and cheer us on. More than one Afrikaner we interviewed said, "I'd like to read your book," or "Maybe you will help us understand ourselves." One man said he knew what we were doing: we were *dwarskykers*, which means "cross-spectators," or "cross-lookers-on." And we adopted that perspective, acknowledging that ours is an outsider's view and that this book is intended primarily for an outsider audience.

We apologize to our interviewees for the condensation and truncation of interviews that were often long, nuanced, and eloquent. From thousands of pages of transcripts we've picked revealing moments and incisive analyses, but we've had to leave out volumes. Even though a few of the people we interviewed are not quoted directly, they all contributed to our deeper understanding. For example, we focused several entire interviews on the issue of censorship and asked many people about their views of it, but in the end, although the urge to censor struck us as revealing of many Afrikaners' thinking, there simply was no room to do the subject justice.

Because many aspects of Afrikaner society and of South African politics are sunk in secrecy, a note of caution: ties between government security forces (police, army, intelligence) and political and cultural elites (within and outside the secret Afrikaner Broederbond) are unclear to outsiders and to Afrikaners themselves. The widely mentioned Third Force in contemporary South African politics refers to several different visions of clandestine organizations operating beneath the surface of society. The term is most often used in the media to describe government-linked intelligence organizations such as the Civil Cooperation Bureau (CCB) and police death squads that carried out political killings during the late 1980s. These are slowly being exposed in court investigations. But Third Force also refers to other even more mysterious associations still capable of executing violent measures aimed at influencing or halting the political transformation of the country. Much remains secret. Our interviews reveal the nationalistic attitudes that have produced the Afrikaner addictions to secrecy, violence, and manipulation.

*   *   *

Heart of Whiteness is divided into seven sections: two introductory sections, then four sections on the topical pillars of the book—the Broederbond, religion, the Afrikaans language, and the police state—and a final section looking toward the future.

Since 1992 Afrikaner society has been changing rapidly, like a river at springtime flood, but what our interviewees discussed then reveals traits, beliefs, and traumas that, while not immutable, have not been eradicated and that remain to affect their future decisions.

We hope this book will help readers understand how Afrikaners could invent the biggest social engineering effort of this last half century, how they could justify it on religious grounds, why they are so fearful of blacks, why they are suspicious of outsiders, why some are obsessed with their language, why secrecy is second nature to many, and how they are embracing, resisting, aiding, and thwarting the ongoing transition.

We listened to Afrikaners' deep feelings, reasoning, and rationalizations. We held their tears in our throats, their hands in prayer, their eyes in both trust and suspicion. Here we give you their words, to know their past, to guess their future.

PART I

INTRODUCING THE AFRIKANERS

CHAPTER ONE

THE SPECTRUM

Afrikaners complain that outsiders depict them monochromatically, as white racists. In fact, until President F. W. de Klerk's February 2, 1990, speech heralding the end of apartheid, it was not widely known that Afrikaners are to be found all across the political spectrum.

On that momentous day, dubbed "Red Friday" by right-wingers who opposed F. W.'s National Party and considered his policies "communistic," the relative silence and conformity of the white tribe shattered. Distressed, hopeful, scared, and ebullient, Afrikaners of all convictions were eager to talk. Their diversity erupted into public view. A handful are members of the African National Congress (ANC), more are neo-Nazis, some refuse to align, many are confused, a few are women who have rebelled against their patriarchal tribe.

The first two Afrikaners in this chapter are a young man and woman, the man mildly right of center, the woman decidedly on the left. Though they are both close to thirty years old, one might have been raised on the moon and the other under a barrel for all their similarity to each other. The third Afrikaner, a man in his fifties, has spent his adult life questioning the authoritarian system, a rare (and discouraged) activity in this constricted society.

A two-and-a-half-hour drive east of Johannesburg across the mildly undulating plains of Africa called the highveld*—tamed to grow potatoes, *mielies* (corn), cattle, and sheep, watered by lonely windmills, mined of its coal and gold, blemished with man-made mountains scraped from inside the earth—lives Dominee (Reverend) Pieter Nel. In 1992, two years after de Klerk's speech, Nel reminisced about "once upon a time" in the days of Hendrik Verwoerd, prime minister from 1958 to 1966.

---

*The highveld, in the center-north of the country, is prairie interspersed with trees; it includes corn-growing farmland. The lowveld, surrounding the highveld to the north, east, and southeast, has more trees but has been heavily deforested and contains scrub.

"I was born in 1962 and I can remember in the days of Dr. Verwoerd, those people were not ashamed to talk about Christianity," he said.

Brown-haired, light-eyed Nel looks scrubbed and cheery and handsome. His wife, Gerda Brits Nel, has the thin physique of the long-distance runner she is. With their two children they live in a middle-class ranch-style house surrounded by a low decorative fence in the small farming town of Bethal.

"Making room for communist atheism to govern," that's where the Nationalist government was going wrong, Nel said. "We're giving the forces of evil, the forces of the antichrist, room in our government. That's the ANC."

Nel believes the white man in South Africa is "asking for the wrath of God." The right-wing Conservative Party (CP) is "misusing the Bible," while the ruling National Party is "forgetting it," he said.

"I'm not saying the CP itself, but many of its members. These fanatics that say the black people are not true human beings, and they're monkeys and can't be saved, you know that's nonsense. I mean, that's terrible. There's no biblical foundation for those arguments. Then, of course, there's a great bit of materialism in this Conservative way of thinking. They don't want to give away what they have."

Nel is slightly right of the fluid middle of the Afrikaner political spectrum. He doesn't believe apartheid can be justified biblically, but "for practical purposes the government should keep people apart" because that way they maintain their Christian values best.

"The Bible is my authority," Dominee Nel said over and over.

What about other people who read and interpret the Bible differently?

"I don't think it is a matter of interpretation," he said. "The Bible says if we don't acknowledge Christ, we are the antichrist. It's not something difficult to understand."

Nel said he had "strong roots in a Voortrek house." He is related to the Voortrekker, or pioneer, Sarel Cillie, who participated in the Great Trek.* He was at the Battle of Blood River on December 16, 1838, an event mythologized in Afrikaans culture. In that battle only three pio-

---

*The Great Trek refers to the large-scale exodus of Dutch-descended people from the Cape Colony east and north away from British control during 1835–1837. These people, thereafter called Voortrekkers, Trekboers, or Trekkers interchangeably in conversation, are regarded as the Afrikaners' pioneer ancestors and were the first whites to settle the interior of what is now South Africa. "Boer" translates as farmer, and the Afrikaners often refer to themselves as Boers with pride, while for English speakers and blacks, "Boer" has been used as a pejorative term.

neers were injured while the Boers and their black servants shot and killed three thousand spear-wielding Zulus, in retribution for the Zulus' killing 270 Boers and their 200 servants in an earlier ambush. In Afrikaner history December 16 became the Day of the Covenant because legend had it that the Voortrekkers had promised God to honor Him if they were victorious.

"God planted the white South Africans here with a purpose," Nel said. "And that was to spread His word, to do missionary work. The French Huguenots came here because of their faith. And Jan van Riebeeck in 1652.* Ever since they landed here, they had churches and people that looked after the sick. Somewhere along the line we neglected missionary work. That's why we are in this crisis. Ever since I was four, I've done missionary work, I spoke to them [blacks] about Christ. I mean, it's part of my life, that's how I read the Bible. But when the government neglects its duty to God, it's asking for trouble."

As a dominee Nel is performing a political juggling act, trying to keep his congregation happy. He ministers to fourteen hundred whites in the Bethal Dutch Reformed Church, who think as he does or, in many cases, are to his political right.

"My congregation is divided into forty sections, where each has an elder and a deacon. Of those forty sections, nine are farming sections and the rest townspeople. But all the people work with the land. We live close to the earth. People here are much closer to the Boers as we know them, you know of a few years back. Biblically as well they are conservative. They are real Calvinists, much more than you get in the cities.

"In the cities you get this individualism. Each one believes what he likes. With the urban people there is more immorality, an antichristian way of living. It's just humanism, like forcing everything together and saying that's New Age. I'm saying why should we all be in one huge pan of scrambled eggs?"

Annica Marincowitz, who lives in the "one huge"—i.e., interracial— "pan" in Yeoville, a bohemian suburb of Johannesburg, is an Afrikaner of a kind scarcely visible a dozen years previously. Her rented apartment spoke for her, because she was far away in Japan, teaching English to the Japanese.

---

*Van Riebeeck worked for the Dutch East India Company, whose trading vessels sailed from Europe around the Cape of Good Hope to India. He established a victualing and supply station at the Cape for the Company.

Books, many more than in Nel's office, are stacked along a shelf in the entrance hall and crammed in boxes under the beds in the three-room apartment. Afrikaans and English books, many used in classes at the Harvard of the Afrikaners, Stellenbosch University, about 850 miles southwest of Johannesburg.

A few rough-hewn antiques from the old Boer days of the Great Trek are sprinkled around the ground-floor apartment: a yellowwood and stinkwood chest, mellow from years of having beeswax smoothed into it; a foldable pioneer table that could easily have been heaved onto an ox-drawn wagon during the mid-1800s trek inland away from British colonial rule. There is an ultramodern hand-painted coffee table, and a large length of Indian fabric is draped on the wall.

Anarchic prints by South African artist Shelly Sacks hang on several of the fifteen-foot-high walls. In the hall outside the kitchen is a collage of snapshots of Annica's family and friends. Posters of Jimi Hendrix and John Coltrane are affixed high in the kitchen, looking down like lords on a cheerful table, hand-painted with daisies. A mammoth portable stereo sits on a hall table. Photos of this woman's heroes and heroines are glued to the walls: the black American Communist Angela Davis, the novelist Nadine Gordimer, the American musician Paul Simon. Pages from a calendar have been spaced around the kitchen walls at chair-back level like decorative tiles: photos of elderly black Namibians in uniform who fought in the 1980s war with South Africa, little boys with toy AK-47s fashioned from scrap wire. In the bathroom is a photo of a flower-toting, naked black man with splendid torso. In a separate, small toilet room the walls are decked with pictures of Renaissance and medieval madonnas and contemporary photocopied articles. One tract is a fable about an era on earth when women were worshiped by men, when men tried to make "holes" in themselves similar to women's so they too could give birth. The result was predictably gruesome. Also plastered to the wall is an enlarged newspaper column on abortion rights and a cartoon that attacks sexism and lauds women who "were built like cars." On one skinny wall a life-size poster of a female Greek statue makes the closet-size room seem crowded with people. On the door is "The Twentieth Century Witch Chant" which ends:

> "As for the boys playing with their power toys,
> Entoad them all."

The woman who decorated these walls is about the same age as Dominee Nel—she turned thirty-two in 1992. Although a daughter of the *volk*, she represents Nel's nightmare, the urban antichrist. In a newspaper photo on the kitchen wall she is shown marching at the second annual "Pride March" organized by the Gay and Lesbian Organization of the Witwatersrand (GLOW). She holds one end of a banner that reads WE LOVE WOMEN, WE ARE WOMANDERFUL. All the O's are transformed into the female symbol.

Like Pieter Nel, Willem Saayman is a Dutch Reformed dominee (minister). Unlike Nel, Saayman, who is in his early fifties, has asked questions all his life and has gotten into trouble for it. He spent years as a missionary in Ovamboland in Namibia, which used to be called South West Africa and was administered by South Africa from 1920 to 1990. Surely Nel, with his missionary concern, would approve of Saayman for carrying out God's intent in Africa. But Saayman turns out to be no ordinary Afrikaner missionary. His questioning began in the hallowed halls of the University of Stellenbosch in the sixties.

"I can very, very well remember the first time that I asked a critical question in a theological class there," Saayman said. "How my heart was absolutely dancing in my chest. Because you don't question authority. And I mean, here I had the authority of the whole church. Stellenbosch, you must remember, has this tremendous dignity as the center of Dutch Reformed theology: it's Calvinist, it's over the ages, and here I, first-year little student from the Free State,* stand up and I say to the prof, 'Sorry, but I don't agree with that.' I knew before I stood up that I'd be the only person that thought so. The others all agreed with him."

What was his objection?

"I can't remember, something about allowing black people into the church, joint worship or something like that."

So what happened?

"Wooh, ja [yes], I got hit on my head from all sides."

For asking a question, or for stating a disagreement?

"Ja, ja, for even questioning why whites have their own church and blacks have theirs. That was not just questioning a human institution, that was questioning the will of God. God willed it so, so how on earth can you be so stupid as to ask such a question?"

You're not supposed to learn the will of God by questioning?

"No, no, no. No."

None of that talmudic stuff?

"No, no, no," Saayman said, grinning. "Our central doctrinal work is

---

*The predominantly rural Orange Free State.

called the Heidelberg Catechism.* You see the German connection. The Heidelberg Catechism gives the question and then provides the answer. You learn them both. So you don't ask your own questions and you don't question the answers. There are fifty-two questions; that's enough. You have to ask nothing more to know in heaven and on earth to be saved.

"Today if I go and teach at the white theological school or even preach in a white church and say, 'Please speak up if you don't agree, please ask me questions,' there is a shocked silence.

"There's another thing about us—the Teutonic. It isn't necessary for us to know: the leaders know. We want to watch rugby on a Saturday and cricket in summer, and we have *braaivleis* [grilled meat], and a few people up there decide what is good for us."

Dominee Saayman lives in Pretoria, that haven of the Afrikaner, and the administrative capital of the country. At the end of the summer, March in the Southern Hemisphere, the grass on the veld glows orange like a Scot's hair. By then the breathy lavender blooms of the jacaranda trees from November's spring have been forgotten in the earth's sienna dust, which floats almost as finely as chalk powder into carpets and curtains and eyelashes.

"I don't think I can last outside of Africa," Saayman said. "It's too green. The land is too green. Land must be brown and dusty."

He was comparing it in his mind to Canada, where he, his wife, and four daughters lived for six months in 1983 while he was a visiting professor at the Atlantic School of Theology in Halifax and the Toronto School of Theology.

Saayman, still a minister in the Dutch Reformed Church, is also a professor in the Department of Missiology at the University of South Africa (UNISA), a mammoth correspondence university consisting of concrete buildings stretched lengthwise, like decks of old computer punch cards, across the southern hills of Pretoria. UNISA's faculty dining room nestles cavelike in the side of the hill, all gloomy inside, and vaguely reminiscent of a monastery. Faculty members sit at long tables eating subsidized, cafeteria-style meals. After a long conversation in the dining hall, Saayman strolled back up the hill to his small office. He murmured, "I want you to know that we're not the only people in my office." He knew his office was bugged. Suddenly it seemed like South Africa in the bad old days of the 1980s State of Emergency, the days of the National Party's ideology of "total onslaught," when communists were suspected

---

*The Heidelberg Cathechism is a profession of faith drawn up by the German Reformed Church in 1563 and adopted by several Reformed churches.

to lurk under every bed and certainly at the universities in the guise of every opponent of apartheid.

Of course his office was bugged. Saayman is, after all, chairman of the Central Pretoria branch of the ANC, which in 1992 had more than three hundred white members, mostly Afrikaners. Somebody out there, the National Party, Military Intelligence, somebody, still wanted dissident Afrikaners in their sight (and sometimes their gunsights).

The tale of Saayman's brave renunciation of apartheid involved his daughters and his wife, a woman who is as pleasing to be around as a favorite flower and who was nearly killed by shots aimed into their house by a death squad called Witwolve (White Wolves). Growing up within the *volk*, knowing the Afrikaners intimately but also having lived and worked closely with blacks, Saayman had the perspective necessary to explain his people.

"Apartheid has not failed," Saayman said. "It has succeeded tremendously well in building two worlds, in keeping the white and black, the rich and poor, worlds apart. Black people always had to move into the white world, so they knew how the white world worked. But white people never had to move into the black world, so they know nothing about the black world. If I begin to tell them some of the things which are going on, they find it more or less impossible to believe." He knew about how most Afrikaners thought, based in part on experiences in his own family.

"Let me tell you a story, that's where I am at my best," he said. "My daughters have always been very active in the liberation [anti-apartheid] movement. One weekend we had to go to Kroonstad in the Free State to my wife's parents, my parents-in-law. It was the weekend of the first public march here in Pretoria, it was a women's march. That was before the legalization of the ANC. They said, 'We are going to march, it will be peaceful, we don't have permission but we are going to march in any case.' So my two eldest daughters stayed behind, and we went to Kroonstad.

"That evening on the eight o'clock TV news, [the announcer] said, ja, it was a violent protest march and the women threw rocks at the police so the police had to retaliate and fourteen women have been arrested. So we immediately phoned home and got my second-eldest daughter. The eldest was one of the fourteen in prison. The second-eldest one saw an old woman being trampled and bent down to try and protect her, and as she bent down a policeman simply ran over her from behind. She said to us, 'You know Pretoria as well as we do, where would we in Schoemann Street find stones to throw at the police?' She said, 'It was totally peaceful, when they just chucked tear gas at us and baton-charged [clubbed] us.'

27

"My eldest daughter was very angry, so she had an altercation [with a policeman] and was arrested. The second one was hit over the head and trampled. My wife spoke to our daughter, then told her father and mother what really happened. My father-in-law said, 'I don't believe your daughters. The police will not do something like that without reason.'

"The police are our great protectors," Saayman said sardonically.

He emphasized that "scores of people" were being killed and injured in black areas of South Africa in 1992 while police failed to protect them, but most whites ignored the carnage, claimed not to know about it, or rejected the idea that whites and the government were somehow responsible for it. "It is incredibly difficult to get people to understand what is really happening because they only know the white world."

Like Saayman's father-in-law, Afrikaners have been socialized to trust their leaders. It's a habit not easily broken.

CHAPTER TWO

A CONSPIRACY THAT WORKS

Who are their leaders?

Sh-h-h. Afrikaners know many hidden things and suspect even more, but they're not going to tell outsiders. Strangers—*uitlanders*, foreigners—are not to be trusted. Outsiders always condemn, attack, condescend.

"Conspiracy theory runs through the back pocket of Afrikaner history," said Zach de Beer Postma, professor of philosophy at UNISA. His office is a cubicle like Dominee Saayman's.

Right-wing and some not-so-right-wing Afrikaners believe in various conspiracies: that the Illuminati, along with Jews, the capitalists, and the Trilateral Commission, run the world; that Nostradamus's predictions are coming true; that the CIA is building a big military base in neighboring Botswana from which to attack South Africa if things get out of control; that the Americans forced the National Party to cave in to the ANC; that international capital seeks the destruction of a strong South Africa so that the country's wealth can more easily be plundered.

The Afrikaners know about conspiracies. To fight the *uitlanders*, especially the English, they fathered, and for more than seventy years nurtured, one of the world's most effective conspiracies, the Afrikaner Broederbond. Founded in 1918 by six young men who sought to promote Afrikaner interests after the disastrous defeat by the British in the Anglo-Boer War*, the Broederbond went underground in 1922. Its

---

*In common use the Boer War, or Anglo-Boer War, refers to the second and larger of two conflicts. The first Anglo-Boer War (called the War of Independence by Afrikaners) began in 1880 when Transvaal Afrikaners rebelled against Britain's 1877 annexation of their independent republic and ended in 1881 when British forces were defeated in the battle of Majuba. The British restored the Transvaal's independence, subject to limitations on its external sovereignty.

Particularly following the discovery of gold in 1886 on the Rand, a tide of English immigrants swept into the Transvaal province and, backed by British mining interests, the British government sought once again to conquer the Boers. The Second Anglo-Boer

leaders were emotionally bound by a fear their language and culture would be suppressed and by a sensitivity to ridicule by the British. The Broederbond was designed to promote Christian values and brotherly love among the *volk*. Members called each other *vriende*, friends. At first a small cultural pressure group, it spread its tentacles to found and control a growing welter of Afrikaner institutions. After the surprise National Party election victory in 1948, the Broederbond became the heart and brain that ran the social engineering experiment of apartheid. To get a picture of what this meant, imagine the U.S. President and his cabinet and the top generals, civil servants, teachers, religious and civic leaders, all males, all of the same race and the same church, all belonging to a secret organization that met monthly to study and discuss implementation of their executive council's latest pronouncements.

A two-tiered society came into being. Law professor Johan van der Vyver explained: "I always refer to it as the 'Broederbond syndrome.' In the Afrikaner community there had always been this kind of idea that there are a privileged few, all men, who are given the information, and who decide what is to be done and where one is to go. And the rest of the population must be kept in ignorance and are expected loyally to follow the leaders. And we were brought up to believe that the people who criticize us either hate us or they don't know, they were ignorant. But we were the ignorami. We didn't know. We were fed. News was withheld from us."

A more benign view comes from Frederick van Zyl Slabbert, an independent politician and former academic. "I saw the Broederbond as a very powerful clearing house for Afrikaner gossip."

And politically useful gossip drips from every leaf of the Afrikaner grapevine. Did you know that Piet Meyer, chairman of the Broederbond through the sixties and for over twenty years head of the South African Broadcasting Corporation (SABC), had a son named Izan—Nazi spelled backward? Who held the gun in that celebrated marital tiff—former Finance Minister Barend du Plessis, or his wife? Or someone else? A well-known cultural leader and dominee grabs women, it's widely

---

War (for Afrikaners, simply the Boer or Anglo-Boer War, 1899–1902) was far bloodier than the first. The British resorted to scorched-earth tactics to eliminate the threat of Afrikaner commando forces. Afrikaner women and children were placed in concentration camps as their farms were destroyed. Mortality due to disease was very high in the camps because of horrible sanitary conditions and inadequate food and medical services. Of an estimated 30,000 Afrikaner casualties in the war, 26,000 were women and children. The war ended with the Peace of Vereeniging, named for the town south of Johannesburg where it was signed.

known among journalists. Marike de Klerk, F. W.'s wife, was fuming when their son Willem got engaged to that colored girl. She had, after all, called coloreds *uitskot*, dregs (also the term for windfall apples).

But the Broederbond is much more than just a gossip factory; for decades the shrouded Broederbond members made all important decisions in the country. Its plans were the basis for Afrikaner domination. Van Zyl Slabbert said, "You know, that's where they met and said, What's going on in education? We must look after our interests there. There would be a meeting of the minds, then out would flow the strategies that would eventually work out in politics, in economics, and in the civil service in particular."

The Broederbond created Christian National Education for the schools, masterminding the indoctrination of the *volk*. It came to control the parastatals (state-owned enterprises) such as Transnet that ran railways and airlines. It established an investment fund called Federale Volksbelegging (Federal Peoples' Investing) that founded insurance companies, one of which became SANLAM (South African Life Insurance Company), a major South African conglomerate. In 1965, Federale Volksbelegging gained control of General Mining, which eventually established Gencor, one of South Africa's biggest mining companies. *Vriende* dominated the Dutch Reformed churches and the National Party. Broederbond academics designed the apartheid laws that tangled blacks in webs of restrictions and injustices, as well as the theories that justified the system. In the late 1980s and early 1990s the Broederbond guided the privatization of the parastatals (especially the Armaments Development and Manufacturing Corporation of South Africa, Armscor) when it became clear that the Afrikaners would have to move aside from government; thus they were able to take government assets into the Afrikaner private sector.

"We were always in a minority and we simply had to plan the future," Dominee Johan Heyns said. A prominent Broederbonder, he explained the Afrikaners' obsession, expressed in the old adage *Die boer maak 'n plan* (The farmer makes a plan). "If you go back in our history, we had the ambushes, the fights with the natives, we had British occupation, we had to fight the British twice at the end of the last century, at the turn of this century they conquered our country. I think it's a quite natural phenomenon for the Afrikaners to design, to plan. Also, we, the Afrikaners, believe that we were planted by God Himself in this country." Their own plans helped implement God's plan.

"Actually, large-scale planning is a very interesting academic exercise. I can see that Karl Marx and Lenin must've had an interesting time," said Elizabeth Bradley, the millionaire vice chairman of Toyota South Africa and a self-described "detribalized" Afrikaner. "But practically, people don't get planned like figures on paper. People unfortunately are rather more selfish than the planning implies." Despite their rabid anti-communism, "Afrikaners are socialists at heart, not businesspeople," Bradley said. "They want free schooling for their children, they want the right to a job, but they don't actually want to be Mr. Oppenheimer* with the responsibilities of earning lots of risk capital. They want security bought with taxes on other people's income," Bradley said. "To me, that's socialism."

With the government as its main tool, the Broederbond succeeded in delivering security to most Afrikaners: jobs in the state sector; exclusive white neighborhoods; protection against competition in the workplace; subsidies for farmers; perks everywhere; and, as a result, endless opportunities for corruption, which led to scandal as a way of life.

"It's what people wanted: order and peace and stratification and central planning," Bradley said. "I think we are risk-averse. Which I think most socialists are. Not work-averse, Afrikaners are quite hard working. When I say socialist I mean a system where everybody looks after each other, and it's the one that makes the fewest waves that's going to be looked after the best."

Broederbond membership grew from 12,000 in 1977 to more than 20,000 in 1992, all of them white males, members of one of the three Dutch Reformed churches or the Apostolic Faith Mission. Of those men, eighteen constituted the national Executive Council (Uitvoerende Raad) that made crucial decisions.

Dominee Pieter Nel in Bethal said he had been approached to join the Broederbond as well as the Conservative Party's equivalent, but he had rebuffed both overtures, believing he must be neutral. The CP's secret brotherhood is "not as organized as the Broederbond, but they're stupid if they haven't got it [a similar secret organization]. There are these people in strategic places now directing the thought of the people," he said.

Nel's former theology professor at the University of Pretoria, Dominee Heyns, thought the Broederbond was a positive force for change. Heyns warned darkly, "You'll make a great mistake if you think that the Broederbond is a monster." In fact, he said, the organization "played a role in the whole process of reform." He knew firsthand the deep resis-

*Harry Oppenheimer is the former chairman of the Anglo-American Corporation, the biggest mining-based conglomerate in South Africa.

32

tance to those reforms, for he was bitterly hated by right-wingers for his success in liberalizing Dutch Reformed Church doctrine. Heyns was a point man in the eighties and early nineties, continually defending the Broederbond and its code of secrecy. And he was central to disseminating new attitudes.

For example, in 1992 Heyns expounded a new theory about the reputed "individualism" of the self-described "stubborn" Afrikaner. It was, he said, a trait left over from the rough pioneer days of his ancestors. "If you read the history of the Voortrekkers you will know that some of them didn't want to join other trekkers; they simply went their own ways, some in this direction, others in that direction. This was due to the fact of their inheritance from their ancestry. I mean, you know that we are a mixed-blood population in this country from the fourteen percent so-called colored blood into the [white] Afrikaners. I think that gives a sort of predisposition of being very individualistic."

"Colored blood" made the Afrikaner individualistic! No wonder the white supremacists hated Heyns. His new theory was a far cry from the days of apartheid, when every person was classified as white/European, African (with a designated tribe), Asian, or colored (with many subcategories of colored). These classifications caused some people who considered themselves white to commit suicide when they were legally declared colored instead.

Heyns and the Broederbond were spreading a new ideology, forming a new attitude among the *volk*. In the nineties, as the National Party faced one-person, one-vote elections, suddenly the Afrikaans-speaking coloreds became acceptable as Afrikaners to the creators of apartheid. Ruthlessly stripped of their voting rights in 1956, the coloreds, who spoke Afrikaans and went to Dutch Reformed churches, were being wooed back by the National Party. The "white" clan of 3 million wanted to remarry the "brown" clan of 3.5 million to claim a "group" or tribe of 6.5 million, doubling their voting clout. The Broederbond was reprogramming the *volk* to expand its sights. In 1992 Heyns was in lockstep, with a new theory of eugenics, extolling "colored blood" instead of condemning it, preparing for 1993.

In November 1993 the secret Afrikaner Broederbond committed suicide.

Or so the Broeders say. They claim they founded a new, open, nonpolitical cultural organization called the Afrikanerbond (Afrikaner Union) to take its place. Coloreds and women who accepted the Bible as the word of the Holy Trinity and the "meaning it has on all aspects of life" could join. Dominee Heyns became deputy chairman of the new, more colorful *bond*.

But did the secret Broederbond really expire?

For more than a decade the National Party, the Broederbond's political sidekick, claimed apartheid was dead, even while its loyalists stalked the land, detaining, killing, corrupting, co-opting. Can ruling Afrikaners break their secrecy addiction? Or are they too hooked by the elixir of the illicit? *Vertroulike*, confidential, was the euphemism injected into conversations by Broeders instead of "secretive," and they always seemed to think that using the euphemism made it acceptable, just as calling apartheid "separate development" convincingly improved the product. After 1948 the real Afrikaner "culture" being protected by the Broederbond was its own, its shadowy culture, which enriched and empowered the Broeders, their families, and fellow travelers. Can they leave the shadows, broaden their membership, and succeed in the light?

In 1992 Sampie Terreblanche was dubious that the Broederbond would really dissolve. He spoke as a former insider, a professor of economics at Stellenbosch University who flamboyantly quit the Broederbond in 1987. "It was originally an underdog organization to fight against the injustices experienced from British imperialism/colonialism. But I have reason to believe that there is a new lease of life in the de Klerk period. They're hand in glove with the corporate sector and they are the upper dogs, but they carry on with the organization."

But when the Afrikaners really lose power, won't people find it detrimental to belong?

"It can cut both ways," Terreblanche said. "If they feel again we are underdogs, then we must close our ranks. So it's possible that it can become stronger. It can dissolve, regroup under a new name, more secret and with more of the old underdog attitude."

That, and more, worries Dominee Saayman, the Pretoria ANC chairman. In 1992 he wondered if President de Klerk was really in control of things, even in control of his own small Afrikaner society; if not, it could bode ill for the transition government, as well as for the second election in 1999.

"Some people simply cannot think that a nice man like de Klerk can have people behind him who are willing to do the things that I'm talking about," Saayman said. "He's a nice old grandfather, he smiles so nicely, he's always humble. I mean, he was the best leader they could have elected. It doesn't happen by chance in the National Party."

Behind de Klerk are the military and police intelligence operatives, "the securocrats, I think that's still the best word for them," Saayman said. "They actually work out the plans and are cold and deliberate about what they are doing. They are deliberately instigating things like the [1991–93] murders in the Vaal [industrial area south of Johannesburg], the involvement with Inkatha [the Zulu political organization headed by Chief Mangosuthu Gatsha Buthelezi].

"Now, in a sense for me, it would be better if de Klerk were in charge, because then you'd still have some political accountability. It is an even more fearful idea that he's not in charge, that he's just the figurehead. Unfortunately, I tend to feel that that is actually the truth."

Does de Klerk know whether or not he's a pawn?

"I don't know. My experience of the military in Angola has been that they are so bloody successful that the politicians don't even realize to what extent they are being used as pawns in that game. That is my fear. Remember Afrikaner history," Saayman said, citing the fact that the first Afrikaner prime minister this century was General Louis Botha (1910–19) and the second, General Jan Christian Smuts (1919–24 and 1939–48). "It's always been generals. You have this very, very strong thing buried somewhere in the Afrikaner psyche of military authority, that the true Afrikaner leader is also a good military leader."

Is that why former President P. W. Botha acted like a general?

"That's exactly right. But for the transition [away from apartheid] in which we are now, P. W. was a disaster. And that is why when it suited them, they took out the knives and they stuck into his back like nothing. It was actually his generals that did it. It's also interesting to me that at the moment, the military is playing mostly an invisible role." During the transition many of the same Afrikaner military men are in their jobs.

"The minister said in Parliament [in 1992] that the CCB* has been administratively disbanded," Saayman said. "Now what the hell does that mean, 'administratively disbanded'? With an Afrikaner, in the church, in politics, you must always read the words very carefully."

What does it mean that the Broederbond is gone, replaced by the Afrikanerbond? Are critics right when they charge that the Broeders just created a new, publicly acceptable face, while burrowing further underground? And what has happened to the links between the Broederbond and the security establishment—soldiers who are officially separated from power but whose networks of influence remain, even after the 1994 elections brought the ANC to power?

*The Civil Cooperation Bureau (CCB), under the ultimate authority of the Ministry of Defense, secretly carried out political activities including assassinations in the 1980s.

*   *   *

Cutting through the political thicket and secrecy to the facts is difficult, if not impossible. But Braam Viljoen is in a unique position to point out trends. Braam is a former theologian and professor who in 1992 carried out peacekeeping efforts for the liberal IDASA (Institute for a Democratic Alternative for South Africa), bringing ANC and Conservative Party people face to face. During the late eighties he had been a target of death squads for his anti-apartheid activities in the African homeland of KwaNdebele.*

Braam's twin brother, the former South African Defense Force (SADF) chief of staff General Constand Viljoen, became a major right-wing leader prior to the 1994 elections. His moderately right-wing views ripped the Conservative Party apart, since he encouraged participation in the elections the CP wanted to boycott. The general's detractors on the right claimed that he was a Broederbond plant to sap the right wing of its power. While Constand rallied support for a right-wing front that would be a responsible opposition in Parliament to the ANC–National Party condominium, Braam worked to assuage the fears on the extremes and to bring political enemies into contact and eventual cooperation.

Although his liberal views are well known, Braam relates well to conservative Afrikaners, and his farmer neighbors had elected him to head the local agricultural association. As wise as an Old Testament prophet, Braam Viljoen looks the part with his thick white hair. But his tanned, crusty hands are those of a cattle rancher, albeit a highly educated one, trained in theology.

"The moment you start with conservatives and you really want their support and their ear, just say something bad about the Broederbond [which conservatives loathe]," Braam Viljoen said. His crow's feet crinkled almost audibly at the edges of his stunningly blue eyes.

What does he think is happening with the Broederbond?

"It's as alive as ever. Have you seen the present chairman of the Broederbond? Piet de Lange? You must see him. It's clear that de Lange initiated this whole change of face of the Broederbond, from the old support of the separate development [apartheid] policy to negotiations. It's nothing but a last-ditch effort to save what can be saved. Within government circles and within very influential positions all over the country the

---

*According to apartheid, thirteen percent of South Africa's land was designated tribal homelands, or *bantustans*. Under the pass laws, or "influx control" laws, every African was made a citizen of one of the ten homelands and could be sent there if his or her identification and work permit documents had lapsed or were not valid for a particular area.

Broederbond is strong. The strategy of political life within the National Party domain is determined by the Broederbond as always. You can be sure that the Broederbond will have its key people in every important organization in the country, including the military. And no final appointment will be made without the Broederbond being involved."

What about the Third Force, that shadowy force fomenting violence in black areas to diminish ANC control, to continue the old tactics of divide and rule, to retain white power?

"Personally I wouldn't say that the Third Force is in the military. I do think that the military is involved in the Third Force. And particularly Military Intelligence. But I think the Third Force is a far wider organization, including big business, including overseas organizations, both political intelligence organizations and also business."

Braam Viljoen is gloomy about prospects. "With this violence and with their mischievous double agendas, I think de Klerk has missed the bus. I don't think he has it in him. He is too light for it. But, say that of him, his lieutenants make me frightened. Frankly they lack humanity, they lack leadership. They are the people forming the inner circle around de Klerk.

"As in the old plays of the Greeks, the old dramas of Aristophanes, Euripides, Sophocles, you see the whole thing developing, the whole intrigue growing to a fatal end," he said. "The choir always warning, warning, warning. Like people have been warning for forty years about apartheid. I mean, there is no excuse. It's not a matter of them not having been warned. But in spite of all these things you see an inevitable progress towards what could be disaster."

Wheels within wheels. Afrikaners believe in conspiracies because they've seen the conspiracies work. Secrecy and operating behind the scenes is a practice not easily abandoned. Along with Willem Saayman and Braam Viljoen, others with reason to know believe in a persisting, broad Afrikaner conspiracy, possibly overlapping with but more dangerous than the liberalizing Broederbond, largely latent but waiting on a hair trigger to go off.

Listen to an Afrikaner, around forty, who had served in the army for over a decade in Namibia. Next to him sat his friend, a decidedly liberal man, intoning like a one-man Greek chorus. The army man asked, at the end of the conversation, to remain anonymous—he was afraid he had talked too much.

ANONYMOUS: There are quite a number of Afrikaners who believe they will have to face the world, telling them, "Look, do your damnedest.

We'll go on our knees, we're not afraid to build up something from scratch again. We've done it in the past, we did it with our ox wagons. We'll do that. We'll face the wrath of the world, go to the final conflict, give them a greater genocide than in the Third Reich."

The true leaders of the Afrikaner nation never forgot to look back to see what was happening with the Afrikaner at grassroots level. My opinion is that with one or two strong leaders—now I'm not talking about the present bunch of Afrikaners, I'm talking of those that are still hidden, unknown to the world and even to de Klerk—

FRIEND: When he talks like that he scares me. My hair stands up.

ANONYMOUS: And you'll have more than half [of all Afrikaners] following. I believe that. De Klerk has lost a great part of Afrikanerdom. He's lost that already and there is no way he's going to win it back.

FRIEND: I'm afraid you're quite right. I've never come across such bitter comments from Afrikaans-speaking friends about any politician as I have with F. W.

ANONYMOUS: Right through history you'll find incidents where there has always been that split of the true Afrikaners and the false Afrikaners.

FRIEND: You've always had this accretive movement toward the right. It started immediately after the Anglo-Boer War. You had people who wanted to go into the union and others who didn't want to go, who saw it as a British creation. These things cast very long shadows. Every white Afrikaner thinks that there is going to be some kind of fierce clash eventually between black and white.

ANONYMOUS: Third Force. Not the Third Force referred to in the press, another Third Force. When that is triggered, I reckon that will make Germany look like—

FRIEND: This is one of the best-armed countries, for private citizens, in the world.

ANONYMOUS: You must remember that every person between the ages twenty-five and forty-five at this stage is an expert in army in one or another fields. If they are triggered by the intelligentsia, the Third Force that I'm talking about, which at this stage is still just looking at the situation—

QUESTION: But what "intelligentsia" is he talking about?

ANONYMOUS: Right up to within the cabinet.

QUESTION: Who are these people?

ANONYMOUS: Certain people. They sit everywhere. In the Broederbond, in the cabinet, in the universities, in every echelon of life.

QUESTION: Do they know they are united?

ANONYMOUS: They work in cells of two or three. I reckon that's what.

FRIEND: I think you know more than "reckon." That's the most I've ever heard him say about this topic.

QUESTION: What is the objective? Chaos?

ANONYMOUS: No. Their objective is if they don't see the result coming that will suit them, and I reckon if they are triggered, they will at all costs go for an *oorwinning*, total victory. Then you won't have any Sowetos left, you won't have any Alexandras left. If anarchy comes, it will be a struggle for who's going to rule, who's going to be warlord.

Saayman's advice, Braam Viljoen's gloom, the hints and fears of the anonymous former soldier hang like Damoclean swords, warnings not to assess the Afrikaner superficially. The Afrikaners who belonged to these secret organizations in 1992 are still there, holding the same beliefs, assessing the political scene to see if it "suits" them. The Afrikaners' faith in secrecy and conspiracy demands that they not be judged lightly. Their plodding reputation, parodied in *dumkopf* stories called "Van der Merwe jokes," which play up a stereotype of a stupid farmer, conceals another trait called *slimheid*, meaning wiliness or astuteness, more devious than the British idea of "clever." *Slimheid* is useful when fighting against great odds, as many Afrikaners think they are.

Secrecy and conspiracy are close cousins of *slimheid*. Afrikaners feel compelled to organize, plan, and control out of sight, beneath the surface of society. Remember Dominee Nel's declaration about the Conservative Party: "They're stupid if they haven't got it [a secret organization]." Although Nel said he hadn't joined the secret organizations into which he was invited, he granted their importance. Afrikaners will find it difficult to get secrecy out of their systems. How will we ever know if they do? *Slimheid*. Conspiracies. Sh-h-h.

CHAPTER THREE

JOHANNESBURG/EGOLI

Afrikaners who met black South Africans in exile in the late eighties were amazed that they cherished the land of South Africa as much as the Afrikaners did, that people described in the press as terrorists nostalgically yearned to go home.

One African woman who spent more than a decade in exile as a soldier in the ANC's uMkhonto we Sizwe, Spear of the Nation, military underground, returned home after F. W.'s February 2 speech, even before details of amnesty were worked out. She was desperate to be home again. Shortly after her return, while walking down a city street, she came face to face with the Afrikaner policeman who had tortured her during imprisonment without trial in 1976. In prison he had bashed her around, bouncing her head like a tennis ball, as she put it, again and again against a concrete cell wall. Sixteen years later her temples still throbbed during debilitating headaches and a scan showed a depression in her skull on the forehead. Wretched slop for food and a cell bucket with green, crawling contents were other memories that his presence evoked. He said cheerily that he'd heard she was coming back, then asked if she could now shoot a gun.

How did that make her feel?

"I had knots inside," she said. But she was home.

South Africa is a lion-colored land—blond sun, yellow grass, rusty earth—with vast empty spaces, much of it semidesert, interrupted suddenly by seething knots of population. Sometimes the knots are former African tribal homelands, the overpopulated, eroded 13 percent of the land designated by law for blacks. Sometimes the knots are "white" cities, towns, and *dorpe* (villages), each one connected umbilically to nearby black townships, the latter lacking in infrastructure because they were considered temporary under apartheid.

The biggest knot of all, in the north center of the country, is the metropolis of Johannesburg or eGoli ("gold" in black patois). A little over one hundred years old, Johannesburg (population, one million) is sibling to Soweto, an even bigger knot (population, two to three million) that was ignored on maps until recently, and to other townships such as Alexandra, Lenasia, Eldorado. Johannesburg was one of the fastest-growing cities in the world after gold was discovered in 1886 in the region surrounding the city, the watershed between the Vaal and the Olifants rivers called the Witwatersrand, or simply the Rand. Twenty-five miles wide and sixty long, the Rand is marked by ridges, called reefs, laden with gold, silver, and other minerals. Its name was given to South Africa's currency, the rand.

Beneath the city wind the tunnels and cells of old mines, like magnified labyrinths of the snouted harvester termites that swarm out of the ground after rains. These mines were exhausted and their human tunnelers moved elsewhere, leaving tobacco-stain-yellow mine-tailing mountains to the city's east and south. Flat on top, resistant to plant growth, the vast eroded dumps are etched deeply with creases like an old smoker's face. Other mine mountains to the northeast in Witbank are grizzly gray and senile. In the bitter highveld winters the winds sometimes whip dust off these mountains, further polluting the smoggy air, exacerbating sinus and lung problems.

Hillbrow, now a roiling, interracial area of high-rise apartment buildings and night clubs, sits halfway up the reef that divides the older Johannesburg, with its central business district and industrial zone, from posh areas to the north. Southwest of the city's central grimy industrial area, spanking new suburbs such as Sunward Park spread beyond the more established Boksburg. The N1 national highway bisects Johannesburg and the country, southwest to northeast. Swooping on it over the central business district, one drives through the shadow of the building called John Vorster Square, the police headquarters. Its tenth floor was notorious as the site of torture and death, the point of departure for "suicides" who "fell" to their deaths while under interrogation for anti-apartheid activities. Several blocks away is the Market Theatre and the jazz bar Kippies, hangouts for black and white sophisticates. Glaring in the sun, like something out of Dallas, is The Diamond, a glass office building monolith whose heat reflection flummoxed the cooling systems of the nearby Johannesburg Stock Exchange and the Chamber of Mines, marshalers of awesome wealth. At The Diamond's base on Diagonal Street, one of the city's original streets laid out by Oom (uncle) Paul Kruger,* are African *muti*, traditional

---

*A founder of the Boer Republic of the Transvaal and its president from 1883 to 1900.

medicine, shops crammed with dried baboons and other foul-smelling paraphernalia.

Back on the N1 riding north, one sees the University of the Witwatersrand's solid, stone buildings to the left; the SABC television tower rises farther to the west, with its radio tower to the east over Hillbrow. Up, up gradually to the crest of that hill, then suddenly the vista is velvety green. Stretching north and west are the well-watered, almost all-white suburbs—Mandela and a few other blacks have moved in here and there. Sturdy, splotchy sycamores line Rosebank's avenues. In the November spring, purple jacaranda blossoms clash with the sky, soon nudged out by the gnarly trees' filigree leaves. Here and there palm trees squat, solid as elephant legs, with pineapple-scale trunks, gray, dangling bottom fronds and upright green ones with amber dates tucked in them like hair baubles.

A lovely park called The Wilds stretches across the hill that falls off toward the north. Overlooking The Wilds with its watered trees and plants, mansions so glorious that they would be at home in Newport, Rhode Island, sprinkle the top of the hill in Houghton Estate. In March the proteas, flowers of a family native to South Africa, bloom in the park; their pink petals with brown tips look fused into chunky thoraxes and they feel furry like mammal pelts. Sprinkled around The Wilds are the ubiquitous thorn trees with deep green, lace leaves that hide toothpick-length, gray thorns too strong to be easily broken and so shockingly sharp that, one imagines, they would make excellent murder weapons. The northern suburbs are cooled by numerous parks, in great contrast to Soweto, fifteen miles to the southwest, which is so unlandscaped that blacks travel to Johannesburg's parks for backdrops to their wedding pictures. Another small park, the Melville Koppies (hillocks) Nature Reserve, was designed to be rain-watered. There archaeologists have dug up and preserved an iron smelting furnace dating back to A.D. 900, proving that Bantu-speaking people have exploited the mineral wealth of these hills for a long time. In layers beneath are an Iron Age floor, 1,000 years old, and a Middle Stone Age camp, maybe 40,000 years old; still farther down, handaxes were unearthed that may be 100,000 years old.

In South Africa a northern exposure is desirable for a home because, of course, the sun crosses the sky to the north. Johannesburg is as far south of the equator as Miami Beach is north of it. However, Johannesburg is on the highveld, a vast grassy plain about a mile above sea level, so its climate is considerably cooler than Miami's. Although South Africa has a brief winter when temperatures can occasionally plunge to freezing at night, most houses lack central heating. Huddling for warmth around electric radiant heaters, or coal heaters where no electricity is available, is a condition of winter life from June through August. When the sycamore leaves, big as hands, fall, they skitter crisply down the streets where they are swept away at night by blacks, the omnipresent people.

From the close-in suburbs, the N1 passes a place not quite visible from the highway, an area less than a mile square that's like a patch from Dante's *Inferno*. Alexandra, a black township originally located miles from any white area, is now completely swallowed up by white-owned factories and housing subdivisions. Its muddy streets, dreadful migrant labor hostels, and cheek-by-jowl living are the legacy of pulsating apartheid Africa. This is what scares the spit out of whites. Whites who live on the fringes of Alexandra have nightmares of robbers and worse. This volatile area, an apartheid concentrate, received regular attention from the Dutch Reformed Church and other Broederbond-approved bodies, lest it explode; because it pricked the conscience, unlike the more remote Soweto; and because Dominee Sam Buti, of the black Dutch Reformed Church, lived there and complained.

Heading farther north on the N1, one cruises past one new, modern office building after another. The unoccupied, gleaming buildings are evidence of government tax incentives that made them good investments while the rest of the economy deteriorated when international sanctions against South Africa were in force.

Here and there off the highway white suburbs spread through the trees, their houses surrounded by tall walls studded with warning signs: PASSOP VIR DIE HOND (Beware of the dog), ARMED RESPONSE SECURITY SYSTEMS. Residents now rely on private security companies to guard them because the police were too busy with problems more serious than burglary and suburban muggings.

Right-wingers blame rising crime on F. W., insisting it didn't exist before his February 2, 1990, speech. But the real change was that after the speech the press began to report more freely on what was happening in the country, including crime and growing unemployment, reaching 50 to 60 percent among blacks. As the number of robberies, car jackings, and incidents of little black children sniffing glue in Hillbrow rise, the heights of the walls in the suburbs are climbing too. For houses without walls, insurance is prohibitively expensive.

But walls cannot solve a fundamental problem of South African life: apartheid produced a terrible housing shortage. The government preserved apartheid's fiction that blacks were citizens of homelands by prohibiting permanent housing development around the cities even as the African workers were brought in to keep South Africa's economy going.

Millions of people have thus become "squatters" and "transients" where they live. Parks, empty lots, and the streets and alleyways are home to growing numbers of urban migrants. "Under the best possible conditions imaginable, we will not be able to wipe out our housing backlog for the next fifteen years," said Philosophy Professor Zach de Beer Postma. "We will have to build as many houses in the next fifteen years to wipe out that backlog as have been built in this country since 1652. That is physically impossible. Even if every other sector of the economy is neglected, we can't do it."

In the northern suburb of Parkhurst one white woman knows she has several homeless people living in her magnificent back garden with its five ponds. She can tell by washed clothes hung out to dry. Years ago when she and her husband purchased the land it was derelict and stacked with car wrecks. To their surprise, when they cleaned it up they found a stream running through it. Her husband, an architect and artist, designed their beautiful garden, now graced with his metal and wood sculptures. She is happy to have her garden lived in and makes sure that its surreptitious residents have access to the water spigot on the side of her house. She regards them as a defense against an invasion by other homeless people; the occupiers' vigilance over what they view as "their" territory protects hers from further encroachment.

Few whites are so sanguine. The "blackening" of the city terrifies many, although they usually express their fears in objectified terms. Standards will fall, whites say. *They* are on a different level. *They* will take years to reach our level, or *they* never will.

"Standards" seems to be the word more often used by English-speaking whites, "level" by Afrikaners. "Standards" can be fairly easily improved with education, but "level" seems to be inherited or almost genetic. "Standards" applies to material conditions and to school quality, while "level" includes culture, customs, manners—such as the often-mentioned use of knives, forks, and spoons. To whites, the erosion of standards can be seen in the presence of black hawkers selling all kinds of items and services, from produce to clothes mending, on street corners all over the city. In the past, under apartheid's Influx Control laws, police would have swooped on them, throwing them into police paddy wagons and carting them off to prisons. This was such a common scene in the white suburbs during the apartheid years that the arrests became nearly invisible to whites, obscured by the calluses on their consciences. With the abolition of the apartheid laws in 1990, the migrant homeless began converging on Johannesburg and other cities, drawn by the hope for jobs like iron filings to magnets.

*   *   *

Johannesburg is a fast-paced, grubby city, where wealth and poverty stare at each other, hating each other. In Rosebank, a hungry woman presses her face against an elegant restaurant window. On either side of the woman's hips a tiny foot is visible, belonging to a baby plastered on her back and obscured by a blanket used to strap him on. In the same Rosebank suburb are splendid art galleries, full of experimental art, shopping malls with expensive imported goods, bookstores, coffee shops, a cinema complex playing the latest American movies, and a shop selling magnificent furniture made from old, hardwood railway ties. You name it, and Johannesburg-Soweto, together the fourth-biggest metropolis on the African continent, probably has it somewhere.

All this consumer lushness was made possible because gold was found on the Witwatersrand, resulting in the fastest-growing economy on the African continent.

But pause in that shop or grocery store and think about uniforms. Orange uniforms, blue uniforms. The effect is to categorize and stereotype, to teach whites to think of blacks as drones, as less able than the whites, who are without uniforms. Uniforms make people ciphers. Like trees in the landscape. But the uniform people are now voting, now disturbing the economy in which the whites had reveled.

When spring comes in the highveld the brown leaves fall off, pushed by the new ones. The winter wind, which made the dirt roar off the mine mountains lounging like mangy lionesses, is quiet. Rains will follow in furious, quick storms, and the dust will lie down with the homeless. Whites are learning that blacks too love this dust, the smell of the earth just before rain. That horizon, those *koppies* were born in them too. They think it the most compelling land in the world. It lies deep in their psyches and, like the arms of a lover, they are loath to leave its allure for long.

CHAPTER FOUR

WHAT IS AN AFRIKANER?

If Afrikaners lie down on their couches and talk about what it means to be an Afrikaner, one thing leads to another and another, until they contradict each other and start pointing fingers at who is and who isn't. Discussing their identity has been an Afrikaner predilection for decades.

The precariousness of the Afrikaners' survival has been a theme played like lachrymose violin music by the Nationalists since the 1920s. Then the Afrikaner was defined vis-a-vis the English speakers and the coloreds.

"I've only been an Afrikaner always, but I don't exactly know what it is," said Dominee Jan van Rooyen, chuckling. The main thing, he said, is that he is Afrikaans-speaking and has a culture that "differed from the English." When he was growing up in the thirties, that was the Nationalists' political emphasis. But if "you go to England, you find out how English we all are in South Africa," he said.

"I've been an Afrikaner for forty-two years and I don't understand what's going on," said journalist and editor Max du Preez. "I try very hard," he added. "We're a mass of deep conflicts." Take Eugene Terreblanche, the neo-Nazi right-wing leader and founder of the African Resistance Movement (Afrikaner Weerstandsbeweging, AWB). At first Terreblanche will "tell you all this white supremacy bullshit." Then switch off the tape recorder and he will "tell you he's an African militarist." His hero is Shaka Zulu, the Zulu military leader who ravaged other African tribes in central South Africa during the mid–nineteenth century. "Now where does white supremacy come in?" du Preez asked rhetorically.

Some Afrikaners insist they are Africans tied to the land.

"There's some truth to that," du Preez said.

Others say, no way, Afrikaners are Europeans through and through.

"That's also right," du Preez said.

Annie Gagiano is a professor at Stellenbosch University who calls herself a South African rather than an Afrikaner "because I grew up in a very Afrikaner family and disliked a lot of it." She is opposed to being jammed into "the narrow category because of the devastating conse- quences. There are geological layers of a very contorted identity which is fiercely maintained [by Afrikaners]. If you try to analyze it, it's full of a great deal of hogwash," she said. "Powerful Afrikaners running the show and at the same time having this romantic notion of being underdogs."

"I'm not an ordinary or conventional Afrikaner," said the former police commissioner Johan Coetzee. It is a frequently heard comment. What he meant by "ordinary" was the stereotype: "The farmer in the countryside, the patriarchal family. Another strange phenomenon that you'll find is that the majority of Afrikaners would be from Dutch extrac- tion, but they don't place a lot of emphasis on that because of the war [World War Two], when Holland fought on the side of England [the Afrikaners' former enemy]. You'll find a tendency amongst Afrikaners to stress, 'I'm from German immigrants.' "

Even when Afrikaners are well-traveled, highly educated urbanites, they can retain the mark of the farm. The wealthy lawyer P. J. T. (Terts) Oosthuizen, who called himself an Afrikaans-speaking South African, grew up on a farm near the Caledon River. The Depression and the drought of the thirties were so dreadful that he vowed never to be a farmer; yet he supervises stock farming on his ranches in his spare time and in 1992 waxed rhapsodic about Simenthaler cattle, akin to Texas longhorn, whose red-haired hide was well adapted to South Africa. He used the terms "stock" and "blood" when discussing his family.

"The Oosthuizen clan is like cattle. If I see an animal, a bull or cow, I would immediately recognize the strains and I would know what I'm getting. That is why in our old families we always insisted on the right breeding."

As for his own marriage, "We believe we made the decision ourselves, but the checking up was done," Oosthuizen said. "My wife is a daughter out of the Steyns and Krugers. The first Oosthuizen came to South Africa in 1691, the third of April. So we're here for more than three hundred years. My grandchildren are ninth generation. There are many old fami- lies that have been here that long, coming mostly from Holland, some from Germany. Of course if you say Holland, you do talk about Germanic origins and the influence of the German side. The French Huguenots, the English, others have come too, of other nations from time to time. Scots, Irish, you name it, Portuguese, plenty.

"I had people in the military with Scottish names that could hardly speak English [Oosthuizen was a brigadier in the army]. And I've had people with Afrikaans names that could hardly speak Afrikaans. My daughter is married to a man of Portuguese origin. She's Afrikaans-speaking, equally at home in English, and is also now learning Portuguese. Their home language is English. So, what is she? She's still an Afrikaner in my book."

One book about Afrikaners widely read in the United States was Rian Malan's *My Traitor's Heart*. The history professor Albert Grundlingh thought that although Malan's book was disturbing for its well-written depiction of violence, its representation of Afrikaners was atypical. Malan "makes a big thing of his Huguenot roots; that's actually an aristocratic sort of view. I think he's posing as an Afrikaner," Grundlingh said. "He went to a multiracial school in the seventies—Woodmead—which is an elitist private [English-language] school. That's quite unusual for Afrikaans speakers.

"You know the Dutch were a fairly rough lot, but the Huguenots were really sort of sophisticated people," Grundlingh said. "Malan played on this, the blood thing comes into it. I just found it a bit corny. If you really want to meet some Afrikaners, go to Pretoria West, these uncultured, uncouth types. I've got more sympathy for them than [for] these sophisticates."

Grundlingh has twinkly eyes and a sense of perspective, appropriate for a historian. Afrikaner ethnicity wasn't invented from scratch, he said, but it was manipulated by a lot of people. "The debate goes back at least to the twenties and thirties," he said, when Nationalists "resuscitated the philosophy of ethnicity during traumatic urbanization and industrialization. The notion of a pure Afrikaner was created. It is an intellectual construct, a product of a historical ideology. I don't think anything like that exists in the real world."

He noted that when the majority of Afrikaners prospered in the massive economic growth of the 1960s, "they didn't need the crutch of ethnicity any longer." White workers who couldn't make it even in those best of times however, fled to the right-wing camp, Jaap Marais's HNP (Herstigte, or Reconstituted, Nasionale Party, which split from the National Party in 1969). Grundlingh recalled that at that time lots of articles fretting about Afrikaner identity flooded the newspapers.

Religion professor Danie Goosen, who in his youth was a staunch HNP supporter, said, "Jaap Marais from the HNP often uses this metaphor of the tree's trunk. In the middle you find the center and then the layers around it, and the center is, of course, the Afrikaner *volk*, the *ware* [true] Afrikaner. This is sort of the holy, or the sacred center."

Goosen was so soft-spoken he nearly whispered as he explained his identity crisis as an HNP youth. He and a few close friends completely rejected Christianity because they thought it incompatible with nationalism, and they yearned toward a European intellectualism, a "holistic approach toward religion." As a professor at UNISA he returned to an iden-tification with Christianity but with an awareness that it is one among many religions. Goosen explained the more usual Afrikaner mentality, "a deep, underlying thought pattern, where we try to create identity and this is seen as sacred, as on a pedestal. This is placed in distinction to the profane world, which is associated with the world of the black people, and the English of course. The 'other' is always seen in a negative light. They are somehow on a lower level. They are the antichrist."

The cataclysms that shook the National Party in the eighties rattled the Afrikaners' self-definitions. Although a thin liberal vein existed within Afrikanerdom—from politician J. H. Hofmeyer in the 1880s to Leo Mar-quand, the founder of the National Union of South African Students (NUSAS), in the forties and fifties—the liberals were outmaneuvered and outshouted after 1948. To many Afrikaners they became tainted by their alliances with English speakers, and were therefore derided by Nationalists as not real Afrikaners. When the Conservative Party (CP) split off in 1982, suddenly it became broadly acceptable to have a differ-ent opinion and still be called an Afrikaner. Questioning spread like wildfire, on the left as well as on the right. The CP built on HNP beliefs and drew membership largely from the lower middle classes, according to Grundlingh.

"The Afrikaner is actually a metaphor for a larger social process at work," he said. "I don't think Afrikaners ever came around to an urban definition of Afrikanerdom. They yearned back to the countryside. That's where the idea of the Boer—Terreblanche and that mob—that's where their ideas come from."

"I call myself a Boer, and I resent the fact that the term was hijacked by the right wing," Max du Preez said. "Because it's an honorary term. It comes from those old days. I'm extremely proud of the history of the Anglo-Boer War. My family on all sides took part."

Du Preez said he and his fellow journalist Jacques Pauw deliberately carried on a knockdown, drag-out fight in the columns of their *Vrye Weekblad*, a dissident weekly newsmagazine, over the hoary issue, 'What is an Afrikaner?' Du Preez took the position, "I'm a Boer and proud of it," while Pauw, a decade younger than du Preez, said, "I don't want to be a bloody Boer. They are conservative and racist."

Pauw grew up in a Nationalist, upper-class suburb of Pretoria. He majored in political science at the University of Pretoria in the early 1980s. It did not occur to him that anything was amiss about apartheid or that he had any reason to question his Afrikaans identity until a controversy erupted over the presence on campus of a young black boy of fifteen who was leading a blind Afrikaner student around to classes. In the end the university council ruled the boy "could be present in the lecture rooms, but he may not use the toilets on the campus." In reaction, Pauw decided, "I'm a South African, I'm not even an Afrikaner."

Many Afrikaners are fond of saying they are members of a white tribe, a notion as elusive as the term "Afrikaner."

"It suits us Afrikaners to be an African tribe when we want to be," said the journalist Marichen Waldner in the softest of sarcastic tones. "But in all other aspects, it suits us to talk of our European ancestors and traditions. I know very few Afrikaners who have become Africanized. Being a tribe, that is not really true. I promise you that it is really not true. Because they are Westerners. It will take them a long time to become Africans."

Oh, but the Afrikaners are too a tribe, said political theory professor André Louw.

"The Afrikaner somehow through historical circumstances turned himself into an African tribe," he said in his office at UNISA in Pretoria. "This is what most outsiders usually don't understand. I can't explain how or why without becoming mystical, but the point is that this actually is what happened."

African tribes are introverted, closed societies, Louw said. Even though the Afrikaners superficially look European, there is "a rigid tribal exclusiveness about them. Or there was up until ten, fifteen years ago when things started opening up," he said. "A tribe isn't the same as a nation. A nation has got boundaries. This is the problem of the Afrikaner, they are not geographically defined. Their cohesion depends on descent and not on where they live. This was the whole problem of apartheid all the time, you know, the fact that they couldn't see their identity in geographic terms. The international community accepts the self-determination of areas. But not of groups.

"The Afrikaner [historically] had two forces to contend with," Louw said. "European imperialism on the one side and African tribes on the other. And he tackled them in succession. The way he tackled them is partly to identify with them and partially to try and transform them."

Louw takes the example of Jan Christiaan Smuts, who was prime minister until 1948; he partially accommodated and partially rejected the British empire by "transforming the Empire into the idea of the [British] Commonwealth." Now the Afrikaners are going through the same process with South Africa's blacks, Louw said. The conservatives would reject the blacks, flee from them into a *Volkstaat*, a state for Afrikaners alone. But the other attitude, that of F. W. and the National Party, is, "Well, let's try and absorb them," Louw said.

The conservatives who clutch to the notion of a separate Afrikaner state often use the terms "free" and "freedom," words with historic resonance because of the Boer fight to be free of British rule.

Koos Botha was a CP Member of Parliament in 1991 when he helped plant a bomb in an empty Pretoria high school that had been designated for use by returning ANC exile children. "There are two types of Afrikaners, those that want to be free—I'm one of those—and those that want to share power within a new dispensation," he said in 1992. "Mr. de Klerk is one of those Afrikaners. I won't say that he's not an Afrikaner. I would say that we've got basic differences."

Manie van Heerden, a founding member of the Conservative Party and a businessman in Johannesburg, sneered about "so-called Afrikaners, people that speak Afrikaans, that are white and that go to the Afrikaans churches, but they have lost the will for freedom or the self-determination struggle. They want to be in a unitary state now. That is why I cannot regard them as Afrikaners."

Dominee Willie Lubbe, right-winger par excellence and the glum head of the Afrikaanse Protestante Kerk, put it this way: "If you want me to explain the Afrikaner to you, I'd say in the first instance the Afrikaner was a Christian from the very beginning. He's a man who has his own language, own culture, own customs, own history. And right through the ages, he was a white man. You can't ignore that.

"Some people prefer to call themselves *boere*," Lubbe said. "Others prefer to speak of Boer-Afrikaners. Because now anybody who belongs to Africa may be called an Afrikaner. If we want to remain Afrikaners, we must have our own Christian government, have our own country, we must have our own future. You see. We must have our own Fatherland."

Was F. W. de Klerk an Afrikaner?

"No, he's definitely not an Afrikaner," Lubbe said.

Why not?

"Because de Klerk has preferred to associate himself with the world opinion and not with his own people in his country. He's not serving his own people. He's serving wider interests. He's trying to accommodate international opinion, international forces."

So who is an Afrikaner? The vicious/mystical/pathetic-verging-on-bathetic debate goes on, presenting a dilemma for anyone writing a book about Afrikaners. One must be arbitrary: this book is about white Afrikaners, whatever that means.

CHAPTER FIVE

THE BOER
INSIDE EVERY AFRIKANER

"I grew up on a farm."

"My parents came from the farm."

"My grandparents were farmers."

Boer means "farmer" in Afrikaans, and for many Afrikaners a farm tie is a point of pride and nostalgia. The strength of the National Party in the thirties and forties lay with the farmers, and even after the Afrikaner population shifted to the cities, the farm ethos clung like mud to politicians' shoes.

When one thinks of rural areas, or *platteland*, in South Africa, usually the image of the highveld rises up. Corn, called *mielies*, is the great cash crop; since it was introduced from North America it has become the subsistence food of Africans north through Zambia. On the highveld, old-fashioned electric lines with their white porcelain insulators stitch for miles down the major—two-lane—highways. Giant sunflowers nod toward the sun through the smog, which in winter months virtually blankets the country from the Cape north to Pietersburg in the north central Transvaal. Windmills suck up ground water, their blades echoing the shape of the sunflowers' faces, whirring in the breezes, which plunge to freezing in the July winters. The *platteland* is tamed land, whereas the wilder bushveld in the north of the country is tangled with acacia scrub and thorn trees, dotted with three-foot-high termite mounds and dollops of rocky hillocks called *koppies*. Much of the veld is devoted to cattle and game (antelopes of various kinds) ranching, although parts such as the Springbok Flats, around Naboomspruit, are used for tobacco, cotton, and peanut farming, and the lowveld down the escarpment toward Kruger National Park specializes in vegetable and fruit farms.

South African farming includes lush, old vineyards and apple orchards in the Cape, sweaty sugar-cane plantations in Natal, tea estates on Drakensberg mountain slopes, sheep-rearing expanses in the Karoo (an extensive plateau in the Cape Province), and a particularly ideal place for ostrich farms around Oudtshoorn in the Little Karoo where the pebbles perfectly suit the big birds' gizzards. In northern Natal and on the Drakensberg mountains in the Transvaal, mile after mile of uniformly high eucalyptus and pines girdle the land as if trying to keep it shapely and under the control of some white plan. The tree farms supply the vast paper needs of Johannesburg's urban and industrial maw.

"In the twenties, seventy to eighty percent of Afrikaners were still rural people, small farmers," according to the Stellenbosch University economics professor Sampie Terreblanche. "Up into the fifties these small Afrikaner farmers were traditionalistic and did not have the capacity to adapt to changing circumstances. The same kind of phenomenon as the Dust Bowl, as you called it in the States. There was a process of forced urbanization."

In the wake of the Anglo-Boer War, the Depression, and the droughts of the 1930s, the Boers crammed into an urban world whose values they despised and where they could compete only as manual laborers. Business had always been an English preoccupation, viewed as a dirty pursuit by the Afrikaners.

Jack Botes, a longtime city manager of Pietersburg in the northern Transvaal and a National Party functionary and regional planning chairman, recalled, "I was born in the heart of the Karoo. My father was a farmer about two hundred miles south of De Aar in Beaufort West, and he went bankrupt [in the drought of 1932–34]. He had standard three [fifth-grade] schooling. He became farm manager for a wealthy farmer just outside De Aar, and that farmer also went under, and then he joined the South Africa Railways as a laborer. Pick-and-shovel work. I had my first pair of shoes when I was in standard nine [eleventh grade]. I was fifteen."

The farmers were "not very well equipped for making it in urban conditions because they had no training, so they had to come in on a very low level as unskilled people," said Jan Lombard, a former governor of the Reserve Bank. But more than a romantic past, the farm is a touchstone of memory and the incubator of values. As liquor-store owner Louw Bezuidenhout put it, "I don't think that there is any one family here in Pretoria who hasn't got family stretched over the whole country on the farms."

Julie Bezuidenhout, Louw's wife, grew up on a *mielie* farm on the Caledon River near Lesotho in the fifties, a far cry from her cozy, middle-class Pretoria home of 1992. "We had no machinery on the farm when I was a child. We had to cut all the corn by hand. I had to work so hard that my back was always sore. And my arms. There was a donkey or a mule or a horse pulling the plow and we had to keep it straight. We had to work very, very hard with our black people on the farm. My grandfather, ohhh, he was a terror. On Sunday, it's an Afrikaans tradition, all the family sits around this huge table, sixteen, eighteen, twenty people. The children were not allowed to eat with the grownups. We ate after."

She broke into merry laughter.

"We had to take peach-tree branches and keep the flies away with that peach branch. We, my cousins and sisters, were having a look at what they were feasting on. And we were hungry."

What did she learn from that?

She laughed and then said very deliberately, smiling, "To hate. Sunday. Dinners.

"I remember looking for eggs," she recalled nostalgically. "I enjoyed that, in the basket, between the hay. I loved the eggs. Still up to today I don't eat eggs, or hardly ever.

"It was nice on the farm; you were free and playing with your black friends," Julie said. She wondered where they were now.

The fortunes of the white farmers are changing as the country alters course; their traditional government support and subsidies are shrinking.

Professor Zach de Beer Postma said, "One of the first things that [Prime Minister] Louis Botha did after the Boer War ended was to go to England to get a loan, I think of three million pounds, a vast fortune in those days, to establish land banks. The land bank became the mainstay of agriculture in this country ever since that time [providing cheap loans to farmers]. Now with the subsidy system and all these things being withdrawn, people have a real sense of betrayal. This is an institution that originally restored them to their lives, got them going again. Now the mat has been pulled out from under them."

The mat of protection and assistance for farmers was a thick, many-layered one. Its first layers were set down as early as 1828 when white authorities in the Cape Colony passed laws to control Africans' movements and drive them off pasture and farmland, which was the beginning of the creation of a landless laboring class. By 1862, labor tenancy laws and customs were well established. Blacks could remain on white-owned territory in exchange for labor, but beginning late in the decade a series of "Location Acts" called for landowners to register the dwellings of tenants and to limit their numbers. The early laws were not rigorously enforced, but registration and eviction of excess "squatters" began in earnest in 1892. In 1894 the Glen Grey Act required that nonowners be evicted from "locations," and the size of African land holdings was limited.

White agricultural and mining interests pressed for laws that would add to the low-wage black labor pool, but in some places their interests clashed with those of white merchants. Historian Colin Bundy, in *The Rise and the Fall of the South African Peasantry*, reported that in Queenstown in the 1880s, English merchants opposed efforts by Dutch farmers to evict African peasants in order to make room for additional white farmers. The merchants found Africans to be a much larger potential consumer market for their businesses than the relatively few whites that would replace them, but the elaboration of laws restricting African land ownership, residency, and mobility continued.

In the 1870s and '80s, drought reduced the productivity of African farming and impoverished tenant workers, while wars between the whites and African tribes brought floods of black refugees looking for jobs.

At the turn of the century, according to contemporaneous white observers noted by Bundy, African agriculture was more efficient and productive than white farming. But the whites used their power in government to destroy African competition and to transform the formerly independent African farmers and pastoralists into a low-wage labor pool for farms and mines. Land value increased as white productivity rose as a result of irrigation and government subsidies, grants, fencing, dams, housing, veterinary and horticulture advice, cheap rail rates, special credits, and tax relief. Former pastureland was enclosed, further reducing Africans' abilities to support themselves through herding.

In 1899, legislation permitted white landowners to keep Africans on their land only if they were continuously (as opposed to seasonally) employed, or if they paid annual leases of £36—quite a lot of money in those days. Bundy cited a commentator who said in 1908, "It is probable that during the last 20 years more money per head of the rural (white) population has been devoted to the relief of farmers in South Africa than in any country in the world." However, in the same year a government commission found that too many Africans were availing themselves of opportunities to remain on white lands. A new act in 1909 raised fees, tightened enforcement, and led to a new round of evictions in 1910. Finally, in the 1913 Land Act, the Union of South Africa, including the Cape Colony, Natal, Orange Free State, and Transvaal, prohibited African land ownership anywhere but in the "native reserves," which amounted to only about 8 percent of the total land area.

The Land Act and its precursors under British administration show, as many Afrikaners argue, that post-1948 apartheid extended a preexisting state of affairs that was largely created by the English. English mining interests promoted the conversion of Africans into wage laborers in collaboration with white farmers who not only wanted cheap labor, but successfully sought to eliminate the efficient African farmers as a competitive threat.

From the Land Act until the Nationalist victory in 1948, laws accumulated that slightly increased the area of the "native reserves" (to about 14 percent of the total area) but further restricted African mobility in white areas, established curfews for Africans, curtailed ownership rights even in the reserves, and progressively limited and destroyed what little representation the Africans had in Parliament.

After the Nationalists' victory in 1948, legislation was no longer piecemeal, but was elaborated into a complicated and comprehensive code intended to protect white "civilization" by controlling every aspect of life for the "nonwhite," and especially the African population. The Immorality Act outlawed racial mixing, from theaters to marriage. "Influx Control" required that to be in white areas, Africans and coloreds had to have proof of employment, be born in the area, or be the spouse of a legal resident, and they could live only in specified townships or as employees on the property of their employers. Forced removals dumped an estimated 3.5 million people into the tribal "independent homelands" and "self-governing territories" from "black spots" (small parcels still owned by Africans) or other areas declared to be "white areas" as the government strove to consolidate white land holdings and to rationalize the black areas. Fourteen categories of race were identified, including "other," and were indicated on passes that every "nonwhite" person had to carry. An estimated 18 million people were arrested for pass-law violations until the laws were abolished in mid-1986.

From being a growing, independent, and productive peasantry in the mid-1800s, the Africans by 1920 had been reduced under white domination to landless, largely unemployed migrant wage laborers. Forced to search for work on white farms, in mines, or as domestic servants, but prevented by law from moving into white areas with wives, husbands, or children, African families were stretched to the breaking point by the welter of restrictions.

An estimated 40 percent of the African population still lives in rural areas, but land redistribution to rectify some of the past inequities faces an uphill battle in the transition to a "new South Africa." The agricultural bureaucracy, divided into fourteen ethnic departments and many parastatals, remains oriented toward large-scale white farms. Privatizations within the meat and dairy industries appear calculated to turn public monopolies into private monopolies, still in the hands of white capital. Where the government privatized state-controlled lands in the homelands, they were sold cheaply or given to the Nationalists' homeland allies. The government's drought relief program in 1992–93, funded with 4 billion rands ($1.48 billion), was used to rescue heavily indebted white landowners, enabling them to stay on land that could have been bought by black farmers. Little of the money went to black farmers.

Afrikaners' eyes often glaze over rapturously when they talk about their land. They are clearly moved, and largely unaware that their encomiums resemble mantras chanted the world over by other agrarian peoples. Like those others', Afrikaners' ties to the land are under pressure. Drought threatens cash cropping. Reductions in government subsidies slash profit margins. And, most worrisome, the new political order threatens to shake up ownership patterns.

Land redistribution began with a trickle in 1991, when laws barring black ownership in areas once deemed "whites only" were abolished. Take the farming area around Naboomspruit, a modest Transvaal town founded in 1910 when a prospector discovered tin among the *nabooms*, cactuslike plants thrusting their forklike tines into the sky. Two Naboomspruit farmers, Ben Steenkamp and Henry Rauch, epitomize opposing Afrikaner sides of the volatile land issue.

Caltex WTS Motors is the first gas station on the right in Naboomspruit, one of the less prepossessing stations on the N1 highway: a few pumps, a garage, a gravel parking area—humble compared to the dark tarmac, shiny pumps, and uniformed attendants of the bigger stations. WTS fixes trucks, and its proprietor, Ben Steenkamp, is a certified mechanic, along with being a farmer six or so miles outside of town. His sweat- and grease-stained khakis sagging in the midday heat seemed of a piece with the slightly basset-hound droop in his face. At a round table in the scuzzy office section of the garage, he sipped coffee and smoked as trucks roared by and his employees stepped in to consult with him about the repair jobs going on outside.

His gas business was picking up again in April 1992. Things had gotten sticky five weeks earlier when local whites began boycotting his station after word spread that he'd helped a black man buy a white-owned farm. Instead of the usual white clientele, more and more black motorists were stopping at WTS. "One of my boys here told me, '*Baas*, when they saw that story in the paper, they come along here and ask, is this the garage the whites are boycotting?' So he reckons 'yes,' and they say, 'Put petrol in.'" Steenkamp laughed. "Ja, 'put petrol in.'"

On his farm, Steenkamp has two center-pivot irrigation machines that spray plenty of water despite the drought, but he thought that he and other farmers probably made a mistake when they cleared the land and pursued cash cropping in this dry place instead of cattle ranching. Like other local farmers who had been socked by rising costs and falling water tables, one of Steenkamp's sons ran into trouble. He then decided to sell to a black man who had been renting grazing rights. Steenkamp's attitude was, "I don't mind. If he's got some money, he can buy it. If you've got money, you can buy anything you want." And when the deal looked good, "We helped the bloke. He paid the outstanding amount on the farm, he paid cash, and we gave him a first bond. So we helped him.

"I didn't expect this kind of trouble because I didn't realize it's such a bad thing to do, to help somebody else. I usually help people here, and they come and greet you by hand and what's wrong with that? There's nothing wrong with it.

"Afterwards, I spoke to one of these [African] taxi drivers. He reckon to me, 'Man, you are one of us, and I'll speak to my people so that they can come and help you.' Because we helped that black man. Some of those Gazankulu [Shangaan homeland] ministers, when they pass they put petrol here. They greet me every time and ask, 'How are you getting on?' They fill up every time. Six, eight Mercedes-Benz cars they park here in front. And they promise me land there. I can start a garage there in that place, Gazankulu.

"I now got three more people that are interested in farming, that want me to help them get nice places where they can buy and stay. I'm on to a new business. That's what's gonna happen now. And I don't care what other whites, especially the real right-wingers, got to say. The hell with their attitude."

One of Steenkamp's mechanics came inside to discuss a problem, talking in a local language. Steenkamp summarized: "A Zimbabwean hasn't got enough money on him for the repairs on the tires. He reckon when he's coming back he'll pay the outstanding balance. You have to trust him. What else do you do? If he runs away, he's gone, and that's all."

What was his experience in similar situations before?

"If they owe you money, they're gone," he said, making it clear he didn't help the Zimbabwean out of generosity, but because he had no choice.

Although property of the black farmer who bought Steenkamp's son's farm had been bombed, local police hadn't apprehended the criminal. Steenkamp was getting threats, but he said he wasn't worried. When one Afrikaner complained about his sale of land to the black man, Steenkamp told the complainer that he'd sell it to him instead, but the man didn't have "that kind of money. I said, 'Okay, suck your milk ring [teething ring], I don't want to hear a thing from you.' " Steenkamp continued, a bit righteously: "De Klerk gave us the right to do this business, and so what's wrong?"

Was there any reaction in his church to what had happened?

"No, the people now boycotting me are in the other church, the APK [Afrikaanse Protestante Kerk]." Steenkamp had faith in the police, even though some of them were right-wingers, but he heaped scorn on the far-rightists.

"I heard this story from my brother. The other day they are leaving the Co-op [agricultural union]. On every end of month the farmers get together and they talk about this and that and this and that, and some do a *bietjie braaivleis* [little barbecue], and have a couple of drinks and hold a party. There they confronted my youngest brother about this business that I sold that farm to the black man. They were swearing at him. So he said to them, 'You know what's your people's trouble? In daytime you like to kill these people. At nighttime you sleep them to hell.' You follow? That's what's going on."

Steenkamp said that unlike many of his white neighbors, he got along well with his black neighbors and workers. He spoke Tswana, Sotho, Shangaan, and a little Venda. "We can communicate with the people, and that's nine out of ten points. You talk nicely and tell him what you want from him. If he's working for you, you can speak to him in his language, and tell him what you want from him, and they do a nice job and that's it. But some of these people don't know their language, get cross to the people, swearing at them. Let me tell you, they respect you properly when you can speak their own language."

"You know, this politics is no good, man. I don't even go to meetings. I don't like it. Sleep nicely at night, tomorrow the brains are nice." Life was fine, apartheid irrelevant, and his treatment of his workers governed by market forces and his own good sense. The few farmworkers' dwellings visible near Steenkamp's house were miserable-looking hovels. "Ag, this apartheid business doesn't trouble me," he said. "Because on the farm, every oke got his own place where he stays. During daytime we work together, at night everyone goes to his place, and that is that. Apartheid doesn't affect me whatsoever."

But doesn't keeping wages low make life better for him?

"Ag, man, if the bloke works nice he gets nice pay. That's what it is. You get skilled people and you get people who don't know nothing."

Could he imagine what it was like to be black under apartheid?

"Well I don't know, I didn't think of it."

Steenkamp walked into his tiny office and proudly lifted a forked tree branch down from a hook on the wall. He had been divining and drilling for water for years and owned drilling rigs. He knew the land intimately, could read its signs. "The stick holds down," he said. "You can grab it in your hand and it turns down. You can't teach it. It works or it doesn't work. My father was divining long ago where I drilled, because I had the machines [for drilling water wells]. And one day I took one of these sticks and I go there and it works and it works and it works," dipping it each time he said "works."

"I don't charge for this. Especially where my machines work. You know, I could tell you, you are walking into the veld, the trees, the ground, the way the trees grow there, the way the upper ground tilts. When you get where the termites make a line, you can drill in one of the holes of them, you get water as well. They know where the water is. I say to the people, I can't divine water, but I think I'm luckier than anyone else."

Who did he think was threatening him and his family with bombs?

Steenkamp peered through his lightly tinted glasses, said nothing for a moment but pressed his lips together. He stood, hitched up his pants, led the way to his Toyota *bakkie* (pickup) and told several black men to hop into the back. He drove to the tiny *dorpie* called Crecy, where his mother owned a little grocery shop built by his father. It had one gas pump. A few black men sat around outside the shop playing games with coins.

Steenkamp didn't know who was threatening him and organizing the boycott, but there were two farmers who might know. One was Hendrik Botha and the other was Henry Rauch. Steenkamp pointed the way toward Rauch's farm, where he cash-crops cotton and tobacco.

Henry Rauch's split-level A-frame house was of shiny new logs. A pack of dogs snarled into action with the approach of a strange car. A short man with a beer belly and a lanky, tall youth strode from the house and called off the dogs. Sure, sure, welcome to talk about the drought and farming, come in, the older man said, leading the way into the house.

Henry Rauch and his twenty-year-old son Loffie (for Rudolph) wore typical Boer clothes: khaki shorts, shirt with epaulets, and khaki-colored kneesocks. Inside the house Rauch called his wife, who shook hands and supplied coffee, then faded into her domestic activities; she was occasionally visible with a black servant up on the balcony of the second floor. A wood carving of Jesus' head hung behind Loffie, who sat in the living room nearest the kitchen door.

Rauch didn't want to talk about neighborhood disputes. He was furious at F. W. and the Nats for reducing agricultural subsidies, driving the farmers out of business, and leaving the farms open to purchase by blacks.

According to Rauch, 20 percent of the local farms had been repossessed and were owned by the agricultural bank. "They are going to give it to the blacks for next to nothing. This year, at Naboomspruit, half of the farms are empty because of government policy. They told everybody it was the drought. I'm farming for fifty-five years. This is not the first drought. But economically, we're out. Ten years ago I bought a new tractor. I paid for it seventy thousand rand. Two years ago, I bought a smaller tractor, I paid for it seventy-five thousand rand. I'm a cotton farmer. Ten years ago I got eighty-five cents for a kilogram of cotton. Now I'm getting eighty cents. Prices are going up. Ten years ago I bought a tank [500 gallons] of diesel for under a thousand rand. Now I'm paying three thousand rand. That's government policy. They want the money to put in these niggers."

Loffie leaned forward, listening intently, his elbows on his knees. The wife passed through the living room, carrying laundry and muttering darkly in Afrikaans.

Rauch knew a lot about black people, he said, employing them on his farm and farming near their homelands. He spoke no African languages, however. Black workers who "work like white men" are very scarce. "It would be wrong to tell you that there are none of them, but they are scarce because of their background. The needs of the man is very little, much smaller than our white man's. If they slept well and their tummy is full, they are quite happy.

"They're not on the same level of civilization as our white people. Our civilization comes over a long period, two, three, four thousand years. This people, they have become civilized over three hundred years and less. You can't lift them. They steal and murder and all that sort of thing. They're not good farmers."

In a family, "Just one or two works and supports the rest. The unemployment they talk about, there's a lot of nonsense about it. I will take you into this black area, the homeland. On a working day there's thousands of them not interested in work. There is work, plenty of work.

"Tobacco, it's all hand labor. It's one of our great problems, to get enough labor. We go in with a lorry to get some people to work. They're not interested. But if they want a wireless or something, they will come and work till they get enough money to buy that item."

How much does he offer them to work?

"We give them piecework, you know. We pay every laborer five rand [$1.85] per oven. You get about thirty and you pay them five rand individually to fill an oven. They must pick the tobacco and bring it to the trailer and fill it. They can fill three to three and a half ovens a day. And for that, they get five rand an oven, they get free meals, and if they come from somewhere else, they get free boarding."

When he drives into the homeland and offers those wages what happens?

"They're not interested."

How much would he have to offer them to get them interested?

"I believe if I offered them a hundred rand, they'd still not be interested, because they're not interested in working."

Henry Rauch's wife became agitated. She marched out to him in the living room and made him go with her into the kitchen, where they argued hotly in Afrikaans. Henry returned, sat down, and acted as if nothing unusual had happened.

Henry and the rest of his family had joined the Afrikaanse Protestante Kerk (APK), which, determined to keep blacks out of their church, split from the Dutch Reformed Church in 1987. Henry still believes in separate development, or apartheid, as does Loffie. The young man had served his national service in urban townships and he was ready to fight if necessary. Henry seeks a *volkstaat* for himself and fellow Afrikaners because "you can't mix a sheep and a goat. It will never work. They'll go together and graze, but tonight when they come to the *kraal*, the sheep will sleep there, the goats will sleep in this corner."

Rauch agreed that blacks and whites are not different species, but said, "There's such a difference—civilization, education, you can't mix them. What is for them good is not good for me. Your niggers in America are a lot more civilized than these people. These people, they want to go tonight and sit there and fight and drink some beer, to have a nice fight with each other and that's it. And they don't want to get forward."

Rauch disparaged the black farmers for running cattle on rangeland rather than growing cash crops. "They haven't got the organizing in them to do tobacco or cotton or maize farming. If they plant maize, they will plant three or four or five or ten acres. That's enough for them to live on. Hell, if I can't plant two or three hundred acres, I'm not interested.

"The Springbok Flats, this area, is the best ground in the world. A long time ago this was a lake, and the soil is the mud of the lake, very, very rich soil. If it gets wet and there's no infrastructure, you can't move here" because of the mud. "The blacks didn't move in here because there were no roads. Now that the whites come and put infrastructure in, now they want it. But two hundred years ago, when they had the chance, they did nothing."

Rauch made veiled threats about what farmers might do in reaction to the loss of government subsidies and the fact that blacks could buy farms in the neighborhood.

"If the government doesn't come back to us, we farmers are organized to do some worse things like we do a year ago in Pretoria." In 1991, thousands of farmers paralyzed Pretoria by driving their tractors and trucks into the town and halting all traffic, as a protest against decreased government subsidies. This time, Rauch promised, "We're going to get the government so that there is nothing they can do in the whole country. Block the roads."

Wouldn't the government send in the army?

"The army can do nothing," he said. "If we block Naboomspruit, the police can't stop us, the army. And who is the army in Naboomspruit?"

Henry's wife screamed in Afrikaans from the balcony on the second floor.

"Henry, Henry. Henry, slow down now. We've got a letter from the South African Agricultural Union that tells us not to say a word."

Henry turned slightly, looked in her direction then repeated, "Who's the army here?"

His wife screamed, "You talked too much already!"

"We are the army," Henry said triumphantly.

Loffie nodded.

During the rest of the discussion Henry's wife scowled from the kitchen while instructing her servant to work. Toward the end, as photographs were being taken and the camera was flashing, she suddenly dashed out of the kitchen as if she'd been set afire.

"Sir, I'm very, very sorry but you don't take photos of my husband and my son," she shouted. "No, I'm not for publication. I talk to reporters much in my life. I don't believe you. No, I'm sorry, no. My husband is talking too much. I told him that but there, okay, he don't listen to me. So I ask you please, no more pictures. No one in the outside world has any sympathy with us. If you come here as tourists, that's all right. But don't as reporters, sorry."

A sign on the front gate of the farm said TURPAN. What did it mean?

"No, no, no, *nee*. No, no, no, I don't want, please." Mrs. Rauch was in flames.

By now Henry was standing, trying to ignore his wife as his visitors edged out of the house.

"There's a hell of a misunderstanding," he said, meaning misunderstanding of Afrikaners. "Therefore I'm glad you come and see for your-self. You people [outside South Africa] don't get the facts, even our local papers don't give you the real facts."

"These white farmers are the laziest things," Elna Trautmann said. In her job as regional director of Operation Hunger, the country's biggest private charity, she had recently returned from a scouting mission into the Karoo semidesert in Cape Province to investigate the plight of the thousands of black farmworkers who were hungry, suffering from mal-nutrition caused by the bad drought and pitiful economy. In some towns Operation Hunger was feeding every single black and colored person, she said. But the newspapers had mostly reported the increasing poverty of white farmers. She found those stories quite false.

"White farmers are pleading poverty there because they've been so used to the absolute wealth, the subsidies and that type of thing. But if you look at the mansions that they live in, there's no poverty there. If you're in dire shape, you don't have thousands of sheep and angora goats, do you? You start clamping down. You sell your Mercedes because there's two *bakkies*."

When the white farmers feel a pinch, they cut workers' pay, she said.

"Farmworkers used to get one hundred rands a month or twenty rands a week, or whatever they pay, plus some sheep. They're not get-ting that anymore."

In addition there is the "company store," owned by the farmers. At the end of the month there's nothing in the pay packets, she said, because the workers owe money to the farmers' stores.

Trautmaun described how she, speaking her Afrikaans *taal* (language) to the hilt, went into the office of a farmer who was in the sixteen-farmer syndicate in Britstown. "He sat back and was telling me about all these 'Hotnots.'* He gets government money and then buys products the gov-ernment prescribes. He buys a huge amount of soya and then distributes it. The people are so hungry they give whatever little bit they have. He's going to make a lot of bucks. He felt good about it."

Outside in the northern veld at night, far away from any houses and cities, the quiet *is*, just is. Even a half-moon throws almost palpable shadows from the mopani, the elephants' favorite munching tree. One can sense multitudes of wild animals breathing out there. It's the land Afrikaners love, but it's being ruined.

*A derogatory term derived from Hottentots, now more properly called Khoikhoi.

The ecological sins of modern agricultural and industrial development weigh heavily on South Africa. Salination from irrigation, water pollution from fertilizers, erosion due to plowing marginal and fragile lands: large-scale agriculture in South Africa now confronts the same problems that face commercial farmers in other countries. Water shortages combine with a booming population to exacerbate the crisis. Mining and metal industries are massive polluters. A pall of smog hangs over the highveld from Bloemfontein to the escarpment and down to the Kruger Park lowlands, in the eastern Transvaal, as well as over the townships of Cape Town and in Natal.

The smog worsens in winter, when millions of coal stoves in the townships are fired up for cooking and heat. Expanding the electrical grid into the townships will eventually help, but housing standards are so low and the people so poor that wood and coal will continue to be burned in huge quantities by people who can afford nothing else.

Added to the coal smoke, black clouds billow over the veld in fall and winter as stubble is set afire in the belief that burning over the rangeland promotes new growth. On even the driest and smoggiest days, fires dot the countryside. The land is well loved, but sorely abused. Lack of opposition to the National Party thwarted development of an environmental movement.

Ton Vosloo, a powerful man in the Afrikaner establishment as the president of the publishing and media company Nasionale Pers (National Press) and M-Net cable television, spoke disparagingly of the Afrikaner and his vaunted love of the land.

"You know, Afrikaners are not that much involved in nature conservation. They love to go to the game reserves, but that's to have a *braai* and a booze-up. I'm involved in nature conservation and ninety, ninety-five percent of the active people in there are English people.

"Oh, they all love the land, they all love nature, but we are the worst exploiters of the bloody land and the nature, I mean, if you look at what my compatriots have done to the soil and in the environment! Jesus, just look at the Transvaal now in the winter. The whole, from Johannesburg down to the Kruger Park, it's polluted. They'll probably crucify me, I'm saying Afrikaners are still in the exploiting phase."

CHAPTER SIX

CLOSE TO THE BLACKS

Regretful, nostalgic, perplexed, racist emotions pour out when Afrikaners speak about Africans. They say they *know* the blacks, especially their tribal characteristics, and the rest of the world doesn't. Afrikaners often believe that outsiders criticize them for relationships that, for the most part, they say, were benevolent.

The experience of growing up with Africans from an early age and then moving into an exclusively white society was common to Afrikaners of the first half of the twentieth century. Many made the transition without reflection. For a few, it was jarring. As an adult, Henning Myburgh, the thirty-something regional director of the Institute for a Democratic Alternative for South Africa (IDASA) in Bloemfontein, still felt the anguish of losing childhood friends. "I grew up on a farm in the Northern Cape. The only other kids were blacks and I used to play with them. They were my only friends. When I went [away] to school at about ten, I was separated from them. We moved to town and took one of the guys with us. It was such a mishap. You know he couldn't live with us in the house because my dad was a Nationalist so he wouldn't contravene the regulations, so this chap had to live in the outroom. Eventually he disappeared into the black township. I felt unhappy in my first years in school, because I wanted my friends and couldn't stand the guys that I was with."

Afrikaners more removed from farms found similar experiences in relationships with their African servants. "I think the Afrikaner really understands the black," said Rena Pretorius, a University of Pretoria professor of literature and a member of the Publications Appeal Board.* "[Blacks were] my playmates when I was a child at my grandfather's farm. So we've known them, we've lived with them all these years.

"Here's Sophie," she said, introducing the woman who helped her in

---

*The state censorship board that had the authority to ban books, magazines, and movies.

See Ina—
growing up.

her Waterkloof Heights house. "She's been with me for fifty-one years now. With my parents and then when my parents died, she came to live with me. And she's like my mother, she's like my sister. I mean I pay for her children. We pay for her one daughter at university in Qwa Qwa. We pay for the husband, who is becoming a preacher. We paid for her younger son until he was at standard nine. So there's no such thing as being not friendly or kind or willing to help them. I'm very unhappy about the whole picture that they try to show of the Afrikaner because it's just not true. I think we're a very kind people. Sometimes there may be incidents that are very, very harsh and I do feel that the way the [apartheid] system worked out is a sad story."

Because Afrikaners rarely bear a personal animus toward the particular Africans they know, they can honestly testify to the fair and honorable attitudes they hold. The idea of structural discrimination, even when understood, is rarely taken as a personal responsibility. In the study of his home in the Parkview section of Johannesburg, standing under a mounted Cape buffalo head and gazing at a painting of a wagon path winding across his ranch on the veld, the lawyer and retired general P. J. T. (Terts) Oosthuizen recalled, "I grew up on a farm and I grew up with the black people. On the farm I was taught to respect a person irrespective of his color. I was not allowed to be impolite to a black man."

But politeness certainly didn't entail a belief in equality. Professor Ben Marais, one of the earliest public dissenters against apartheid within the Dutch Reformed Church, sat in his Pretoria living room telling old stories, occasionally prompted sweetly by his wife, Tannie (Aunt) Sebs, for Sebastiana. "I was raised on a Karoo farm. I was born in 1909, seven years after the conclusion of the Anglo-Boer War. My parents suffered a lot during the war, as did almost all Afrikaans people outside of the Western Province, the Western Cape. I grew up with the general approach of Afrikaans people at that time, anti-English, and that, well, we are whites and the blacks are . . ." Tannie Sebs supplied the next word: ". . . inferior." Marais uncomfortably agreed. "No, ja, ja, inferior, or backward. If one of their family visited them, you'd never think of inviting them into your house. But my parents would never have allowed me to act in an unfriendly personal way."

The relationship between Afrikaner and African was at base like that of medieval lord and vassal, according to the novelist and travel writer Elsa Joubert, the author of *The Long Journey of Poppie Nongena*.

"It was a feudal relationship on the farms," she said approvingly. "How many times a night did laborers come and knock and wake up the farmer? Had a child that's got croup. The farmer takes out his *bakkie* or his motorcar, takes the child to the doctor. That's not exceptions, it was the rule. How do you think we would've lived for three hundred years if this relationship hadn't been good?" Evidence of the benign relationship had been unearthed by her husband's father, the historian F. W. Steytler. "He proved that the Boers in the Anglo-Boer War left their wives and their children on the farm with the black laborers. The fact that those women weren't murdered on their farms and the farm taken over by the blacks proves there was a good and loyal relationship." Only since 1948, with apartheid, Joubert argued, had the relationship soured. (Other historians, such as Stanley Trapido and Dan O'Meara, assert that African peasants did seize Afrikaner land in large quantities during the Anglo-Boer War, but that after the war, armed by their former British enemies, special Boer commandos retook the land.)

In the wake of February 2, 1990, National Party people are particularly at pains to argue that, even if there had been mistakes in the past, Afrikaners have learned and aren't basically racist. It isn't racist to understand reality, and different groups are, well, different. Now that there are Africans who can deal with modern society, the structures of the past can be changed. A National Party city councilman and real estate agent in Phalaborwa in the eastern Transvaal, Manie Kriel is an enthusiastic "new Nat." For him, other whites, not the Afrikaners, are the problem, because the others don't know the blacks, hadn't grown up on the farm with them.

"We Afrikaners are not racists," Kriel insisted. "The racist people are the people from the U.K. and the German people. Even the Greeks, you must be careful of the Greeks, and the Portuguese. And I mean it, they are the real racists. You know, and the Hollanders. My ex-wife was a Hollander, and her mother is a big CP because she hates the blacks. But we grew up with them and we used to play with them in the streets, on the farm, and you know, they don't bother us anymore, we've accepted them. We are part of Africa."

In contrast to Elsa Joubert's righteous defense of the Afrikaners' goodwill and positive relations with Africans, the novelist Jeanne Goosen is possessed with collective guilt, convinced of the whites' constant betrayal of Africans. The author of the CNA (Central News Agency) prizewinning novel *Ons Is Nie Almal So Nie* (We Are Not All Like That) and for a time a medical worker in townships consumed by apartheid violence, she has solid anti-apartheid credentials. Goosen grew distraught as she talked about a black woman who had approached her on the street in Johannesburg.

"I passed a café and there was an old black woman asking where is the direction to Rustenburg. I said, 'Oh, I can't even explain to you, to-hell-and-gone away.' She told me that her husband helped a farmer in Rustenburg. He got sick and the farmer one day said, 'You must plow now.' He died of a heart attack on the thing. Then the farmer said to her, 'There's no more place for you to stay.' But she's old this old woman! So she came here. She's a bit senile too. I've seen her about six times after that. Every time she stops people, [she asks], 'What's the best way to Rustenburg?' She sleeps outside. I don't know what I must do. I phoned people along there, 'Please, haven't you got a room, won't you take her in?' We've been living like that [under apartheid] for forty-four years! Get old in two days' time with experiences like that! It's so terrible! And it's not nice to feel so terrible all these years about things!"

Elna Trautmann told a similar tale, sitting in an unassuming tea room behind the very assuming Cecil Rhodes Memorial on the mountainside overlooking Cape Town.

"On the family farm that my aunt inherited after my grandfather died, we had old Jacob. I grew up with Jacob. Jacob was a Sotho man and he was old when I was a toddler. So Jacob was very old."

In 1988 while visiting South Africa from Namibia, Elna went back to the farm. "We found Jacob there looking after the [unoccupied] house. Grandfather died when I was standard six or seven [eighth or ninth grade]. The farmhouse was fairly furnished. Grandmother still had some of her linen in plastic covers that she bought new, within her linen cupboard. We had a bee problem and it was very dusty, but otherwise everything was just like I remembered it from years ago! Jacob was living a few kilometers away in his mud hut. For years he kept the garden going. The flowers were beautiful. We used to play in this garden when I was a kid. As we left I gave Jacob fifty rands and he nearly cried. He couldn't believe it. I said 'Well Jacob what do you get? Who pays you?' " Elna said a relative was paying Jacob ten rands a month [$4.60] until the farm was closed in 1991. "I sent home immediately and I asked what happened to Jacob? But no one in the family can tell me what happened to Jacob. And he was faithful all those years."

On her trips into the Karoo for Operation Hunger, Trautmann and her deputy frequently talked to people on the road. "We stopped at one of the people on a donkey cart, camping next to the road," she said. "And in front of my eyes I saw another Jacob. An old man and his grandchildren. He stood on very bent legs. He said, 'I can't take it in my knees anymore.' He said, 'I've been farming with sheep throughout my life for the white farmers and now that I'm too old to work I'm asking them, can't I live with my son? Let my sons work for you, I will train them.' [The farmer said] the sons can come and live there, but not the whole family. And he says, 'Where must I go and live? Where?' There he was on his donkey cart, his two sons and his three grandchildren and his wife. That's how the Afrikaner treats his labor and they can't see anything wrong with it."

South Africa can make a white foreigner feel so colonial, from the awareness of whites' puny presence in rural areas to the visible discrepancies in living conditions between whites and blacks. At the exquisite Magoebaskloof Hotel in the Transvaal province's northern Drakensberg Mountains, guests' cars get washed overnight even if they're not Mercedes. The hotel has a swimming pool, an English-ish rose garden, four-poster beds, and fog foaming up the mountain clefts in the early morning. Hadidah ibis, with their curved knitting-needle beaks and calls that sound like their name, tromp around the hotel grounds. An elegant dining room serves smoked trout from the Sabie River for dinner, and Japanese businessmen in the mining industry joke with beefy white men over their meals. Everywhere one is served by blacks. It all costs about $100 for two per night, including breakfast.

Just to the east, the highveld falls off the Drakensberg escarpment to the subtropical lowveld. On the way down, chartreuse tea bushes hug the rolling, reddish earth like an afro. The lowveld farming town of Tzaneen is surrounded by vegetable and fruit plantations growing bananas, mangoes, avocados. Farther east, on the Mozambique border, lies Kruger National Park, one of the world's biggest game preserves. Made a national park in 1926, Kruger is about the size of New Jersey. Its road complex makes observing animals from cars easy. In the lowveld area the shallow rivers are wallows for hippos, with their little wiggly ears, and crocodiles. Elephants, giraffes, baboons, and lions meander among the green thorn trees, the beloved *groen doringboom* of Afrikaner folk songs. And here are the southernmost baobab, those Falstaff-fat trees whose arthritic branches look like roots when the leaves fall off, often called upside-down trees. Almost every part of the baobab can be used by humans: the leaves as a vegetable, the pollen as glue, the fruit pod as a source of tartaric acid, the wood for ropes or paper.

One such old tree broods, splendid and lonely, halfway between Tzaneen and Phalaborwa, a copper-mining town on the edge of Kruger Park. The entrance to its hollow center, used as a bar during the gold rush days, is growing closed, and initials are chiseled all over its bark. Ten people could easily stand inside it.

Nearby lies the cattle, game, and sheep ranch of prosperous Piet War-ren. Directly inside Warren's mansion on his ranch named Josephine is his study, chockablock with stuffed wild animals. At the entrance "stands" a giraffe neck and head, with giant chin hairs seven feet above the floor. Then there is the front half of a female lion. A spotted, stuffed lion fetus the size of a house cat rests on a file cabinet. On the walls hang heads of zebra, warthog, several impala (or elands), a Cape buffalo, and a stud bull from the United States that Warren had used in cattle breed-ing. Elephant-foot footstools with dinner plate–sized toenails stand next to the desk. A CB radio, used to communicate around the farm, blares from a shelf.

Piet Warren is an Afrikaner farmer nicknamed "the white Shangaan," for his comprehension of local languages and his reputed knowledge of black people. The Shangaan is a local tribe with members also in neigh-boring Mozambique, where it is called Tsonga. Warren is wealthy; besides the ranch, he owns a garage in the nearby small town of Grav-elotte, employs four hundred workers, owns a slaughterhouse in the tribal homeland of Gazankulu, and has a butchery in the black township of Lulekani near Phalaborwa. Warren's "boys" call him *baas* (boss), in keeping with colonial tradition.

Reflecting a farmer's genetically oriented mentality, Warren described his father as coming from "rather well bred people," a descen-dant of 1820 settlers in the Cape from Britain, and his mother as coming "from very good Afrikaans stock." She was educated in Stellenbosch to be a teacher and was "teaching kids somewhere between nowhere and nowhere" and "became nearly an old maid" of twenty-four when his father married her.

Warren is haunted by his dead father. Like many South African men, Warren seemed obsessed with appearing strong and manly. His father, he claimed, was a "man's man."

"You had to get malaria once a year or twice a year and live through it and nearly die and they push you around in a wheelbarrow for a week and stuff like that," Warren said of his dad. "Those guys, they just had that much more guts, hey? My Dad used to say, 'You can kill me but you can't scare me.'"

Warren said white South Africa was like America. "Two generations ago everybody was farming stock and land meant everything. When you had ten cents, you bought ground." His father arrived in the Gravelotte area impoverished by the Depression, fired from a job for refusing to join the army in World War II, and forced to become a miner. "Right down to the bottom of the ladder, that's a dirty, dirty, dirty coal miner, hey? Absolutely dig with his hands. So he then became very anti the establishment. He was a very hard man, my dad; nobody ever gave him any lip.

"He came to this part of the country because you could get any amount of land. Quinine had just been found out then, the thing that stops malaria, so you stop dying. He came to this part in 1939 and started farming."

Living up to his nickname as well as illustrating Afrikaners' convictions that they understand the Africans, Warren talked at length about the attributes of various tribes in South Africa. It boiled down to this: Zulus are strong and don't give a shit about human life, Sothos are sneaky and better educated, all blacks steal (except Freddy, one of his employees who'd been with his family since the age of three and "thinks like a European"), and no Africans are disciplined enough to make plans. It is nearly a universal belief of Afrikaners that Africans can't plan.

"The difference in people comes such a long way," Warren explained. "The Zulu people are such tough people. I have a boy by the name of Gumtree, a big Zulu. Gumtree is now running a deboning factory. He thinks less of a Shangaan than I think of my dog. I don't think he even wants to greet them. One Zulu with a knobkerry [a heavy stick with a knob on one end] is a better war machine than five Sothos with AKs. That is the truth. Without the Zulu nation, and without the Afrikaners, you can do nothing in this country. Because those are the only okes [blokes] that can stand and physically fight. They're not afraid to die. Dying is nothing. A Zulu doesn't even speak another man's language. Even till today I have to speak Zulu to Gumtree."

The Zulus seem to be the traditional Afrikaner's favorite Africans because of their admired courage and willingness to fight. Imprinted on Afrikaners' thinking is the 1836 slaughter of trekkers and their servants when the Zulu chief Dingane did not trust a Boer attempt to negotiate a land deal.

"Now the Sothos are quite different," Warren said. "They are the educated people." When, in the late 1800s, wars between African tribes ravaged the countryside, "the guys who ran away and made a plan, lived on a hill, made spears and traded and lived in holes, were all Sotho people. They are yellower. They are a mixture of the runaway Hottentots [Khoikhoi]. Look, the Xhosas hate Hottentots and that's where the humped cattle came from. The Zulus didn't have humped cattle. They had flat-necked cattle. So, but the Sothos now ran away and hid and they were all the wise guys, and without guts. The Zulus had the guts. The guys behind them were the Swazis, which had a little less guts, and the Shangaans had a little less guts, eh, in a sequence like that. But the Sothos have no guts, as a group."

Warren is a staunch F. W. supporter, deeming negotiations the best tactic. He is optimistic about the future of South Africa because he believes Africans understand that they depend on the whites. "There is nothing more that I need than a black man's ability to work for little money. And there is nothing he needs more than my ability to plan, so that we can get out of this hole. We have to put it together to attract and make capital."

While much of Warren's wisdom is sweeping and racist, some clichés about tribal characteristics cannot be dismissed out of hand. Braam Viljoen, the farmer and very liberal IDASA worker in Pretoria, agreed that ethnic or tribal differences mattered. "It is still there, oh yes. Some farmers say that the Tswana is a good worker. It may be due not to intrinsic qualities but history. I don't know, but there are characteristics like this. And the most awful type of thing is in hospitals. You cannot trust a black nurse of a certain tribe to take care of a patient of another tribe. Even in urban areas. The Zulus particularly will not easily accept other people among them.

"You do have intermarriage," he noted. Then he cautioned, "You have to keep in mind how much the ethnic-based policy of government perpetuated and strengthened the ethnic feelings. Wherever you had urbanization, you have the breakdown of ethnic preoccupations."

Some farmers, even politically very conservative ones, have discovered that Africans are not the threat that Nationalist propaganda taught them—that in fact the Nat government stood between them and cooperation with their black neighbors. In the northern Transvaal, Braam Viljoen discovered sincere outrage among his conservative farming peers against the Nationalist government's mistreatment of local Africans who resisted its homeland machinations.

These Afrikaners' deep mistrust of the Nationalists seems incongruous but it was heartening to Viljoen. He described the way the apartheid system bizarrely and arbitrarily shuffled land and people. His story shows that some whites, even Viljoen's conservative farmer friends, can cut through Nat propaganda to accept that blacks were victimized and killed by the government.

"I was chairman of the local farmers' union for quite some time," he said. "KwaNdebele was the latecomer of the homelands. In planning the homeland they included another tribe's land, the Pedi, Northern Sotho people. This area was called Mutsi, with 126,000 Pedis living there.

"When the Ndebele king, who just died last week—I was at his funeral last Saturday—when this king moved to the area, he had nowhere to live. The Pedi chief gave him hospitality and a place to stay. Then the Pretoria government took this Pedi chief's land and gave it to the Ndebele. Of course that caused havoc.

"It was a land swap, you know. You take Mutsi because it's adjacent to KwaNdebele and you give it to KwaNdebele, but then you take the land of KwaNdebele which is adjacent to Lebowa and give it to the Pedis, and then they must be satisfied, why not, you know? Funny how these people worked.

"That was '85. It meant resettling a hundred twenty-six thousand people against their will without having consulted them, and those people refused to move. They [the government forces] created a vigilante group within the Ndebele called Mbogodo. Now, Mbogodo was the word for 'millstone,' which would grind the people into submission. That was also to be used against the obstinate Pedis who didn't want to move away to make room for the Ndebele kingdom.

"That caused a war because while the [KwaNdebele] homeland government used this Mbogodo organization against the Pedis, the Ndebele people refused to go along. Particularly the old king, who we buried last Saturday.

"Eventually my area [in Rust de Winter] was also demarcated for inclusion into KwaNdebele. There were thirty-four thousand acres of land with a very good irrigation scheme; sixty-three [white] farmers live there. They were up in arms because the farming community was not consulted. In the end we would not sell, so they expropriated the land and we lost the whole area.

"But now I want to come to a very interesting phenomenon, that's why I give you the background. I was chairman of the farmers' union, and I'm perhaps the only real liberal amongst the farmers. The fascinating thing was that archconservative farmers in the end found themselves opposing the government. First it happened because of this seizure of their land. But when the Ndebeles rose up on the issue of Mutsi and against the security force, those farmers came to me and said, 'Look, there are some quite horrible things happening. We cannot allow this to happen.' Conservative farmers.

"I went to investigate and I found that they were right," Viljoen said. "Horrible things that the security forces did. Attacks on certain communities, an effort to wipe out the comrades [ANC-aligned youths]. In this battle the comrades burnt down seventy percent of the businesses in KwaNdebele in one day, every business of a member of the Mbogodo organization. So then the security forces went for the comrades and for the civics [United Democratic Front local organizations]. It was terrible. Many were arrested.

"Even myself, a warrant for my arrest was out because we farmers took the side of the Ndebele," Viljoen said. "Under the emergency regulations those things could not be made public. In fact, after the first meeting we as a farmers' union had with the security chiefs in KwaNdebele, a new rule was issued allowing no one to say anything about what any member of the security forces did in KwaNdebele. Those conservative farmers found themselves siding with the comrades in a struggle against the government.

"For a whole year we fought this issue. And when I had to go down to Cape Town to meet with a commission of Parliament, those conservative farmers gave me a mandate. They said, 'Tell the government to make this an integrated farming area. We will help those farmers with whatever advice they may need.' "

Viljoen looked and spoke like a latter-day Moses, with his shock of pure white hair and Biblical cadences.

"So I went down, in the days of apartheid, and of homelands, grand designed policy, and came in the holy Parliament of South Africa, met this commission, and came up with this suggestion. So I said to them, 'Look, you need not consolidate this area into the homeland, just bring in the black farmers. We are quite happy to accept them.'

"So the Nats came up and they went for us. Not the Conservative Party, but the Nats. 'Where do you get this from? Since when is integration the policy of the agricultural union which you represent? Did you get a mandate?'

"When the Nat spokesman Mr. Mentz said to one of my farmer colleagues, 'Mr. van der Walt, will you accept a black farmer as your neighbor?' Van der Walt said to him, 'Mr. Mentz, I have ten black families living on my farm. I have black neighbors.' And he said, 'To the north of my boundary you have created the homeland of Bophuthatswana. I have lots of black neighbors there.' He said, 'I must be frank with you. I have less problems with my black neighbors than I do with some of my white neighbors.'

"Those farmers really got appalled, absolutely shocked by what the security forces did in KwaNdebele," Viljoen said. "When they saw what was happening, it was not 'agitators,' or 'lying in the English press.' They saw the victims. At times they saw the bodies. You know, there is a sense of fair play and a sense of religious duty with these people, and they simply become confused. That type of existential experience helped them to move to the point where they said, 'Look, they may be black, but given the fact that we have to share land, we might as well do it with these people.'

"Whereas you can sit there every night of the week for the whole year with academic arguments and get nowhere, I am quite convinced that when you are in the existential position over a number of years, a period of five or ten, I think most people will be able to shed their prejudices."

PART II

APARTHEID
CULTURE

CHAPTER SEVEN

A CULTURE OF TORMENT

"Fear hath torment," it says in First John 4:18. White Afrikaner fears are torments passed down from generation to generation; they are elabo-rate, nuanced, and endemic. At the febrile heart of white panic pulses the numerical fact that the black population is 35 million and growing, and the white population is 4.5 million and shrinking.

The classic Afrikaner terror is commonly expressed in two verbs with flooding connotations: "swamp" and "engulf." In the 1948 elections that brought the Nats to power, the sloganized threats suspended over the whites' heads were *oorstrooming*, swamping (of the cities by blacks seek-ing jobs), and *swart gevaar*, black peril. Ever since then fear has been drummed into whites' brains and remains a main tactic of politicking. In fact the Nats are masters at fostering fear among their own people and using ruthless tactics against their adversaries.

Yet sympathy—and perhaps pity—for the Afrikaners may be in order. H. W. (pronounced "Hah-Veeh" in Afrikaans) van der Merwe, the direc-tor of the Center for Intergroup Studies, has disagreed for years with a fellow Cape Town Quaker over the reasons for the Afrikaners' cruel poli-cies and tactics. H. W. said his coreligionist "always attributed the Afrikaner's wrongdoing to greed. I attributed it to fear. If you attribute it to fear, you are much more sympathetic to the person, but if you think it was greed, you hate him."

The novelist Jeanne Goosen, raised in the working-class heart of the Afrikaner tribe, sympathizes with Afrikaners but also accuses them, say-ing fear and hate are seminal attributes of the *volk*. Apartheid was very harsh in the fifties and sixties of her childhood in the Cape Town suburb of Parow.

"We were all taught since the age of two to be frightened of blacks and coloreds. It is a fear I think most whites still have and you cannot get rid of because of Dingane, how they murdered the Voortrekkers. 'The *kaf-firs* will catch you and cut out your tongue,' and 'They use white children as *muti.*' *Muti* is a Zulu word for Sangoma (traditional) medicine. Every black, colored, and Indian was a potential murderer or rapist. Newspapers gave such a hell of a coverage to these horrors black people do, with the result we all had this fear.

"But everybody had servants, and you did not actually experience it with servants, you were not frightened of them. For them you used to feel sorry, helluva sorry because everything was so inhuman.

"I remember my father was very much befriended with a colored man, Piet van Staden, Afrikaans name. He and my father worked together, they'd build things, fix gardens and so on. He could play piano. Syncopation, you know. He used to play for us on the piano, but before he can do that, we must lock all the doors and the windows, close the gates, everything: you could expect a policeman there because we are socially together."

That was illegal?

"It was absolutely illegal," she said firmly. "Our culture in Afrikaans started with hate. Your whole upbringing, even at home, schools, the church. There's always hidings, there's 'Don't play with those kids, they're Indians.' If you insist on playing with them, 'You're the devil's child.' That was more or less the way we were all brought up. This whole culture of hate is still there. It's being reflected today in faces and deeds of the AWB [Afrikaner Resistance Movement]. And of the CP."

Does that come from fear?

"I think the two go together," Goosen said. "But I think it started with hate, the Calvinistic upbringing: God is jealous, don't get His hate on you, or His violence or His wrath. There is fear of God, fear of black people, Roman Catholics, Jews, a fear of British people, *uitlanders*, fear of absolutely everything. A fear of communism."

How did she throw off that education, even so far as to become a member of the ANC?

"I'm very fortunate because my mother was a Nationalist but she always questioned it. She was a minister's daughter who was rebellious. She could never come to terms with that passage in Job, 'Those who have, will receive more, while those who have not, it will still be taken away from them even that which they have.' "

Poor and ill-educated in the thirties and forties and consequently holding menial jobs, many Afrikaners feared Africans' willingness to take their jobs at lower pay. Goosen's father was a train engineer. "An engine driver in those days had prestige," she said. "Because it was something like the pilots in the sixties, you know, they opened up the world. But then all these things came, Afrikaners had pensions all of a sudden, sick funds and all that. To that they clutched, and what better political strategy could one have than fear and hate for everything that was different?"

Goosen asserted that to her apartheid was worse than Nazism, but she immediately explained that was because of the time element, the more than forty years blacks were driven into the wilderness by the social engineering of Verwoerd and his disciples.

"The time," she said. "Apartheid affected twenty-six million people in this country. It affected everything. It took away white people's souls. And the blacks got a culture of, what is the word? *Ellende*, not mourning, not sorrow, torment. They've got nothing to lose."

What does *ellende* mean?

"I'll look it up in the dictionary . . . 'misery, distress, wretchedness,'" she read out. "That's why there is a PAC [Pan-Africanist Congress, which allows no white members]. They don't believe in reform because the whites, they have no soul. Reform is only a strategy. A sort of a survival kit now to be friendly to everybody. But the fear is still there, and the hate is still there."

Does she think the PAC is right?

"I think so. It'll take another generation or two, new schools" to eradicate the fear and hate.

Sometimes Afrikaners' comments on their concerns have a tone verging on self-pity.

"Afrikaners have a very real fear: to be plowed under," said Frans van Rensburg, a retired professor of Afrikaans at Rand Afrikaans University.

Dominee Johan Heyns, prominent leader of the Dutch Reformed Church, sympathized with whites: "I think we have had up till now, and still have in our country, two basic emotions: that of hatred and that of fear. Fear from the side of the whites and hatred from the side of the blacks."

F. W.'s brother Wimpie de Klerk listed some whites' fears: "There is fear for survival, a fear of being overruled by the majority, the fear of lowering standards, the fear of being pushed out of jobs, especially at the middle and lower level." He said his son, who is "not very well educated, he's a cameraman at the SABC [television]," faced that possibility.

"Apartheid was born out of fear," said Professor Pieter Potgieter, who teaches political science at Potschefstroom University and is also a Broederbond member. "People came up with funny ideas like [in the late seventies] these fast-moving trains, just to get the labor from the black homelands [to the 'white' cities]. It's unbelievable the kind of stuff that they came up with, so obsessed were they with the idea that it [apartheid] must work. They couldn't think of a situation in which the white population could live in open competition with the mass of black people."

Johann Rissik, an agricultural development expert, said, "A lot of them got where they got because of the color of their skin, not through their ability." Of course they'd fear a system that destroyed that advantage.

Many Afrikaners say they are not afraid of blacks physically. Rather, a deeper psychological fear lurks inside connected to a conviction that Afrikaner identity is tenuous, prone to erosion.

The linguist and professor Hans du Plessis delicately put his finger on this terror that is seldom voiced: "There is the fear of becoming like they are. In our thinking there were only two groups, black and white, and there's no diversity in the black group. The fear is that the moment you speak to a black person you must become like they are. And they are heathen and uncivilized."

So it's not a fear that blacks will kill whites or hurt them?

"No, no, I don't think so. It's never been my fear. No. My father was a building contractor. He always had something like one hundred twenty black people working for him. I never feared them. There are very few Afrikaners that fear them in a physical sense."

The threat is that you become like them, perhaps even racially?

"Even racially, yes, right, and I think, when I was a kid, you didn't think of those people as diverse kinds of people."

Afrikaners fear their own disappearance by mixing, a result of their own lust and lack of control. An apprehension about contamination by mere association is certainly a sign of an insecure people, a remnant from their "poor white" past. The fear was enlarged to a huge tapestry by elaborate apartheid laws that banned mixing of the races.

Similarities to the apartheid system existed in the United States, such as the barring of blacks from restaurants and other public places, but apartheid spawned its own idiosyncracies. Dominee Jan van Rooyen and his wife, Joupie, remembered that in Cape Town, audiences at the national orchestra were suddenly segregated in the 1950s. "They put a room divider in the town hall in such a way that no white would see a colored. The coloreds sat there in the back of a corner," the minister said.

"You can't believe it, but it really happened," his wife murmured.

"Serving liquor at any party," Dominee van Rooyen continued. "If the security police caught me offering a black friend a glass of champagne, I would have gone to prison."

The couple remembered a colored friend, Dr. Jan Metle from the Cape, whom they invited to supper in the late sixties. "When Jan came in he was uptight, but terribly uptight," Joupie van Rooyen recalled.

"We didn't know what had gone wrong; we thought perhaps he'd had a difference with his wife or something like that. After a while, my husband said, 'Jan, man, what's the matter?' Jan said, 'Don't ever do this to me again. Can you imagine the anxiety me and my wife have had, coming into this white building, having to come up with the elevator and never knowing when somebody is going to say, "What are you doing here, get out!" ' There was a tremendous amount of anxiety and fear, I think, on both sides," she concluded.

"Our nationalism is built on hate, or aversion rather, of blacks," said Kobus van Rooyen, a lawyer and professor at the University of Pretoria. Van Rooyen became famous in the eighties as chairman of the Publications Appeal (censorship) Board, which by banning books, magazines, and movies, helped to keep the Afrikaners isolated from their fears. No longer on the board, he was excited about his new associations with educated blacks.

"The aversion to blacks has a lot to do with class," he said. "It's easier for us people in cities to integrate. I have some sympathy for the guys in the rural areas to really integrate with your lowly worker who may not have gone to school. But once again it's that fear which is instilled. People would see pictures in their mind of their children marrying blacks. Or their grandchildren sitting on their laps, you know, little colored children.

"It's the lack of communication, for example, between a white man and a black woman. I grew up in a home where it was a tradition to say no more than good morning [to a female servant], although they would look after you when you were a baby and when you're grown up. People would never give a lift to a black woman, alone, because that could've created the impression something was going on that wasn't quite right. It was a crime [under the Immorality Act] to have sex there [between the races]. For me it's just a fascinating exercise to start talking with black women during the last ten years," van Rooyen said.

Where does he meet them?

"SABC for example," he said, citing the national television station. "At the American embassy. Here in our home, people invited for dinner. One of our big problems in this country was we didn't really communicate on an equal level with blacks."

Not all Afrikaners were so insulated. Marianne de Jong, a professor of Afrikaans and a leading feminist literary critic, was flouting apartheid strictures in the seventies while she was a professor at the black Fort Hare University. A blond, tall, compelling woman who thumbed her nose at the establishment that educated her, de Jong said "they" when she meant the

Security Police instead of the usual blacks. The Security Police kept tabs on her—and a dossier—because she was "mixing with blacks.

"I was being very friendly with black students, whether that was sexual or not," she said. "If it is sexual, it is just what they want. At that stage there was still a so-called Immorality Act, which we all trespassed. They couldn't do much about it because they would have to arrest people who were sponsored by the British Council, who were not South African citizens," she said, laughing merrily at the memory. "I was called in by the rector [university president] for mixing with blacks, being leftish inclined. I'm one of thousands and thousands and thousands of South Africans who the police kept tabs on. I mean, I'm totally unimportant. You know, even if you are unimportant they keep a tab on you."

Johann Rissik recalled a conservative Afrikaner whose aversion to blacks was typical—quite the opposite of Marianne de Jong. "I remember a guy who was with us in the army," Rissik said. "He'd been to university as well, Potchefstroom or somewhere. He was an extreme right-winger, but not a violent one. He said that white boys must not have black nannies, because when those men become adolescents they would yearn after black women and the smell of black women. That's the sort of thing they were taught. They probably discussed this in their Christian National Education in school. He was quite serious. We just laughed at him. When we wanted a bit of entertainment, we'd go and enter into a political discussion with him. He wasn't violent, he wasn't a Eugene Terreblanche type of scum, he was a serious Christian. He would be first in line to go to church on Sunday, and he'd pull us up often for swearing and things like that."

Rissik and his companion, Belinda Blaine, mentioned some of the sexual fears of the whites: that "All black men want to rape white women," Blaine said.

Also, "there's nothing an Afrikaner can do, no lower act, than sleep with a black woman," Rissik said. "That's a serious offense."

"A hell of a lot of them do it," Blaine mused.

"Ja, a hell of a lot of them do it," Rissik agreed.

Such ideas about blacks may not be on the Christian National Education* curriculum instituted by the Nats, but teachers supplied a little

*Soon after the NP won power in 1948, the Broederbond established the Institute for Christian National Education with a teacher-training college in Potchefstroom. Christian National Education policies—eliminating mixed English-Afrikaans schools while establishing tribal African elementary schools, a Christian orientation to the curriculum, and stress on separate "nations"—were slowly extended through the country. Christian Nationalism can be traced to theologian and politician Abraham Kuyper (1837–1920), who founded a Christian National movement in the Netherlands.

extra education. Mimi and Lisa Saayman remembered teachers who "made lots of racist jokes.

"I had this teacher who said things like 'Why do black people smell? So that white blind people can also hate them,' " Mimi said.

"In the history class," Lisa stressed.

Marichen Waldner, a journalist a generation older than Lisa and Mimi, said, "It has been a thing in people's minds that black men always want to rape white women and white women have to be protected against that." But in fact, "If you look at the statistics, there are almost no interracial rapes in this country. It is only black-on-black rape or white-on-white rape. Every year the newspaper publishes these statistics when we get them. And people still don't believe."

Afrikaners' fear of Africans is rooted in the belief that, as Professor Hans du Plessis said, "We were with the Dutch world, the civilized world. In Afrikaner terms 'civilized world' also meant the Christian world. The Dark Continent meant the heathen world. You can't mix the two. You've got to fear that one and therefore you've got to rule it."

In Afrikaners' minds in the twentieth century, heathenism was melded with communism, again to threaten their Christianity. "You are born in this country with this communist fear, you were brought up with it," said John Horak. Horak said he had been a police spy on English-language newspapers for twenty-seven years because of his hatred of communism.

"Especially if you are committed to a religion, it becomes a zeal. You went for Communists. Communism, as far as I was concerned, stood against everything I stood for, and that was Christianity," Horak explained. The journalist Jacques Pauw said in 1992, "Even today it's so deeply embedded in people that they talk about the ANC and its Communist allies."

With the 1970s and '80s military buildup in South Africa and the deaths of white "boys on the border" fighting in Namibia and Angola, fear was ratcheted to hysterical levels. Every disruption in black townships was blamed on communism. The Security Police cast their net wide, monitoring and terrifying people who opposed government policies. Fear of Security Police increased among left-leaning Afrikaners, as among black activists.

Dutch Reformed Church dominee Willem Saayman spoke out against the government in the late seventies. His were impeccable Afrikaner credentials, from his grandfather, who fought in the Anglo-Boer War, to his grandmother, who was imprisoned in one of the British concentration camps. But from the perspective of mainstream and right-wing Afrikanerdom, Saayman betrayed his people.

"Throughout our history always the single greatest sin was being a traitor to the *volk*," he said. "That a dominee is a traitor to the *volk*, that is always even worse."

Saayman was forced out of his job as a missionary of the Dutch Reformed Church because of his opposition to the war in Namibia and Angola in the 1970s. "We lived right on the border on the Okavango River," he said. "That was '74. Then the war broke out. I saw that the stories I'd been told about SWAPO* were nonsense. They were not Communist terrorists. They were eighty percent Christian; fifty percent of my congregation were SWAPO members.

"Our church's members lived on both sides of the border, both in Angola and Namibia. So I heard for the first time of the atrocities committed by South African soldiers. Full of youthful idealism, I decided the military commanders don't know about this, so I must go and tell them that the men are doing bad things in their name.

"The chief of the secret police there is now chief of police here in the Witwatersrand: General Gerrit Erasmus. He had the deadest gray eyes that I've ever seen, absolutely lifeless. He called me in, he was sitting in a swingchair behind his desk, and he let me stand there like a schoolboy. By then I was in my thirties.

"He swung around and looked at me with his dead eyes and said, 'Dominee, you mustn't think I am a friend of missionaries.' Those were his first words, I'll never forget. I have seldom been so afraid in my life.

"So it was that kind of thing. Scaring you, shutting you up, saying there is a law, you are not allowed to tell anybody about this. In any case, 'We don't believe your sources.' "

Saayman's days as a missionary crashed to an end. Stress caused a breakdown in his health, and his family decided to move from Namibia back to South Africa. There, in the lovely, purple-blooming jacaranda-treed heart of Afrikanerdom, the Saayman family was "victimized much more.

"They shot at us, they shot at our house. One evening it was just the grace of God that they didn't kill my wife."

Who is "they"?

"Those days they called themselves the Witwolve, the White Wolves. But nowadays I am convinced that that was the CCB, and that they used this white wolves thing as a very good cover, disguise. I am quite sure

*The South West Africa People's Organization, the Namibian liberation movement.

that if ever one day the files are opened, we will be able to find it there. Because it was very professionally done. Not the slightest trace, nothing ever. They came quietly. The one night they shot at our bedroom when they nearly killed my wife. I mean, they couldn't have been further than that filing cabinet [about seven feet] because we have a wall around. And yet the moment the shots had been fired he was out again and we just heard the car roaring away. I wouldn't say he necessarily tried to kill, but if they killed, they wouldn't have worried.

"My daughters the same. My eldest daughter was often detained. That's where I got the high regard for the Canadian embassy. Sometimes it was just a hearing just to postpone and they would be in court for five minutes. But the moment they came in court, John Schram [a Canadian diplomat] would be sitting there. That was a wonderful feeling of comfort in those years. This was now after '85. You know it was a rough time after '85. I mean, it was much rougher for the black people, I don't try to pretend it was rough for me, it was much rougher for them, but it was rough for us as well. That was when nothing [information on killings, detentions, etc.] got out. That's the time when [black community leader Matthew] Goniwe and the others were murdered. That's when people just disappeared.

"They try to scare you, because that is our national characteristic," Saayman said. "We fear authority. So they try to scare you into submission. In a sense they are a little bit hopeless when they can't do that. That's why I also say they are going to fail politically. Because they don't understand African people. They can't scare the Africans into submission. But that's what they try to do with us."

Willem Saayman has a brother-in-law who faced similar run-ins and intimidation from police and other more shadowy figures. As editor of *Vrye Weekblad*, Max du Preez has shepherded into print crusading exposés of misdeeds, murders, and plots carried out by security forces, including the Civil Cooperation Bureau (CCB). The first exposés, based on interviews with the Security Branch captain Dirk Coetzee, put the struggling weekly newsmagazine on the map. They were written in 1989 by Jacques Pauw and subsequently collected and published in a book called *In the Heart of the Whore: The Story of Apartheid's Death Squads*.

"They would sneak into your yard and loosen your car's wheel nuts," du Preez said. "Then when you drive off, your wheels fall off. This happened to me several times. Or letters come to your door, under your window. Walking around your house at night, trying to break into your house. Breaking in when you are not there. That kind of stuff. A lot of that happened. Was that right wing? CCB? Security Police? Was that

Military Intelligence, or was it somebody's husband whose wife I've made a pass at? I don't know."

Does he fear for his life?

"Ag, I did at some point, but you know, you can't really let that occupy your mind. It's the easiest thing to become paranoid. I soon realized that there is nothing you can do about it. They have a spy in my office [in 1992]. If somebody writes me a letter and I open it and the guy [who wrote the letter] phones me half an hour later and says, 'That letter you just opened, please don't publish it because I've just been threatened.' I don't know if [the spy] is a person, if it's a bug. I'm just going to have to live my life. Otherwise you are going to be paralyzed, and that's what they want."

Afrikaners' fears were pervasive in the eighties, but in the nineties they deepened. Apartheid laws were lifted and censorship decreased, and whites confronted the likelihood of a completely black-ruled future in 1999 and the certainty of violence that accompanies change. They feared ANC "mass action" campaigns, tactics of civil disobedience, and protest marches. It was *swart gevaar* all over again. The Dark Continent was lapping around the ankles of the Christian white man. They also feared the militant white right-wingers who, lurking underground, fomented violence, often through black surrogates. Most Afrikaners have not had enough time to digest the National Party's 180-degree turn.

For the very long run Dominee Willem Saayman is optimistic. But for the short run he's gloomy. "I base that on my centuries of Afrikaner blood in my veins," he said. "Afrikaners will not give up power in this country, because bred into our bones is the visceral fear of black domination. I can remember vividly from my earliest childhood that I was taught to be afraid of these people and therefore to dominate them. You have to remain *baas*.

"When I went to a small farm school, we were always told by the teachers: 'See how the small blacks are running to the school? If you don't keep up, they are going to pass you. You must remain in front.' There is no way that a National Party is going to negotiate itself out of power. There is no way."

Thus, fear remains the engine of National Party emotion. The Stellenbosch economist Sampie Terreblanche, watching the initial campaigning for the 1994 elections, noted that the NP was "creating a kind of fear psychosis in the colored community" in an attempt to turn them against the ANC.

Then there's the new fear of losing wealth gained in the past forty years under apartheid's aegis. While eating at Pizza Hut in an affluent shopping mall in the eastern suburbs of Pretoria, journalist Dries van Heerden, who was a Nieman Fellow at Harvard in 1987, addressed the issue.

"What white people, particularly Afrikaners, fear about changing South Africa is the whole system of economic privileges that we have built up around us," he said. "Two cars, swimming pool, tennis court in the backyard. It's a very, very capitalist vision which has got nothing to do with all these protestations about the *volk* and the *taal* [language], and the culture. I'll go so far as to say that if whites can be guaranteed some sort of economic security, I don't think that they'll care whether Mandela runs the country or de Klerk runs the country. The primal fear of white people in this country is that blacks are going to treat them the way in which they treated blacks."

CHAPTER EIGHT

A Few Words
About Women

"The developed black woman really has a tough time," Louw Alberts mused as he sat in his Pretoria condominium apartment filled with lovely Persian rugs. "Black women had three systems suppressing them: the tribal system, which is even worse than the patriarchal one; the church, where there's no room for a woman to get to the top; and the apartheid system. There is very definitely a rising feminism amongst black women. I'm happy about that."

Alberts, a retired physicist, is in his late sixties. In the Nationalist political context he is enlightened on black-white relations and has been a central figure in organizing multiracial church conferences.

"What I'm saying now I'd better not say in public because I'm being 'liberal,'" he said with a sardonic smile. "When it comes to common sense, black women do as well if not better than black men. They are extremely balanced, common-sense people. Maybe something to do with the fact that they haven't got that urge for power the way the black male leadership has. They have a more balanced approach."

What about white women and power? How does he feel about Afrikaner women proclaiming they are feminists?

"That's a very difficult question, because I can't escape my own biases. I have raised a patriarchal home. My wife is a great woman and she's raised a great bunch of kids. Okay, she's involved in her women's group and study groups and what have you, and I encourage her for all I'm worth. But what would my reaction be if Else said, 'I want to be the wage earner and you stay at home and run the home'? I'm not sure that I could handle that."

He blamed it on being a Christian.

"If I understand the Bible, God is going to hold the father responsible ultimately for the spiritual welfare of the family. He's going to be called to account before anybody else is. The woman is the support structure.

This means that the career woman is a schizophrenic in a sense. When she's out there she's in command, men report to her and that's great, she can be more intelligent, more capable. But the moment she steps inside the home, she has to take the biblical approach of being the infrastructure and not the boss."

The "biblical" roles have to be maintained for another reason, he said. "Now you're getting some basic Afrikaner thinking: I think little boys need to identify with their father, girls with their mother." The roles were "genetically constructed."

"You see what I'm worried about is, let me come back to my own kids. If my sons thought that 'Mom is taking responsibility, she's bearing the burden, she's really making the decisions,' they would have been better candidates for becoming homosexuals, because they are not identifying physically with the right one."

Women are infrastructure! Ina van der Linde and Marichen Waldner, two Afrikaner women journalists, laughed and laughed, like wind chimes in a breeze.

"You really made my day by telling me that story," van der Linde laughed.

Then she sobered. "You shouldn't look around at Afrikaner women for real feminists," she said.

The Calvinist fundamentalists "really and honestly believe a woman's place is in a kitchen and that one should not do anything on Sunday. Racism is part of it, and anti-Semitism. You're not allowed to play sport on Sundays. They are conservative to the bone."

Mimi and Lisa Saayman, sisters in their early twenties who live in Cape Town, know the fundamentalist type quite well. Although they are themselves highly unusual in that they belonged to the ANC, they have family who were farmers and members of the neo-Nazi AWB.

"We visit them about once a year," Mimi said. "One visit was on a Sunday. My sister and I were knitting, of all things, and my uncle walks in. He says, 'Oh, do you knit on Sundays now?' You're not allowed to knit on Sundays because you're doing work. Meanwhile, my aunt gets up at six in the morning and she's cooking the whole day, slaving away in the kitchen."

"My mother's family are *verligte* [enlightened] Afrikaners," Lisa said. "They're still National Party but they can see we must change. They asked me what I'm studying at university, so I say I'm doing a B.A. They said, 'B.A.: man catch.' That's the only reason you do a B.A. is to—"

"—get married." Mimi ended the sentence.

Mimi and Lisa are two of the four girls raised by the Dutch Reformed missionary couple Willem and Cecilia Saayman. The girls, now women, are eloquently enlarging the definition of Afrikaners. It isn't easy. They had spent many miserable years in Afrikaans schools under the educational system called Christian National Education. Their descriptions of school practices as recently as 1986 hinted at the high hurdles any girl faced in trying to overcome the patriarchal system.

"All Afrikaans schools are very authoritarian," Mimi said.

Girls' hair could not touch their collars and boys' hair had to be above their ears. At school assemblies, students were called forward and "their hair cut in front of everyone to show we won't stand for this." In another example, the two sisters said that during initiation, when students moved to high school, older students "took all the girls who hadn't yet started shaving onto the stage and said they were going to have a competition to see which had the longest hair on their legs. The winner, they said, got a lawn mower." Public humiliation enforced conformity.

Commingling sexual fears with racism left permanent psychological scars. On certain commemorative days honored by blacks, such as the anniversary of the June 16, 1976, Soweto uprising, "All girls in the school were told that we were not allowed to cycle or walk to school. Pamphlets went out warning that black men have to rape one white woman [on that day].

"And this doesn't just stay with you for that day," Mimi said. "All the years of Christian National Education has still done something to me," Lisa said. "You grow up seeing black people and hearing about them in a certain context—you have to consciously break that down, you have to work at it."

The two young and attractive women were every day beset by the general sexual harassment and lewdness prevalent in the South African society—a burden few men fathom.

"It's really something that bothers me very much," Mimi said. When she walks down the street, "there are thousands of men along the street and they all feel compelled to make kissing noises, to shout something from the car, to hoot, whatever. Every single day."

In their spare time the sisters worked at Cape Town's Rape Crisis Center, which had two shelters for battered women. "Statistics are that at any one time one hundred thousand women are being battered in Cape Town," Mimi said. "I'm counseling one woman who's gone to the church for help and the church said she must accommodate her husband, please him, appease him.

"The reason I decided to do Rape Crisis is because I was feeling so helpless."

As a woman?

"Yes, on the streets, everything. It really gets to me. I felt to empower myself and to help empower other women I wanted to do it. So we did the training course together," she said, nodding to Lisa.

Lisa, a student at the University of Cape Town, said there was a "big drinking culture" at universities. "A lot of harassment happens at university parties where lots of drinking goes on," Lisa said.

"It reflects the society we live in, rape, I mean," she went on. "Johan Heyns [the dominee who headed the Dutch Reformed Church during the mid-eighties] said that it's a woman's fault when she gets raped because she could just cross her legs. I think that's what most people feel."

The rise of hundreds of thousands of Afrikaner women from abysmal poverty and ignorance to riches and education was relatively quick, fueled as it was by the National Party government's policy to funnel economic advantages to Afrikaners.

Elsabe Brink's family was not among the poor, but as a historian she has studied them. She has written articles and a master's thesis about the newly urbanized women of the early forties who belonged to the Garment Workers' Union and who had at best only basic primary school educations.

"Women have been 'used' a lot in Afrikaner nationalism," Brink said. "We're all called 'volksmoeders,' mothers of the nation. It was a fictitiously created and socially engineered position which gave you respectability and standing in the community. In the middle class you got these volksmoeder buttons for twenty years of service in the South African Women's Federation."

Much nonideological research still needs to be carried out if the history of Afrikaner women's role is to be understood. Brink said there are three main streams of historical methodology in the country—"the Marxist stream, the old liberal school, and the Nationalist stream"—and she is considered suspect by all of them because she doesn't properly fit their academic stereotypes. She abandoned history study her first year at Stellenbosch University because it was boring Nationalist pablum. Later, at UNISA, she "was as alien to them as a UFO" because she was ten years older than most students and pregnant. Fascinated by Marxist approaches, she switched to the University of the Witwatersrand for her master's. Then she taught briefly at Rand Afrikaans University, "but there I was radical, a Communist. And I'm not even faintly pale pink in the eyes of the radicals [at Wits]."

It doesn't take much deviation from the norm to be viewed as a radical in the mainstream Afrikaans community. Feminism is so suspect that few women will admit to it.

Does Brink consider herself a feminist?

"It's such a broad question," she said. "I think it's a label and what you mean by feminist and what I mean are two different things."

Feminist is a bad word in this country, isn't it?

"That's precisely why I'm hedging around."

Why is it a bad word?

"Because feminism here was burning your bra, that old view. Violent, we hate men, that kind of attitude."

Who is the purveyor of that view of feminism?

"White men," she said. "Feminism here is very much academic. Women have been excluded from the political process, especially from the fifties onwards, where you got this thing of mothers of the nation, go back to the kitchen and to bearing children. Which I think was a world-wide trend after the Second World War. Then in the high apartheid of the sixties and the seventies there were very few women in politics. They licked the stamps and baked the *koeksisters* [crullers] for the elections. That was how they took part in the political process, as a subordinate group. You have that subservience and obedience to male patriarchy and authority."

"You certainly do not have anything like a [feminist] movement as you might have in the States or in Western Europe," said professor of Afrikaans Marianne de Jong.

De Jong is herself one of the few Afrikaner feminists willing to say so publicly. She is up to date with all the literary and feminist trends in Europe and is frequently quoted on the radio and in publications. But she is far more progressive than most Afrikaner women.

"The ANC is pledged [to be] antisexist, but its structures are sexist and its Women's League is horrifyingly conservative," de Jong explained. "But the interesting point is that that kind of nonfeminist attitude is causing a stir even amongst members of the ANC. You cannot associate feminism with the ANC, or the PAC, least of all Inkatha or the Nationalists."

Elaine Botha, a professor of Calvinist philosophy at Potchefstroom University, is an elder in her local Dutch Reformed Church.

"Now this is quite strange to have a woman elder," she said. "Women in positions of authority are frowned upon."

She said that in her ethics course at the university she talks about "the typical Calvinistic understanding of marriage and family. I often try and get the students to understand that in marriage, where the Bible teaches that the man is so-called the head—which it doesn't teach—it teaches mutual reciprocity or mutual empowerment. The students get all uptight about that because they grew up in households where even if the father said this was yellow and it's green, then it's yellow. That's the way I grew up, too. Honestly, if I think of my own upbringing, it never crossed my mind to criticize my father."

Botha is an impressive woman in her late fifties, an internationally known religious academic, whose protestations about her lack of courage belie her success at overcoming the subservience thrust on Afrikaner women, while also revealing the residual mental baggage she can't quite jettison. She lives alone in a town house bedecked with shelves and shelves of books and a computer at her desk.

"For a long time, as a woman, I just suffered basic feelings of inferiority in thinking I don't represent anything so it doesn't matter whether I have an opinion or not. That takes a long time [to overcome]. I think it's a blessing of becoming older and really not caring, which I think is so liberating.

"As I experience myself as a woman now being invisible, I'm astonished at how invisible blacks were for me for a long, long time in my life."

She noted that she'd met Louw Alberts, the retired physicist, several times and each time he didn't remember who she was, probably not a problem he would have had with a man.

"The fortunate thing about my life is that I'm single," Botha said. "If I were married, I would have to worry about what would happen to my poor husband in the Broederbond and what sort of image am I projecting of him. The people of my age grew up with the notion that the man is the head and what he decides is final."

She said it was hypocritical for women to pretend to acknowledge male authority and then have little mechanisms and attitudes that undermine the so-called authority. "There are expressions like, 'He's the head of the household but she's the neck.' Then everybody laughs and the man laughs. I can't stand it. Those are very prevalent ideas."

Is the younger generation of women any different?

"Duu! There are younger women. There's one young student who the day Nelson Mandela was liberated, a couple days later he spoke at Soweto soccer stadium, and that young girl from Potchefstroom got into a black taxi and went all the way to that rally, the ANC rally, left her little car standing here in front of the Pickin Chicken, Pickin Lickin [fast-food store]. The Security Police put sniffer dogs around the car and what-not. She just went. She said she wanted to be part of a momentous occasion of the country. I mean I could never have been that way, and I don't think in my generation there are many women of that kind."

Women like Botha are frowned on, labeled "humanist" and called un-biblical by the likes of Dominee Pieter Nel. Nel listed symptoms of humanism: advocating abortion, homosexuality, governmental abdica-tion of religious responsibility, the dilution of censorship, and allowing women to be elders and ministers.

"Paul says it clearly," Nel said. "The women should not lead or have any authority or teach over the men. And now we are doing that. The church is giving room for individual interpretation and liberalism.

"God in His wisdom knew that there's got to be a hierarchy. When there is not such a structure anymore in our society, it's going to go to rubble, and that's what's happening. The more women turn to profes-sional jobs and moving out of their houses, you get children living loose, doing what they want, there's not acceptance of authority anymore. The first priority of the wife is to submit to her husband, that's what the Bible says."

Nel was twenty-nine years old. His generation's time was about to come.

Political science professor Pieter Potgieter, a colleague of Elaine Botha's at the University of Potchefstroom, is a top Broeder. A patriarch, defi-nitely not infrastructure. "We are traditionally a male-dominated society and the issue of taking women seriously into the system is not very important. We are not so concerned about that as the Americans are," he said.

CHAPTER NINE

HEALTHY APARTHEID
AND OTHER CLICHÉS

Like an artist examining an object from various angles to paint it, Marianne de Jong worked her mind around a particular Afrikaner conviction that is perplexing for outsiders to grasp. Then she elaborated on how Afrikaner nationalists argue that since apartheid protected every tribe and every nationalism, it could not be racist. And since "South Africa never thought it was racist, so it never thought it was immoral. If they had thought that was racist, they would not have pursued it because they are a fundamentalistic kind of species, the Afrikaners. So if they had thought that this was really wrong in the eyes of God, an 'ism' of the worst kind, they would have prayed about it. It was not because the Afrikaner was bluffing himself, or being mean and crude and stupid. There is a structure to it, call it myth, call it an ideology, call it something else. I can't say."

She thought some more, talked about other topics, then rounded again on racism. She realized that to outsiders apartheid looked so patently racist that repetition was necessary to pinpoint the prevailing white state of mind, even if it stretched credulity.

"People are not prepared to admit that they did wrong," she said. "Because they have not understood yet that they did it. They thought this was a democracy. The blacks were an issue of the Department of Native Affairs, exercising their voting rights in their homelands. There was always a white democracy. The Progressive Party [of Helen Suzman] became the party of opposition in Parliament, so you always had a measure of public debate.

"What happened in [Prime Minister Hendrik] Verwoerd's head [in the 1960s] was not an immoral thing," de Jong explained. "It was a perfectly abstract scheme. It wasn't intended to kill a lot of people."

How could anybody rationally think it was fair to reserve 87 percent of the land for the small number of white people?

"Because the eighty-seven percent was poor land. And they were black. They were not people. What can you say about racism of any kind? What happens when a people decide something else is not a people? What did the Germans do? It is the same thing."

The Afrikaans word *skepsel* used to be quite widely applied to blacks, and still is, among the more right-wing Afrikaners. It means a creature, even a creature of God, but of a lower sort than normal humanity. A similar racism, perhaps deepened by apartheid, is reflected in some African languages too. For example, in Venda one term for whites is *makua*, meaning nonhuman things.

In the farming town of Bethal, Dominee Pieter Nel, an Afrikaner Everyman in the center of the political spectrum, said, "Apartheid has got many beautiful things in it, and that is what's happening in Europe, what's happening in Russia. People believe and see again that they've got identity, they've got a culture that's unique to them."

Why doesn't the majority of the population in South Africa see it that way?

"They see it that way," Nel insisted.

They liked apartheid?

"But they see the word 'apartheid' not as it was meant, they see apartheid as a bull sees a red flag. They don't think about all communities living on their own in peace and love as it was intended. They see it as this mean instrument, because it was not practiced in all its facets, it was not done right."

So the ideal version of apartheid has to do with self-determination and communitarian self-sufficiency?

"Ja, that's right. What I see as a healthy apartheid."

Dominee Willie Jonker, a professor of theology at Stellenbosch University, calmly analyzed why most Afrikaners had thought apartheid was innately good. He spoke gently, as if explaining to believers that they are heretics, but trying not to offend them too much.

"If you look at Verwoerd, Verwoerd was of course of Dutch origin, the Dutch people are prone to be people of principle. So his plan in principle was equal-but-separate. But we know that it is impossible. People voted for ideals in this country, not for realities.

"Think about the Transkei [homeland]. The Transkei was set apart, that's for the Xhosa people. Anton Rupert, the industrialist [founder of Rembrandt tobacco company], went to Verwoerd and said to him, 'Give me the opportunity to go into the Transkei and develop it.' Verwoerd said no. He said, 'You are going again as a white man and making profit out of the blacks. No, they must start their own business and they must have the profit.' That's an academical argument that is very far removed from the reality," Jonker said.

"So I think maybe the Afrikaner didn't think clear enough. He was emotional, didn't look at the realities. That was immoral, too. If you don't look at the realities, you are immoral.

"I would say there is nothing wrong with the intention of having your own culture preserved," Jonker said. "That is what the Conservative Party people mean when they say that apartheid is morally defendable— they think only of that element. In Afrikaans we say '*Die maak van die nood 'n deug*'—What is need is turned around to become a virtue. So we made a virtue of fostering the Afrikaner heritage in such a way that it was detrimental to other people."

Johan Heyns remembered Verwoerd. He had been a minister in Verwoerd's Cape Town church.

"I visited him the same way I would visit any other member of my parish," Heyns said. "Read the Bible, prayed with him, talked about religion. I once invited him to deliver a speech to my students at the University of Cape Town. I had about eighty students in my lounge and dining room. It was a remarkable experience to hear him talk about 'Is our policy Christian or not?' "

Did he say that it was?

"He said it was. Due to the love command: 'Love your neighbor as you love yourself.' Verwoerd said apartheid is based on neighborly love. That sounds to me very acceptable. Even morally defendable. Yet we at that time didn't realize that that would imply injustice to the majority of blacks who were to be expatriated from the so-called white areas to the black."

How could it be? The formulators of apartheid had to know how unjust it was, didn't they? Injustice was the point, wasn't it?

"But in order to survive, in order to maintain one's own identity, we had to do it," Heyns said. "If there is injustice, then it is injustice only for a short period because the ulterior motive is to create a just society."

Does the end justify the means then? Is there a strong basis in Calvinism for that kind of thinking?

"According to Christian ethics, Calvinistic Christian ethics, you cannot justify the means by the end," Heyns conceded. His explanation grew murkier.

"But if you inherited a position, a political position, where you cannot disentangle it without justifying the means by the end, then you are justified to apply unjust means," he said, defending his predecessors. "The position from the thirties was unjust, as far as the relation between blacks and whites was concerned. 'For a time we have to be satisfied with these things in order to create a just society,' that would be the moral argument. Although in principle it would be wrong."

So it is acceptable to make compromises if one is acting toward a situation of greater morality?

"That's right."

And was the greater morality articulated by Verwoerd total separation?

"That's right. Total separation, territorial separation was the idea," Heyns said. "In order to achieve just that, you have to bear temporary injustices."

Did Afrikaners have to do that because their identity was in danger?

Heyns nodded yes. "And if your identity is in danger you cannot fulfill God's calling," he said. "That is to say, to be an effective missionary of the cause of the gospel."

How was identity in danger? Was race-mixing the threat? Were they trying to avoid producing "colored" babies?

"Oh yes. Yes, very much so. Some of our theologians and cultural leaders studied in Germany in the thirties. When they came back to this country they incorporated some of those ideas within the framework of the Calvinistic world and life we had here. Purity of blood, purity of the nation was of paramount importance in order to fulfill God's calling in this country. They had a very interesting example. Some of the British missionaries came out, inspired by the French Revolution ideas of equality, brotherhood, whatever. Some of them even married black women. And what was the result of that? They couldn't go on with their missionary work."

Why not?

"People didn't accept them," Heyns said.

What people?

"The blacks simply didn't accept them. Because, um, they thought that a missionary would be something, let me put it very simple, from a different world. And here they come and they are the same flesh as we are."

Griet Verhoef, a professor of American history at Rand Afrikaans University, could have been Marianne de Jong's art object, the perfect example of glistening pure fundamentalism.

Verhoef and her lawyer husband are upwardly mobile, living elegantly in the northern Johannesburg suburb of Linden in an airy house with high wood ceilings, shiny wood floors, and an antique organ.

At the center of her political beliefs is the idea of a *volkstaat* where Afrikaners can run their own affairs and not have blacks around. She feels uneasy hiring household help because it violates her desire for Afrikaner self-sufficiency. For seven years a black woman had worked for her one day a week. Verhoef considers it un-Christian to hire a live-in nanny, since that would destroy the woman's own family life. The professor really wants to hire a "European" (Afrikaner) woman, who could help her children with their homework, in addition to doing household chores. But she said the image that house cleaning was *kaffirwerk* (nigger's work) made this difficult.

"Something that's very important to me is that real Afrikaner nationalists are not racists," Verhoef said. "They really are Christian people. If Afrikaner nationalists would act in an unchristian manner toward people who are living in their state, it won't be justifiable."

Verhoef's English is impeccable. She went to a dual English-Afrikaans school in Natal and in fact was worried that her children were not learning English well in their Afrikaans school.

She pointed out that 870,000 whites, mostly Afrikaners, had voted "no" in the all-white referendum in March 1992, against F. W. de Klerk's negotiations with the ANC. "They don't want to go into a unitary state," such as the one envisioned by the ANC and the Nats, Verhoef claimed.

"The people who think about the Afrikaners' future the way I do are definitely not in the majority," she said. "Many people out on the streets still think that they must dominate to exist. There is no justification for that to my mind."

She doesn't favor domination, preferring separation. She is correct in believing that, judging from the 1992 referendum, at least half of all Afrikaners believe that apartheid—domination or separation—is fair in principle but had perhaps been misapplied. Her utopian dream of "equal equality," where all nations (tribes) could live in peace and Christian harmony, is the idealist version of apartheid and appeals to Afrikaners' yearning to feel moral and good.

"The way the policy of separate development developed was definitely not the way Verwoerd wanted it," Professor Verhoef said. "Verwoerd was taken away from his people far too soon. [He was assassinated in Parliament in 1966 by a mentally deranged Greek-Portuguese immigrant.]

"The politicians in the National Party that took over then governed this country with *kragdadeheid* [strength], with strong white control: influx control, security laws. They were absolutely dominating whoever was in this state, black and white. In order to keep white wealth increasing, and to keep the votes coming toward the National Party, the National Party did not work systematically toward the making of independent [black] states.

"I've never been a supporter of white power because that is racist and I'm not a racist," she added.

Who are the racists?

"Many of the people who talk about violence, violence, violence are rather more white racists than they are really Afrikaner nationalists. Blowing up minibuses or taxi ranks, things like that. It's senseless. That's simply racist.

"If they're talking about a war for the independence of their people, a war directed at another state which is not prepared to acknowledge their right of self-determination, that's something of a different kind, and I would be more prepared to support that.

"I think a state for Afrikaners is a real possibility. One must not see a state like that as a geographical area that would overnight be populated only by the Afrikaner. Of course, the development in this country since the sixties has been such that it's going to be difficult to disentangle again.

"But the idealism that made me believe that separate development can succeed is the same that now makes me believe that this one [of a *volkstaat*] can succeed." Professor Verhoef strongly supported Dr. Carel Boshoff's effort to create a *volkstaat* at Orania, a small enclave near the Hendrik Verwoerd dam in the Karoo.

Professor Carel Boshoff was for ten years a Dutch Reformed Church missionary to blacks in Lebowa and Soweto; he is married to Hendrik Verwoerd's daughter, Anna. His academic career began with the Broederbond's pulling strings. In 1966 Boshoff was hired as a professor of missionary science at the University of Pretoria instead of the more qualified and internationally eminent theologian David Bosch. Boshoff eventually became chairman of the South African Bureau for Racial Affairs (SABRA), a think tank set up by the Broederbond's front organization, the Federasie van Afrikaanse Kultuurverenigings (Federation of Afrikaans Cultural Organizations), which espoused conservative positions under his leadership. He was chairman of the Broederbond from 1980 until mid-1983. At the end of 1983 he resigned from the Broederbond, joining CP members who opposed the organization's and the government's course toward a multiracial constitutional system. He resigned his professorship in 1988 to enter politics full time, becoming the first chairman of the Afrikaner Volkswag (People's Way), the conservative answer to the FAK, and the head of Afstig (Breakaway), a think tank for right-wing Afrikaners churning out plans. He is a man with a long résumé.

Boshoff personifies the proper, polite right-winger and looks appropriately Voortrekker-like. A burly man with thick, white, wavy hair, Boshoff paced beneath the thick straw thatch of his rondavel office, a bookcase-and-basket-lined, African-style giant circular hut detached from his house in Pretoria. He and his wife were reputed not to have any servants: two indications were the untypical dust and messiness of the office and the serving of coffee by Anna Verwoerd Boshoff herself. Boshoff seemed bored with his own talk, so deliberately did he proceed, like a church minister with a long time to fill. He'd been over this material so many times. It was his duty to do it again, though. Wielding a long wooden pointer, he showed on a giant map what Orania contained.

Not much. It was, after all, located on the edge of the semidesert Karoo south of Kimberley. A small *dorpie*, tiny town, originally built by the government in the sixties for whites working on irrigation projects that sucked water from South Africa's longest river, the Orange River, it was purchased, all 1,167 acres, by Boshoff's followers. A few families had resettled there, but even goats found the scrub vegetation only slightly more nutritious than eating cloth.

Professor Boshoff is an idealist who has picked up the torch of his father-in-law, Verwoerd. "I think that Dr. Verwoerd was on the way to acceptance by the black nations. But it was necessary to give much more land to the blacks. I think it was not his intention for a white minority to keep the whole area, the whole vast land for themselves."

Boshoff's primary concern is "survival." He considers the biggest threat to Afrikanerdom to be "this social revolution threatening the identity of the Afrikaans nation.

"Now I think they [the ANC and Nats] are trying to bring people in an unnatural way together and working towards integrated community, mixing children in camping and in conferences. We may have a Latin American situation, where the Spanish immigrants almost vanished in the local communities. The Afrikaners are a small nation, and it's not difficult to break down the borders between children and young people and make them used to mixing and putting the accent on living together rather than living apart. Sharing common goals and common values and trying to create a common society, an open society. Now, I don't think it is wrong to be open towards other people, but if the Afrikaner nation is going to lose its identity, then, well, then the question is what is your future? Do you accept the disappearance of your people, or would you like to have good relations and Christian attitudes without being absorbed in mainstream Africanized society?"

There in a philosophical nutshell is the centuries-old torment, the fear of being "swamped." The fluorescent light over Boshoff's desk flickered as if this was a remote part of Africa, instead of being hooked up to Pretoria's system. Somehow, in this hut—where the top thatch had to be regularly changed and the chill wind whistled through—the vagaries of a developing country seemed close. Boshoff seemed like an old-time missionary. Outside, in the parking area where right-wingers gathered to consult with their fading guru and the daughter of their revered forefather Verwoerd, the giant roots of an indigenous tree had writhed and shifted the flagstones into tortuous upheaval.

"We love him very much."

Marichen Waldner loved Professor Boshoff very much? This seemed anomalous, for the speaker was far from right-wing. A journalist who for many years considered herself opposed to the policy of the Nats, let alone of the Conservatives, she covered religious affairs for the Afrikaans newspaper *Rapport*.

"He is such a kind old gentleman," she explained. "My friend Ina van der Linde and I were having lunch with him at the synod, at the last big synod of the Dutch Reformed Church in Bloemfontein about two years ago. When he made the appointment, he said he would show us his secret weapon that would make that country [Orania] a success. After we were sitting cozily around the table, he threw out this piece of paper on the table. It looked to us like a big phallic symbol and we asked him to explain. He said, 'Here, that's the Orange River, and that's the land that you can cultivate by irrigation around the river.'"

She chuckled infectiously and sweetly, in a muffled tone as if she'd taken a bite of cotton candy.

"He is one of the most civilized people in South Africa," Waldner said. "He's very soft-spoken. He's a wonderful old gentleman. He's not like the other Afrikaner politicians. He listens. He was a missionary in his younger days. He is not a racist in the ordinary, in the Afrikaner sense of the word. He is one of the few people in the right wing I have never heard make a racist remark."

Waldner wrote a newspaper story about the colored community that currently lives on the land planned for Orania. For Boshoff's plans to be fulfilled, the coloreds would have to move away. "I wrote one of the best stories I ever wrote about these people because they speak Afrikaans, a wonderful Afrikaans. They had no idea where they were going, and they were telling me the most tragic stories I have ever heard. Their houses were like Afrikaner houses in the Depression days, with all the religious pictures. Just a beautiful little town. And I wrote a story that made many people cry.

"Before it was published I phoned Carel Boshoff and said to him, 'I have just listened to these people, and I think that you are committing a sin.' It became very quiet on the other side of the telephone for a few seconds and I began to feel bad myself because Carel Boshoff is a just and fair person.

"It was silent and it was silent and it was silent. Then he said to me, 'Well, then you must write the story.' He answered the questions about the development company and what have you. But I knew that I hurt him. And I knew that story would hurt him very much. Now I see that whenever he makes a speech about his new Afrikaner homeland, he always addresses the question of forced removals, and he says they must not be forced and they must not hurt people."

Doesn't she think he knew forced removals have been going on in South Africa for years?

"I have asked myself the question about forced removals a hundred times," Waldner said. "Because forced removals are the most horrendous things that happened in this country. It is comparable to anything that you found in Nazi Germany. If you ever stood there and watched the forced removal, you will know.

"The Germans must have watched the Jews being removed from their streets. And they must have known, but after the war many of them said they didn't know anything about this. In this country, twelve million people were touched by forced removals. It is too large a number of people not to be noticeable. It was published in newspapers. Photos were published. In the eighties Afrikaans newspapers joined the fight to stop the forced removals. People must have known. The only thing I can think of why they didn't protest or why they kept silent or why they tolerated it, was because they had this idea that it was for the good of the country. Or for the good of the government.

"Between 1950 and 1970, it was very difficult for an Afrikaner to criticize anything. He could have done it, but he would have been labeled a Communist immediately and all sorts of other bad names. So not many people had the courage to do it and it also was not very wise to do it. F. W. de Klerk certainly didn't do it, and look what he turned out to be. Yet I often think there must have been among the people enough to keep a conscience alive. Even if they didn't say anything."

*   *   *

The economist and professor Sampie Terreblanche at Stellenbosch University drew an analogy to explain those Afrikaners—most of them—who refused to admit they did something dreadful by supporting apartheid and all its trappings. He said it was like a man who, while helping another person repair a broken-down car, had blown it up.

"The man then said, 'Oh I know so little about these things, I tried to help, but sorry, sorry, sorry, it's a technical mistake. The whole thing is messed up now.' If apartheid was a mistake, it was that kind of mistake: it was not intentional," Terreblanche said.

He thinks it important that the Afrikaner have a conversion, "make a confession and a commitment towards restitution."

President de Klerk hasn't done that. He has only said he "made mistakes. But he has not acknowledged that our intention was wrong," Terreblanche said.

"They did not intend to exploit the blacks—for heaven's sake!" he sputtered in indignation. "And they claim to be Calvinists! in the true sense of the word. How on earth! It was a systematic process of exploitation."

CHAPTER TEN

SCENERY
(DON'T THINK ABOUT POLITICS)

You need to get away from it all in South Africa—the tension, the horror, the tears: go for a swim in the Endless Summer surf of the Indian Ocean, hike high into the desolate mountains, camp in a private game park and track a lion (with a radio transmitter on it) to a leonine banquet, and forget.

But it won't work, you can't escape: once you've seen a toy monkey's head stuck on a spike with a sign labeling it MANDELA bobbing in the hands of a white teenager at a right-wing rally in Church Square, Pretoria; once you've been elbow to elbow in an angry crowd of thirty thousand blacks at a funeral in Boipatong township and noticed young boys passing around bullets like baseball cards; once you've read the newspapers for a week.

Of course, other countries are harsh too, even more brutal at times. But in South Africa the apartheid cruelty was so—well, so black and white, and it echoed profoundly in the United States and Europe. When one is in South Africa just a dab of knowledge makes it difficult to relax, to take a vacation in the fullest, lethargic sense of the word. Even the scenery has been steeped in myth and polemics for so long that the blood won't wash off, the dead won't die but, instead, rise in memory: reprimands haunting the living. Reprimands such as the Khoikhoi people who were hunted like rock rabbits on Cape Town's Table Mountain in the seventeenth century; such as the people killed in the Border wars between white settlers and African tribes; in the nineteenth-century wars of the Zulu clan Mtetwa led by the military commander Shaka that ravaged southern Africa; in the Anglo-Boer wars over control of the mining riches on the great reefs; in the twentieth-century struggle of the anti-apartheid resistors; in the wars in Namibia, Angola, Mozambique; and in the chaos of the Third Force in the 1990s.

*   *   *

But try. Pick a few places in South Africa and try to experience them as a relaxed observer. Hike up Table Mountain, that famous landmark in lovely Cape Town, along Skeleton Gorge to the top, or till the clouds roll down. Sometimes the mountain can be seen from one hundred miles out at sea, a welcome sight centuries ago to thirsty sailors on ships rounding the Cape of Good Hope on the way to and from India.

Step off that lichened boulder onto the edge of the gurgling stream and hold a fern in your palm, fold it over. This one looks so primitive. Study the meticulous spore lines on the back.

Skeleton Gorge lies in Kirstenbosch Gardens, a property that was owned by the British imperialist Cecil Rhodes almost a hundred years ago. Now a world-class botanical garden that covers over two square miles and lies on the wet side of the mountain, it contains specimens of more than four thousand of southern Africa's eighteen thousand plant species. Most prominent are the family Proteaceae, probably the most ancient of flowering plants. There are 329 South African protea species. One, the silver tree, has soft, aluminum-green leaves that beg to be stroked. Another, the wild almond, is a tough bush transplanted by the first whites to dishearten cattle thieves. The king protea, *Protea cynaroides*, was named South Africa's national flower in 1976 (don't think of that as the year Soweto school children exploded in political protest). The pineal, often bulbous, flower can now be found in up-market flower shops in Manhattan and London. The wood of the *waboom* ("wagon" tree), *Protea nitida*, was used in building wagons, especially those of the Boers who trekked north out of the British colony. (*Sis*, watch out—politics again.)

In Kirstenbosch, nature lovers amble about, ooh and aahing over the flowers of the season, picnicking on the grass while the polka-dotted, pear-bottomed guinea fowl skitter hither and thither, tilting their baboon-blue and red heads. Kirstenbosch is a haven, a peaceful place. (Don't think about the fact that many people can't afford the entry fee.) Admire the *fynbos* (fine bush), which has rolled, or ericoid, leaves caused by dry, hot periods and lack of water in the growing season. The chaparral of California is a *fynbos* cousin.

And the cycads, *sigh*, the cycads, palmlike plants that can seduce your imagination back to an age before dinosaurs. Evolved in the Permian period, they are the most primitive of surviving seed-bearing plants. Their slow growth has heightened their value and their allure to cycad thieves, who steal them from their natural habitat in the Cape's Mediterranean scrub area that receives rain in the winter instead of summer.

*   *   *

The coves and *kloofs*, ravines, around Cape Town can be so beautiful on sunny days, or when a rainbow lilts through the mist, that the mind flows out. Here one can almost escape. The amazing thing about Cape Town is that within a short drive one can be walking up a wild mountainside, high above the Cape flats that in winter are often covered by appalling smog. Down there lie townships and squatter camps and soggy misery. Up on the mountain, one could weep for the beauty. And for the contrast.

Because South Africa is in Africa, one might think the weather would always be warm, if not hot. But a bone-chilling day in Cape Town, or in the highveld winter, for that matter, creates a yearning for the tropics. Central heating is not a South African concept, not even in whites' houses. People grit their teeth, huddle around space heaters, stoves, or fires, and mutter that the winter is short, spring is coming.

In Western Cape Province, called the Boland, spring means flowers galore, wild arum lilies and daisies that in some places blanket sandy fields down to the Atlantic Ocean tidal pools, where their color and variety are then swiped by those Fabergé brooches of the ocean, the sea anemones. You can lie down in those flowery beds of white and purple and orange and think you've been transported to the Elysian fields.

In the three centuries after Jan van Riebeeck arrived to establish a supply station for the Dutch East India Company, the native wild animals of the Eastern Cape area retreated from "civilization," laying trails east of Stellenbosch through Hottentots–Holland Mountain passes, trails that would be plastered with tarmac a few generations later. Here and there baboons crop up, leopards cruise through the Swartberg range, a hundred or so elephants are clustered in the Addo Elephant National Park in the Eastern Cape, and ostriches are now an industry in the Little Karoo.

Cape Town, the "mother city," pseudo-British in its humid weather and genteel British trappings, is the parliamentary capital of South Africa. Although white settlement began in 1652, only three decades after the Puritans stepped off the Mayflower in North America, it soon stagnated. Intense white pressure on indigenous peoples' lands did not emerge until after Britain took the colony over from Holland in 1806, and from 1820 on settlers began pushing the boundaries of the colony north.

The rise of a vigorous capitalist, trading economy; the imposition of British laws, including the abolition of slavery in 1834; and the extension of legal recognition to blacks so that servants could take their white masters to court for mistreatment—these and more blows against traditional

Boer society impelled the Great Trek from the Cape area. The Boers spewed north, as if squeezed from a tube, through the mountain passes all along the coast of the Indian Ocean northeast into Natal, heading away from the British into the scrubby, thirsty interior of the country. They trekked into the dusty expanse of Africa, although they had no idea just how huge it was. In 1866 about fifty miles north of Pretoria the Voortrekkers founded a town they called Nylstroom (Nile stream) because, unlike all the other rivers they'd crossed, this one flowed north; after consulting their Bibles, they decided it was the source of the Nile River.

In fact, it flows into the Limpopo River, as do all streams north of the great mineral-rich reefs around Johannesburg. The part of the Limpopo that serves as South Africa's northern border disappears seasonally, sucked dry by the bushveld. Farther downstream, over the border in Mozambique, winds Rudyard Kipling's "great, gray-green, greasy Limpopo," the last 130 miles of the river that lazes its way into the Indian Ocean. (Don't think about South Africa's support for the war that devastated the first Mozambique government after the Portuguese colonists left.)

In the face of this great, dusty unknown, how could the Boers bring themselves to leave the lovely Cape? Some couldn't. Thirty miles east of Cape Town glistens that Afrikaner town of towns, Stellenbosch (pronounced "Stellenbos," with a rising inflection at the end, if one is being snooty in Afrikaans). The second city to be established by the Dutch East India Company (1680), Stellenbosch was once at the white frontier. Now its eighteenth-century whitewashed, thatch-roofed, stucco buildings with grand hardwood doors and window trim stand primly against the spectacular mountains jutting up just to the east, the beginning of the geological transition to the highveld.

The crème de la crème of Afrikaner society is educated at Stellenbosch University, which was established in 1918. About fourteen thousand or so very large, book-toting white students, clean-cut mesomorphs, roam the town. At the university's center an amphitheater of brick steps, terraced like an open-pit mine, is chiseled down into the ground. At the bottom, where the stage would be in a real amphitheater, is the door to an underground library. Nearby, in the student union building, music like "Birdland" from the American fusion band Weather Report throbs into the ears of the mesomorphs, and five or six colored students sitting at one table. They are all relaxing between classes, perhaps debating the controversial policy of officially declaring Stellenbosch an Afrikaans-speaking university, entrenching ethnicity.

University buildings around town carry the names of prominent Afrikaner men such as Verwoerd and Vorster. (A Verwoerd grandson named Wilhelm was a student here in the early 1990s, and he and his wife were among the few student members of the ANC.) Many other buildings hark back to earlier times, from a 1709 white-built house, the oldest in the country, to the Dutch Reformed Mother Church, dating from 1717, to the 1851 Lutheran church, now an art museum for the university.

Stellenbosch is in wine country. More than twenty estates and co-operatives, imbued with all the beauty and intrigues reminiscent of the American TV soap opera *Dynasty* set in California's Napa Valley, dot the town's outskirts. In the July winter, the dark skeletons of grape vines stalk the vineyards, their drastically pruned, bare branches tied up with twine. Between the rows succulent green rye or other grains spring up like fine, static-electrified hair. Cows browse there.

All around the town in winter, acres and acres of tidy, quiescent vine-yards hint at the labor-intensive nature of wine making. Coloreds' houses can be seen along the rural roads from Stellenbosch to Paarl and Franschhoek, a town settled in 1688 by Huguenots who had escaped religious persecution in France, via Holland. These roads and houses resemble scenery in the back hills of western Arkansas, far more conge-nial than the big-city townships.

(Don't think about the fact that the manual laborers, the most visible workers, are almost all black.) Whites seem permanently to be on vaca-tion. Of course many of them work quite hard, but almost always inside buildings, out of sight of the casual traveler. White South Africans, when they travel in the United States, are jarred at the sight of white men actu-ally digging ditches, doing heavy construction work, getting dirty.

Travelers anywhere can seek their scenery at whim, slide from city to countryside with abandon. So slide to "the Garden Route" east of Cape Town, a two-hundred-mile-long, slender strip of glorious greenery; giant hardwood trees such as yellowwood, stinkwood, and ironwood; bay after bay of sandy beaches carved out, lapped and lulled by the Indian Ocean, backdropped by the Swartberg mountain range. This is vacation land for many white South Africans. (And retirement land for a bitter, ousted President P. W. Botha.) This sliver of vacation bliss is no more glorious than some other lovely properties in the world, but for most white South Africans, at home in the plant penury and parched earth of the veld, the "Garden Route" is their oasis.

Driving east along the coast one comes to the industrial city of Port Elizabeth, traditionally the center of the automobile industry. It was in

Zubeida

Port Elizabeth in 1977 in the SANLAM (insurance company) building downtown that the Black Consciousness leader Steve Biko was beaten by police until he suffered major brain damage. They threw him naked and alone into the back of a Land Rover and sped frantically 710 miles north through the night to Pretoria, where he died on a mat in the corner of a stone-floored prison cell. The N6 highway north from Port Elizabeth, tracing a Voortrekker route, will enter the history books stained by the blood of the self-possessed and generous young leader whose death shook the West. (Don't think about the convulsing, dying, naked man bouncing on the Land Rover floor.)

In winter the wind whips through the Stormberg Mountains, stirring an occasional snow. Not much can grow in these arid parts. As one drives north on the two-lane highway, the idea of the vastness of Africa sinks like a premonition into the body, inexorable as rust. In contrast to the traditional diminished depictions of Africa on Mercator projection maps, a Peters projection renders its true monumentality vis-à-vis Europe and the United States.

The town of Aliwal North, on the Orange River, site of a rather seedy hot spring spa, has a jail right across from the Juana Maria Hotel. One can almost hear the daydreams of the local young people, yearning to get out of this little *dorp*, just get out, go to the city, escape the remoteness, the boredom.

Continuing north the scratchy landscape gradually softens into the topography you might find in Ohio, but with fewer trees and the odd ostrich heads pivoting like periscopes with eyelashes from behind wire farm fences. Dingy sheep are lumps across the landscape, like the rusty-colored termite mounds of the northern Transvaal. Toward Bloemfontein, the *mielie* and wheat farms of the Orange Free State grow more lush, encouraged by water from wind-driven pumps and from the lake behind the Hendrik Verwoerd Dam on the Orange River.

The gracious facades of Bloemfontein, the capital of the former Orange Free State and the judicial capital of South Africa, come from a series of nineteenth-century sandstone buildings, including the Appeal Court and the old Boer Republic government buildings. On the southern rim of the town, buses regularly disgorge white tourists at the site of the old-fashioned Vroue, women's, monument with a pointy obelisk and traditional bronze figures—a memorial to the more than twenty-six thousand Boer women and children who died in British concentration camps during the Anglo-Boer War. The ashes of the Englishwoman Emily Hobhouse are here. She is revered by even the most conservative of Afrikaners—in 1994 she was called an Afrikaner by the right-wing *Volksfront* president Constand Viljoen—as the woman who roused the British conscience against the war. But many choose to ignore that part of her 1913 speech in which she dedicated the monument that espoused liberty as the "equal right of every child of man, without distinction of race, color or sex."

Bloemfontein seems such a white and placid city, it's hard to believe that there in 1912, in a community hall in the black "location," was launched the ANC's precursor, the South African Native Congress. A chasm divides the white and black worlds, the white being virtually oblivious of the black. Only thirty-eight miles east of Bloemfontein festers one of the most miserable, crowded homelands for blacks in the country. Thaba Nchu, a shard of Bophuthatswana, seethes with unemployed Africans, some from Orange Free State farms, some from more remote mines. And people starve. In 1991, a drought year, Operation Hunger viewed Thaba Nchu as a world-class malnutrition disaster.

The Boers' beloved heartland, the Transvaal, stretches inhospitably north and east, an arid plain interrupted by the gold reef and its jewel, Johannesburg, 250 miles away. Swoop through Johannesburg then, through the white coal smoke of the townships, through the gray smog of the factory emissions, through the brash city with more scams per minute than the Wild West, through the commercial heart of South Africa: Johannesburg, the capital of nothing. Go thirty-six miles north of Johannesburg, to Pretoria, the Magaliesberg Mountains slicing it in two. It is the third, the administrative, capital of South Africa.

Pretoria is clogged with Afrikaner bureaucrats and their retinues. During the week the city is stiff as a child's piano lesson, but on weekends pent-up energy escapes in testosterone clouds from rugby stadiums, so that one journalist imagined the chemical could light the hundreds of backyard *braais* that are stoked up in the suburbs.

During the days of the 1980s, when the whites were at war against the "total onslaught" of communism (broadly defined), Pretoria was full of Afrikaners wearing military and police uniforms, status outfits quite in contrast to blacks' drone or worker uniforms. But in the 1990s of the "New South Africa," fewer whites in uniforms were evident.

Named after the Voortrekker leader Andries Pretorius (1798–1853), Pretoria is *the* Afrikaner boomtown, which ballooned during the drought of the thirties and after the Nats won power in 1948. Before that it was a sleepy farm town that was the capital of the first South African Republic from 1860 to 1910, then of the Union of South Africa, best symbolized by the grandiose British colonial Union Buildings on a landscaped *koppie*.

In Pretoria's hot nationalist climate, the virus of apartheid prospered. Hydra-headed bureaucracies sucked up Afrikaner civil servants, transforming the State into the great welfare queen of the National Party. During the twenties, thirties, and forties, whole segments of farm communities flocked into Pretoria, replicating their former villages, clinging like velcro to their *volk* thinking and concentrating in an area called Die Moot (The Valley) in the north of the city, forming a suburb that was very conservative and lower-to-middle class. Die Moot still often determines the city's mood more than east Pretoria's yuppie classes, who prospered most from the state's largesse.

Crammed together downtown, most of the apartheid-era office buildings are architecturally boring (except for the undulating pink-and-mauve facade of the government think tank, the Human Sciences Research Council), and they seem full of zoned-out bureaucrats and furtive police spies. Underneath the buildings are arcades with tidy shops, including one that sells South African police memorabilia and many that sell the salted dried meat of cattle, ostriches, antelopes, zebras, and other creatures. Pretoria is the *biltong* (jerky) capital.

At the heart of the city is the old Church Square, studded with ginger-colored buildings with cake-icing architecture. A statue of Paul Kruger (a founder and president of the Transvaal republic), sporting a cane, top hat, and pigeons, has scowled over Nationalist rallies and, since 1982, gatherings of the neo-Nazi AWB and the Conservative Party. In a typical example, on March 7, 1992, at a protest of right-wingers dressed in khaki brown, a woman in Sunday school dress warmed the audience up (to lukewarm). After each hymn sung, she trilled in a prissy voice used for obedient children "Dit was pratig" (That was beautiful). After the rally, AWB leader Eugene Terreblanche's horse's footing slipped on the paving stones and the charismatic neo-Nazi toppled off. He was snatched back to his saddle by his colleagues, who charged through a police cordon down a side street bellowing the worst epithet they could think of at the Afrikaner police: "Fuckin' *Engels*!"—English.

From the noisy Grapevine pastry shop on Esselen Street to the Voortrekker Monument, a gigantic, dun-colored rectangle, fuzzed pink with veld dust and shaped like an old-fashioned radio, on a hill south of the city, Pretoria is belligerently Afrikaans. Sidewalkless suburbs such as Wierda Park and Verwoerdburg look like white suburbs in Kansas City. Almost every house has black servants. In some of the houses the operatives of the old apartheid security apparatus cower, each day driving to work by a different route, living in fear that their black victims will search them out and take revenge for torture and worse.

In the highveld, with its warm days and cool nights, people live outside as much as in, cooking *braais*, swimming in backyard pools, and fanatically playing and watching sports. For Afrikaners, rugby is the main addiction. (Don't think of Attridgeville and Mamelodi, two black townships looming on the outskirts of Pretoria. To the north of that, in the Transvaal province, lies the overstuffed homeland of Bophuthatswana, and farther north, Lebowa and Venda, then the countries of Zimbabwe, Zambia, Zaïre, stretching on and on across vasty Africa.)

"These Transvalers eat *mieliepap* [corn porridge] with their meat and people from the Cape don't. One thing that I've retained from the Cape is that I can't eat this bloody *mieliepap* with a *braaivleis*. It's just not on, so, but apart from that, I think I'm a better Transvaler."

Jack Botes, the town father in Pietersburg in the northern Transvaal, was not talking about blacks, whose staple food is *mieliepap*, but about the Transvaler Afrikaners versus the Cape Afrikaners.

Botes's personal trek from De Aar, a small town in the desolate Karoo that is the great railroad hub of the country—the Namibia rail line linking up to the South African, the Cape line, the Port Elizabeth line, and the Natal line all meet there—to Pietersburg is unusual for an Afrikaner. Few Afrikaners his age, mid-sixties, had ventured so far from where they were born. As a consequence, Afrikaners' loyalties are local, and they find even their own people a bit strange when they come from a faraway province. The urban quadrumvirate of Cape Town, Johannesburg, Pretoria, and Stellenbosch vie for Afrikaners' affection, and each city has its aficionados who deride the others.

Elizabeth Bradley, the millionaire part owner of Toyota South Africa, was a Johannesburg defender.

"Everybody who comes from Cape Town thinks it's the only part of the world. I don't like Cape Town, I don't like the people, I hate the weather. Johannesburg's an ugly city, I can't deny that. It has no natural features to recommend it. It is the largest city in the world with no natural body of water at all. I have a funny feeling about Cape Town. To me that is the last colonial outpost. It's going to be the last part of South Africa that's going to get to grips with the fact that life is not quite what it used to be.

"Cape Town is full of people who're more interested in where you come from, who your forefathers were than what you do. Or what you earn. Which in Johannesburg is not such a rude question. But in Cape Town one never discusses money because that's trade. It's an old-fashioned and strange attitude for a highly developed country. It's not a personal thing with me. I actually come from quite a respectable Cape family. I can talk with the best of them."

Bradley's mother, the much praised poet Elizabeth Eybers, has lived for years in the Netherlands and received awards there for her Afrikaans poetry. Her father came from a Dutch, Orange Free State trekker family. On her mother's side she inherited the necessary pedigree to prove that her dislike of the Cape cannot be chalked up to sour grapes. From her father she inherited leadership of Toyota South Africa's holding company. Bradley bristled at the pretensions of Afrikaners from the Cape and especially those who combined higher academic degrees with disdain for people in industry.

"We need everybody, obviously we need the writers, we need the university people. But our distribution in South Africa is skewed. Too many people thinking about things, and too few doing something about it," Bradley said.

"Pretoria is more reverent about titles than Johannesburg is. Many people in Johannesburg have the honorary doctor's degrees, but in Pretoria, boy, if you have it, it's engraved on your door the next day. We laugh about it, but I think we also understand where it comes from," Bradley said.

The craving for degrees is reflected in the high number of full-fledged Afrikaans universities in the country for the small population: five. Stellenbosch, the most prestigious, has been joined by the Universities of Bloemfontein, Potchefstroom, Pretoria, and Rand Afrikaans University. The latter three have been dubbed, respectively, the Dopper university, the Trekker University, and the Broederbond University. All of them, of course, plus the black universities, were Broederbond-controlled.

The common characterizations of the different Afrikaner areas run something like this: Johannesburg is aggressive; Cape Town is more relaxed and Anglo, whereas the rest of Cape Province is Afrikaans; Stellenbosch is snobbish—all those people with French names; Natal is vacationland, where people wear sneakers and shorts; and in Pretoria people rise early for work, and women wear their "farmer's pride" hats to the State Opera House.

"You must definitely not quote me on this," said one sophisticated Democratic Party supporter, as if a state secret were about to be unveiled, "but they say people in the Cape are the elite, people in the Free State were the good solid ones who wanted to get away from the English government. But the ones who went to the Transvaal were the *biltong boere*, the hunters."

Traditionally, the main divide in Afrikaner society has been between those who trekked and those who stayed in the Cape. That great split forged the Cape-Transvaal struggles in the National Party, the Broederbond, and the Dutch Reformed Churches. In the 1990s the trekkers' Nederduitse Hervormde Kerk (NHK) still refused to allow blacks or coloreds to attend services.

"The northern Afrikaner and southern Afrikaner, we are almost a different ethnicity," journalist Max du Preez said, chuckling as he laid claim to being a "blueblood" Transvaler because his mother was a great-granddaughter of the eminent Boer forefather Paul Kruger. Du Preez, born in the Free State and a self-described anarchist as a Stellenbosch student, was himself one of the great rebels of late twentieth-century Afrikanerdom, proclaiming his Afrikanerness to the skies while flamboyantly attacking the policies of the NP and the Broederbond.

"We like to say they came to Johannesburg by train," he said of the Cape Afrikaners. "We walked here. The romantic view is, my forefathers couldn't stand British colonial rule. The truth is they wanted to keep their slaves, and some of them were criminals running away from colonial government in the Cape. But the wealthy landowners remained. So the rough people came up. Then we went through that whole generation of trekking. No teachers, no schooling, no personal hygiene, no dominees, a lot of incest. For two, three generations, that's what happened. And then we got caught in the Anglo-Boer War."

The Afrikaners divided: some fought, some remained sympathetic to the British. "I grew up not talking to certain families because their great-grandfather was a jingo, or was a *hanskhaki*, as we called them," du Preez said.

Is that the same as a *handsopper*?

"Well, *handsopper* is one thing, he just stopped fighting [put his hands up]. A *hanskhaki* becomes a tame Englishman. The uniforms the British wore were khaki. And *hans* is tame. When you have a goat or a sheep and you rear him in the house, you know, the ewe had left him, then you call that a *hanslam*, and that's where the word *hans* comes from, it's kind of pet, a pet khaki. It's a very derogatory term."

Aside from some forays by Afrikaner commandos from the Orange Free State into the Cape Province, the Cape was generally quiescent under British rule during the Boer War. The trekkers' mistrust of the Cape deepened. Transvalers still think of themselves as the real Boers, both because of the Anglo-Boer War and because they, not the Cape Afrikaners, have faced the "real" Africa.

"The so-called Afrikaner liberals in the Cape, there is nothing liberal about them," du Preez said. "They grew up with colored people who spoke Afrikaans, went to the same church, had the same culture. So in a sense they could afford to be liberal.

"In the war, in the Free State and Transvaal people had lost all their property. They were forced to compete with people who they knew as savages, to compete for labor in the mines and on the roads," du Preez explained. "It was unfair to them then, because they wore proper clothes and ate certain foods, yet the tribal person was prepared to work for ten cents a month. All he needed was a bag of *mieliemeel* a month. So the relative deprivation was much higher for Afrikaners.

"Then you had all these people in the western Transvaal, for instance, parts of the Free State, parts of eastern and northern Transvaal. Communities that sort of became odd. There are a couple of genetic diseases that you only see among Afrikaners. Northern Afrikaners are mostly descendants of sixty thousand people. That's why we all look the same, you know, we all do. Most Afrikaners look the same, don't you think?"

Not really.

"They do," he insisted, grinning.

Du Preez emphasized how the vast spaces of the highveld led to isolated, backward Afrikaner enclaves. "You've got to understand that incest in Afrikanerdom is an extremely serious problem. The most prominent one is called Afrikaner *dik-kopsike* [thick-head sickness]. Your bone structure doesn't stop growing and you get giants of seven foot with these huge jaws and thick foreheads. They die at thirty, thirty-two, thirty-three when their brain gets squashed."

Eugene Marais, a writer and doctor, documented this, du Preez said, adding that Marais found that 99 percent of the children he examined in small towns were the products of incest. "Brother and sister, father and daughter. They were completely illiterate. They were absolutely poor," du Preez said.

When the Afrikaner Nationalists came to power, they made sure that those unfortunates weren't ignored. "We created the South African railways as a huge, labor-intensive organization, and all those people were employed there. Let me tell you a little story about where I grew up. There was a little community near to the farm where I grew up, it's called Geneva. It was a siding, an agricultural siding, between the towns of Kroonstad and Hennenman. There were probably ten, fifteen families living there, all working for the railways. There were probably jobs for about four of them, but they all worked there. Shunters and firemen and whatever, and just hangers-on. They were all retarded. All one hundred fifty to two hundred people. They were in the same congregation in town as ours. There was an unwritten rule that they wouldn't come to church every Sunday. But for communion they would, because you can't have communion on the farm. So they would come and we would all sit down and then the dominee would stand up and say, 'Can we have our people from Geneva.' Then all these retarded families would walk in, and they would sing a song and we would sit there and snigger. They all look the same and have the same surname and, you know, that story you can repeat twenty, forty, fifty times in the Free State, western Transvaal, northern Transvaal, even in the Northwestern Cape. Nobody writes about this stuff," du Preez said. "Nobody was ever really interested in our history. We had to write it ourselves and we really screwed it up. We wrote what we wanted people to believe."

Far from the Cape, the trekboers finally "uplifted" themselves with the help of the state they captured at the voting booth. Their Cape relatives were tame by comparison and hadn't developed the trekkers' inferiority complexes.

"I grew up in Cape Town," Ina van der Linde said. "What you have here in Transvaal is the Afrikaner that really fought the battles against the English. They were taken to concentration camps and their houses were burned down. The Cape is like another culture. They never took part in the *Groot Trek*, never took part in the Boer War, and they don't have those insecurities. You're uneducated and whatever if you trekked. Landless. They're sort of boorish, that's why they trekked.

"I think Cape people see themselves as not really racists, and they are. They are terribly frightened of the blacks [as opposed to the col-oreds] and the first thing they'd say is that 'we don't know them [blacks].'

"I think you would find the people are very friendly in the Cape, con-genial, wonderful people, but they would rather not have a straightfor-ward argument or get cross or emotional about things. They would rather make jokes about it and flow over it lightly. 'Just don't embarrass me. Don't get argumentative. Don't say unkind things. Be cultured.' But in being genteel you are not very honest with yourself, or with the future."

Still, as professor of economics at Stellenbosch Servaas van der Berg pointed out, the far right wing, and particularly the Transvaal's most famous neo-Nazi, Eugene Terreblanche, had really drawn quite large audiences in the Cape.

In Cape Town, Ton Vosloo of Nasionale Pers simply couldn't fathom the likes of Terreblanche and his neo-Nazi AWB supporters. "Some-times I despair that it's changed at all," Vosloo said. "I saw this television documentary called 'The Leader and the Driver and the Driver's Wife' on Terreblanche. The Afrikaner typified there, most of them were overweight, drinking hard liquor, and all smoking. And you know, I've come to the conclusion that I'm out of touch with Afrikanerdom, sitting here in Cape Town, or at least not living in the rural areas anymore."

Vosloo was born in the industrial town of Uitenhage just outside Port Elizabeth in the Eastern Cape, far from the snootiest part of the Cape.

"If you live in the Cape, there's a standard joke that you have to be born behind the Hex River Mountains and on the other side of Worcester to be a 'Kapie' [a genuine Cape native]. I'm from the other side. You have to have a passport to get in," he said. "The heart of aristocratic Afrikanerdom is Paarl and Stellenbosch. You have to be born there to be accepted as one. Even [multimillionaire businessman] Anton Rupert jokes he's never been accepted in Stellenbosch because he's an outsider. After forty years he's still an outsider. Wasn't born there. It's like your Boston Brahmins or Philadelphians or whatever."

Vosloo did concede that maybe he could by now be considered an insider.

"I suppose I'm accepted," he said. "But Afrikanerdom has opened up you see, in the sense that at least if there is still a conservative lot, there is also a much greater fluid lot, a mobile lot in terms of political thinking. Over the last decade and a half, you must include [P. W.] Botha, give him his credit, for breaking the logjam, an openness and fermentation was created in the ranks of Afrikaners and we'll never go back to the old hegemony. The Conservative Party lost out. The battle was for, as I termed it once in a newspaper column, the holy grail of Afrikanerdom: possession of the Broederbond, the church, of the political establishment. They lost out on all of them."

Perhaps. But up north there are hundreds of thousands of Afrikaners who hate F. W. They may be a crude lot by Stellenbosch standards but they are a lot. Hilda Burnett, the retired principal of the Women's Army College in George, Eastern Cape, is a large woman with a delicacy, an abundant fairness, and clear eye. She thought the weather might have something to do with people's attitudes.

"Life is hard in Africa," she said. "There's drought and extremes in temperature. I think the climate has had an effect. You must have tremendous perseverance to stay on the land with all these conditions. Also they are like the Americans who trekked across the country to the West. They weren't soft like the people in the East, who are the same as the people down in the Cape."

No, in the Cape, the air is moist, the fields are green, and the Afrikaners have their very own architecture, called Cape Dutch; their houses have facades with gentle curves like those of a powdered wig from a

French imperial court. Cape Dutch buildings are painted white as white can be.

Burnett was elected as an unopposed NP candidate to the George City Council in the early eighties, became disenchanted with apartheid, fought vicious character assassination smears from the Nats when she switched to the Democratic Party, and in 1989 joined about sixty people on a trip to Zambia to talk to the military wing of the ANC.

"I just grabbed the opportunity to go because I wanted to know what they were thinking," she said. "I think it's terribly important; we whites don't really know what it's like to be black or the way blacks think and their perceptions. That's why I went."

That sentiment, so simple and so sensible, was rare among Afrikaners, who often assume, "We know the blacks because we grew up with them."

"What I say to people is we are so stupid because we don't realize that South Africa is actually an African country," Burnett said. "I have accepted that this is a black country. Otherwise we must move out. Go live in some European or some other country."

A lovely restaurant called the Copper Pot in the town of George is one of those places known only to the cognoscenti. Reservations required. Starched linen. Everything is cooked individually, the lobster mousse-line, the freshest fish. The oysters were local, harvested wild from the bay, instead of from the oyster farms at Knysna. Mrs. Burnett ordered a perfect fumé blanc, South African of course. This was probably not exactly what Jack Botes in Pietersburg meant when he said that in the Cape they don't serve *mieliepap*. But, no, there was not a *mielie*—or a black—in sight. The waitresses were all white.

One could almost forget politics. Almost not remember certain words heard in a conversation. The words were uttered by an anti-apartheid activist who was talking about Jeanette Schoon and her six-year-old daughter, Katryn, the wife and daughter of the Afrikaner anti-apartheid activist Marius Schoon. On June 28, 1984, in Lubango, Angola, Jeanette Schoon opened a parcel sent by the South African Security Police. It blew her apart and killed Katryn, as a toddler son watched.

Why is Mummy's head on the floor? little Fritz Schoon asked.

Those words.

Interviewing Marius Schoon at his home in Bez Valley in Johannesburg, after he'd played cards with his young son and put him to bed, was like trying to hold a feral cat: scratching at the face, clawing veins, and yowling hideously. Schoon had been the ANC military wing's organizer in Botswana in the 1980s, and a Communist Party member. He himself was spared assassination when he learned from British authorities that the South African Police had a plan to kill him. He said that he had joined the ANC resistance for his people, for his *volk*, and for the friend he'd met during his twelve years in prison, the Afrikaner lawyer and Communist Bram Fischer, one of the earliest white anti-apartheid rebels.

Schoon could talk to the leaves and they would listen, he could twist things in elegant knots, play psychological warfare to the screaming point. "With Marius you can't tell what is myth and what is fact," said a Communist Party acquaintance. In 1992 he reveled in the fact that old enemies now came to him to ingratiate themselves with the ANC.

The reef that rips through Johannesburg lies just north of Malvern, where Marius Schoon returned home in the early nineties after fourteen years of exile. He had grown up nearby, among these tidy, tin-roofed working-class houses jammed fence by wall. In a private home in that suburb the Broederbond was born in 1918.

When raindrops clonk on the corrugated metal roofs, hundreds of elves seem to be stomping overhead. Just before the rain slams the dust to the ground in the highveld, it exudes a special smell. A lot of people mention that. It's the dust's last gasp, just as a flower smells stronger when crushed. South Africa's dust, its scenery, smites passion into many.

(Don't think about young Fritz Schoon's question.)

PART III

THE BROEDERBOND

South Africa is the terrain of double-think, double-talk, double-do, of hidden agendas, where birds sit in the tree like severed hands and fly up to scribble inscrutable truths. Drops of blood on the trees. The only way to see South Africa is to close the eyes.

—BREYTEN BREYTENBACH,
Return to Paradise

Nee, ek was gelukkig. Ek kom uit 'n armblanke-omgewing, so ek was nooit goed genoeg vir hulle nie.
No, I was lucky. I came from a poor white environment, so I was never good enough for them.

—PIET GOUWS,
chairman of the Free State Agricultural Union,
when asked if the Broederbond had ever
approached him to be a member
(quoted in *Vrye Weekblad*, September 16, 1993)

CHAPTER ELEVEN

MODUS OPERANDI

More than fifty years ago, in March 1936, the Afrikaner Broederbond swore it was abandoning secrecy, fourteen years after adopting it. That's what *bond* chairman J. C. van Rooy promised the Boer War hero General Barry Hertzog after he denounced the *bond*'s secrecy, exposed its ties to the (purified) National Party, excoriated its infiltration of the teaching profession, and condemned teachers' indoctrinating Afrikaner children in hatred of English speakers. On the strength of van Rooy's promise, Hertzog wished the Broederbond well in a letter to him.

Hertzog was fooled. Broederbond secrecy deepened, double dealing became its norm, *vriende* became obsessed with the oath that bound them for life. Because Broederbond members hid their activities, they bred superstitions about power, who wields it, and how it can cast into oblivion those who challenge it.

Occasionally the Broederbond's mask slipped. In January 1944 Prime Minister Jan Smuts received a Military Intelligence report arguing that the Broederbond infiltration of the civil service and teaching profession was so serious a threat to peace in South Africa that the organization needed to be destroyed. Late that same year, Smuts declared the Broederbond to be a subversive organization, and by the following March the government had been notified that more than five hundred civil servants and teachers had resigned from the Broederbond. But when the Nationalists came to power in 1948, membership became an asset, and those who had resigned were reinstated.

In 1963, secret *bond* documents were published in the *Sunday Times* newspaper. Ivor Wilkins and Hans Strydom's 1977 book *SuperAfrikaners* and Hennie Serfontein's 1978 *Brotherhood of Power* detailed the structures and exposed members' names. In 1989, Charles Bloomberg's posthumously published *Christian Nationalism and the Rise of the Afrikaner Broederbond in South Africa 1918–48* brought out more details of the tight links between the *bond* and other leading Afrikaner institutions. In the 1990s, *Vrye Weekblad* and *Die Suid-Afrikaan* magazines continued the exposés.

Sociology professor Louwrens Pretorius of UNISA described the Broederbond of 1992 in terms that would have been familiar to Smuts in 1944. Referring to analyses by Frederick van Zyl Slabbert and a book called *Volkskapitalisme: Class, Capital and Ideology in the Development of Afrikaner Nationalism 1934–1948*, by Dan O'Meara, he said that Afrikaner life was controlled by "interlocking directorates, with overlapping memberships at the top levels and with the Broederbond as a kind of nodal point. Mobilizing [the *volk*] is done by organizations which revolve around the Broederbond nexus," Pretorius said. "You organize teachers via churches. You get the schools, the youth organizations. You know, we are all members of the Voortrekkers, a sort of Afrikaner Boy Scouts [Girls Scouts too]. With the consequence that you have a fairly tightly knit population group. You grow up literally from the cradle to the grave within the Afrikaner community, which is an organized community."

In late 1993, when the Broederbond declared itself to be a new organization, called the Afrikanerbond, open to Afrikaans-speaking women and coloreds as well as white males, critics greeted the announcement with skepticism, saying the move was merely made to appear to comply with an expected new Bill of Rights that would outlaw discrimination by race or gender. Meanwhile, they figured, a core group of Broeders would remain, secretly wielding political influence, directing the brothers and others.

Information on how the Broeders operate has leaked out slowly over the years and reveals the Afrikaner Nationalists' mentality. Time-honored devious tactics and coercive attitudes will be difficult to change, even if genuine change is intended—and some observers doubt that it is.

Ben and Sebastiana Marais knew about Broederbond tactics from long ago, from the forties, before the Nationalists came to power. They told their stories over tea in their old home in Brooklyn, around the corner from the University of Pretoria where Dominee Marais used to teach theology.

It was an autumn day in May as the chill from the south, from Johannesburg, crept into Pretoria with early twilight. The moon, already up, hung low over the yellow hibiscus bush in the yard. A giant, eight-foot-high sisal plant sprawled nearby like a flat-armed octopus holding a ballet position.

The Maraises have many friends in Pretoria who call them Oom (Uncle) Ben and Tannie (Aunt) Sebs. If the makers of Ken and Barbie dolls decided to produce grandparent dolls they would look like this genteel pair—he, properly dressed in a suit and tie, and she, in a smashing bright blue flowery dress, standing arm in loving arm. They were married back in the days of Afrikaner poverty, in the church where the British explorer David Livingstone wed Mary Moffat, in the town of Kuruman, northwest of Kimberley, the diamond city.

Incongruously, this serene couple had over the years provoked into action a number of anonymous enemies, called "they."

Tannie Sebs pointed to their steel mailbox with a pronounced dent in it. "They smashed one of my friend's postboxes and they tried to smash mine," Ben Marais explained. "But it is made of steel plate and they couldn't. They dented it."

The couple has received ominous anonymous phone calls in the middle of the night and threatening letters with the childlike contour of a hand next to the word WITHAND (white hand), suggesting a terrorist organization. Ben Marais has been called names such as *kaffirboetie* (nigger brother), Communist, khaki (someone who favored the British), and humanist. What had he done to raise the ire of some of the *volk*?

"You know, the Broederbond was very powerful," Ben Marais said. "It's still powerful. I finished my theological course in 1936 and within two or three years probably two thirds of my classmates were members of the Broederbond." This was immediately after J. C. van Rooy had promised General Hertzog that the Broederbond would emerge into the light.

"They had wonderful principles: to serve the people and build the nation," Marais said. "But the moment you have this element of secrecy, then some people within that group begin to plot against other individuals.

"I once bought a book at a second-hand auction, and in it I found the principles of the Broederbond. The book probably belonged to a Broederbonder. Reading through them, I said to myself, there's very little in this I couldn't subscribe to, apart from the secrecy and that it was an out and out factional thing. In a country like South Africa, with all the varieties of groups and peoples, this is never a thing I could support. The Broederbond became a sinister movement. I would never think of joining."

Has it been easy, down through the years, to guess who was a Broederbonder?

"No, it wasn't easy," Marais said. "You never knew if your next-door neighbor is a Broederbonder, that is the problem."

"Even your own son," Mrs. Marais chimed in.

"Ja, you know, many good people belonged to the Broederbond," Dominee Marais mused. "Honorable people. I could never quite understand it. In the forties the old Smuts government had a commission to work on [investigate] the Broederbond. And one of the members of that commission told my friend Danie Craven at Stellenbosch—the head of the rugby board, he's also never been a Broederbonder—that in the early forties a circular was sent out by the Broederbond in which they mentioned three names and said, 'We must keep these people small,' the Afrikaans word *klein*, 'because they are our enemies.' They mentioned my name, the name of a general in the army who was prominent at the time, and Craven. So I knew these things."

Why was Marais regarded as a threat?

"Because he was an outstanding student at Stellenbosch," his wife offered.

"Ja, and as a student pastor at that time, I had very intimate contacts with hundreds and thousands of students, and they knew I was outspoken," he said.

"When I wrote the book *The Color Problem in the West* in 1952, one of my elders, a very prominent man in Afrikaans culture, came to me one night at about ten-thirty or eleven. He knocked at the door, and I thought, 'Well, it's a queer time to visit the minister, did this man murder his wife or what happened?' And he came in and he says, 'I must talk to you about a personal matter, something that greatly bothers me. We had a meeting of a secret society two nights ago, and your book was discussed. A number of people got up and said that book is going to do great harm to the Nationalist Party.' I never mentioned the Nationalist Party in the book, but of course it was against their basic philosophy."

One chapter of Marais's book was a survey of twenty-four internationally eminent theologians such as Karl Barth and Reinhold Niebuhr. "Every single one of them was negative, to say, you can't base apartheid on Scripture, you can't have apartheid in a church," Marais said.

After the Sunday Transvaal newspaper *Dagbreek* (*Daybreak*) had published a very positive review, Marais said the Broederbond decided the two Johannesburg Afrikaans dailies *Die Transvaler* and *Die Vaderland* had to quash his book. Marais sipped his tea as he remembered. His giant hands, which once snatched rugby balls from the air, dwarfed the tea cup.

"One of the subeditors who handled this part of [*Die Vaderland*] said, 'Well, I've already written the review, and I have some criticisms but I wrote positively.' It took them an hour and a half to get him to delete all the positive elements. With the second editor they had no trouble convincing him what he should do."

Dominee Marais described how in 1953 the jobs-for-pals Broederbond had tried to prevent his getting a professorship at the University of

Pretoria. In the end, one of the Broeders cracked. "You know, often a man's conscience works," Marais said. "One of my old classmates who was a Broeder told me years later, 'You know, I actually voted you into this professorship. The night before, I promised the organizers of the Broederbond that I would vote against you. But that night I woke up and I told my wife, 'I can't vote against Ben. I just can't do it.' The next day he voted for me and that swung it."

Marais said that to further their church careers, dominees had to go along with the Broederbond-controlled leadership in synod meetings; however, many of them privately told Marais they agreed with his position. "I had a lot of them," he said, chuckling. "Now, of course, it's quite different. Any man can stand up now and say 'I'm against apartheid.' But twenty years ago it was quite another matter."

The youth groups Voortrekkers and junior Rapportryers (Dispatch Riders) are crèches for the Broederbond, nurturing future Afrikaner Nationalists from an early age. The final grooming organization is the Ruiterwag (Mounted Guard) for men between twenty and thirty-three, established in 1956 and patterned on the Broederbond. After that, if a man is chosen, he takes the Broederbond's oath never to reveal anything about the organization to outsiders, learns the secret handshake, and is launched into the life of the elite.

Journalist Dries van Heerden was in the Ruiterwag as a young Afrikaans newspaper reporter in the late 1970s and early '80s. It was the era when the Conservative Party, led by the cabinet minister and former head of the Broederbond Dr. Andries Treurnicht, hived off from the National Party to protest the new Tricameral Parliament that allowed coloreds and Asians to vote. Van Heerden recalled, "The fights in our cell were such that we were suspended for a year because we were considered a security risk. We were not allowed access to documents at one stage.

"It was the junior cell in Parliament. There were a number of private secretaries of ministers belonging to this cell. The only reason I stayed on in the end—I mean, I hated the organization at one stage—but I stayed on just to be privy to all the information because the fights that we had on every second Tuesday of the month mirrored the fights that they must have had in cabinet. Jesus, we had fist fights between [Minister for Cooperation and Development] Piet Koornhof's and Andries Treurnicht's private secretaries. I said to myself, 'Hell, if the private secretaries go on about this, what must Piet Koornhof and Andries Treurnicht be doing to each other?'

"During the eighties the Broederbond and its front organization [the FAK] had been fairly paralyzed by that [political split in the NP]." The organization's influence waned under P. W. Botha, but waxed again as the CP members were drummed out and then finally P. W. was replaced by F. W. de Klerk in 1989. "The Broederbond is very influential in de Klerk's thinking," van Heerden said. "You must remember that the Broederbond is predominantly a Transvaal phenomenon. There are branches in the Cape, but it has always been dominated by the Transvaal. De Klerk is a Transvaal man. In the P. W. Botha era the Broederbond played no role, or a very, very small role. Reason: Botha was a Cape man and a National Party man first and foremost. He was a party political organizer. Botha surrounded himself with the securocrats, the Defense Force, the police and national intelligence service."

Lanky, disheveled, gregarious, van Heerden had been fired from the Afrikaans daily *Die Vaderland* in 1986 along with its editor, Harald Pakendorf, for being too critical of the Botha regime's perpetuation of apartheid. Van Heerden believed that the then cabinet minister F. W. de Klerk had a hand in their firing, because de Klerk was on the paper's board of directors at the time.

"There is no objectivity in newspapers in this country," van Heerden said. "We are campaigning newspapers."

Van Heerden has come a long way. He'd grown up in Die Moot, the valley in Pretoria on the north side of the Magaliesberg Mountains that is a hotbed of middle-class nationalism. He had dabbled as a young man in politics more conservative than the National Party's and still viewed Carel Boshoff, the *volkstaat* advocate, with affection.

"I come from a Broederbond home. The strength of the Broederbond has always been the fact that you have a fixed set of ideas that is given from above and then dispersed among its members. You have the Head Committee, which sends out circulars to each and every cell, or local branch. Eighty percent of the time spent at a Broederbond meeting is to listen to the circular, which often is a sixteen- to twenty-page document. That circular covers every conceivable aspect of political development for the past month and for the coming month.

"In the late sixties, when the Broederbond was at its pinnacle, all the important people in the community received exactly the same message in the same way—the local attorney, the chairman of the farmers' co-op, the headmasters of schools, the three dominees of the three Afrikaans churches. Their job is then to disperse the message, not actively by going out and telling people about that, but just through their actions."

Van Heerden doesn't see the Broederbond as a particularly malign

130

influence in Afrikaner politics, especially since in recent years it has been more reformist than the military men advising P. W. Botha. But van Heerden had seen firsthand how the *vriende* secretly organized the *volk*.

"When my father was minister of the church and the time came for school committees to be elected, the Broederbond decided, okay, there are twelve members of the school committee to be elected, let's make it eight for the Dutch Reformed Church, two for the Gereformeerde Kerk [Doppers] and two for the Hervormde Kerk [Reconstituted Church, NHK]. This happened all over the country."

On the Sunday before the election van Heerden's father announced the agreed names from his pulpit. Never did van Heerden hear of anyone contesting the process or one of the nominees not being elected. If a school committee member ever got any political ideas other than approved ones, he would find his name off the list the next time around. The process is duplicated at all levels, van Heerden said. "On higher levels, obviously, guys were denied promotion in the bank or in the civil service" if the Broederbond decided.

"They [Broeders] will never again be the same strong force that they were in the sixties under Verwoerd and Vorster, because the power of patronage is gone. They are not drawing the best and the brightest in Afrikaner circles today. On the *platteland*, the rural areas, the most very important people are CP members, not National Party. In the cities they may still have the headmaster and the dominee, but the local bank manager or the CEO of a huge company has no interest in the Broederbond anymore. He doesn't need it.

"In the old days, I'm talking about the seventies, church, party, Broederbond, all these were so absolutely intertwined that if you dissented on one level, you were immediately taken out of the loop in all spheres. You become a loner.

"The best guy to talk about that is the former cabinet minister called Theo Gerdener. Still living. Poor guy. He was administrator of Natal at the age of forty-three or something like that, was brought into the cabinet two or three years later, then had a very serious car accident, had to undergo brain surgery. When he returned to the cabinet, everyone still thought very highly of him. But then he started thinking apartheid's not going to work. He broke away in the early seventies and formed the then Democratic Party, which was a liberal offshoot of the National Party. Immediately the propaganda that came out was, the guy's a little cuckoo—you know, he had a brain operation so don't take him seriously. The guy's whole political future was destroyed.

"He's still living. In his late seventies or something, at least now he's got the knowledge that he was right. Interesting family, his father was one of the guys who translated the Bible into Afrikaans."

Theo Gerdener was in the phone book and was easily reached, but he didn't want to talk about his past, or the present—not even if history had proved him right and saner than the men who questioned his mental capacities and buried him in calumny, a common Broeder tactic. They'd made him small.

The slur and the smear are, as elsewhere, weapons of the political trade. The men who made it to the top in the Broederbond were first-rate insinuators.

As Stellenbosch professor of political philosophy Johan Degenaar said, "They try to label you and put you within a certain frame of reference. I would always say if you want to put me in a frame of reference, it is that of philosophy, which can ask the crucial questions that people don't like."

Degenaar noted that men in the Dutch Reformed churches advised students not to take his classes. He and his colleague André du Toit were labeled *oorbeligte* (overenlightened, with a connotation of going overboard) and considered far too "liberal" in a society in which "liberal" was often equated with libertine. Conflation of the two words "liberal/libertine" is common among Afrikaners.

One of the men adept at insinuation is Piet Cillie, the editor for twenty-three years of the newspaper *Die Burger* and chairman of Nasionale Pers, the paramount Afrikaans newspaper and magazine publishing conglomerate that now includes M-Net television. When Cillie retired as chairman, he started a journalism school at Stellenbosch patterned on the Columbia School of Journalism.

Stellenbosch professor of English literature Annie Gagiano depicted Cillie vividly: "I think he said two or three years ago that apartheid was an experiment that had to be tried to find out that it didn't work. To me, that's a statement almost more shocking than many of the shocking things that have been done. He's as hard as nails, you know. Fiercely proud, dignified. I think it was he who said that here at Stellenbosch you can have a broomstick as NP candidate and it would be voted in. I think that's a psychopathic person, to use a very crude, harsh sort of comment."

Does she think Piet Cillie knew perfectly well about the killings of anti-apartheid activists by police and death squads that went on?

"Yes, I think [he knew about it] without having had an organizing hand in it, I'm pretty sure," Gagiano said. "He's Machiavellian. He might not use the term himself, but that's the way his mind works."

*　　　　*　　　　*

Sampie Terreblanche, the chairman of the department of economics at Stellenbosch University, knows Piet Cillie well. Terreblanche is described as "bitter" by numerous Afrikaners. He quit the Broederbond and the National Party in 1987, turning into a sharp polemicist against them, though he had earlier been one of their most acid-tongued defenders.

When Terreblanche slipped through the door of his office, he seemed gleeful rather than embittered. Of medium height, he has an academic slump, owl-rounded shoulders. His blue-green eyes behind bifocals are lively, peering around for a choice morsel of an idea or phrase. His thick, feathery white hair adds to the owlet effect.

Ebullient, funny, incisive, Terreblanche relishes polemics and is expert at dishing them out. He had practiced his skills for the Broederbond "in my sometimes ignoble past," as he put it, and his old targets still remember his attacks. Terreblanche had dubbed *oorbeligte* a group of academic critics of the government, the Stellenbosch professors André du Toit, Johan Degenaar, and F. van Zyl Slabbert, who had argued in 1982 that the *verligtes* (enlightened Nationalists)—of which Terreblanche was a leading member—were actually giving legitimacy to the regime while claiming to be changing the apartheid system from inside.

After slamming them in the early 1980s on behalf of the Broederbond and National Party, in 1987 Terreblanche concluded that they were right. Slabbert and Degenaar accepted Terreblanche's apologies, but du Toit can't forget how those exchanges in the early eighties were "vicious at personal levels." The attacks were carried out in Broederbond-run media, using ruses such as the publication of viperous anonymous letters to editors. Since the Afrikaans papers are controlled by the Broederbond establishment, du Toit and his associates had great trouble refuting these "letters" and getting their message across.

By the nineties there were other media, including *Die Suid-Afrikaan*, a liberal opinion magazine edited by du Toit, and *Vrye Weekblad* in Johannesburg. In the 1990s, Terreblanche pitched his polemical pies at the Broederbond and the Nats in *Vrye Weekblad* and in the English press. His hands dance while he talks, molding his thoughts. He claimed he was much more persona non grata to the Broederbond than those Afrikaner academics who never were members.

"My sin in their eyes was that I was one of them and could dare to make such a clean break and to criticize them the way I'm doing," he said.

His journalist daughter bumped into Piet Cillie of Nasionale Pers at a cocktail party and Cillie launched into an hour-long attack, saying her father was a "troublemaker." "Be forewarned," Terreblanche said, "if you have an interview with Cillie, don't mention my name until the end, or the whole interview will be spoiled."

Terreblanche's eyes gleamed as he chuckled. He was especially delighted that, unlike in his Broeder days, he could write any article he pleased and send it off to a newspaper without consulting anybody. He is having a jolly good time, turning the tables, spilling the beans—but not all of them. The old Broederbond oath still hangs in his body like a chromosome, keeping him silent on the subjects of his erstwhile Broeder buddies, how the Broeders decided whom to attack, and when, and how it had felt to sling mud at the liberals and *oorbeligtes*.

As editor until 1978 of the influential Cape Town daily, *Die Burger*, Piet Cillie was a maker and breaker of Afrikaner reputations. Then until 1992, as chairman of Nasionale Pers, he exercised his biases more broadly. "Machiavellian," Professor Gagiano had said of him. Her adjective was more subtle than he deserved.

"You're talking like an intellectual," Cillie jibed, when it was suggested that the Democratic Party's policy in favor of negotiations with the ANC conquered the National Party, and that policies were more important than individuals. He argued that in politics what counted was who ruled, not for what.

"Politics is about power for me and not about power for you," he declared.

He wore a well-fitting three-piece suit the color of French mustard. He is about five foot four, sturdy, with a bit of a strut, like a Calvinist bantam rooster. He has thin lips, light brown plastic glasses, and a grandfatherly air, with a hint—no, less than a hint, a soupçon—of rakishness. He smacks of the machine politician. He does what he has to do, and without much finesse.

"A newspaper has to carry its readers with it," said Cillie. "So you have to give them the truth in small doses. Not push it down their throats. It's like a preacher, he can't go and say 'You're all going to hell' every Sunday, they won't attend his church any longer.

"All newspapers are partisan," he said. "Ours is. We follow the government line as far as we can. We regard ourselves as the [Nationalist] government's best friend."

He appeared surprised when asked whether he thought the Afrikaans press should have exposed the killings and excesses of the security forces in the 1970s and '80s.

Afrikaans press

"No, this is the opposition's function. That is why you have an opposition."

Asked whether his newspapers had ever published any major exposés, Cillie replied, "As soon as any exposé starts, we've got to get in."

But Cillie couldn't cite any investigative journalism that his papers had initiated against the government in all the years of his leadership. "You have to be very careful if you're very powerful, especially if you're close to an authority like we are to the governing party."

Everybody has his role. Everybody is to fit in his box properly. And Cillie's job was to mold opinion for the government. Smearing seemed to be a specialty.

Take Dominee Beyers Naudé. Naudé is a prominent Dutch Reformed Church leader who was a top Broeder until he broke with the church over its stand in favor of apartheid, criticized it for being the tool of the Broederbond, and leaked Broederbond documents in the early sixties. From Cillie's standpoint, it appears Naudé deserves the best of smears.

"What I resent, or what I don't like about him because I have a different philosophy, I believe that you must stay inside as long as you possibly can, till it becomes utterly impossible. Why does the other side make a fuss of him? Because they saw him as an instrument of dividing the Afrikaners. You can work from the inside or you can work from the outside," Cillie continued. "And the outside man gets all the publicity and gets all the glamour. He becomes a sort of Christ. Naudé had what I would call the Christ syndrome. I think he likes being crucified."

Cillie laughed at his own cleverness to come.

"But there were two murderers crucified next to Christ, so it's really difficult to distinguish," he said, grinning like a schoolboy and sounding as if he'd used this locution many times before.

Naudé has a brilliant Afrikaner pedigree, which is one reason his defection was so startling to the establishment. His father was one of the Broederbond's founders. But Cillie applied a pseudo-Freudian analysis to the situation.

"Where do you look for the trouble?" Cillie let the question hang like a riddle, then answered himself: "The mother." He laughed triumphantly. "The mother is what we call a van Huystein. They're a very difficult family. They're hard-headed people. She dominated the old man, his father. I wouldn't like you to mention that because you may anger some of the van Huysteins if you say they are hard-headed. But she dominated the old man."

When pressed that it was surely poor journalism to attack Beyers Naudé in print while never having spoken to him, Cillie exploded in anger.

"I never got any protest from him. He never said that I was not telling the truth." It was irrelevant to Cillie that during many of the years when his papers attacked Naudé, the latter was prevented by government banning orders from being quoted, speaking in public, or having his letters published.

Cillie views himself as a proponent for change, having "quite a lot of sympathy with him [Naudé] because many of his ideas were my ideas." But unlike Naudé, he pursued change from within the establishment. The moderation he pushed could have barely been recognized by apartheid's real foes and victims. He proudly claimed, "I was very much involved in politics and especially in changing the Afrikaner outlook from white supremacy to separate freedoms, what was called the bantustan policy."

What does Cillie think about later defectors from the National Party/Broederbond establishment, such as Sampie Terreblanche?

Cillie pulled out his rhetorical tools to make Terreblanche "small." "He is a frustrated man," Cillie said. "He didn't reach what he wanted to do. He's also got the martyr's syndrome. He was pulled up very sharply by the prime minister once and he can't forget this. In several ways he missed the bus. He didn't get what he wanted."

But wasn't Terreblanche pushing the National Party policy in the same direction as the *verligtes*—he was just a little further along?

"Yeah and he did it the wrong way, of course," Cillie said.

What's the wrong way?

"When you don't succeed."

Terreblanche's attacks on the Broederbond seemed particularly to annoy Cillie. "He's isolated himself, by the way. Ag, he writes for *Vrye Weekblad*. He's terribly against the Broederbond influence. He sees Broederbond influence almost everywhere."

Maybe Terreblanche knows because he had been inside.

"He pretends that he knows, you see. The Broederbond has been a whipping boy right through Afrikaner history."

It was hard to empathize with this claim of victimization, as Cillie sat in his office high above Cape Town harbor in the Nasionale Pers building. Here is a man who for so long made men "small" and worse, under the apartheid regime that he helped make big and grand.

The Broederbond's declining popularity among Afrikaners was exposed in 1992 in Stellenbosch when it became known that the university's rector (president or chancellor), Andreas van Wyk, was to become the new national head of the Broederbond. Students, liberals, and ex-Broeders on the faculty signed petitions and wrote letters to newspapers complaining about the "double agenda" that the rector would have.

Rector van Wyk denied assertions that being rector and a Broeder represented a conflict. "I don't see anything incompatible about it," he said, sitting in his office at Stellenbosch. "Never has it played a role in the high decision-making of the university. I've appointed many people at this university over the years and they range from all political views. I don't see that it has any relevance to my position. This issue was raised against me before my nomination as rector and in spite of that I was the only candidate nominated by the synod of the university. So I think I can say that I have overwhelming support from the university's community.

"What I do resent very strongly is the implication that if you are a member of such an organization that means you are *verkrampt* [hardline or right-wing]. I mean, I think I've played a very important part in this country in bringing about change. I was the chap who was instrumental in abolishing the pass laws [Influx Control laws abolished in 1986] when I was in government as director general of Constitutional Affairs." As director general he was a civil servant and thus followed political orders, instead of being a policy-maker. Also, by 1986 so many blacks disobeyed the pass laws that they were unenforceable.

Although van Wyk was defensive about the Broederbond's reputation, he acknowledged that its secrecy created resentment and suspicion.

"I can't tell you what the situation will be in a year or two's time," he said; less than a year later he publicly resigned from the Broederbond. Shortly thereafter the Broederbond declared itself reborn as the Afrikanerbond.

Annie Gagiano led the battle against van Wyk at Stellenbosch. "I keep emphasizing that the Broederbond represents white Afrikaner males," she said. "There are so many people who detest or are merely indifferent to the Broederbond. It's an interventionist organization that operates by placing its people in positions of influence. Plus it is narrowly exclusive. So obviously it's incommensurate with academic interests, which ought to value free inquiry.

"I would guess the Broederbond has very little involvement with the real command structure of ordering so-and-so to be tortured or killed," she said. "The morality structure [of Afrikaner society] is very Victorian, not allowing the knowledge of what the ordinary cop is up to in the cell to sully the conscience up here. Of course it's hypocritical. That's what has allowed Afrikaners at the top to maintain this tremendous air of self-righteousness whilst the world is outraged at what actually goes on.

"The Broederbond really is something that has only become an issue for me quite lately," Gagiano said in 1992, although she'd known for years that her father was a member. "Because I think there is a danger in laying the guilt at the door only of the Broederbond, like thinking of the Nazi thing as only a matter of the SS. One shouldn't do that. Obviously, the Afrikaners aren't the only people to blame for apartheid."

"When I was young, sixteen years old, I just remember acknowledging to myself one particular day: of course apartheid is unjust. It's an indoctrinating concept—school, Sunday School, equivalent of Boy Scouts, the Voortrekkers. This is where the Broederbond, as we now know, consciously set things up.

"I always used to say that apartheid is maintained in a threefold way: by the structure of laws, by the structure of education, and by the media. Very close control is kept on the nonstate part of it through the Broederbond network. The education. Also when you grow up in an Afrikaans-speaking household, *Die Burger* is the only newspaper.

"Now, of course, they're entering a new ball game and they are already setting themselves up to be victims. This is while they are actually top dog. It's an amazing situation where insecurity's a strength." She paused. "Not a strength. But it generates the will to hang on to power."

CHAPTER TWELVE

SCRAMBLING
TO KEEP CONTROL

In the late 1970s, Prime Minister Balthazar John Vorster spoke of a future under black rule as a "future too ghastly to contemplate."

"The operative word there is you don't *contemplate* it," said history professor André du Toit. "For twenty-odd years under Vorster and P. W. Botha, political decision making was in the hands of the gerontocrats who never thought further than five years [ahead]. Now you get de Klerk, he's in his early fifties, suddenly the blinkers fall away, and you begin to think about the National Party as a political force in a wider arena than whites." The "future too ghastly" is rapidly arriving, and the Broeders are racing to make up for lost time.

They should have begun much earlier, according to Potchefstroom political science professor Pieter Potgieter. "Old John Vorster had the authority to tell the South African nation, 'Look, I have decided that apartheid is over and done with, we need to look for another path.' But he didn't have the guts to do so." After the far-right HNP (Herstigte Nasionale Party) split from the NP in 1969, Vorster "was so fearful of another split that he became a lame duck," Potgieter said. "He introduced the Wiehahn commission [a study that suggested legalizing black unions] and he started the process of 'normalizing' sport [slowly eroding segregation], but he could have gone much further."

Vorster's pattern of minor liberalizations that led to schism and a halt in reform was repeated during the presidency of P. W. Botha. When Botha took over in 1979, he legalized black unions as recommended by the Wiehahn commission, in order to enable orderly relations between business and increasingly restive African labor. In 1982 his government proposed to the public a new constitution that would create parallel representation for coloreds and Asians, but still freeze the black majority out of politics. The government's "tricameral parliament" proposal was "liberal" enough to drive conservative Afrikaners—led by Andries Treurnicht—out of the NP and into the new CP, and the Broederbond split along the same lines. In 1983, after being approved in an all-white referendum, the new constitution came into effect. But because of the split, Botha's taste for reform soured and the importance of the Broederbond waned as he turned to the military and the police to maintain order as black protest spread.

As South Africa's economy declined, damaged by the international recession of the early 1980s, by domestic industrial protests, by international sanctions, and finally by loan refusals by major international banks, Botha became increasingly intransigent. Even the military leaders upon whom he depended came to agree that change was needed, and when he was finally weakened by a stroke in 1989, the Broeders, the military, and the NP shoved him from office and replaced him with F. W. de Klerk. After Botha's fall, the *verligte* Broederbonders started popping up again like mushrooms, and after de Klerk's political opening on February 2, 1990, some of the most unlikely people suddenly began to claim that they had opposed apartheid all along.

Henno Cronje, head of the FAK (Federation of Afrikaner Cultural Organizations), the Broederbond's public face, asserted in 1992: "To be quite frank, when I came back from America in the end of 1957, I knew in my heart we'll have to change."

Jan Lombard, a former economic adviser to Hendrik Verwoerd and former deputy governor of the South African Reserve Bank, said that at first he supported separateness but thought it wasn't being adequately implemented. "Later on, when I came to the conclusion that it couldn't work, then I really did say my piece and I got into serious trouble." He was "marginalized in the establishment." (It was after his "marginalization" that he was appointed deputy governor of the Reserve Bank.) He added, "I would state almost categorically that diehard Afrikaners were as outspoken and worked as much, if not more, than anybody else to get rid of these unjust laws."

The most impressive retroactive conversion was that of the head of the Broederbond, Professor Piet de Lange, who said he had opposed apartheid since 1950. It was a quiet, within-the-system kind of opposition, so subtle that critics might be pardoned for not finding his claim believable. (See Chapter 14, "The Chairman," for more on de Lange.)

Some Afrikaners, non-Broeders, were sour about these apartheid supporters who turned their personal histories upside down and also claimed that they suffered for their opposition to apartheid.

Dominee and ANC leader Willem Saayman, who really did oppose apartheid at risk to his health, life, and livelihood, said, "There is no room for real dissidence within Afrikanerdom, within the structures. It's breaking down a little bit now." He disparaged "new Afrikaners who now suddenly pop up and are friends with ANC black leaders, inviting them to dinner. You have that kind of charlatan. Those are people who've not faced their guilt yet. Those are the people who say, 'We've closed the books on apartheid.' But they never even opened it. They didn't dare to look at what was in those books of apartheid. So for them it's very easy now to say it's closed."

F. W. de Klerk and company didn't abandon apartheid out of moral conviction. As André du Toit put it, their motives were "pragmatic and opportunistic." Sociology professor Louwrens Pretorius also didn't believe the change constituted a victory of ideas or a change in moral sense. "The resistance on the ground [to apartheid] was becoming too strong here in the eighties," he said, sitting in his minuscule office at UNISA in Pretoria. "You couldn't constrain the township rebellion; people just weren't paying their rent. Then obviously the lack of confidence that went with [international] sanctions and divestment, and ultimately the financial sanctions: South Africa lost its banker. That turned it."

Journalist Dries van Heerden said de Klerk's shift was precipitated by three factors: "Sanctions, sanctions, and sanctions. The economy did the trick. I don't think politicians really allow themselves to be swayed by moral arguments. De Klerk is not a crusader. He's very cool and calculated. Botha detested de Klerk and de Klerk was never in the inner circle of Botha's cabinet, so he never really knew the extent of the country's problems until he found himself in a chair where everything was available."

Willem Saayman said, "I can still remember vividly the collective shudder which went through Afrikanerdom the morning Chase Manhattan announced it was not going to renew our [short-term, commercial] loans. The sanctions worked, especially the financial sanctions. Not the others. The others we got around."

The economist Jan Lombard, who had been right at the heart of the Broederbond's attempt to defy sanctions, said, "The pressures that were put on the economy were beginning to bite, especially the financial sanctions, which ironically enough were never thought out by any government in the world. They were thought out by the bankers themselves. I landed up in the Reserve Bank the very day Chase called the standstill [halt in loans]. I walked in the front door and the back door fell off. They said to me, 'This is your desk, so administer the standstill.' I did that for six years. It was a nerve-racking business, but I'm very glad that I had that opportunity to go through it. I think one can write a book about that.

"We had to depress the domestic economy deliberately to be able to produce a surplus on the balance of payments so that we could service our debt. That depression brought about the feeling that we couldn't get out of this. But I do want to give as much weight to the morality of the people in government."*

The economist Sampie Terreblanche, a Broederbonder until 1987, argued that the sanctions cemented an alliance between English business and Afrikaner government. The alliance ultimately opened de Klerk to pressure from British Prime Minister Margaret Thatcher to embark on reform. Terreblanche claimed that English speakers and the Afrikaners had begun their courtship as far back as the economically "roaring sixties." They cohabited in the seventies, and when business was co-opted into the weapons boom during P. W. Botha's era, they entered into "unholy marriage, what I like to call the English-speaking, capitalistic man of Johannesburg and the Afrikaans-speaking bureaucratic woman of Pretoria," Terreblanche said. "The National Party in the mid-eighties became a free-marketeer party. I think the business community played quite a role to prepare the atmosphere for that meeting [in June 1989] between Thatcher and de Klerk. She pressurized him with her iron arms to such an extent that he agreed to start with reform. Then after the second of February [when de Klerk promised to unban the ANC] the two [Afrikaners and English] became one establishment."

De Klerk's goal was to maintain that English-Afrikaans compact against the new enemy, the ANC.

"It is a race war," Terreblanche declared. "It now is starting to develop into a typical class struggle with a capitalist upper class and a very big underclass. Those in control of the economy are in a position to dominate, to set terms."

Down the hall from Sampie Terreblanche's office at Stellenbosch, economist Servaas van der Berg exuded a Buddhalike serenity that counterbalanced Terreblanche's frantic exuberance. While Terreblanche was amusing, *slim* (sly), and on the attack, van der Berg was wry, understated, and steady. Van der Berg had never been a Broederbonder. He was educated in dual-language schools in that haven of the English,

---

*Lombard was interviewed on a day when, according to *Business Day*, his brother was in court indicted on charges of fraud for using his Reserve Bank connections to bypass foreign currency rules.

Natal Province, and was a friend of the Anglo American Corporation official Bobby Godsell and a sometime member of the Progressive Federal Party. He had tried the establishment, had worked for a while at the Bureau for Economic Research for Cooperation and Development, a parastatal think tank on homeland development. But he soured on the homeland scheme, and in the nineties he advised the COSATU (Congress of South African Trade Unions) labor federation and the ANC, epitomizing a new role for Afrikaners in politics.

Van der Berg agreed with Terreblanche's argument that business definitely had influenced the apartheid government, despite businesspeople's persistent declarations of political neutrality. And van der Berg agreed that external pressures, though perhaps not Thatcher alone, were important in changing de Klerk's view.

"There was a lot of speculation as to how strongly he was put under pressure by Thatcher. We also had all sorts of strange Americans out here trying to do that," van der Berg said. "A lot of us were more skeptical about de Klerk than were many of the foreigners who had spoken to him and his cabinet. I think they [the foreigners] were probably closer to what happened there. There are theories that the script was written somewhere else, not here. Some of that may be true, because I cannot think of who within government could come out with that whole package [releasing Mandela and unbanning the anti-apartheid organizations]. It does not fit de Klerk's previous style, but he adapted very well. There was a lot of talk about CIA influence."

If de Klerk's change came about for pragmatic and economic reasons, how will the Nationalists pursue their interests in the future?

Van der Berg argues that the Nats won't mind if the government stays heavily involved in the economy under a black government—as long as whites' living standards hold up. Afrikaners are traditionally economic socialists, not the individualist entrepreneurs they had recently begun extolling, he said.

"You find for instance that in 1987 and thereafter, Afrikaners who left the National Party jumped across the liberal position and ended up in what were broadly social democratic groups. We are in that sense closer to the ANC. That was part of the problem of Afrikaners in the Democratic Party in that the DP was dominated by laissez-faire thinking."*

Van der Berg described Anglo-Saxon economic thought as emphasiz-

---

*In 1988 white liberal parties amalgamated with dissident Afrikaners to form the Democratic Party, under Broederbond impetus and Wimpie de Klerk's planning; then the DP's reform policies were adopted by the Nats.

ing individualism, whereas the dominant system in the rest of Europe is more a social market economy. South Africa has had a social welfare net for whites that can't continue, he said. That is where tension will arise between Afrikaner interests and a majority-dominated government. To close the black-white gap, "We would require about a threefold increase in social spending, from about twelve percent of GDP to well above thirty percent. Now that cannot be accommodated." Health, social pensions, and housing could be provided for blacks, but not education, he said. Education for all blacks at the same level as whites would just cost too much.

Under majority rule, it can thus be expected that standards for whites will fall. Therefore, the Broederbond is scrambling to devise ways to retain as much political power as it can, and to grab as much wealth as possible before power slips away.

Tales of corruption make upright Afrikaners wince. But with the end of their dominance in view, corruption is flourishing. From the first great public scandal in the late 1970s—the Information Scandal* that brought down Prime Minister John Vorster's government and destroyed the career of his potential heir, Connie Mulder—to the siphoning off of public money to taxpayer-funded business fronts for death-squad activity, the supposedly honest, incorruptible Calvinist leaders' feet of clay trod heavier and heavier.

According to Sampie Terreblanche, forty-four years of NP control created a "whole process of patronage and nepotism that got derailed into corruption, networks of patronage in Afrikaner circles since the fifties, and in the eighties as part of 'total strategy' and Armscor [the weapons industry parastatal]. The business community was drawn into it. This is part of the cement that is binding the establishment." To truly transform South Africa, he argued, "We will have to unhook this whole thing."

While the NP harangued the public with the threat that the ANC could not be trusted to govern, its own leaders emerged as part of the corruption syndrome. Dr. Gerrit Viljoen, a former Broederbond chairman, Rand Afrikaans University rector, minister of Education, minister

---

*Under Information Minister Mulder, government money was secretly spent on propaganda drives designed to improve the government's image at home and abroad. Despite public denials, investigations revealed that the Information Ministry pursued approximately two hundred projects, including financing the pro-government English language daily *The Citizen* and attempting to buy a controlling interest in the U.S. newspaper the *Washington Star*.

of Cooperation and Development, and in 1992 the minister of Constitutional Planning, was dubbed by the English press the "minister of toilets" because of the extensive corruption in the Department of Development Aid when it was under his Ministry of Cooperation and Development. The ministry had assigned massive contracts to favored Afrikaner firms for construction of schools and outhouses in planned townships which, as was shown on TV, turned out to be vacant fields where blacks were to be deposited under the Group Areas Act. The "towns" remained empty, though millions of rands had been spent on construction. School buildings were condemned as unusable even before they were completed. The outhouses stood derelict. Viljoen became a minister without portfolio, fading from public view for "health reasons." He reemerged in 1993 on the executive board of the new, rainbow-hued Afrikanerbond.

Many Afrikaners excused Viljoen, saying he was a professor and not really an administrator, and he didn't intend the crimes. Or it was someone else's fault: according to Professor Pieter Potgieter, when Viljoen told P. W. Botha it was unacceptable to dump people in the middle of nowhere without facilities, Botha said, "If you must build a new town in six months, then you do it, you have the money, do so." Potgieter thus blamed the corruption on Botha and apartheid, not Viljoen.

In addition to petty corruption—such as the bribes blacks had to pay to Afrikaner civil servants to acquire the endless documents demanded by the apartheid bureaucracy—the government squandered billions of rands on other efforts of dubious economic and political value that enriched primarily those with the connections to absorb cash from the government. For example, 11 billion rands were sunk into a futile gas exploration project in the Indian Ocean called Mossgas; an estimated 70 billion rands were spent on destabilizing neighboring black countries; and, most fundamental of all, the apartheid system necessitated duplication of government civil services for the ten "native" homelands in addition to the South African government itself. The system itself created illegality of massive proportions: the enforced migratory labor system forced an estimated 90 percent of black workers to break laws in order to secure their livelihoods.

The system's patent injustices and waste led even the Afrikaners to lose respect for the governing institutions, adding to the rise of corruption and disregard for law. One major Afrikaner businessman said, "As we got more concerned about the way in which the government was spending our money we became less and less keen as taxpayers. I'm not talking about legal tax avoidance. I'm talking about tax evasion. We're not down to the practices of southern Indian states, but there is already a crack that's very wide. I think that somewhere along the line people lost hope things would ever be run on a proper, regular, ordered, planned way as most Afrikaners would've liked it. Then they started losing their self-respect and that led to a lot of corruption. It's evident right throughout society.

"I think it was probably exaggerated that we were all such upright, Christian, honest people. By and large, honest, upright people are the ones who don't have the opportunities to be otherwise. I think that the moral corruption of the last years of the apartheid society, when everybody knew what we did was wrong, no matter what they said, corrupted people's morals generally. A cynicism set in."

In 1992, reports of corporate fraud had skyrocketed, according to newspapers. The Witwatersrand attorney general claimed in September that there were almost twenty thousand fraud cases under police investigation nationwide, involving a potential loss of 374 billion rands, and he believed that half of the cases were not being reported.

Many Afrikaners are "holding thumbs," as the South Africans say—keeping their fingers crossed—against societal chaos. The chaos could come from Afrikaners disappointed that, despite promises made to them, their standards of living are falling and their insularity eroding. "The lunatics may become more loony," Piet van der Merwe, head of the civil service, said in 1992 of what the right-wingers might do in the future. To forestall that, the Broederbond, with its mania for control, is producing plans in litters, trying to convince Afrikaners their material conditions will not plummet, and trying to keep as much power for Afrikaners as they can.

"De Klerk has always believed that he can manage the change," said Dries van Heerden. "The National Party still believes that they can manage the change, that what we have is not a handing over of power, but a sharing of power." From February 2, 1990, until the scheduled elections in 1999 that will end the period of unity government and transition, the Afrikaner establishment will conduct its most important struggle since the Boer War.

"The relevancy of the Broederbond is restricted to the transitional period [until 1999]," said Stellenbosch law professor and ANC member Louwrens du Plessis, "where Afrikanerdom are going to try and pull together all the resources and all the forces they have in order to maintain as much as possible."

Servaas van der Berg said, "They think that it's possible to control everything from the center. And it is not, as the Soviet Union showed us. But that the Broederbond is very influential I would not doubt at all, sometimes not through formal means, but because of networking."

The plans are hidden, but men all over the country are putting it about that the Nats promise to keep control. According to the ex-Broeder Sampie Terreblanche, the Nats are "telling their supporters, 'No, we will outwit them, we will not give up power, control.' We have de Klerk saying often, 'We saw all the damage that was done by a minority monopoly of power; we can't allow there to be a majority monopoly of power doing the same kind of harm.' "

There are hints everywhere as to just how the Broeders hope to keep control.

One of the ways is to circle the wagons around as much of the economy as possible. Ina Perlman, executive director of Operation Hunger, South Africa's biggest private charity, had extensive dealings with the economic community in her fund-raising efforts and saw lots of clues.

"The U.S. disinvestment handed them [Nats and Broederbond members] economic control of the country on a plate," she said. "If you look at all those companies that actually sold out, if you track them through, you'll find at the bottom of it all they are [the Afrikaner banking, insurance, and financial holding company conglomerates] SANLAM and Old Mutual. And Old Mutual, even though it's officially not an Afrikaner company, with Jannie van der Horst, that is probably, in terms of spiderweb, the most powerful group in the country. They own for example seven percent of Anglo-American. Now that's a huge shareholding in economic terms. They own ten percent of Barlow Rand. They own ten percent of SANLAM, they own ten percent of Gencor.

"It's actually fascinating. Look at what they bought up—Delta [the former General Motors subsidiary in South Africa] is SANLAM, which is Broederbond. Mobil. Every one of the major U.S. disinvestments. Even IBM, if you track that, it ends up with big Afrikaner money. I would say not even twenty-five percent went outside the Afrikaner community. There was the biggest mobilization of right-wing capital for that buyout."

The Afrikaners were moving into the private sector after 1990 as they saw government jobs receding from their grasp. This required turning Afrikaners into businessmen and "privatizing" government parastatals. Under a black leadership, government service would no longer be an option for young educated Afrikaners. What will the Broederbond do for them?

The FAK, the public front for the Broederbond, is organizing conferences to try to train Afrikaners to think more like businessmen, according to its chairman, Henno Cronje. The FAK has its work cut out for it, for the Afrikaner has generally been more comfortable in more socialistic enterprises, state-run businesses or the civil service, than in the competitive world of free enterprise. Anti-English, anti-Hoggenheimer (as anti-Semitism was called), and antibusiness attitudes still cling to the culture like onion odors.

"Business still is mainly English run," said Professor van der Berg. "Historically, the route that Afrikaners took into business was through state structures. Sometimes when they talk about Afrikaner-run concerns, that means the ISCORs [Iron and Steel Corporation of South Africa, employing 68,000 people], and the SASOLs [the oil-from-coal corporation, designed to circumvent oil import sanctions] and so forth, so that it's not really been private-sector business, but parastatals. But that has also acted as a training ground."

Under the NP the government expanded the British model of rule by running the broadcasting, railways, the airline, the iron and steel industry, telecommunications, the post office, energy production and distribution, the harbors, and meat slaughterhouses.

For Cronje and the FAK, training entrepreneurs is more than helping Afrikaners to survive economically. It is vital for preservation of the *volk*'s existence in South Africa. "We feel that we must help our people to be not just employees, but to be entrepreneurs," Cronje said. "To start things themselves. And to make themselves *onmissbaar*. What's the word in English for that? It's very important for a country to have these people, we call it *onmissbaar*."

Indispensable.

"We feel that we must prove that the Afrikaner is indispensable for the future of South Africa," Cronje said. "That's not arrogance, please, don't misunderstand me, it's not out of arrogance that I say this. But I think that this country needs the Afrikaners, as this country needed the Afrikaners to start the reform through people like F. W. de Klerk and others."

In addition to trying to keep its fingers in every economic pie to make the Afrikaner *onmissbaar*, the Broederbond's second major strategy to retain power while losing control of the government is to entrench "regionalism" in the constitution. Regionalism means that South Africa's provinces, much more than states in the U.S., would gain major power over government expenditures and functions. Regionalism gained ground among Broederbond theoreticians as they discovered that the ANC would not accept a constitution in which rights for ethnic "groups" were entrenched. Regionalism is intended to substitute a geographic concept for a racial one. The problem for the Afrikaners, however, remains that they do not constitute a majority of the population in any sizable area of the country.

From the Afrikaners' standpoint, regionalism is intended to maximize what influence they can muster even from their minority position. South Africa's new provinces would reflect existing ethnic concentrations, so in each province the (minority) whites deal with one or two African, colored, or Asian "groups," rather than the full array of the majority population. And in each region the Broederbond apparently hopes it can co-opt the local majority and thus control policy.

The word "regionalism" seemed to float around the country like Muzak in 1992. It was discussed on TV news, appeared in newspapers, and was mentioned, mentioned, mentioned. Who turned this word on? In Pietersburg, Jack Botes, who regretted he was never asked to be a member of the Broederbond, was dealing in "regionalism" in his role as a city father and National Party stalwart, trying to convince blacks in the area that they would like "regionalism" too, if only they'd listen to its melody.

Finally, on a cold winter day in June at the University of Potchefstroom south of Johannesburg, on the *platteland*, the Broederbond admitted to playing the word "regionalism" the way teenagers play lyrics of love till finally they are heartsick and moondrunk.

Professor Pieter Potgieter said yes, he was in the Broederbond and was trying to implement "regionalism." He spoke tediously slowly, as if ponderousness equaled profundity. Calling the Broederbond an "attitude-forming net," Potgieter said the organization has launched a program called "Action 2000," presumably for the year 2000.

"I'm on a committee that tries to coordinate this whole thing from the top," he said. He writes a short newsletter every month, coming up with ideas on how to reach other "groups" with information and patronage—for instance, if a colored school needs a library, setting out to provide one.

"One of the most important things is to create the idea that we will have to have regional government," he said.

Ah, "create the idea." That's how the regional government notion permeated the country. Potgieter's region included Afrikaners in the Western Transvaal and Tswanas from the homeland of Bophuthatswana. In 1992 he was organizing a "Satswa Forum," which was "working towards a regional government for Region J," a temporary designation, based on a South African Development Bank map, referring to the Western Transvaal and parts of the Bophuthatswana homeland.

How did he pick blacks to get them to the forum?

149

"I don't pick them," he said.

How then does he get them?

"Uh, well, I am in contact with the ANC people in this region and I give them a number of invitations, say, five hundred, and they distribute it in their own thinking."

What does he say to them—"I'm implementing Action Two Thousand, this is a Broederbond operation"?

"Oh no," Potgieter said, shocked at the suggestion.

No? Does the ANC know he was acting on Action 2000?

"No."

In April 1993, Hennie Serfontein, writing in *Vrye Weekblad*, said Action 2000 had been launched in 1988. He quoted from a secret Broederbond circular of May 1992 called "Compass 4," which said that in the upcoming nonracial elections, Action 2000 must "help shape that sentiment on the part of black and brown people which will make it possible for them to go along with Christian democratic whites. . . . All Afrikaners must be persuaded to work with grit and determination for the establishment of strong regional and local government. . . . The idea of regional government is well developed in the Western Transvaal. [Broederbond] cells which want to know what role they can play in their own regions in this regard, can contact A. van der Venter at telephone number (0148) 992765."

That was the telephone area code for Potchefstroom, evidently for somebody in Potgieter's Broederbond cell.

Regionalism faces serious problems. First, the ANC properly regards it with suspicion in constitutional negotiations, having always campaigned for a unified South Africa under a strong central government. Until the new constitution is finished, however, it remains unclear how much power the regions can gain from the center. Second, there are major practical problems with the idea. According to the economist Servaas van der Berg, the real difficulty with regionalism is that the PWV (Pretoria, Witwatersrand, Vereeniging) area, renamed Gauteng in 1994, generates South Africa's great wealth and will have to serve as the paymaster for the other regions.

"That won't work because it is likely to give you conflict between regions, rather than races," he said. "The difficulty is that you have to determine what goes into the pool to be redistributed. Whereas in a central system everything goes into the pool."

What then is the purpose of the Broederbond plan?

"To retain at least some control," van der Berg said. "But I think it would make for very great economic conflict. If you want federalism to function well, it needs to be constitutionally built into the system. That means you need a formula for revenue sharing or for revenue transfers."

What does van der Berg's effervescent colleague, Sampie Terreblanche, think?

"I have never been enthusiastic about this idea of regionalism. To think that in this way they can keep control," Terreblanche said.

Is that what the Broederbond was trying to do?

"Everything is to keep control," he said.

Afrikaners adore planning. The northern Transvaal rancher Piet Warren, like so many Afrikaners, claims that blacks simply haven't the ability to plan. That's why blacks need the white man.

This attitude, so arrogant, so blind, is the Broederbond's Achilles' heel. One of the first rules for effective planning is to have good intelligence regarding one's opposition. This is almost impossible for the Nats, according to Max du Preez.

"You've got to remember that they never understood what was going on here," du Preez said. "I mean—this is not an anecdote, it's the real truth: the first black leader that F. W. de Klerk really met, outside of three or four corrupt homeland leaders that he had a chat with, was Nelson Mandela. He was apparently—and this comes from his family—he was stunned. He didn't know that black people could be so clever. He met Mandela and [ANC information director] Thabo Mbeki. They're the two smoothest politicians around, and they are extremely charming. De Klerk was completely bowled over.

"Now, how can you make a plan, how can you be a strategist if you know your opposition that badly? If you think they are all savages and sweaty dumb people who work—that's what he thought," said du Preez. "The idea of the planning is to have a South Africa with mostly black faces run by whites. That's why we are privatizing so quickly," he said.

But during the 1990s, the ANC moved so fast and effectively, also planning, that the Broederbonders were thrown off balance. "It is ad hoc thinking all the time [by the Broederbond]," du Preez said.

Strategize. Plan. Control. That's how the *volk* was molded and that's what the Afrikaner Nationalist thinks he does best. Wimpie de Klerk, F. W.'s brother and a top Nat strategist, said, "As you know, democracy is an elitist business all over the world. The masses can't rule a country, a government must rule a country. We haven't got the democratic tradition, not the Nationalist Party. We are very used to authoritarian rule. So I see democracy in the future, but not around the first or second corner."

*　　　*　　　*

On April 27–29, 1994, South Africa held its first-ever nonracial election for the transitional, power-sharing government that will rule until 1999. F. W. de Klerk helped his and Wimpie's eighty-nine-year-old mother walk unsteadily to a voting booth. F. W. turned a starched smile toward the cameras, and a few words that sounded rehearsed slipped between his teeth. He clipped them off like bites of something acrid: "I feel a sense of achievement," de Klerk said. "My plan has been accepted, and my plan is being put into operation."

CHAPTER THIRTEEN

PAYING THE PRICE

No matter how many beneficial things the Broederbond might accomplish, either for the Afrikaner *volk* or in reforming apartheid, its effect on the thinking and psychology of individual men is often dire. Membership makes men timorous, fearful they'll say something they shouldn't, and arrogant when they speak the party line. Being a Broeder compromises professors' academic independence, undermines families, and debases personal integrity. So say men who were asked to join but refused, men who weren't asked to join, men who quit the organization, and women who resent it.

Bobby Godsell, the executive director for industrial and public relations at the giant, monopolistic Anglo American Corporation, who has a lot of contact with Afrikaners, said, "I think it is probably true that you'll not find the best Afrikaners at the heads of Afrikaner organizations." He noted that in 1957 the poet and writer N. P. van Wyk Louw said that those politicians who claimed to be "defending Afrikaner interests, that's crap. He said what they should say is I'm defending the crass material interests of the ruling group of Afrikaners."

The dominant impression left after talking to a Broeder is that of a man constricted, often even in voice timbre, and certainly in any willingness to probe and discuss with free range. Broeders either seem afraid that they will utter a "wrong" idea, or they speak in clichés. The most creative and relaxed Afrikaner men are those outside the *bond*.

Some Afrikaners use repellent adjectives to describe the atmosphere and effect of the Broederbond and its tentacles throughout the society, in the churches, the schools, the farm unions, the media.

"A suffocating environment," said Kobus van Loggerenberg, who once was in the Ruiterwag organization and whose father was a Broederbonder.

"This absolutely murderous environment," said Henning Myburgh, speaking of the Broederbond elements in the church and NP. "Either you have to be dead to live in it, or you will die, or you will drop out."

Broeders' creativity is "severely harmed without their realizing it," said Dominee Beyers Naudé, who quit the Broederbond in the early sixties. "It's a process of moral, intellectual, and spiritual disintegration. Sometimes it's so subtle and it's so slow in the beginning that you do not realize it."

Another minister, Willem Saayman, said, "People like Beyers Naudé, Willem Kleynhans in political science, were chopped early on because they were too critical. Those who were good at saying 'Yes, *baas*' got to the top. That's how people like Pik Botha, Gerrit Viljoen, and even F. W. can get to the top. In their professions they never would have made it to the top, never [without their Broederbond connection]."

F. van Zyl Slabbert, who rebuffed Broederbond overtures twice and became an opposition Progressive Federal Party leader, said he was "fascinated" at Broederbond tactics, the "vilification campaigns" against him, where they took the attitude that you were "lobotomized and out of your mind, an enemy of the Afrikaner, boom, go for you. They would invite me to pre-set-up meetings and then just hammer me, irrespective of the merits of my arguments. Ah, heavens, ja." He said that often Broederbonders in the church "are trapped. It's really a ravaging experience emotionally for many of them."

Elizabeth Bradley, the millionaire part owner of Toyota South Africa, said, "My father wasn't a Broederbonder and I rather resent we don't have a family connection, and quite often there are family connections."

Zach de Beer Postma, a UNISA professor of philosophy, described himself as cynical about the Broederbond, doubting "that they were ever really a Christian organization. It was a self-serving organization no matter how they tried to cover it up. I know lots of old men in this country who should have been heads of schools or other things, but were kept away when they were United Party adherents, Progressive adherents. I don't come from an old United Party family for nothing."

Political adherents to the right also suffered from Broederbond censure. UNISA religion professor Danie Goosen remembered when his father was expelled from the Broederbond in the late seventies because he joined the right-wing HNP. "It was rather traumatic because he was closely involved and he was high up within the Broederbond."

Stellenbosch law professor Louwrens du Plessis, now an ANC member, was approached to join the Broederbond during the late eighties when he was editor of the Calvinist magazine *Woord en Daad* (*Word and Deed*). He thought the man approaching him was discussing another man's case.

"I told him, 'Look, if they were really to approach me to become a member of the Broederbond I will ask myself a question: Do I have one evening a month to waste on nonsense? Because that has been my experience in Ruiterwag and my answer would be no, I'm too busy.' He was embarrassed and said, 'But I'm coming to approach you.'

"I'm not one of those Afrikaners who feel excluded because I've not been approached," du Plessis continued. "I know what's going on inside. I know in a sense they are very helpless and in another sense they're extremely powerful. And they have this hold on people."

He then described the "hold" it had on a friend of his, a political science professor at the Potchefstroom University.

"In 1987 a small number of us in Potchefstroom signed a declaration that we're not going to participate in the elections until they are free and fair. That was tough medicine at the time.

"Then my Broederbond friend dropped me, saying his academic integrity didn't allow him to sign that. But that's nonsense, the excuse many people use when they don't have the guts or when they don't see their way open to do it."

Did the man remain a friend?

"Yes, but it cooled down."

Is he still in the Broederbond?

"Still in the Broederbond, we're still friends. We still visit each other, but we no longer share our confidences. What do you call that?"

Confidants?

"Confidants, yeah.

"I mean we had holidays together. I remember one December–January on a day we were spending in the Transkei, we went on a hike and he told me he had this one New Year's resolution, and that's that he wanted to end his membership of the Broederbond."

As du Plessis talked further, it became clear the friend is Professor Pieter Potgieter, a main organizer of the Broederbond's regionalism plans under Action 2000.

Is the Broederbond to blame for the lack of Afrikaner academic opposition to apartheid?

Albert Grundlingh, a history professor at UNISA, doesn't think so.

A man definitely outside of the Broederbond fold, Grundlingh had a light brown loopy mustache and a sly sense of humor. He described UNISA's giant conglomeration of cubicle offices in Pretoria as a hen battery, with all the professors laying their academic eggs.

"The Broederbond could jeopardize their [academics'] positions, but it couldn't stop intellectual curiosity. It was more a pliant academe that allowed the Broederbond to rule, rather than the Broederbond being all that powerful," he said. "Broederbond ideas were never taken on intellectually."

UNISA political science professor Pierre Hugo attributed academics' lack of vocal dissent to their own timidity. "Afrikaner academics usually waited for the green light from politicians, waited until it was quite obvious to anybody that apartheid had failed, that the homeland concept had become derisible, that the outside world had had enough. And then they said, 'You better do something.' "

In an attempt to provide intellectual underpinnings for the new, reform stance of the Broederbond in the 1990s, the works of several earlier Afrikaner intellectuals, the most prominent being N. P. van Wyk Louw, are being resurrected and refurbished to prove there had been opposition to apartheid, even within the Broederbond.

Professor Potgieter spoke of one Broeder, L. J. du Plessis (no relation of Louwrens), a professor at the Potchefstroom University, who in the 1950s was "crown prince" to succeed D. F. Malan as leader of the National Party, instead of Dr. Verwoerd (who was himself once a sociology professor). L. J. was one of the founder-members of the Broederbond and a leading light in the Ossewabrandwag (Ox Wagon Brigade, a pro-Nazi World War II organization).

"Du Plessis was called the prophet of Potchefstroom," said Potgieter, who wrote a master's thesis on him. "Du Plessis left a large volume of writing which was very, very provocative at that time. What is happening now, he appealed for in the 1960s. But it was so unacceptable at that stage that it was just impossible to think about it.

"Du Plessis thought that Verwoerd was the most awful thing that could ever have happened with the Afrikaner people. He wrote a manuscript for a book which was never published. The title is *Towards One World, How?* The basic thesis of the manuscript was that as the world had become unified just before the coming of Christ, under the Roman Empire, the world is again starting to unify with the view of the Second Coming. From that he spun all kinds of scenarios concerning how we as South Africans should react in a world like that. It's really fascinating stuff."

Potgieter said the Afrikaner would not be accurately portrayed if what is called *die stem van Potchefstroom*, the voice of Potchefstroom, is ignored. (See Chapter 21.) L. J. du Plessis was part of that voice in the late 1950s and early '60s.

What Potgieter didn't say, his friend Louwrens du Plessis in Stellenbosch did: L. J. quit the Broederbond.

"Potty gave me his [L. J.'s] letter of resignation from the Broeder-bond—it's a thirty-two-page document. I found that very insightful. He was accusing them that their nationalism is no longer a popular national-ism, it's an elitist nationalism."

Although it was run by Broeders and funded by Broederbond institu-tions, Stellenbosch University's *verligt* reputation rested during the late 1970s and '80s on the teaching of a handful of men, most prominently the non-Broederbond philosophy professors Johannes Degenaar and André du Toit, history professor Hermann Giliomee, and, briefly, F. van Zyl Slabbert when he was professor of sociology there.

In 1966 Johannes Degenaar established a discussion group, which became a serious and lively tradition, with debates occurring often into the wee morning hours. "In the group was Sampie Terreblanche, Willie Esterhuyse, Johan Heyns, myself, Piet Cillie [editor] of *Die Burger* used to come, and so on," van Zyl Slabbert recalled, listing mostly the Broeders.

At these discussions, verbally rambunctious affairs, the academic Broeders went head to head with the non-Broeder academics. Some-times there were vicious personal attacks that spilled into the public arena, especially in 1982 in a battle completely out of proportion to the actual ideological differences between the combatants.

Professor André du Toit, subsequently at the University of Cape Town, described the differences between them this way: "I think that one of the things that must be most difficult for outside observers to understand is that the differences were much more a question of strat-egy. Take someone like Sampie Terreblanche or Willie Esterhuyse. If you tried to establish my conviction and Willie Esterhuyse's conviction, they would be fairly close together. The difference was that that Broederbond group was firmly convinced you had to work through the party and the Broederbond to have any political effect.

"Their criticism of us was that we marginalized ourselves. Our criti-cism of them was that [working through the system] meant you had to pay a price. You had to take certain actions, and that in the end contra-dicted what you personally said you believed in."

Du Toit noted that Sampie Terreblanche, whom he still couldn't quite forgive, "now recognizes and says that we were right and they were wrong at that stage. But others in that grouping still pursue that policy. Willie Esterhuyse for example would still pursue that line."

Professor Degenaar, the epitome of politeness, said that the Broeders "are critical within a certain way of speaking, so that they can think that they're on the move."

He noted that when an academic Broeder breaks out, as Sampie Ter-reblanche did, "that really is liberating, but he can't just leave it at that. Terreblanche wants to hit those people hard because they have hurt him, they've stultified him, there was no development of his personality. The way in which he fulminates is not my style. He can't be an academic. He has a cause, you see."

And Terreblanche himself described the Broederbond as "a way to let information through, and to make propaganda and to consolidate opinions." He said it's a debating society where members can freely say what they want, but their opinions are not going up to the top in the same way directives and policies are coming down. "This is the way one blocked oneself over the years.

"Peer pressure worked in a rather structured way," Terreblanche claimed. Also, members "talk each other into a specific state of mind." When he was a Broeder, Terreblanche said, he knew perfectly well that he was compromising his academic integrity. He'd written speeches for the cabinet minister Chris Heunis over the years. And when it became clear on August 15, 1985, that President P. W. Botha was not going to abolish apartheid, a new discussion group led by Terreblanche called for the unbanning of the ANC and the start of negotiations with blacks. Highly distressed at government intransigence, Terreblanche met with Heunis.

"I told him I have given my academic independence as a pawn to him. 'I'm here today to tell you that I'm taking it back,' " Terreblanche said. "We had a long discussion but it was clear that he did not really understand what I was saying."

Henning Myburgh, who had long been "incredibly cynical" about the Broederbond, said, "I've come to realize it's not worthwhile feeling this way, that in fact these people are also prisoners of the system. I think being Broeders disadvantages them in terms of the wider South Africa. I understand better the fear that goes with this. But it's still not my idea of the free individual."

Vrye Weekblad editor Max du Preez is anathema to many Broeders (although his newsmagazine was highly appreciated by Professor Potgieter). Du Preez said that his Broederbonder father admitted that he knew about apartheid atrocities. "We have become such schizophrenic people, Afrikaners, that you are actually dealing with two personalities," du Preez explained. "We say, 'I am a sophisticated, church-going family man, I never kick my dog, I'm kind to my children, I'm a patriotic South African, I don't crook, I don't cheat on my wife, and I'm kind to my servants.'

"Then there's the other personality, which goes for most Afrikaners: knowing about death squads, dirty tricks, Mozambique destabilization, Angola, Namibia, knowing about corruption, especially in the Broeder-bond. The Broederbond people all know about it, and my father's one too. But not confronting that."

history of not admitting

Did his father's admitting this privately do anything to his psyche?

"Ja, ja, I think so. I think so, but it's kind of subtle. If he had to admit this openly and publicly, it would have so many consequences for his public position."

What does his father do?

"He was a farmer and he's now a businessman. He's retired."

Was he a Broederbonder for a long time?

"Mmmm. In Kroonstad in the Free State."

Did Max's attacks on the establishment damage his relationship with his father?

"Well, basically he denied that I was his son," du Preez said.

159

CHAPTER FOURTEEN

THE CHAIRMAN

It is hard to imagine the Broederbond chairman Piet de Lange, a retired professor of education, ever bobbing up and down on the aerobic trampoline that is stuck like an oversized postage stamp on the floor of his office. But no doubt he needs exercise to deal with the tension of his job. He was the top keeper of the Broeders' secrets in 1992.

He appears calm, but hardly relaxed. He knows what to say and what not to say, what to imply, what not to imply, what to hint, and what not. This is the man who ran the Broederbond for a decade, from 1983 to 1993, surviving the poison of the Conservative Party split, the deadly squeeze of the securocrats during P. W. Botha's era, and the cracking of the NP glacier under F. W.

He sat in a tight-lipped, stately way. His wrists hung, as if broken, over the arms of a velveteen wingback pickle-green chair in front of shelves of books. The titles on his bookshelf included *Future Shock*, *The Pictorial History of the Jewish People*, *The Afrikaners*, by Graham Leach, *The Apartheid Psychology*, by Brian Pottinger, Alan Bloom's *Closing of the American Mind*. De Lange said that he had just read Arthur Schlesinger's *Disuniting of the United States*.

In interviewing de Lange one had to be prepared to read between the lines. He said, "I am not really a political person."

Surely, there can be no position in South Africa more political than his.

He elaborated: "[I'm not] ready to spend all my time organizing little things." Not for him, stuffing National Party envelopes. Rather, the grand sweep of philosophy.

He claimed he had opposed apartheid ever since 1950, "ever since I heard Verwoerd the first time."

Really?

"Yes. I always opposed it [apartheid]. But it's one thing to go and stand and shout on the outside. It's another thing to try and change things from the inside. It's a choice Afrikaners had to make. I decided to do it from the inside."

160

But how did he actually oppose the system?

"Well, I was building a career of course at the same time," he explained. "And building a family and therefore you are fairly preoccupied with other things. But in every opportunity I obtained, I criticized certain things. One was the urbanization policy, another was the economic policy, which I believed to be bordering on the silly. If anybody has criticized the educational system, in a basic sense, it is myself. There is a report, the twenty-volume report of criticism of the educational system, which I led, using eight hundred researchers. It was commissioned in June 1980 and I brought it out in July '81."

Suppose men with his critical views had joined together much earlier and publicly denounced the system of apartheid? After all, so many men say that they worked within the system for change, perhaps if they'd stepped out publicly, the system would have changed much sooner.

"I don't know how many are honest about this, but certainly some of us did," he said. "I took this as a conscious decision. In hindsight, I can imagine that it wouldn't have been so easy to go against a strong political party, riding on a wave of economic success as it did in the 1960s and '70s."

De Lange laughed about being called a *verligte*, a word invented, along with *verkrampte*, by Wimpie de Klerk in the late sixties to describe the divisions inside the National Party. "I have no objection to it being used," de Lange said, then explained the split.

"In the sixties there were, in certain sections of the Broederbond, convictions that apartheid would not work, and that certain aspects of it were in fact immoral. The immoral side was 'influx control,' which forced people [blacks] to come [into urban areas] as singles. That, in terms of our beliefs, was a direct assault on family life. The stability of the family. This view, which had nothing to do with politics as such but with a view of society, grew in the sixties. By the early seventies, there was a growing conviction among the economists in our membership and also some political scientists, lawyers, whatever, that apartheid wasn't working.

"A little-known factor then came into play," de Lange said. "Apartheid by the early seventies was dying of intellectual starvation. There was an attempt to mobilize the research power of Afrikaners to give support to apartheid."

As an example, de Lange recalled that in the 1970s the government wanted Afrikaner researchers to determine the viability of developing high-speed trains to bring black laborers from their "homelands" to work in the so-called white urban areas. But few were willing to even consider the idea. "I wonder if half a dozen Afrikaner academics were interested to devoting research time, which is their bread, to [sympathetic study of] apartheid," de Lange said. "There were a few odd people who would, you know, and eventually they were from the Boshoff group.* In the late seventies the politicians started to think about what they called 'rolling democracy.' Which led to the inclusion of coloreds and blacks [into political positions]."

De Lange was rector of Rand Afrikaanse University when he was appointed to head one of the government's many commissions empaneled to tell it what was going wrong. The De Lange Commission's forty-volume report on education suggested many changes in the extremely segregated and financially lopsided system. The De Lange Report, whose recommendations were largely ignored by the government and rejected by the Afrikaner mainstream, was de Lange's main claim to being a critic of the system. While battling against Afrikaner conservatism, publicly clashing with Boshoff and others over the idea of government reform and a more egalitarian educational system, de Lange became chairman of the Broederbond in 1983, following the Boshoff faction's walkout. "I think I achieved quite a lot by becoming leader of the Broederbond and being able to effect change from inside. The making ripe of the Afrikaners for change was effected through the Broederbond," de Lange said.

He viewed himself within a historical tradition of Broederbond protection of Afrikaner interests that is intended for constructive, not divisive, purposes. "In the forties the unity of Afrikanerdom was to the fore [in the Broederbond's plans]. After '48 the main thrust was to become a republic and not have a king in England. After '61 [when the Republic was achieved] there was some doubt as to what was the thrust." Blithely skipping ten years, during which apartheid laws clamped down tighter and tighter on blacks' movements and aspirations, de Lange said: "By the seventies the discussion on apartheid and its viability and its morality was strongly in the focus. And by the eighties, when I came into the leadership of the Broederbond, the focus was, could you isolate Afrikaner interests from South African interests? This defined the [1982] split [between NP and Conservatives] which took place. Boshoff took the position that you had to seek Afrikaner survival and interests in isolation, as it were. I took the position that if I wanted to promote Afrikaner interests, I had to promote economic and cultural interests of everybody." The new South Africa necessitated a reoriented Broederbond, and de Lange was the leading pitchman.

*The Broederbond think tank on racial affairs, South African Bureau of Racial Affairs (SABRA), founded in 1947, was taken over by Boshoff in 1972.

"We have redefined our mission: I'll try and translate into English— 'We accept the responsibility of promoting Afrikaner interests in such a manner that it serves everybody's interests.'

"I think that at the ground level and at the macro level, we need a lot of creativity and tolerance for diversity, otherwise this place will simply blow up. There is a place for the Broederbond, which will look at the diversity, but also the commonality."

Haven't the Afrikaners delegitimated themselves not only by instituting apartheid, but with their rampant corruption toward the end of their rule?

De Lange doesn't like questions posed abrasively. He fumed, "Corruption is one thing, but extreme poverty and absolute chaos is, well, you know Africa." He was upholding a common tendency to point at someone else's problems when accused of faults one's self.

What if the ANC says to whites in South Africa: Emigrate, we don't care about your skills.

"Look, we are not asking them," de Lange said, jaw clenched. "I'm an African. I'm as much an African as they are. That's my position. And I won't be asking them whether I might stay or not. I demand a place here."

What if they say: We want power, we don't care what you do.

"We would not be prepared to go along with that," he said.

What would he do?

"We would resist it politically—" he said, clipping his words.

He paused. After all, he wasn't a political man. The Broederbond billed itself as a cultural organization.

"—as the National Party is trying to do now, by building up a voter base. The assumption that there is going to be an overpowering homogeneity in the black power base I think is not true." De Lange's Broederbond was tightly in gear with the National Party's effort to attract black and colored voters away from the ANC.

Then he threatened: "If the Afrikaners are found guilty as a people, I think one must take into account the anger that could evoke that could be destructive of this country." The Nationalists' favorite threat remained the potential violence of the Afrikaner right wing, which might go berserk.

De Lange's "diversity" didn't seem to include women. In his April 1992 *Die Burger* article, de Lange said the women question "didn't have to be answered now."

When will it be time?

De Lange gave a pseudoscientific-sounding answer about the "commonality amongst women" and the "commonality amongst males."

"Whether you should suddenly disband all male organizations and all female organizations in the name of nondiscrimination is a doubtful thing to my mind," he said with a dry, sarcastic inhalation, as if one would have to be an idiot to believe such a thing.

But isn't he cutting off the intellect and creativity and experience of half of the smart people in his community?

"Yes. Yes, it boils down to that. And therefore, in that same article I mentioned that we have meetings where women are included."

Twice a year, the newspaper article said.

"Twice a year and more. But on average, twice a year."

Are these women separately recruited, or are they related to the Broederbonders?

"They are related."

So they are wives?

"Yes. Mostly, yes."

Are they recruited on merit?

"At present, no."

Does he think women have little to contribute, or doesn't he trust them, or is the price of admitting them too high? On the word "trust" de Lange spoke angrily through the rest of the question.

"I'm known in South Africa," he said, "as a supporter of the feminist movement. So please don't ascribe antifeminism to me. I had three girls and they were all very bright. I was principal of a teachers' college, of a university, and I promoted the emancipation of the female, intellectually and otherwise.

"I've also supported bursaries [scholarships] for women. There was a time when doctoral bursaries in South Africa, the six top doctoral bursaries in South Africa in the natural sciences, went to women for seventy percent. Over sixty-six percent. And I think that's still the case. I say there is place also for a male organization as there is place for female organization. And there is place for mixed organizations, and why don't we have that?"

But is there an analogue to the Broederbond among females, an organization for them as powerful as the Broederbond?

"Not that I know of, not that I know of. We bring in . . ." He paused, then his tongue roamed over possible words. Then he said in irritation, "I needn't answer this question. But let's put this thing off and let me go off the record."

And so he did. De Lange asked two more times that the tape recorder be switched off over the course of the interview. After such exercises in self-censorship, over issues that wouldn't have been controversial in other societies, de Lange's comment on secrecy in the Broederbond, that "it's become a bad habit, to my mind," rang hollow. And he attacked those who had leveled very similar charges against the Broederbond, along with their broader criticisms of the organization's role in South African politics.

Two of the most prominent Afrikaner Broederbond debunkers are the journalists Hans Strydom and Hennie Serfontein. Strydom, with Ivor Wilkins, wrote *SuperAfrikaners*, published in 1978, which gave names and membership numbers of over seven thousand Broederbond members. Serfontein's 1979 book, *Brotherhood of Power*, also reveals the workings of the Broederbond and tells of perils he and his wife and children faced for his criticism of the organization. In 1994 Serfontein was writing for *Vrye Weekblad*, continuing his years of journalistic exposés of the Broederbond. (For financial reasons, *Vrye Weekblad* ceased publication on February 2, 1994.) The Broederbond's response to the exposés evidenced a police-state mentality: witch-hunts to discover the leakers and exacting retribution against critics.

How does de Lange view the role or effect of Strydom and Serfontein's criticisms?

"I think the only effect it's really had is that many people who belong to the Broederbond have become known and have discovered that it's not such a terrible thing to be known. They [the critics] didn't add anything constructively to the Broederbond. I know both these chaps and they had their own axes to grind in this revealing of the Broederbond, as it were."

Their own axes being that they don't like the secretiveness and the decisions made, and all of that?

"Well, I, partly because they were not members."

So they resent it, that's why—?

"That certainly is part of it. They would deny it but I know both of them."

Why does he believe that?

"You are asking me to say things on record here which—"

De Lange was irritated at being pressed on the matter and spoke with aggravation. He stopped in midsentence.

He is, then, just analyzing them that way?

"Ja."

Innuendo hung heavy in the air, piquant as vinegar. De Lange the insider wouldn't allow these men who had exposed the Broederbond any legitimate motives for their attacks on his brotherhood, even as the Broederbond set about reconstituting itself, publicly proclaiming its new openness.

CHAPTER FIFTEEN

DEEPER UNDERGROUND

When the supposedly aboveboard, newly diverse Afrikanerbond opened its doors in 1993, critics were convinced that the Broederbond still survived, addicted to its secretive ways. But Hans Strydom had already deduced that the Broeders were engaged in burrowing deeper in 1990, when his ongoing exploration of Broederbond operational procedures revealed that secrecy was increasing.

Strydom considers himself an Afrikaner loyalist and views the Broederbond as the Afrikaners' enemy. His revelatory book and subsequent journalistic forays sought to bring home to the *volk* how they were being manipulated. While the Broeders tried to ignore what he reported, or, in Piet de Lange's case, to discredit the source of the revelations, other Afrikaners held Strydom and his activities in high regard.

Did his book blow the Broederbond out of the water?

"Not out of the water, but it certainly made a hole in the boat," said Louw Alberts, a non-Broeder whom F. W. liked to appoint to church and peacemaking committees. "It certainly did. The very concept super-Afrikaner made the masses feel we are being short-looped. You see, the way that book was written indicated that the authors knew what they were talking about. It was never completely or thoroughly denied by the Broederbond. They figured that the best way to deal with that book was to smother it with quietness."

Publication of Broederbonders' names in *SuperAfrikaners* alarmed some Afrikaners and rattled many, reverberating in *dorpe* (towns) across the land. Manie Kriel, a real estate agent in the copper-mining town of Phalaborwa, said, "Funny, the one guy in town here, Verhoef, when the book came out in Phalaborwa, he went down and bought them all." That's L. H. Verhoef, who was a geologist and who joined the Broederbond in 1963.

Hans Strydom lives in the diamond-mining town of Cullinan, about sixteen miles east of Pretoria. Cullinan's main street is lined with old, tan stone houses with colonial-style corrugated tin roofs. Mine tailings bulge here and there through the town, the ground having been turned inside out for ninety years. The waitress at an incongruous yuppie restaurant called La Casa, with pine floors and booths, tells visitors that Cullinan's main claim to fame is that a colossal diamond, known as the Cullinan Diamond, or the Star of Africa, was found here and now nestles in the Queen of England's scepter.

Hans Strydom has a very deep, relaxed voice. Clusters of bright yellow birds flutter in and out of a birdbath outside the window of his lovely old house. Over the years he has collected some German Mausers once carried by Boer commandos in the Anglo-Boer War, and he proudly displays them in his hallway.

Strydom seems tired, a bit beaten down. He is a one-man research empire with contacts inside the Broederbond. He doesn't smear, he doesn't prevaricate, he bases his observations on leaked documents and statements by people whose credibility he has checked. In 1990 he found the track of the Broeders leading deeper underneath South African society, not to its surface. When he began talking about his discovery, he said, it was "like throwing a stone in the bush and a lion jumps out."

In 1990 Strydom was a Democratic Party member of the Johannesburg City Council. Through his sources in the Broederbond, he discovered that his prominent Democratic Party colleague and member of Parliament from Randburg, Wynand Malan, was a Broederbonder. At a party meeting Strydom charged that Malan's dual loyalties—to the party that espoused openness, negotiation, and democracy and to the secret, racist, and sexist organization—were incompatible. Strydom recalled in 1992 that he challenged Malan: "I said that this society is so secretive that they actually have to burn certain documents in front of witnesses. He said, 'It's rubbish, it's not so.' I, at the meeting, pulled out the Broederbond circular and I said to him, 'You don't know what is going on in your own organization. Either you don't know or you're lying to us, because here it is.'

"I said to Wynand it's quite possible—and he conceded that—that I know more about the workings of the Broederbond than he did, attending his branch meeting once a month. Because I've also got documents from head office.

"There are certain documents that are marked, that once it's been dealt with at the branch meeting or a cell meeting, it's got to be burned in front of everybody and the secretary's got to fill out a form signed by others and sent back to head office that this document has been destroyed.

"This is how far the whole secrecy bit has developed. You have a cabal who need to put very little nowadays on paper and if they do, sometimes they burn it."

Strydom had demanded that Malan should stay in the DP only if he quit the Broederbond because only then, according to Strydom, could he be trusted to put DP interests first. Malan resigned from the party, gave up his parliamentary seat, retired from politics, and in 1992 was a practicing lawyer.

Strydom saw that as a strategic move by the Broederbond. "By withdrawing, he cut the ground from under my feet and it [the issue of Broederbond secrecy and penetration of the DP] died down very quickly after that," Strydom said. "I hear talk that Wynand says his day is still coming, he will come back later. My feeling is that he was told by the executive to pull out."

Strydom quit the Democratic Party, disillusioned with the DP because Malan had said there were other Broederbonders in it. In 1992, Piet de Lange confirmed that there were Broeders in all the white parties, claiming that this showed the Broederbond was not merely an Afrikaner Nationalist tool.

A train hooted through the small mining town, blotting out conversation for a moment. The brilliant yellow birds flapped water drops through their wing feathers in avian bliss, then flitted off to a clump of pine trees at one side of Strydom's little plot of wire-fenced land that he rented from De Beers diamond-mining company. Bougainvillea cascaded through the garden and a couple of glorious, gnarled jacaranda trees spread their branches like proprietary matrons. Strydom figured they must have been planted around 1903, when the diamond mine was started. From the first, jacaranda, which was imported to South Africa from Brazil in 1888, prospered, and a man nicknamed Jacaranda Jim Clark planted the trees with their oily lavender blooms across Pretoria.

Strydom was researching how the Broederbond managed to switch directions away from apartheid. "It's purely a matter of survival and keeping control because that's one thing they will never give up."

F. W. de Klerk joined the Broederbond when he was twenty-eight. His father was a member and his brother Wimpie too, until he had to resign in the early nineties because his divorce might have caused revelations, through court appearances, that would have exposed the Broederbond. When F. W. came to power, he knew he had little clout with the generals and soldiers, so he turned to his *vriende*. The word went out for them to study everything and report back.

"So that was done for the military, police, economic, trade unions, overseas investment, boycotts, sanctions," Strydom said. "Everything that could be studied was studied. The message came back and without exception, even from the military, that the status quo can't be maintained."

Former Broederbond chairman Gerrit Viljoen at one stage said the National Party may even lose control and disappear in a coalition. "They are prepared to do that as long as they can save the Broederbond," Strydom said. "That was not a change of heart or a vision. Behind the scenes, [they have] got to at all costs protect this Broederbond."

Strydom believed that any potential rogue military elements "can be isolated," but that the Broederbond was a more insidious element because "they are so strong, they are everywhere."

Strydom looks older than he is—fifty-six—for his hair is nearly white. His beard and mustache make him look like a *platteland oom*, rural Afrikaner uncle, rather than the sophisticated, well-educated man he is. He grew up on a farm not far from Cullinan, "in the bushveld," attended an Afrikaans teacher-training college—in fact, set out on a typical cradle-to-grave Afrikaans life, "very isolated from any other viewpoints. I was a big Nat," he said. "Dr. Verwoerd was our member of Parliament. I was chairman of the student branch [of the NP]. Late fifties, ja. And I was secretary of the FAK, which is a front organization of the Broederbond. So I played a leading role in those circles. I was obviously the kind of person that if I stayed on I would have been in the Broederbond. There's no doubt about it. And would've entered politics on the Nat side. There's no doubt about that.

"I was very simplistic," Strydom said of his youth. "I mean, if you're exposed to only one side . . ." His voice trailed off. But instead of going into teaching, he switched to journalism and "that exposure changed my views in a year or two. The one thing I did believe in was that, when Verwoerd talked about separate but equal, that there was such a thing."

Then Strydom met a black doctor, the first black eye specialist in Africa, who asked him about his politics. "I sat with him and talked about the separate but equal thing, saying it sounds to me morally defensible. 'But it isn't like that,' he said, and explained his salary and his living conditions and that of nurses. I came home and said to my wife, 'I want to go into this, find who is lying.' "

Strydom's wife, Gertie, helped him with the research and they concluded, "This knocks the moral base from the thing [apartheid] and there was nothing we could defend. We immediately resigned from the [National] party. That was about 1960, before the shocks of Sharpeville."*

*On March 21, 1960, at Sharpeville, a township south of Johannesburg, police opened fire on a group of Africans who were protesting the pass laws; 68 were killed and 186 wounded, most shot in the back. The incident spurred the ANC to abandon its policy of nonviolence and launch its guerrilla war.

How did his family receive his moral conversion?

"They thought I was mad or something. At one stage I think there was a bit of a disgrace on the family. Those were the days when they easily called you a Communist if you disagreed with the Nats, you know."

Could one reason for the Broeders' extreme hatred of Communists be because they use the same organizational tactics?

"Absolutely, absolutely. Except with communism, I don't know too much about it, but if you don't agree they'll just lock you up and kick you around. Here they're doing that with the blacks but not with the Afrikaners who oppose them."

But what happens to Afrikaners who are ostracized?

"It's a long story, it's a sad story. It's not important to you."

But it is. For example, Beyers Naudé and Fred van Wyk, of the Christian Institute and the Institute of Race Relations, were very badly treated.

"Ja, I'm not in that league," Strydom said. "Those guys really suffered you know. I've had a few things to my advantage and that was that I wasn't made vulnerable by my occupation. And secondly, I always believed that your best protection in a situation like that is to have a high profile. They never expect anybody to stand up to them because they've been so secretive and they've been so powerful. But things happen. You actually become aware more and more of the power of this thing [the Broederbond].

"You see the Broeders are not alone. You have also what I call fellow travelers. There's the Broeder ring of membership and you have a large gray area surrounding it of fellow travelers who will never do anything against them and are very aware of their dependence on the gravy train. You even find that in English circles."

Strydom didn't want to be specific about the harrassment he faced, but finally he gave an example. His daughter Grietjie had six distinctions in her senior year high school work and yet never was awarded a bursary for university study, as could ordinarily be expected. Then, after six years as a medical student at Bloemfontein Free State University, "she was given an oral examination in her strongest subject, she was known for it."

A lecturer from the University of Pretoria was conducting the exam. "His opening remark was, 'Oh so your father is a famous author, isn't he, and worked for the English-language press,' which is very much a swearword. She was too good to fail, but he gave her fifty-one percent, just the bloody pass rate. Then when their own lecturer read out the results in the class, and Grietjie's was mentioned, the students started booing. One chap jumped up and he said, 'Look, if Grietjie gets fifty-one percent then I should have had twenty-one. And I got seventy-eight percent. There's something wrong here.' "

Strydom's daughter mentioned all this to her mother and told her not to tell her father because she thought he would take action and aggravate the situation. His wife did mention it a few days later, and, true to his philosophy, Strydom went into action.

"I got on the phone to Professor [Gerrit] Viljoen, who was then chairman of the Broederbond. He was having a *braai* in the garden and he's got very prominent people. His wife wouldn't call him, you know. I said, 'Well I'm sorry he's going to be very cross with you when he finds out you didn't call him to this important call.' "

Strydom laughed happily as he rendered his recollection of the conversation.

"She said okay and she called him. I said, 'Professor Viljoen, it's Hans Strydom.'

" 'Ja, hoe gaan dit?' [Yes, how's it going?] and so on.

" 'You know me?'

" 'Ja.'

" 'You know my daughter?'

" 'Ja. Grietjie. Lovely child.'

" 'You know that I also wrote a book about the Broederbond.'

" 'Ja.'

"I said, 'I know that you are chairman of the Broederbond.'

" 'Ja, of course.'

"I said, 'The organization claims it doesn't intimidate people who are not members, is very aboveboard, very decent cultural society, etcetera, etcetera, won't tolerate any sort of interference, or nepotism or anything like that.'

" 'No, of course.'

"I said, 'Well what do you think of a situation like this?' and I then just repeated exactly what happened.

" 'No,' he said, 'that can't be tolerated. I'm going to phone the dean of the faculty now.'

"An hour later the dean of the faculty phoned, also highly apologetic. He said, 'It can't be tolerated. I'm going to show you our organization doesn't do that sort of thing.'

"So the upshot was that some steps were taken against this lecturer, I don't know what. And my daughter got fairly good marks afterward."

Strydom's story showed how a lower-down Broederbonder, probably following a general directive to "make Strydom small," went a bit too far and how his superiors then righteously denied responsibility and appeared to discipline him. But few other fathers would have the knowledge, courage, or clout to go to the top and complain, as Strydom did.

"Gossip is a great weapon," Strydom said, when it was mentioned that the former editor of *Die Burger*, Piet Cillie, was quick with the character smear.

"Ja, Piet Cillie was the *Judasbok* [Judas goat] of the Afrikaner," he said. Strydom explained that farmers, in order to induce sheep to the slaughter, train a goat with a bell to lead them through a little gate to their deaths. "They wouldn't go in their on their own. We call it the Judasbok. Piet Cillie would say, 'I was in the vanguard of change.' I say it's nonsense. I say if it wasn't for him, people would have faced realities a long time ago."

Strydom was amazed when he was told that Piet de Lange also claimed to be in the "vanguard of change" and to have opposed apartheid as long ago as 1950.

"Good heavens, would he say it on record?"

Yes, he did.

"They say it so often that they start believing it," Strydom said, smiling. "Next time you see them they'll be absolutely convinced. De Lange was never in favor of change as far as I knew. He never urged any Afrikaner to change in 1950. That's nonsense. I don't believe it happened. Otherwise he wouldn't have become chairman of the Broederbond. He'd have been regarded as too liberal. 1950! No ways.

"It's hard for us to swallow after going through what we did and confronting these people for so many years, and being on the bad end of the stick all the time, while they were just living the good life, and now claim that they were the ones to lead the way."

Has Strydom had apologies from anybody?

"Yes, I have," he said. "I've had two from friends. The one guy used to be a friend, then he did something awful to me. And he said he was very sorry about that. Not that it can help now but . . . I'm not sentimental."

Strydom's deep voice became very soft.

"I believe they must confess, and it must be a deep-seated conviction, and we must believe it when they say it. The horrible thing they have done in this country. Before we can start again, and get rid of the Broederbond.

"You may find me to a certain extent an apologist for the ordinary Afrikaner. It's indoctrination on an insidious scale like you've never seen before. Nobody was put into work camps or forced labor or brainwashing sessions or anything. Try and imagine this mass psychosis. How do the mass get out of it? No, they don't. Individuals like I do, get out of it.

We even get rejected and ostracized as a result of that and now you find a lot of people saying to you, 'You were right all along' and 'I'm sorry for what I've done to you.' "

Again Strydom's large voice shrank to gentleness when he talked about contrition. But when he switched to the reputed Christianity of the Broederbond, his voice was flat, lightly laced with sarcasm.

"It's a highly 'moral' organization," he said. "Every [Broederbond] meeting is opened with prayer. At that meeting they can decide the most vicious, they can break all ten commandments at one meeting, but it's opened with prayer. The white [clean] hands, you know.

"They've persuaded themselves that they talk on behalf of the Afrikaner. That's what they tell the ANC and that's why the ANC is so scared to tackle that issue of the Broederbond. They think they will be attacking the Afrikaners' cultural heritage. They've been told that the Broederbond talks on behalf of the Afrikaner. They got away with that lie, and a lot of English speakers believe the same thing.

"I made more Afrikaner friends, many, many more since I exposed the Broederbond, than I had before. The ordinary Afrikaner may not speak a lot about it, may not know a lot about it. Those who do know, in small communities like this, hate the Broederbond for what they've done."

Strydom saw the gossip mill being cranked up to provide cover for the Broederbond's move farther underground. "The word is quietly going out that the Broeders mean nothing today," Strydom said. "Which is nonsense. They don't want to attract attention. They want people to think that they're not powerful. You must never underestimate them," he said. "This is a lesson I learned very early on. Their public relations is fantastic. You'll detect in me a tremendous admiration from the organizational point of view. It's a fine-tuned organization. It's adjusted every day and they learn from mistakes. To think the Broederbond was started by six young Afrikaners all under the age of eighteen," Strydom mused. "It's an amazing thing, and [it is] holding thirty-five million people's future in the balance. People think it can't be true.

"If you don't understand the Broederbond, you'll never understand what has happened to the Afrikaner."

CHAPTER SIXTEEN

MUSIC WARS

Thousands of humans sprawled, sometimes entangled, sometimes comatose, on blankets spread here and there on the veld at the 1992 Houtstok (Woodstock) music festival. Shadowy figures stumbled about, singly, in pairs and groups, unsteadily traversing the dusty shallow slope. Hundreds of fires lapped at the dark night sky, and shadows wafted across their flickerings like subversive emotions. Gray, black, and fire-colored, the scene seemed a painting of purgatory, or a dire medieval battlefield with the wounded staggering through the devastation. Wood smoke surged in and out of the lungs, stung the eyes, and made breathing haphazard. Whiffs of *boerewors* drifted from grills where the sausages cooked, curled like giant lion intestines.

Way, way over there was a stage, supporting stacks of loudspeaker and amplifier equipment, flanked on one side by a giant inflated beer-can balloon and on the other by a trailer that served as a dressing room for the musicians. Rock, pop, and blues music blared into the darkness and Afrikaners waded through it thickly. As the sun squashed out in an orangy-pink flare, a man played a *treklavier*, a trek piano, supposedly the Voortrekkers' main musical instrument, backed by a rock band.

As night seeped out of the veld and gradually covered the sky, people began to have fun. Grim fun. They were determined to have fun. They gritted their teeth, sloshed down more beers, took drags on *dagga* (marijuana) butts, felt up somebody. This was freedom from Calvinism. *Sjoe!* The Afrikaner has freedom in his blood. Fuck the dominees. Hear that band, the Naaimasjien. Sewing machine, ha ha, nudge nudge. The dictionary defines *naai* as: "(vulg.) have sexual intercourse with." That's "fuck," but the *woordeboek* is too proper to say that. The Naaimasjien claimed to be from Potch, home of the Doppers, the more-Calvinist-than-thou church.

The crowd chanted, "You're not from Potch, you're not from Potch." The leader of the band said, "Okay, okay, you're right, we're not from Potch, we're from Johannesburg. But if the National Party could lie to us

174

for all those years, we can lie too." Then the musician said his name was F. L. de Klerk, and the audience guffawed. F. L. was the brand name of a condom.

The 1992 Houtstok was the second alternative Afrikaans music festival. (Houtstok I took place in May 1990.) Twenty-five thousand people (nearly one percent of the Afrikaner population) drove eighteen miles north of Pretoria, four miles of it over bumpy, rusty-dusty road, to get there. A truck sprinkled water along the road to lay the dust. The thorn trees, the yuccas, the bushes were fuzzed with it, and the grass had dried up in the drought. The dust was so powdery that when people danced, it floated up and drifted in the air. Rows of outdoor toilets bordered the festival field. Lion Lager was sponsoring the event, but everyone seemed to be downing Castle beer, Carling Red Label, Coke, or Fanta.

Houtstok's 1992 slogan was "We're too sexy for the FAK music festival," a takeoff on the popular song "I'm Too Sexy for My Shirt." This was war between David and Goliath. Vicious and intricate, it could ruin people's careers. On one side were the young Afrikaners who, while speaking and singing in Afrikaans, welcomed English-speaking and black musicians, and called themselves South Africans. On the other side was the Federasie van Afrikaanse Kultuurverenigings (Federation of Afrikaans Cultural Organizations), the FAK, the public face of the Broederbond.

Every year the FAK runs a festival that stages only *Afrikaanse musiek*. "It's not opera, it's more the popular music," said the FAK head, Dominee Henno Cronje. "To encourage young people to sing group nice music, happy music, although modern. We don't mean the hillbilly songs, I mean more popular nice songs."

Held in an outdoor Pretoria stadium several weeks before Houtstok II, the FAK festival was squeaky-clean. Starting at ten in the morning, lower school choirs sang Afrikaans songs, then in the afternoon high school choruses paraded on and off the stage. Toward evening the program with popular singers began. All was seemly and Lawrence Welky, with tweedly songs such as "Believe in Yourself" and "The Most Beautiful Language." A TV camera on a dolly-mounted gantry rose and fell in long swoops, rolled back and forth by technicians. Many more instruments seemed to be producing the music than were visible on the stage. Sometimes the singers' lip movements were out of synch with the songs.

The only blacks visible were either selling candied apples and balloons or stiffly singing onstage in the blue-uniformed Soweto Police Choir. The only unplanned moment was when a girl with long hair stood up facing the stage in front of the crowd of five thousand, swaying as if transported. The audience buzzed. "She" turned around, revealing herself to be a long-haired young man. The audience quieted. He turned back around and continued gyrating, then flung a pair of black lace panties onto the stage at the feet of the tuxedoed brothers Innes and Franna Benade, who continued singing their saccharine song. The "girl" was a Houtstok organizer, mocking the FAK.

A less spontaneous, and vaguely anti-Jewish, event took place when a man called "Volga" came onstage in a Cossack costume with a giant black beard and boots and started lip-synching fake Russian words to the tune of "Havah Nagilah," perhaps the world's best-known Hebrew folk song. The sound system repeatedly cut out, leaving "Volga" without amplification. He put on a great show of increasing fury, chewing out the master of ceremonies in slapstick fashion. Finally the sound came back, but the music that blared forth was a rock and roll hit by the "heartthrob of the *platteland*," Steve Hofmeyer. "Volga" began dancing, and as he twirled, his coat flew up to expose his blue boxer shorts. Flinging off his coat, the bearded one stood in just shorts and boots. Then the emcee announced the arrival of Steve Hofmeyer himself! The crowd cheered and girls screamed. Then, "Volga" removed his beard and, lo and behold, he was blond Steve Hofmeyer!

Traditional Cossacks, infamous for killing Jews in nineteenth-century pogroms, wouldn't sing "Havah Nagilah." And black-coated orthodox Jews wouldn't strip their clothes in public. The skit might show ignorance rather than malice, but by omission or commission, it indicated the latent anti-Jewishness of Afrikaner society.

Founded in 1929, the FAK is the Broederbond's public front for coordinating associations created to implement Broederbond economic, educational, and cultural policies. Its symbol is a flame, like those on the *fakkels*, torches, carried in 1938 at the dedication ceremonies of the Voortrekker Monument in Pretoria. The FAK operated in 1992 out of a nondescript building called Die Eike, The Oaks, not coincidently also the headquarters of the Broederbond, slap against the English-speaking Johannesburg Club and across from the SABC television station.

Few English-speaking South Africans seem to know about the FAK, a case of not knowing there was an Afrikaans thought-control office in their police state. That is a sign of FAK's success. Although it aims primarily at taking care of the Afrikaner, its complete control of the SABC radio and TV (until 1994) affects the entire population.

The FAK is a federation of more than three thousand officially autonomous organizations with specific areas of operation. Prime examples of some were the Afrikaanse Studentebond (ASB), the Voortrekkers, the Handelsinstituut (Commerce Institute), the women's federation, the teachers' union, the three Dutch Reformed churches and many religious bodies, the Afrikaanse Taal en Kultuurvereniging (ATKV, Afrikaans Language and Cultural Organization), postal, police, and defense force organizations, the Institute for Christian National Education. You name it, the FAK keeps tabs on it.

What is this Afrikaner culture that the FAK promotes?

"I spend a lot of time doing the few traditional Afrikaner things that have survived: watching rugby and having a nice *braai* afterwards," said journalist Dries van Heerden. "That's about the only part of Afrikaner culture that has survived."

Journalist Jacques Pauw said, "Previously, Afrikaner culture was apartheid. There was nothing else, that was the unifying factor. At the moment I don't know what Afrikaans culture is anymore."

UNISA history professor Albert Grundlingh said that the Afrikaner and any attendant culture did not really exist until after the Anglo-Boer War. The Boers were unified, to the feeble extent that they were, by being anticolonial. "They fought for what they called the survival of the *volk* and that sort of thing. But that wasn't necessarily an Afrikaner *volk*; it was just the survival of the republics. It was anticolonial and had a very weakly developed cultural baggage."

He noted that "cultural entrepreneurs" in the thirties and forties launched "a conscious attempt to stamp out other cultural forms" than ones they chose. In a minor example, they tried to stamp out dog racing and promote the indigenous game of *juskei*, resembling ten-pin bowling. The Broederbond moved in to promote and control all *juskei* in the country.

"A lot of the culture was artificial," said journalist Max du Preez. "Look at our traditional dance, we call it *volkspiele*. It's a joke. It's from Nazi Germany. They [Broeder Nationalists] sent a commission out to study all the dances of Holland, the Flemish dances, and German. The Great Trek people didn't dance any *volkspiele*. They didn't even wear those clothes. All our traditional songs are German songs of the thirties.

"That stretch of history is so important. The Afrikaners got their pride back and started speaking their language and started practicing their culture and started writing poetry and songs and things."

But something went badly wrong.

"We didn't have our own resident intellectuals so we sent some students over to Germany in the twenties and the thirties. Verwoerd, [D. F.] Malan, they all studied in the thirties in Germany and came back with this disease: you judge a person by his race. You start measuring people's skulls and that kind of crap. They came back and they had a receptive audience here because we didn't have any education. Then with the war breaking out, we couldn't possibly fight for the British. My father was a guerrilla in the Ossewabrandwag [Ox Wagon Brigade]. They called it the Stormjaers [Stormtroopers]. He blew up bridges in our town. But the problem was, you can't only be against somebody. When you're against somebody, you're with somebody else. And that was Germany."

Potch Professor Elaine Botha wrote her master's thesis in the sixties about the ideals and structure of the FAK. She admitted that the "very strong religious undertone" in the organization could turn into narrow-mindedness and censorship, but she liked to think of it as "moral responsibility."

She worked from 1960 to 1965 with the FAK affiliate the ATKV as a social worker, traveling around the country to small stations on the rail lines, for at that time it was a railway organization.

"You'd arrive there and the only two learned people in the entire community would be the minister and his wife and sometimes a teacher or two. The type of Afrikaners that we were trying to adult-educate were very simple people in little, way-out stations along the Karoo or other places, where they had minimal resources. You had to teach them how to write minutes, how to organize a meeting, how to send out notices for a meeting.

"Now what do you do if you're living on a little railway siding and there's nothing to do? How do you get any culture going? The way people were motivated were the ideals of the Afrikaner.

"I was quite amazed now, in April [1992], I bought a copy of the *New Nation,* the pro-ANC weekly newspaper. The middle page could've been taken from the 1938 Afrikaners' struggle: 'This is the way you set up an agenda for a meeting, this is the way you send out notices.' You know, I could've written that."

But Botha was talking about FAK history. Some sophisticated, urbanized Afrikaners belittled the current clout of the FAK's organizations. "Poor guys in the FAK, they often make pronouncements on language and on Afrikaner cultural days," said Dries van Heerden. "Jesus man, we've got May Day today. It's the Communist holiday!" He added, though, that FAK-approved student organizations still got out the vote for the University of Pretoria's student government.

FAK power is everywhere evident among Afrikaners—expressed as orchestrating peer pressure to controlling purse strings. The Rand Afrikaans University professor of education Martin Trümpelmann said,

"The moment I resigned from the FAK and the Rapportryers and other cultural organizations [in the late eighties], I felt that many of my colleagues felt in a certain sense I joined the enemy. Ja, ja, you will be marginalized [when you quit]."

Professor Hans du Plessis, head of the writing program at Potchefstroom University, said the ATKV, which funds his program, has "got more influence because they are giving away prizes. They are inviting black and brown choirs to do something and we are trying to cater in creative writing for everybody in the country." It has money and it dishes it out to people who write in an approved way.

In 1989 a group of musicians who came to be known as the alternative Afrikaans music movement launched the Voelvry (Feel Free) performance tour, which was a roaring success among young Afrikaners. Voelvry brought particular acclaim to a young singer calling himself Johannes Kerkorrel (Church Organ) and his Gereformeerde Blues Band (as in Gereformeerde Kerk, Reformed Church or the Doppers). In one song Kerkorrel said that when the face of president P. W. Botha came onto TV, people should switch it off.

"Voelvry just made a mockery of the government," said Attie van Wyk, a music impresario. "They toured the campuses and got a huge following. Kerkorrel is a very, very intelligent guy, and funny. They are very much ANC as well."

The FAK was not amused. The alternative musicians' songs vanished from the SABC airwaves, and planned university appearances were canceled. Then on May 31, 1990, came the first Houtstok.

Theunis Englebrecht, whose stage name is Randy Rambo, played there. (Englebrecht is also a music critic at the *Beeld, Image,* newspaper.) He said the musicians and the organizers "got intimidated, their telephones were bugged. The people from the FAK and the ATKV tried their best to undermine [the event] by having newspapers print articles about the lyrics, saying they are terrible and people must not allow their children to go there. It was a smear campaign."

"I think they started this Houtstok as a reaction against the more conservative way in which we held our festivals," Henno Cronje said. "I'm not really a great admirer of their kind of music, but that's my taste and I think that's my privilege."

What about the Houtstok organizers' contention that the FAK closed the Afrikaans university stages to alternative performances?

"I don't know anything about it. But that's the privilege of the university too, that's not the FAK."

What about the SABC boycott?

"If the SABC decides they don't like this kind of music because, and I must say this, the lyrics of some of the singers, I'll definitely not allow at the FAK [festival] because they were not in the best of good taste. Most of us as parents will not be happy if our children have got to listen to this kind of, I don't want to use the word 'pornography,' but, not in good taste. And I'm pretty sure you will not like it too."

Henno Cronje didn't smile, his eyes never softened. He was, after all, a dominee, the *volk*'s cultural commissar.

Some Afrikaners thought he was poorly qualified to guard their virtue. One journalist, whose claims were echoed by others, said of Cronje:

"He's a slimy guy. If you want to buy a cheap diamond just go and ask Henno Cronje. He's that kind of guy. Cronje's a Broederbonder through and through," the journalist continued, adding that as a chaplain Cronje reported on Afrikaner foreign service employees' personal lives when he was living in England and traveling around to South African embassies in Europe.

Houtstok I took place on the same day as the 1990 FAK music festival, the former claiming an attendance of twenty-five thousand while FAK got only eleven thousand.

"Their [FAK] music is not even Afrikaans music," Englebrecht said. "They take European melodies and write new lyrics. It's European music."

Anton Goosen, the first Afrikaner to sing rock songs back in the mid-seventies, agreed, saying money for the FAK copyrights went overseas. "Thirty-seven and a half percent goes back overseas, twelve and a half stays here for the translator, and the other fifty percent goes to the publisher. It's funny, they've never recognized me for what I've done for Afrikaans music. I've written five hundred songs, I've had probably thirty hits."

Goosen, in his forties, is older than the other alternative musicians. He is thin, has long brown hair and a trim beard, and dresses in fraying jeans, a dingy baseball hat, and high-topped *takkies*, as tennis shoes are called. "My drummer wants me to get boots, because our blacks identify there." But Goosen keeps his casual dress. He speaks in riffs, so the conversation is more like jazz than talk.

Goosen has a big following among coloreds. "I was fourteen years old [born in the Great Karoo] and a colored by the name of Jantjie, he was a Griqua [descendant of the Khoisan], taught me to play the guitar. I became part of his culture and I considered myself like a semicolored. Then when I was at college, there was a [1973] book by Dr. [J. A.] Heese that came out and disappeared overnight, on the origin of the Afrikaner and how many had colored blood. Paul Kruger looked very dodgy to me. He had an earring in his ear, that is another indication." (Heese's son, Professor Hans Heese at the University of the Western Cape, wrote *Group without Borders* in 1984, extending the genetic research.)

Goosen wears a loop earring in his left ear.

"I mentioned this [about Kruger] to my father and he took his cup of tea and chucked it on me, saying, 'How dare you imply that about our first leaders.' Ja, we didn't dig each other much. [My father had] the FAK attitude."

The real FAK attacked Goosen early on, after he was invited to sing at the State Civic Theatre in Pretoria and made jokes about the flag. "I got a letter from the ATKV that said, 'Many unfavorable complaints were received after your appearance at the State Civic Theatre.' They said I was not allowed to go on any of their stages."

In 1989, after the first Houtstok: "What Henno Cronje and his company did to me after Houtstok! Just one phone call: 'Don't allow him on the box.'" Suddenly Goosen's songs were off the SABC radio stations. "My manager went and asked, 'What's going on here? Anton's one of the most popular artists in the country.' Then the story came out and the guy [Henno Cronje] said, 'I'm gonna put him back on.' That is very, very, very immoral to do that."

Goosen and Cronje go back, in the way everyone seems to know everyone else among the elite. "Ja, I've known Henno Cronje for a long time," Goosen said. "His wife borrowed bras from my first girlfriend in college."

Goosen's manager, a twenty-two-year-old woman named Ansie Kamffer, the chief organizer of the two Houtstoks, also became an FAK target, as did Theunis Englebrecht, who according to Goosen is "one of the best Afrikaans music critics in this country."

Kamffer began organizing musicians at age nineteen, after attending Rand Afrikaans University, the Broederbond university. She escaped being brainwashed by Christian National Education because, she said, "I was lucky, I read nice books, and I always had quite interesting friends." She looked like a tired porcelain doll, with a luminous complexion but dark circles around her eyes. Houtstok II had sapped her energy, but not killed her chutzpa and political acumen. Englebrecht, twenty-seven, had long brown hair and fuzz on his upper lip trying to become a mustache; he was not very athletic-looking. He'd published two volumes of poetry and two novels by the time he was twenty-one. His voice was soft and he was utterly gracious, an impression completely at odds with his image as the scatological Randy Rambo.

"A lot of people tried to get me out of my job [at *Beeld*]," Englebrecht said. "Ja, two singers called Innes and Franna Benade [the tuxedoed two at the FAK festival]. They sing all these songs about girls and sunrises. Innes took the Randy Rambo lyrics sheet after it was banned and faxed it through to the managing director of Nasionale Pers in Cape Town." Englebrecht's editors at *Beeld* then told him he could no longer review mainstream Afrikaans music, those tunes based on European songs.

Kamffer recounted how she once went to Church Square in Pretoria for some publicity shots with Anton Goosen, a cameraman from SABC, Jan de Klerk (son of Wimpie), and Piet Botha (Foreign Minister Pik Botha's son, also a rock musician): "This guy came up to us and said, 'Hello I'm so-and- so from National Intelligence. We've got information that a group of activists are coming here and we just want to tell you that we're aware of it.' So we realized that these people were watching us," she said.

Englebrecht said that National Intelligence had tapped Kamffer's phone while she was organizing the first Houtstok, and they both got a lot of anonymous phone calls from people calling them things like *kaffirboetie*.

In 1990 Kamffer discovered that the singers at the FAK music festival were going to lip-synch their words instead of actually sing them, and she spread the story to the front pages of the Afrikaans press. The FAK retaliated by threatening to read Englebrecht's Randy Rambo lyrics on *Agenda*, a popular prime-time TV program, to warn parents to keep their children away from Houtstok. Then the TV channel M-Net (run by the Broederbonder-controlled Nasionale Pers), which had agreed to film Houtstok, called Kamffer and told her to be noncombative on *Agenda*; otherwise M-Net would not televise Houtstok. She was polite on TV, she said, but "It was a nightmare, it was painful." Englebrecht's lyrics weren't read on TV, but they were published just before the concert in the *Transvaler* newspaper. M-Net, under contract with the Houtstok performers, did broadcast the festival.

The FAK didn't flare into action just because of the alternative musicians' antiestablishment or scatological lyrics. The culture battle went to the heart of the *volk*'s identity, as that identity had been cultivated by the Afrikaner Nationalists since the 1920s. Back then, Prime Minister Jan Smuts wanted to be leader of united South Africans—that is, both Afrikaans- and English-speaking whites. He and his approach were anathema to the Broederbonders and their National Party, which turned drastically inward, to "uplift" the white Afrikaner tribe in opposition to the English. Now, these young, modern Afrikaners Kamffer and Englebrecht kept talking about how Houtstok fit into the "broader spectrum" of South Africa, consciously rejecting the Nationalists' *volk* ideology. Reaching out to Afrikaners to encourage them out of their isolation, Houtstok organizers constituted a real threat to the FAK ethos, and the FAK knew it. By 1992, Kamffer, Englebrecht, and Goosen were ANC members. Kamffer was going to work for the ANC, to protect "alternative" artists. She recalled how moved she was when she and Anton Goosen met Barbara Masekela, the ANC's cultural representative abroad, after years of exile.

"When she came into the country for the first time, she was here for about two days and we had a meeting with her. We freaked, you know, and we were just so glad to see this woman," Kamffer said. "She's forty-seven years old and she's just amazing. She's a black woman you know. She said to Anton, 'Well, Anton, I'm your people.' And that was one of the most wonderful statements, at that stage."

Did Masekela say that because she spoke Afrikaans?

"We're in the same country, we're in the same boat you know," Kamffer explained. "I don't think Afrikaners are my people, actually."

"I don't feel any loyalty towards them," Englebrecht concurred.

That's why the FAK is worried.

"Ja, what can they expect after what they've done to this country?" Englebrecht said. "You don't know who you can trust anymore. You get suspicious about everybody. Everything's changing in the country and they're afraid that they're going to lose their power. But they're very much more subtle now and that's why they're dangerous."

"They're doing it on all levels," Kamffer said. "Cultural levels, sports, political, the church. The Afrikaners are a very small part of South Africa, so they can't afford to lose any of their people. If their own people actually betray them, there's nothing left, and that's why I think they're so heavy with us."

"We're very young but we're so cynical and fed up," Englebrecht said. "Being exposed to a culture of violence you lose your faith in humanity. I've lost my faith in humanity. We're cultural terrorists, we're planting mind bombs, because apartheid's got its roots in Afrikaner culture. That culture has to be destroyed because it's like a cancer. It won't go away."

Kamffer was bitterly exhausted by Houtstok II tribulations. She just wanted to plant flowers in her garden, cook food, and listen to nice music.

"I love this country, although it hurts me," she said softly.

PART IV

RELIGION

The Afrikaner believes that it is the will of God that there should be a diversity of races and nations and that obedience to the will of God therefore requires the acknowledgment and maintenance of that diversity.

> —GEOFF CRONJÉ,
> sociology professor who helped
> craft apartheid, 1945

The church never says "I'm sorry."
> —DOMINEE WILLIE JONKER

CHAPTER SEVENTEEN

HOW APARTHEID
BECAME GOD'S WILL

Traditional Afrikaner history is a combination of fact and myth. The official Nationalist version went like this:

In 1652 a Dutchman named Jan van Riebeeck came by ship to the southern tip of Africa. He and his Calvinist Dutch colleagues launched the Afrikaners' mission to convert the heathen hordes. In their Cape home, the Afrikaners cleaved tightly to their Calvinist traditions.

In the early 1800s British imperialists took control of the Cape Colony, and British immigrants began pouring in. While the Afrikaners cultivated, the Crown legislated, and in 1836 some of the first settlers' stalwart descendants bravely marched to the interior on the Great Trek, family Bibles tucked in their ox-drawn wagons, seeking land and freedom from despised British laws, such as one abolishing slavery. Escaping the British, the Afrikaners repeatedly confronted armies of Africans. When the gun-toting Voortrekkers killed three thousand spear-wielding Zulus at Blood River in 1838, losing none of their own, clearly God was with them. A Covenant with Him was sealed and the Boers vowed eternally to honor it. Every December 16 the Afrikaners, still staunch Calvinists, pray and celebrate the Day of the Covenant, also called the Day of the Vow.

God was still with the Afrikaners in 1881 when they defeated superior British forces at Majuba Hill in a battle springing from British efforts to exert sovereignty over Afrikaner lands where diamonds had been found. When the Afrikaners again refused to knuckle under at the end of the century when the British sought to claim newly discovered gold-bearing real estate, they must have been doing something contrary to God's will: they lost the Anglo-Boer War (1899–1902), and the toll was ferocious, including more than twenty-six thousand women and children who died of illnesses while sequestered in British concentration camps, separated from their gallant commandos.

Reconstruction from the British scorched-earth military tactics was slow, Afrikaner impoverishment was widespread, and the upliftment of the *volk* became the task of the Broederbond, formed in 1918. By the late 1930s, Afrikaner nationalism blossomed, blessed by the church. The Great Trek was reenacted in 1938, ox wagons wending through town after town across the country, converging on the site of the soon-to-be-built Voortrekker Monument just outside Pretoria. Almost every white city and town and *dorpie* has a Eeufees (century celebration) Street to mark the 1938 Great Trek centenary. The street signs went up as the myths solidified into dogma. In 1948, the Afrikaners clearly emerged with God's blessing when the Nationalists defeated Jan Smuts's pro-British government, and the Broederbonder and Dutch Reformed Church dominee D. F. Malan became prime minister.

Afrikaner identity was not invented out of whole cloth, but, as the historian Albert Grundlingh said, "Cultural entrepreneurs, ministers of religion, teachers, etcetera, manipulated Afrikaner history to create a sort of ethnic affiliation to counter insecurities that went along with urbanization and industrialization." Afrikaners started to identify and understand the myths as myths only in the 1980s, as Afrikaner academics began tentatively to explore their own history. This revisionism loosened the straitjacket of official *volk* history (*volksgeskiedenis*) but was largely ignored by those in power.

The revisionists observed that Broederbond-based Nationalists had forged the new nation's myths during the 1920s, '30s, and '40s. The major beliefs, which resembled the British imperialist Cecil Rhodes's conviction that God made the English superior to all, are that Afrikaners are a "chosen people" with their own "Exodus," the Great Trek, who have been staunch Calvinists from the moment they landed at Cape Town in 1652; that in pursuing God's commands, they avoid and seek to prevent race mixing; and that they establish institutions of government that are, first and foremost, Christian in nature and action. Christian government entails supporting the spread of the gospel, but not the integration of Christians of different races. Thus, apartheid was the institutional expression of God's will: it kept the races separate, but made possible the spread of the Word.

Historian André du Toit's revisionism has been so incisive that the Dutch Reformed Church pretended his debunking of the Calvinist myth didn't occur. Bury it with silence and maybe fewer of the faithful would notice. Du Toit argues that in contrast to European Calvinism,

188

which emphasizes finding the right theological principles and applying them, the Afrikaners' Calvinism "is pragmatic, opportunistic, ad hoc." He notes that Afrikaner Calvinism is quite recent. It certainly doesn't date back to the arrival of the Dutch at the Cape in 1652.

"Dutch Reformed religiosity is a relatively late development and can be dated from the 1860s," du Toit said. "Pre-1860s [Afrikaner] religiosity is almost unknown." Early South African Christians lacked some typical Calvinist traits. The structure of early Cape society was based more on the legal relations of individuals to the Dutch East India Company than on Calvin's distinction between the elect and the damned. And, while in Calvinist parts of Europe the clergy was independent, in the early Cape the clergy was dominated by the state and paid by the Company.

Early Cape settlers, unlike New England's Puritans, were not highly educated religious zealots or utopians. Van Riebeeck himself was a medical doctor, but, as Albert Grundlingh has written, the supposedly exemplary forefather took the Cape Town job with the Dutch East India Company to rehabilitate himself because the Company had previously fired him for corruption. And van Riebeeck complained about his fellow Dutch workers in Cape Town, most of whom came from among the rabble of Dutch society or were illiterate vagrants press-ganged into service at sea. Van Riebeeck wished for some hard-working Chinese instead, and as soon as he could, he fled to the Far East.

Early Afrikaners did not develop their own institutions for training religious leaders. The Dutch Reformed Church hired outsiders, mostly Dutch or Scottish, to care for the Afrikaners' spiritual needs. The Calvinism that developed after 1860 was informed by a pietistic revivalism largely inspired by an influx of Scottish ministers, such as the Reverend Andrew Murray, who fashioned a new orthodox evangelical piety in the Cape Dutch Reformed Church. In the 1870s, the Cape Colony government stopped supporting the church. The church resisted the state's withdrawal, for economic reasons, among others, and argued that ministers would have to be supported by local congregations and that this would change the whole relation between minister and congregation. They were right. The church became more closely identified with the Afrikaner people.

Once the Afrikaners gained control of the state in the election of 1948, the church and state were reunited in the sense that they both were controlled by the Afrikaner Broederbond elite. Nationalist Afrikaners completely rejected the concepts of individual rights that grew out of the French and American revolutions and instead adopted a messianic vision of God-sanctioned, ethnically pure nations. In the religiously based nationalism of the Afrikaner neo-Calvinist creed, the elect among the Afrikaners guide the community, which itself stands as an elect above the other nations, and within it, individual Afrikaners are depreciated and submerged in favor of the collective personality, the *volk*.

From the time of the Voortrekkers' departure from the Cape in the mid-1830s, Afrikaners differed over how God's will was to be carried out. The Cape Dutch Reformed Church supported the British colonial government and abhorred schism and thus refused the Boers' request for official blessings and dominees to come along on the Trek. By the time the Trekkers were established in the interior in the 1850s and '60s, intense theological controversy sundered the church. Three sects emerged, vying for the mantle of the true religious tradition, each with its own interpretation of Calvinism. Today these are the Dutch Reformed Church (Nederduitse Gereformeerde Kerk, NGK), the Dutch Reconstituted Church (Nederduitsch Hervormde Kerk, NHK), and the Reformed Church (Gereformeerde Kerk, or Doppers). The name "Dopper" may derive from *domper*, a candle damper. For clarity, in this book the three churches are called the Dutch Reformed Church, the NHK, and the Doppers.

The Dutch Reformed Church is the largest of the three sects with 1.3 to 1.7 million adherents, or about 70 percent of all Afrikaners. Because of its close identification with the government and ruling party since 1948, it is frequently referred to as the National Party at prayer. It shows all the stretch marks and strains of trying to cover the theological and political spectrum. Racial separation within the church dates from the mid-1800s. Until then, it accommodated all races in its congregations. In 1857, the synod, the highest governing body of the church, divided the church into four parts: the white mother church, and the colored, African, and Indian daughter churches.

The late Johan Heyns, an ardent Broeder and former moderator, or top official, of the church, in 1992 quoted from the minutes of that fateful synod: "Although we know that according to Scripture we should be in one church, 'due to the weakness of some of our members,' we allow you to organize different worship services for so-called people of color. They knew that it was wrong, that it was against Scripture. But the weakness eventually became a principle."

The NHK, the second-largest white church, was established in the Transvaal in 1853 in reaction to suspicions that the Cape Dutch Reformed Church was too close to the colonial government. The NHK now claims 225,000 members and is politically and racially the most conservative of the three, forbidding blacks to enter a white church, even for funerals or weddings.

The Dopper church, established in 1859 and now with a mere 120,000 adherents, draws on its mother church in Holland for its theology. The Doppers are the most rigid in social manners, frowning on dancing and limiting church music to the recitation of psalms, and the most Calvinist in theology. Their theology centers on the 1618 Synod of Dort in Holland that produced an orthodox Calvinistic dogma emphasizing predestination—the belief people enter the world either saved or damned. The Doppers follow the teachings of the late-nineteenth-century Dutch theologian and politician Abraham Kuyper of Amsterdam (who became prime minister of the Netherlands). Dopper ministers latched on to conservative aspects of Kuyper's theology and honed their brand of Christianity into an exclusionist, antirevolutionary, authoritarian, elitist neo-Calvinism. They believed that all life was divided into "spheres"— politics, culture, religion, home, education—each sphere governed directly by God. The term "own affairs" that was used by the National Party as late as the 1980s—as in each "population group" should control its "own affairs"—comes from Kuyperian thought. The Doppers' influence in apartheid politics has been disproportionate to their numbers, beginning with J. D. du Toit, a translator of the Bible into Afrikaans. According to Dominee Jan van Rooyen, du Toit "gave apartheid feet in the Bible" when he referred in 1944 to God as The Divider.

The theological differences between the three churches hinge on distinctions as small as motes to outsiders, but gigantic to the church members themselves. "The three Afrikaans churches have the same doctrinal creed," explains Professor Elaine Botha of the Potchefstroom University, an expert in Calvinist philosophy. "So emphases and interpretations of either the creed or Scripture would be the distinguishing things. The Dutch Reformed Church is the typical reformed church in Holland but with an influx of Scottish Calvinism and a strong influence of Methodism and pietism. I think the reason the Doppers broke away from the Dutch Reformed Church was because of pietistic and so called Methodistic emphases, such as the hymns." The Doppers sing psalms from the Bible instead of hymns.

"The Dutch Reformed Church also emphasizes strongly that a person could make a choice for the Lord or against the Lord, whereas with the Doppers, the doctrine of the elect is far more emphasized. You have been chosen beforehand. In the [Dutch Reformed] church I belong to, every year we have a series of evangelization services in the church where you have typical Billy Graham hammering of people to become converted, even though they are full-blown members of the church. Now the Doppers would not even think of that. Once you're baptized, you are a member of the church of the Lord, you're part of the Covenant; you've chosen, you don't have to think about it again."

Another difference of emphasis lies in mission work. "The Dutch Reformed Church has always had a very strong emphasis on mission work, going out toward people who are not Christianized," Botha said. "The NHK, which is stronger into the mold of Afrikaner nationalism, has hardly done mission work—they have this exclusive closed-shop mentality. In the Dopper church there have been very strong racist overtones. Not in official documents—they are the most trustworthy and certainly the most balanced scripturally—but outlying [Dopper] churches have very strong racist tendencies. It's very hard for the Doppers to stomach the pious, spiritual types of Christian people. They are extremely down-to-earth, concrete believers."

Common wisdom had it, said Botha, that "If there's a new fad around theologically, the NHK people try it out. The Dutch Reformed people hang in there for about two decades and then they try it out. The Doppers could care less. They just do their own thing." In all three churches, however, "Nationalism is the hidden agenda in our religion. It's always there," Botha said, regretfully.

Nuances of faith were major issues to dominees who carried out theological warfare between the churches. But beyond the religious divide was a power rivalry born of similarity. The former Potchefstroom (now University of the Witwatersrand) law professor Johan van der Vyver said, "When churches are close to one another, then they really hate each other. There is a kind of excessive competition and therefore also disliking each other and trying to do each other in. It was very strong between the three Dutch Reformed churches. I can tell you long stories of how appointments of school principals and teachers are influenced by the church committees." Each church sought to stack local committees in its own favor, aiming to control the messages received by the *volk*.

At the national level too, the interchurch rivalries had political manifestations. Until the election of 1989, van der Vyver said, "I always said that F. W. de Klerk had no chance of becoming state president because he's of the wrong church." He's a Dopper. Van der Vyver strongly believed, moreover, that the fall of the Vorster government in the 1978 Information Scandal was engineered by Dutch Reformed Church politicians who sought to sabotage the succession of Vorster's heir-apparent, Information Minister Connie Mulder, because Mulder was a Dopper.

The historical revisionists showed that Afrikaner racial purity was also a myth, as was the idea that the Afrikaners had always sought ethnic separation as a consequence of God's injunction to retain diversity. "Race consciousness came with the Englishman," editor and journalist Piet Muller insisted, and it eventually resulted in the splitting off of the colored, black, and Indian churches from the main Dutch Reformed Church.

The Dutch Reformed Church was not originally segregated. "Early church registers say things like 'so-and-so married to so-and-so *van die Kaap*'" ['of the Cape,' which meant colored], Muller said. "It took three years for the Dutch East India Company fleet to go from Amsterdam to Java. Would you leave your job, go back to Holland, another three years, scout for a wife, come back for another three years, and settle again? You wouldn't. The Dutch weren't bothered about it. The black women were baptized, that was okay.

"A professor in Amsterdam said he is sure that lots of the founding mothers of Afrikanerdom with their Dutch-sounding names were actually Eurasians," Muller said. "If you think, at that stage, when Europeans for the first time met Chinese, Europeans still believed bathing is very bad for your health. They still had bloodletting, while the Chinese bathed every day, they had pulse diagnosis. And the Chinese are such wonderfully open people, I mean, they wouldn't mind at all, the Chinese could just, they could absorb anything. And they were married.

"The family who produced most of the heroic figures of Afrikaner history came from a black man and a black woman," Muller said. "That was Jan van Bengal, the father, and I think Elizabeth van die Kaap was the mother. She was a slave from West Africa. They had a couple of daughters. Those daughters married off to various families. They became the direct ancestors. All the Bothas, all the Potgieters, you know Hendrik Potgieter, the famous Voortrekker leader, even the famous Boer general, General de la Rey, was from that stock. Paul Kruger is from that stock. And even the Free State president, Martinus Steyn, is from mixed stock. At the beginning women were in very short supply. The slave quarters in Cape Town were first used as a brothel but then as a marriage bureau."

Hans Heese, a genealogist at the University of the Western Cape, got into trouble in the 1980s when he published articles continuing his father's work, articles that documented the mixed parentage of hundreds of Afrikaner families. He was harassed and threatened with lawsuits and violence, but his archival evidence irrefutably bore out his claims.

As the early Broederbond leaders developed their political agendas, they turned to Dutch Reformed ministers to devise theological justifications for apartheid. The cardinal biblical text used to support apartheid is the story of the tower of Babel from Genesis 11:1–9. The exegesis goes like this: God's destruction of the tower that men were building to reach heaven shows that God was angry that mankind wanted to speak one language, defying an implicit command to maintain "diversity" (Genesis 1:28). God struck mankind down and divided it into different *volk* speaking diverse languages. Punishment wasn't the point. God did not want the nations of man to seek unity, much less achieve it.

Dominee Johan Heyns elaborated the apartheid theology as he and his colleagues had preached it for years, and as his antagonist Dominee Willie Lubbe still preached it. Lubbe broke away from the Dutch Reformed Church in 1987.

"God was Yaweh HaMabdil, that is the Hebrew for God the Big Divider," Heyns said. "He made divisions in creation, created different animals, different plants, different people. Therefore the division between whites and blacks was to be accepted as God's will. It was our God-given calling to keep our blood pure.

"Apartheid was legally enforced diversity," Heyns said. "In 1948 my church had a synod here in Pretoria where a first report was adopted which justified apartheid on biblical grounds. So it was very easy for candidates for Parliament to go to their constituencies and say, 'Look, even the church said that apartheid is correct, therefore you must vote for us.' "

That synod met in April. A month later the National Party was elected to power. Over the next ten years the party organized and institutionalized apartheid. Adding to the theological justifications, Afrikaner academics were called on to develop its scholarly underpinnings. The anthropologist W. W. M. Eiselen wrote a report on Bantu Education in 1948 that used social-science language to support the tribal bantustan or homeland policy.

A student of Eiselen's, P. J. Coertze, worked closely with Dutch Reformed Church policy-making bodies. He published his work almost exclusively in theological journals. His "ethnos theory," claiming that mankind can survive and lead a happy life only inside ethnic units, became orthodoxy within Afrikaans universities and in the churches.

Dopper Kuyperians initially dominated the Broederbond, and their justifications for Afrikaner exclusivity were adopted by the drafters of legal apartheid. After World War II Dopper influence waned because so many of them had belonged to the discredited pro-Nazi Ossewabrandwag (Ox Wagon Brigade). Nevertheless, their idea of Christian National Education, institutionalized in the 1930s at a teachers' training institute in Potchefstroom, held sway under the aegis of the Broederbond.

As nation worshippers, the Christian Nationalists had been drawn to nazism and fascism, but apartheid differed from those political ideologies in its religious base. The neo-Calvinist Afrikaners would not accept subordination of church to state as happened in Germany. Rather the state and churches were run by essentially the same people. The leaders self-consciously used theology to justify government actions. The prime minister most revered by right-wingers, Hendrik Verwoerd, "cynically made use of religion," according to Dominee Willem Saayman. "Verwoerd, the grand architect of apartheid, which was supposed to be God's will, was a totally secularized man. He was actually himself an unbeliever."

Dominee Jan van Rooyen said, "Verwoerd invoked the name of God continuously. Well, the same was done by Hitler. And Professor Cronjé [quoted at the start of this section], I do know that he never visited church. The same with Nico Diederichs [a main architect of apartheid and a vice-chairman of the Broederbond]. He was a member of a parish that I served in. People told me that he never ever set his foot in a church. But he always referred to God's will in apartheid."

Most right-wing Afrikaners—well over 850,000, to judge by voting patterns in 1994—still held these beliefs even as the system crumbled. When in 1986, with Moderator Johan Heyns at the helm, the church issued the "Church and Society" document, which argued that apartheid was not a Biblical imperative, the conservatives protested vigorously.

Dutch Reformed Church dominee Willie Lubbe believed so strongly in the old ways that in 1987 he led a schism and formed an altogether new church called the Afrikaanse Protestante Kerk (APK). A large group of dominees and congregants joined the new church. A dour man, an Afrikaner Gothic mimicking an Old Testament patriarch, Lubbe sat rigid as the smell of creosote and wearing a macadam-colored suit, in his office at the APK's theological seminary in Pretoria. He intoned: "It was always the belief of the Afrikaner people, they firmly believed in this principle, diversity, derived from biblical convictions.

"In God's nature you see a great diversity. You see it amongst plants, animals, people. If you go to the Kruger National Park where you see the animals walking and grazing, you will never see them integrating. You've got the springbok, you've got the impala, you've got the kudu, they're always on their own. They're always separate."

Lubbe's congregations must have found solace in the repetition: they'd heard this all their lives; they wanted to keep hearing it. "Now the diversity of God's creation and of people is written in Scriptures. You can't deny it, you can't ignore it. Ja, for instance Deuteronomy 32:8 and in the Acts of Paul 17:26, where it exactly says God has ordained differ-ent peoples and countries."

When Dominee Lubbe said "you can't deny" diversity, it was clear that to him anyone who disagreed was a fool. For him the Afrikaners' covenant with God was alive, if not well. It was threatened, in his view, by dangerous liberals such as F. W. de Klerk and former Dutch Reformed Church moderator and Pretoria University theology profes-sor Heyns. ("I was too liberal for many of my dominees," Johan Heyns said, smiling. The sentence resembled the title of the popular song "I'm Too Sexy for My Shirt.")

"The rot, the liberal rot, I'm sorry to call it that, but the liberal rot started in the theological schools," Dominee Lubbe said.

He made it sound as if this stuff would pollute even a garbage dump.

"The idea that you can't support separate development biblically, that is evidence of the liberal rot," Lubbe said. "Sowing the seeds of skepticism."

One thing Lubbe didn't like was liberals. With his Afrikaans accent, he pronounced the word "luberal," so it seemed as clumsy as a sea lion out of water. As used by the right wing, it was essentially synonymous with "unbeliever." Liberals, by definition, were un-Christian, unbiblical, humanist, even Communist—labels flung around even by the National Party into the nineties. "Liberal" covered many issues, such as abortion, homosexuality, living in cities, most TV programs, rock and roll music apart from the tame Afrikaans versions, feminism, integration.

Nationalist Afrikaners grew up viewing "liberal" as such a swearword that they would shrink in horror at being tarred with the liberal brush. In 1966, when the newspaper editor Wimpie de Klerk, the elder brother of F. W., wanted to categorize and encourage those like himself who believed that apartheid had to be eased, he couldn't use "liberal." He invented a new word. *Verligte* was translated as "enlightened." Those who opposed change he called *verkrampte*, meaning cramped, stiff, or rigid. Especially for the *verkrampte*, religion and politics formed a seam-less web.

Manie van Heerden, owner of the Shirt Bar, a men's haberdashery in a Johannesburg suburb, is so *verkrampt* you could plow with him. Proud to have been a founding member of the Conservative Party in 1982, he holds the old dogmas dear, expounding them in the upstairs back room of his shop amid the smell of bolts of fine wool used to make tailored suits. He detests F. W. de Klerk's politics and believes God's will requires a separation of the races.

"I was never taught that we were *the* chosen race," he said. "But we were taught that we were possibly *a* chosen race. A chosen race in the sense not that we could make demands on special treatment by God, but in the sense that we were planted here with a specific purpose, an *opdrag*, an instruction. That instruction obviously was to make Christians of the black people."

Isn't that still the Dutch Reformed Church's purpose?

"I'm sure that they would say that, but they also now say that the church has to function as a unitary organization [with other races]. I believe differently." Van Heerden had switched to the NHK at the same time he quit the National Party and helped to found the CP.

Van Heerden had a precise understanding of God's will, and thus also knew when people were un-Christian. "Mass action is out," he said, referring to ANC civil disobedience tactics that included strikes, boycotts, and marches to show the ruling whites just how dependent they were on black economic clout and cooperation. "You can't give that freedom to everybody that wants to disagree with a government, to resort to mass action. It's un-Christian. It's not furthering the ends of the people that they so-called 'want to help,' the poor. It's actually having a devastating effect on their lives. They're losing their jobs. There's no investment coming into the country because of that."

What makes it un-Christian?

"You take the food from people's mouths and the family's mouths, I think it's un-Christian. Or don't you?" he said nastily.

Isn't it a political strategy? To say that it was Christian or un-Christian is dragging in the Bible inappropriately. What is the connection with Christ?

"I think you better fly back to America," he slashed out. "I think then you must keep out of South Africa and you should stop writing about South Africa."

If Nelson Mandela came to power, van Heerden said he would obey the authority of the day because the Bible commands obedience to government. Still, it would come to no good. He believes that blacks are "more violent people than you get anywhere else in the world, when they're in crowds, in masses." Crowd-control methods that include using live ammunition are appropriate, in his opinion, "because these people don't have First World, Western, Christian type of standards."

Is there other proof of their un-Christian standards?

"Yes. Yes. I've seen how they maltreat their children."

By 1992, even Afrikaners who insisted apartheid had many good elements often conceded that the Influx Control (pass) laws, which strictly regulated the movements of blacks, were unfair. Other Afrikaners, such as Professor Elaine Botha, were appalled at how ignorant and credulous Afrikaners, including herself, had been, believing in the goodness, the Christian nature of their laws and leaders.

"I'm sometimes amazed, even now after these many years, how much apartheid is still stuck in me," she said. "There's this TV series now [1992] called *Konings* [*Kings*] and in it is a certain little scene set in the early fifties, the time that I was a young person. A black woman is living in the back room [servants' quarters] and the black man comes to visit her, stays over for the night. The kids in the household notice this and go get the father. He takes a whip and goes out and hammers the black man, says, 'You're not allowed to sleep with this woman.' The black woman is standing there in her underwear. I see it and suddenly I remember how many times this happened in our household. We sincerely believed black men were not supposed to be sleeping with black women in white areas and they ought not to be there. My dad would hammer the guy and chase him out—my dad was a policeman. It never crossed my mind, even as a Christian, that that was wrong.

"Now you would think such a person would be crazy. When I saw this on TV a couple weeks ago, I thought, God help, you know how your eyes can be closed with ideology. There was a law that said men shouldn't be staying with their women. You were obeying the law. Terrible. I think gradually people are coming to see this."

She paused, deeply anguished. Then she asked a question. Was it asked of herself? Of God? Of her conscience?

"But how do you make amends?" she said.

CHAPTER EIGHTEEN

OSTRACISM OF A *VOLKS VERRAAIER* (TRAITOR)

C. F. Beyers Naudé, O most reviled and O best beloved. Your wide smiley mouth stretches like a rubber band. Your silvery hair is slicked back like a fifties crooner's. You liberated yourself from "group think" and saved the name of Afrikaners from total ignominy among blacks. O avuncular oracle, you drove the Broederbond batty.

Famous in international church circles, Beyers Naudé is infamous among the *volk*, for years the most publicly invisible of all Afrikaners. In the 1960s the Broederbond waved its propaganda wand over him and transformed him from an Afrikaner prince into a liberal frog, or worse: a traitor, a *volks verraaier*.

Naudé began life in 1915 with a sterling Boer pedigree. His father, Jozua, was one of only six out of sixty Boer leaders who voted to continue the Anglo-Boer War rather than capitulate to the British. Jozua named his son after his friend and hero, the Boer general Christiaan Frederik Beyers. One of the first ministers to preach in Afrikaans instead of Dutch, which caused a split in his congregation, Jozua was elected the first president of the Broederbond in 1918. Beyers followed his father to become a dominee and a Broeder; he was praised for his clear, elegant sermons and loved for his compassion. Elevated to moderator of the Southern Transvaal synod of the white Dutch Reformed Church, Beyers Naudé was set to become national moderator. But he deviated from that path when he found that the price of power was conformity with the apartheid creed.

Naudé didn't move precipitously. As his doubts about apartheid accumulated, he challenged leading Afrikaner theologians to convince him that apartheid could be biblically justified. He found their reasoning unpersuasive. There were others who agreed with him but they wouldn't go public because they accurately understood that, as Naudé later recalled their words, " 'we would be totally rejected by our people.' "

Naudé's apostasy bloomed during the 1960 Cottesloe conference, which was called by the World Council of Churches after sixty-eight demonstrating Africans were shot dead by police in Sharpeville while protesting the apartheid pass laws. The Anglican archbishop of Cape Town condemned the apartheid-supporting Dutch Reformed Church and demanded its expulsion from the World Council of Churches. Trying to mediate the dispute, the WCC helped arrange an interracial and ecumenical "consultation," which met in the Johannesburg suburb of Cottesloe in December 1960. As one of the Dutch Reformed Church's representatives who came from the heart of Afrikaner nationalism, Naudé found the discussions with ministers of other faiths extremely enlightening.

The final Cottesloe declaration argued that people should have equal rights regardless of race, that Scripture did not prohibit racially mixed marriages, and that land ownership, jobs, and participation in government should be available to all people.

Naudé and his Dutch Reformed Church colleagues supported the declaration but argued that it did not contradict the government's apartheid policy, hoping that that tactic would prevent outright rejection of the declaration by their church synods.

Prime Minister Hendrik Verwoerd went ballistic. He knew that if the declaration were adopted by synods of the Dutch Reformed churches, apartheid was doomed. Rousing the dominees to denounce Cottesloe, Verwoerd portrayed it as coercion of the Afrikaners from the outside. The faithful scuttled for cover.

Dominee Jan van Rooyen recalled: "At that stage the Afrikaans church leaders [who represented the church at Cottesloe] were people of integrity, rocks in our society, people you could look up to. They were absolutely ostracized. Verwoerd, in his New Year's message in 1961, started the whole thing. He said, 'You must remember that Cottesloe is only the opinion of a few.' He didn't say unreliable people, but it boiled down to that. Treacherous people. I sort of signed my own death sentence by signing it [the Cottesloe declaration]. We were all marked, the people who felt sympathy or showed they understood something about Cottesloe."

Cottesloe convinced Naudé that more contact between churches and races was needed in South Africa. In May 1962 he founded a religious newspaper called *Pro Veritate* (*For Truth*) as an alternative to the Dutch Reformed Church's *Die Kerkbode* (*The Church Foundation*).

On August 1, 1962, the Broederbond issued a circular instructing church members to oppose "onslaughts against our continued existence as an independent Christian-National Western Community in South

Africa." Two months later a circular stressed that the churches needed to suppress dissident voices.

Naudé aimed to develop an ongoing interracial, ecumenical movement, and in August 1963 he and a few colleagues launched the Christian Institute. Its purpose was to bring together black and white Christians of various denominations to "seek Christian unity and be concerned about the Christian concept of social justice."

Disturbed by Naudé's activities, the Dutch Reformed Church leadership gave him a choice: if he gave up *Pro Veritate* and resigned from leadership of the Institute, he would ascend to the top of the church. If he continued his dangerously idiosyncratic path, he'd be driven out. Naudé tried to persuade the hierarchy to let him stay in the ministry and head the Christian Institute, but they wouldn't budge. They defrocked him. Convinced that the church based its policies on Broederbond power calculations rather than on Scripture, Naudé then resigned from the Broederbond. He was the highest Broeder ever to renounce the organization, declaring it immoral for a Christian minister to belong.

After Naudé was forced from the ministry, he and his family joined the Dutch Reformed Church congregation in the Johannesburg suburb of Parkhurst, where Jan van Rooyen was the minister.

"There were only three families from the Parkhurst congregation who would have any contact with us, nobody else wanted to," Naudé recalled. "I don't blame them. I feel sad for them. But I understand why.

"On occasion when I met church ministers or members of the congregation and I wanted to greet them, they turned their backs on me. Or they made as if they didn't see me. That was hard in the beginning." Naudé realized that change was going to take much longer than he thought.

"Then there was the way our children, especially Liesel, were treated at school by some of the teachers. She suffered very, very seriously. I mean the emotional scars which this left. It took her many, many years before she could recover from that. You know when your own child is affected, perhaps you feel it deepest.

"Two motorcars were burned you know. Quite a number of times our house was attacked, and they smashed the window and so on." Threatening and abusive anonymous phone calls were so frequent that the children had instructions not to answer the phone when their parents were out.

The few men who stood up with Naudé did so at the risk of their careers. The dominees Willie Jonker and Jan van Rooyen were two of the victims.

Dominee Jan van Rooyen's Parkhurst congregation eventually chose Naudé as an elder, which made him eligible for election to synods. Although the congregation did elect him, church authorities voided that vote to prevent Naudé from ever holding any leadership position. Van Rooyen supported Naudé, arguing that criticism of government policy was not an offense against the church. (Later he thought Naudé went too far in calling for sanctions against South Africa.) Because of his position on Naudé and his own statements and actions condemning apartheid, van Rooyen was isolated in the church and attacked in the press, and his family too became the target of threatening phone calls and harassment.

Dominee Willie Jonker and Naudé had become friends at the University of Pretoria in the early fifties when Naudé was the students' pastor. While still a Broederbond member, Naudé advised Jonker to join the organization, but Jonker demurred. Later, as a synod official, Jonker had to handle Naudé's request to remain a minister while heading the Christian Institute. He favored the request on the basis of precedent. Dominees, especially missionaries in tribal homelands, were serving in many nonecclesiastical jobs. When Naudé's request was denied, Jonker advised an appeal. Naudé appealed but was rejected again.

As chairman of the church circuit that included van Rooyen's congregation, Jonker also had to deal with complaints against Naudé's election as an elder. "I took the position that this man had done nothing that disqualified him to become an elder," Jonker said. But he lost that argument too. "Everything that I did was against the dynamics of group coherence," he said. His support of Naudé precluded him from advancement in the church hierarchy. "In the end I just couldn't bear it physically and psychologically. I was involved in the inner workings of the church and I knew I was unwanted. It was really very, very difficult for me, because as long as you are in the inner scrum [as on a rugby team], it's okay. [Outside] you know you are very, very lonely.

"I've always had a great admiration for Beyers Naudé, that he just carried on. I think he must be a very strong man, because he just went on."

Naudé's condemnation of the church was a mighty thunderclap, his resignation from the Broederbond a stunning deviation from the ways of the *volk*. When the Security Police found that he was the source of secret Broederbond documents published as exposés in the *Sunday Times* newspaper, the Broeders retaliated by smearing him as a traitor. He'd violated the Broederbond's secrecy code.

In early 1963 Naudé had lent the documents to his friend University of Pretoria Professor Albert Geyser, not expecting them to become public. Geyser, who was accused of heresy by the NHK hierarchy and defrocked, was convinced that the Broederbond had orchestrated the charges, and was looking for evidence of the organization's control of Afrikaans churches to take his case to the Supreme Court in Pretoria. (He eventually reached an out-of-court settlement with the NHK.) Geyser photographed the documents, returned them to Naudé, and passed copies to journalist Charles Bloomberg. Security police agents followed Bloomberg to Israel and, sitting next to him in a bar, heard him give Naudé's name as the source of the documents, according to Braam Viljoen. Naudé apologized publicly for the leak, but the Broederbond sought revenge, hoping by example to intimidate potential dissidents.

Still, Naudé wouldn't keep quiet. He kept speaking in that very level, loving, firm, mellow voice. He was judicious, careful, and kind, entirely unlike the Broederbond-controlled media image of him as a rabidly radical liberal, which in the Afrikaner context meant Communist. A small number of sympathetic Afrikaners initially supported the Christian Institute, but after the Broederbond revelations, most dribbled away.

Throughout the sixties Naudé continued to lead the Institute into uncharted waters. It held interracial church meetings, helped independent African churches to develop their Bible knowledge and teaching, and in the 1970s provided sympathy and support for Steve Biko and the burgeoning Black Consciousness movement. *Pro Veritate*, which became de facto the Institute's paper, brought liberation theology to South Africa. When police guns crackled across Soweto in 1976, the Institute was almost the only bridge from the white to the black community.

As protests, killings, detentions, and torture raged across the land in 1977, the Christian Institute, with its two hundred or so members and with overseas funding, scrambled to help blacks in their fight and to explain to the outside world what was happening. Finally, on October 19, 1977, the government pounced, closing the Institute; it outlawed it, along with Black Consciousness organizations, banned Beyers Naudé, and banned, detained, and arrested many other individuals.

Under the government's security legislation, a banned person could not be quoted in the media or meet with more than one person at a time. To most South African whites a banned person seemed untouchable or contagious. After he was banned, Naudé was careful not to speak to, and thus taint, Afrikaners who were trying to work for change within the system. "That was also misunderstood, because then some Afrikaners felt I didn't want to approach them," Naudé said. "I wanted to. There were so many times. The burning longing in my heart."

To talk to Naudé when he was banned, a person arrived at his modest Greenside home in Johannesburg, was greeted by his long-suffering wife, Ilse, and had to wait, while two people murmured in the next room. Beyers was talking to someone else. When that person was ushered out, the next was shown in alone. Not even Ilse could be present. One of his friends recalled how, when he wanted to see Beyers along with other friends, they had to play "cowboys and crooks and absolutely stupid schoolboy games in order to meet each other." It was mighty strange, especially because Beyers Naudé's manner was so calm, so clear. He was supposed to be evil and dangerous! It made the government look crazed. Naudé talked to an endless stream of people, including foreigners and a few brave Afrikaners.

He made his silence speak, and his opposition to apartheid deepened. Appalled when the white Dutch Reformed Church national synod voted 202 to 6 against uniting into one multiracial church in 1978, Naudé said he could no longer remain a member with a clear conscience. "How could the church reject the fruits of its own mission?" In 1980 he joined the African Dutch Reformed Church, attended services in the township of Alexandra, and in 1987 became a minister there. For apartheid's opponents, banning was a badge of courage.

"Surely Beyers Naudé must have shaken the moral grounds of the Afrikaners, of the church," said the sociologist H. W. van der Merwe, who himself had played an active role in undermining apartheid. "There was little public acknowledgment of his role, but surely in the inner circles there was great discomfort and some realization that things are wrong. I would say he is one of the great men of our time."

In 1970 van der Merwe conducted a study of Afrikaner elites, including about thirty top Dutch Reformed Church leaders. "The vast majority of those thirty people all expressed admiration for Beyers Naudé," he said. "But they never did it in public. Their position was that the time was not ripe for taking such a stand. I have always argued that if those thirty people, and of course there are many more, had come out in public at the time, in support of Beyers Naudé, they would have reformed the whole church. They failed to stand up and be counted. If they had, they would have made the time ripe."

But the insider syndrome prevailed throughout Afrikaner society; the notion was that it was better to work gradually for change inside the system.

"We were not prepared to do a Beyers Naudé," said Jan Lombard, former deputy governor of the South African Reserve Bank. "Beyers Naudé went whole hog, you know. He became a complete rebel. He refused to obey the laws, got himself arrested."

What laws did he break?

"I'm not sure what laws he broke, but he certainly did break some, because he was, must have lived in a Bantu area or something."

But Naudé wasn't banned or arrested for breaking laws, and he never lived in a "Bantu" area. He was banned because the government decided that the Christian Institute was subversive. And he was briefly jailed because he refused to give evidence to secret hearings of a government commission empaneled to investigate possibly subversive organizations.

Lombard believes Naudé had little effect on the Afrikaner community.

"Not on the government, not on the establishment," Lombard said. "Because the establishment excommunicated him. But on individuals. Some of the clergymen who knew him very well retained respect for him. He made them wonder, you know, what's going on."

Vilifying Naudé for rejecting his own people, the Broederbond's condemnation stuck. Annemarie Nutt, head of the Afrikaans women's organization Kontak, still mouthed the traditional Broederbond accusations in 1992. Her attitude typified that of thousands of very proper, obedient, churchgoing Afrikaners.

"People felt Beyers was not very ethical because he did certain things. It's the fact he made a promise which he broke," she said in reference to breaking the Broederbond oath of secrecy. Somehow that made her suspect the rest of what he stood for.

Despite the Broederbond's thirty-year record of vilifying Naudé, Broederbond head Piet de Lange said in 1992, "We never punished Beyers Naudé. He forced himself out of the Broederbond."

Some of the insider Afrikaners who inched toward Naudé's political stance still resented him. In 1992, Dominee Johan Heyns, the man often credited with nudging the church to admit that apartheid was a sin, still saw Naudé as a traitor. To Heyns, Naudé "made one great mistake, and that is he sided with the blacks to the extent that he couldn't act as an agent of reconciliation. We live on our own little island, Beyers Naudé left that island. And therefore we consider him to be a traitor."

Was Naudé's mistake tactical, or is there something morally wrong with his position?

"I won't say it's morally wrong, I would say it's a mistake in tactics," Heyns said. "I'm not saying that Bey Naudé was not a prophet. I would say he wasn't a very effective prophet." He should have worked within the system.

Another top Afrikaner in the system, F. W.'s brother Wimpie de Klerk, praised Naudé in retrospect. "He was really a very beloved preacher. Personally, Beyers Naudé is one of my heroes. When he broke away, I was very upset about it."

The two men lived in the Johannesburg suburb of Greenside, and gradually started talking to each other when they met on the street. Eventually Wimpie de Klerk campaigned in *Die Transvaler* to lift Naudé's banning orders.

Naudé was "the conscience of the ANC," Wimpie de Klerk said. But even in his praise he still rejected Naudé as a voice speaking to the Afrikaners. *Verligte* power-mongers thought *they* should be the conscience of the Afrikaners.

There was higher praise from Afrikaners not in the "inner scrum." Elaine Botha, professor of philosophy at Potchefstroom University, saw Naudé as an example for Afrikaners.

"That is such a painful thing, Beyers Naudé," she said. "He was minister here [in Potchefstroom] in the Dutch Reformed Church at the time that I was a student. Beautiful minister, excellent sermons. [After Cottesloe] the majority of us were scared to be in any contact with him. I always felt such a damn heel, you know. I would meet up with him at times at meetings, and I'd feel so dreadful because I always admired him and loved him as a pastor and thought that he was an excellent person.

"I think he was very prophetic in a very unpretentious and untheoretical way. He had a very deep sense there was injustice going on and that as Christians something had to be done. That, coupled with his courage to break away from the Broederbond, maybe that was the crucial thing, made him a very pivotal person in the changes that took place."

But how could he be pivotal? People claimed that once ostracized he had no clout with Afrikaners. Elaine Botha disagreed.

"He was always there sticking out like a sore thumb, like a thorn that you stepped on. You know he was always there, not allowed to be quoted. It made him a stumbling block for everybody around him, which meant they had to go in a different direction. He was just bloody well *there* all the time. I can remember having Dutch friends over, everybody who ever visited with me wanted to go and visit with Beyers Naudé. Then I had to arrange this. I found it so embarrassing, I'd speak to him on the phone and I'd know the phone would be tapped, and I would feel so horrible because I was actually not wanting to go there. I was just basically hypocritical because I didn't have the courage to associate with him."

Did that mean she thought he was right?

"Ja, I think I had the sinking feeling he was right."

Martin Trümpelmann, professor of education at the conservative Rand Afrikaans University, quit the Broederbond after several years of membership, having decided that "any form of secrecy is to me in any society a very dangerous thing." He admires Naudé tremendously. "You see, they don't want to acknowledge that he's the savior of the Afrikaner's image. They will do it forty or fifty years hence. Because I believe when the ANC takes over, far more Afrikaner atrocities will be exposed, and then we will need somebody who says no, it's not all Afrikaners. I believe at that stage Beyers Naudé will become a hero."

The full story of Beyers Naudé's activities in opposition to apartheid has yet to be told, says the journalist Jacques Pauw. Pauw shot to fame writing for the dissident Afrikaans newspaper *Vrye Weekblad*, digging up stories of blood-curdling security force misdeeds. The facts were widely known within the "inner scrum," but until Pauw and *Vrye Weekblad*, they were never put into print.

"I only met Beyers after we started the newspaper [in 1988]," Pauw said. "When we eventually took [ex-death-squad policeman Dirk] Coetzee out of the country [to protect him from being killed], November '89, it was also the State of Emergency and it was highly illegal to assist or to advise the ANC. I only found out afterwards that he [Naudé] played a major role in providing finances or whatever for Coetzee to leave the country. We worked through a regional director of IDASA in Pretoria, André Snyman. It was only afterwards that I discovered that he again worked with Beyers Naudé. So he's always played a major role in underground resistance. I think more so than most people realize."

Even when Nelson Mandela was released from prison in 1990 and liberation organizations were unbanned, Naudé declined political party membership and returned to work in the African Dutch Reformed Church, renamed the United Reformed Church of Southern Africa. He continued his efforts to unite the races in one church. One day in 1992, traffic noise seeped through the poorly insulated window of his modest office on the seventh floor of Auckland House in the Johannesburg suburb Braamfontein. A red cross woven into a heavy tapestry hung on one wall, a certificate and some prize and a group photograph inscribed with love on another. He'd just been visited in his Ecumenical Advice office by two hulking young blond dominees from the Free State town of Welkom. They wanted to find out the facts about the South African Council of Churches, about the ANC, about the man-myth, Beyers Naudé.

"Why am I doing this? I've asked myself many times," Naudé mused. His cheeks were rosy.

"You know, at my age, because I'm seventy-seven, and I would love normally rather to sit at home, enjoy life a little bit with my wife. We have very little time with one another. And in that sense I feel guilty toward Ilse. But in this crisis situation, I find it very difficult to stay at home. If I go to Alexandra, as I was there again yesterday, the poverty, the tension, the conflict, the unemployment—how can I go home, have a nice meal and sit down? I just can't do it."

Recalling his departure from the Broederbond fold in the sixties, Naudé said, "I gave them such a fright, you know."

His laugh was merry and sweet. Soaring.

" 'Look what happened to Beyers,' how many thousands of Afrikaners have said that? 'Kyk wat met hom gebeur het [Look what happened to him],' " he imitated them. "I say, 'Yes, kyk wat met my gebeur het [look what happened to me], please. Look at me. In comparison to you, well I'm a poor person, but that's no worry to me. I'm a free person. I've got a freedom towards not only people of my own church and my own denomination and my own religion but also a freedom with regard to people of other religions.' You've got a liberty to be open to other people."

In October 1994, the Dutch Reformed Church apologized to three of its most famous dominees who rejected apartheid: Ben Marais, Beyers Naudé, and the late Professor Ben Keet of Stellenbosch. Marais and Naudé had lived long enough to hear the motion that was passed almost unanimously by the synod that said the church had disregarded their prophetic witness.

Naudé and his wife, Ilse, received the apology in Pretoria together and Naudé said it was a "wonderful moment. . . . There is no doubt that there is a new spirit in the synod which reflects a new spirit in the church."

O Beyers Naudé, true subversive, you saved people's lives. You helped smuggle some to safety, cured sick souls, aggravated complaisant whites. An Afrikaner willing to absorb abuse from your *volk*, you represent the best in your people. Alchemist turning the nasty in human nature to nectar, for that you were a man reviled and revered.

CHAPTER NINETEEN

CONFIDENTIALLY, THE BROEDERBOND RUNS THE CHURCH

Afrikaner society is chockablock with dominees. For the Afrikaners who in midcentury were making the transition from a rural peasantry to an educated elite, the ministry looked clean, learned, and powerful as a career and a calling. Mothers and fathers could be proud of dominee sons in a way they couldn't admire men of the material world. The allure of the ministry was enhanced by the churchman's prestige, his influence among his *volk*, and the good chance of becoming a Broederbond member.

Johan Heyns was born in 1928, ordained in the Dutch Reformed Church in 1954, and joined the Broederbond in the early 1960s. He rose in both organizations, becoming moderator of the Dutch Reformed Church in 1986 and serving as a vice chairman of the Broederbond. He was one of many dominees who have been on the Broederbond's executive committee. The church has always been well represented at the top of the organization—or perhaps it's the other way around. It goes back to Dominee Jozua Naudé, Beyers's father. Two dominees were recent chairmen of the Broederbond, Carel Boshoff and Andries Treurnicht. In 1982 about 60 percent of all Dutch Reformed dominees were Broederbonders.

Heyns put on his smile that did not curve at all, so straight across it was, as he posed for a photograph in his cinnamon-colored leather chair in 1992. He sat self-referentially beneath a large photo of himself sitting in the same chair in the same pose in his same office with his same smile. Books on shelves were plastered over one wall, sumptuous to bibliophiles.

"We have in our church warned our people against joining the Freemasonry because of its secrecy," Heyns said. The Freemasons, an international secret organization dating from the Middle Ages that originated in England and Scotland is thought by many Afrikaners to be part of the conspiracy by which the British controlled South Africa. "We even closed the office of deacon and elder to everyone who belongs to the Freemasonry."

Why doesn't the proscription against secrecy also apply to Broeder-bond membership?

"Ja, ja," he said. "That's a very good question. It didn't come up."

Give him credit for his gall. The issue had come up many times, and Heyns was a leading actor in the drama.

Journalist Max du Preez used strong terms to describe Heyns: not only that Heyns was a "very strange man" for saying on the record that 90 percent of all women who got raped asked for it, but also that "he's a very dishonest man. Ask Hennie Serfontein about that."

Serfontein, a journalist who wrote for du Preez's *Vrye Weekblad*, was one of the first journalists to write extensively about the Broederbond. His 1982 book, *Apartheid, Change, and the NG Church*, exposes Broederbond control of the Dutch Reformed churches. Serfontein wrote that "members of the Broederbond occupy virtually all the top and key posts" in the Dutch Reformed Church, including top posts in theological faculties at the Afrikaans universities. "A popular notion has always been that the Broederbond dictated to the government, the church, the schools, etc. But that was wrong. Because one cannot dictate to oneself. It co-ordinated the leadership in each sector, taking joint decisions and gave the general or specific directives of a line to be followed."

The single most insistent criticism of the Broederbond by Afrikaners has been the issue of church ministers belonging to a secret (*vertroulike*, confidential) organization. In his book, Serfontein details a series of attempts by churchmen to bring the Dutch Reformed Church hierarchy to prohibit membership in secret organizations, and efforts to initiate objective investigations into the Broederbond's grip on the church. One such attempt in 1979 was neutralized when Johan Heyns, from his position as chairman of the Church's Commission for Doctrine and Current Affairs, successfully opposed an investigation proposal. Instead, he successfully pushed the synod to ask the executive of the Broederbond (on which he served) to consider abandoning its secrecy policy, and gained a statement from the synod in which it assured its members that those in the Broederbond were not participating in an organization which "holds any dangers to the church with regards to discharging its basic tasks."

Long before Heyns got into the business of defending the Broederbond and leading the church, dominees and eminent theology professors were warning that a Christian church should not support apartheid and should operate in the sunshine.

Professor Ben Marais said that even as a student at Stellenbosch in

1934 he worried "that nationalism was becoming an alternative religion to many of our people." He also knew that from the moment in 1948 when he spoke up against apartheid, any hope for promotion in the church was doomed. "I served on very few church commissions through my whole career."

In 1955 Marais led the charge against the Broederbond in the Dutch Reformed Church. "In 1955 we had a great debate in our synod about Freemasonry," he recalled. "The report on Freemasonry, put out by Dr. [Koot] Vorster, who was moderator of the Cape Church and Prime Minister Vorster's brother, condemned Freemasonry in the most violent terms. They listed four main objections. The second one was its secrecy.

"As I sat in the synod, four or five men spoke violently against the Freemasons' sinister organization and about its secrecy. I suddenly realized that these men were the leaders of the Broederbond in the church. I got up and I said, 'As Christians we believe in the brotherhood of believers. The moment you bring in a thing like the Broederbond, you create a smaller, inner circle, a secret circle within the broader brotherhood. To me it is wrong.'

"I said I hadn't intended to speak on this thing, 'but now I want to make a proposal, that the church decide that no member of the church may belong to any organization that has a basis of secrecy,' or the Afrikaans word *vertroulik*. Confidential.

"Whoa! Now, the moderator at that time, I knew he would have difficulties with this proposal. So he said, 'Brother, I don't know whether I can accept this proposal, you must give me time to consider the issue.' It was an hour before the synod normally disbanded for the day. So he said, 'Well, I think we'll just disband for the day.'

"The next morning he entered the hall and after the preliminary announcements were made, he said, 'As far as Professor Marais's proposal is concerned, I have decided it is not acceptable.' He didn't give any reason, he just put it to the synod, and by about a three to two majority, his ruling was accepted. So it was off the table.

"Now that night Beyers Naudé came to see me. And Beyers said, 'Ben, you know, I must be honest with you about certain things.' So I said, 'Oh, well, I didn't know you had any secrets.' Then he said, 'You know, last night after that synod meeting was adjourned, there was quick organization among the Broeders.' They met that night to discuss what attitude they should take the next day if the moderator accepted my proposal, how they would counter it. And then he told me what people said in that meeting, how Ben Marais must be stopped.

"In all the years that I have been in the church, there was only one moderator who was not a Broederbonder, and he was willing to become a Broeder. His sympathies were with the Broeders, and of course they knew."

If anything succinctly shows that the Broederbond ruled the church, it is Beyers Naudé's story of how he found that the church was being run not by its theology but by the secret organization.

"When I discovered that the theological justification of apartheid could never be biblically in order, I didn't go to the highest theological commission of the church to deal with these problems, I went to members of the Broederbond," Naudé said. "Your deepest loyalty and where the power lies were with the Broederbond, not with the church. For me, a theological problem arose, the whole question of whether one could remain a member in principle of an organization which in principle was secret."

As thick-skinned as a rhino, Heyns served as the country's primary apologist for the Broederbond in the 1980s and '90s. "Ja, I am a member," he said. "I have never ever experienced that as something contradictory to my religious beliefs or my association with the church. I personally believe that the Broederbond has had a tremendous influence as far as the reformation policy is concerned."

Why does he think other people had such strong feelings that one could not belong to a secret organization and be a Christian? They claim that Christians should be open and totally honest.

"What does that mean? To be totally open?" Heyns shot back. "Surely I'm not going to tell you anything about our married life. I'm not going to tell anybody what is going on in the inner circles of our faculty of theology. For the simple reason that every social institution has its, if you like to use that word, secrets."

But the Broederbond has such power over people's lives in the country as to whether or not they get promoted or into certain jobs.

"Okay, just put a full stop there. Is that true?"

There certainly are people who claim it is true.

"Ja, okay, but that is their interpretation. From inside, that isn't and never was true. If people misused their position, that runs contrary to the policy of that organization."

Intentions don't necessarily get carried out. For example, the intention of apartheid, some argue, was never as bad as it turned out.

"What I'm saying is that individuals could have misused it," Heyns vehemently repeated.

*   *   *

Dutch Reformed Church dominee Willem Saayman confronted Broederbond-church power when, as a missionary in Namibia, he told church leaders that Afrikaners were committing terrible crimes. His health broke under their harassment, which included being accused in the press of supporting communism, but he recovered and, after becoming a professor at UNISA, was elected an ANC leader in Pretoria. He said one reason for Afrikaners' authoritarianism was "the whole idea of predestination. God has told you what He wants. He wants you in heaven, [or] He wants you in hell. So I mean, that's it. I mean, hard luck, you can try as hard as you like but nothing is going to change about it."

Saayman describes himself as both a conservative and a radical. He wants to preserve and respect life, which he thinks of as conservative, but he opposed apartheid and the war South Africa waged in Angola and Namibia (previously South West Africa) during the 1970s and '80s, which in his society was a decidedly radical stance. At bottom the Afrikaner ideology fostered a certain split mentality in a religious people.

"Having been a missionary myself, I often thought about this tremendous, so-called tremendous sacrifice, for mission. Giving so much money, so many millions every year. Sending our best sons and daughters, all that whole kind of romantic story." During the last half of the seventies, Saayman, his wife, Cecilia, and his four daughters lived on a remote mission station on the Namibian border with Angola where he was a minister in the Dutch Reformed Church. Elna Trautmann, who grew up in Namibia as the daughter of the missions secretary, Peet Strauss, recalled that "the Saaymans were poor, oooh, were they poor!" But Saayman himself said nothing of that when analyzing the Afrikaners' evangelizing penchant.

"It is this strange thing that you hate black people, but at the same time you want to save their souls," he said. "It's got to do something with keeping them at a distance. Therefore you send missionaries, and you pay a lot of money, but it must remain there, out there. The moment they move in here, and they come too close, 'Uh-uh, that's not what we paid for. No, no, no, no, we paid to keep them separate. They must go to heaven but they must go separately.' It's a strange ambivalence."

He used a recent example: "My sister, who is in the [neo-Nazi] AWB, goes to holiday in Namibia. So she phones me to say, 'What black languages are spoken in Namibia?' because she wants to take Bible tracts along so that she can spread it among the people."

Saayman told a story about his time in Namibia to illustrate how the Broederbond and church operated to demolish opposition. As the war in Namibia and Angola escalated in the late seventies, he said, "I heard now firsthand of the atrocities committed by the South African soldiers. It's no longer just a story, you know, spread by the United Nations or by the World Council of Churches. It's my own trusted church members or my own beloved students who come and tell me, this and this happened, and show me the proof."

Saayman protested first to the military authorities and was menacingly rebuffed. Then he turned to the church leaders. "So I go and say, 'Listen guys, these are our members. I know the chaplains who go in with those people. Some of those stories have been told to me by the chaplains! We must do something about this.'

"So then the church comes down on me, even tramps harder than the army. To say, you know, it's not in the national interest you know, it's a few individuals, you know."

Following his efforts to alert the church hierarchy to atrocities being perpetrated by South African troops in Namibia, Saayman said, the church "decided they'd had enough of me so they worked me out. We had a synod in Windhoek for the first time." Windhoek, in central Namibia, was hundreds of miles south of where most church members lived. "We are a small church, not so well known, so we want to have a proper good synod for the first time. The white church insists on inviting this [Frans] Geldenhuys [secretary of the white church in South Africa] to open our synod, because they pay for the whole thing. So he's coming to speak to open our synod, which is generally a good sermon. In the end he falls ill, but he sends his speech to be read by the moderator of the white church, who was actually a man I trusted and liked very much and who was not a Broederbonder. Of the nine Dutch Reformed [regional] moderators at that stage, he was the only one who was not a Broederbonder.

"So he read Geldenhuys's speech, a fulmination against communism. Within our context, that's a fulmination against SWAPO.* At least fifty percent of our [Dutch Reformed Church in Namibia] members, but certainly more, are SWAPO. Now I'm sitting in the synod, I'm moderator of the synod, and the other three guys [synod officials] are black. The moment it is over, the people come to me and say, 'Look, we can't allow this to get into the press, that our synod is opened with a speech against communism.' So I said, 'No, of course, we can't allow this.' So we draw up a press statement to say we distance ourselves completely from what has been said.

*South West Africa People's Organization, the liberation movement for Namibia. Since 1919 South Africa had ruled the country under a League of Nations mandate, but it was terminated by the U.N. in 1966. South Africa continued to rule in defiance of the U.N.

"The next morning, I get called by the local press and South African press and by all kinds of other people with other connections who say, 'So, we hear you are in favor of communism.' That's how they do it, you see. I said, 'No, of course I'm not in favor of communism.'

" 'Sorry pal, [they say] this is what it says here. And you have signed your name underneath this statement.' Now actually supporting communism is a punishable offense."

Having been accused of supporting communism, and under tremendous pressure, Saayman resigned his position and left Namibia, moving his family to Pretoria and taking up a job at UNISA.*

"That's part of the way we got out of Namibia and part of the reason why my health broke down," Saayman said. "So then we came here to Pretoria, and it was total culture shock for my children, who had grown up on mission stations where despite all the bad things, the one good thing was we were always in a black world. The eldest was then nine, and the youngest was about three or four, and suddenly they're in a white world.

"My father-in-law came to pick us up at Jan Smuts Airport in December. As we drive to Kroonstad a typical highveld thunderstorm bursts out you know, and it r-r-rains nicely!" he said, rolling his r's like a drumming of raindrops. "And right in front of us is a farmer in his *bakkie*. He's alone in [the cab of] his *bakkie* and at the back is his farm laborer, black farm laborer. It rains, and this poor black man is wet through. My father-in-law, just as an observation, says, 'Ay, but now that little *kaffir* is getting wet, heh?' And my daughters bump me and say, 'What is a kaffir?' "

Saayman whispered as the little girls did.

"You know, it's one of the times in my life when I very nearly cried," he said. "Because I realized my children had this wonderful opportunity to grow up for a few years not knowing what a *kaffir* is. And here they are, back in it. We're not back half an hour, but they're back in it."

Dominee Johan Heyns told a tale intended to show his enlightenment and how in the early 1970s he began working within the system to

---

*Many months after this interview the claustrophobic nature of the Afrikaner society sank in. Elna Trautmann, a regional director for Operation Hunger and an ex-SWAPO member (see Chapter 33), mentioned that her father, Peet Strauss, a leader in the Namibia Dutch Reformed Church, had for a while been a Broederbonder. Was he one of the churchmen who had hounded Willem Saayman out? Dominee Saayman said in a fax: "[He] was indeed the missions secretary who gave me so many problems in Namibia. And most of the problems were caused exactly by the fact that he belonged to a secret organization, and always claimed to be working for change from inside."

change apartheid. "I belonged to a Calvinist organization in Potchef-stroom, Afrikaanse Christelike Beweging [Afrikaans Christian Move-ment]," he said. "We had a meeting at Potchefstroom and we analyzed the concept of social justice and applied it to apartheid. We said, in the light of this principle, biblical principle of social justice, you cannot defend apartheid on any grounds. We were called to Pretoria by the then Prime Minister John Vorster. [Philosophy professor] Tjaart van der Walt, myself."

Had they issued a statement?

"Ja, oh yes. It was published in the papers."

Why was a prime minister summoning a dominee?

"Why not? He's a member of my church," Heyns said and laughed. "And when we came out, Tjaart van der Walt said, 'I feel like a schoolboy called in by the principal to be caned.' "

That "caning" must have taught Heyns and Tjaart van der Walt a thing or two about how the system works. A few years later, in 1977, van der Walt turned around and did the same thing to a group of Calvinists at Potchefstroom University who published a statement called "Koinonia," which said that elements of apartheid could not be biblically condoned. Van der Walt, who was then newly being groomed by the Broederbond, rubbed "Koinonia" into a little grease spot and made the signatories recant, like schoolboys and one schoolgirl, Elaine Botha.

CHAPTER TWENTY

SMASHING GNATS
WITH BRICKS

"We lived encapsulated in apartheid," said historian André du Toit, describing the 1960s and '70s. "This seemed to be permanent, this was the South African order."

By 1976 Nelson Mandela had been in prison for thirteen years of his life sentence. The initials ANC did not cross anyone's lips, even in sleep, so banned was the organization. Only about 6 percent of the Afrikaner population read the political articles in newspapers. Sports was a different matter—the sports pages sold the papers. Most whites sat in their cocoons and hoped nothing would ever change.

Then the riots of Soweto exploded. On June 16, 1976, black children defied their parents and subsequently hundreds were killed protesting apartheid. Steve Biko's head was bashed in by security police in 1977. Black Consciousness organizations were banned, along with Beyers Naudé and the Christian Institute. The prominent Afrikaner economist Robert Smit and his wife were mysteriously murdered, with rumors of a cover-up of corruption. A lot was rotten in the country, and a few Afrikaners began to notice the stench. Nonetheless, in November 1977, elections were due and the National Party was cocksure it would win again.

This was the context for the Koinonia Declaration, a mildly dissident document issued in 1977 by an interdenominational group of young Calvinists including some Afrikaners from the university town of Potchefstroom. The Koinonia document stated, among other things, that banning interracial marriage under the Mixed Marriages Act was not supported by Scripture, that schooling for nonwhites was inadequate and inequitable, and that detention without trial was not being handled well.

People outside Afrikaner society looked at Koinonia as a mild statement that apartheid was basically sound but needed some adjustments

217

because it sometimes was not correctly implemented. But in Afrikaner circles Koinonia roused such scandal that one would have thought it was a Communist manifesto rather than the miragelike shimmerings of doubt among a few idealistic young people living in the straitlaced white university town in the western Transvaal. The Dopper university of Potchefstroom serves about nine thousand students. Near the town there is a prison, and out of sight, as with every apartheid city, is the black township called Ikageng.

Koinonia began almost as a Calvinist gambol, if that's not a contradiction in terms. Elaine Botha, a professor in her forties at the time, remembers the events well. She constantly apologizes for her own timidity, but compared to limp-willed ja-Broeders, she has real nerve. Her English is fast and fluent, as if the words were trying to move rapidly to keep warm in the cold winter on the highveld.

"It started out as a very innocent little exercise," Botha recalled. "We met up with a bunch of English-speaking Calvinists from the East Rand in a group called The Loft, which was interesting, because [to our minds] only Afrikaners are Calvinists. We had them over one weekend."

Botha was one of the oldest of the group of twenty-five from Potchefstroom that included Louwrens du Plessis, then twenty-nine, who subsequently became a law professor at Stellenbosch University; Pieter Potgieter, a professor of political science at Potchefstroom University, of about Botha's age; and Theuns Eloff, nineteen, the youngest of the group and a student leader at Potch.

The Loft Calvinists included a few coloreds and blacks, and, Botha said, because of apartheid laws, "It was hard to know what to do with them. They had to find a place outside of town to stay. We had a wonderful weekend, we had a *braaivleis* and really got to know Christians from other communities, face to face.

"We were invited by them to a Roman Catholic conference center called the Koinonia Center east of Johannesburg. At some point we said, 'Look, we can't just clap hands and glory hallelujah, we must do something. Can't we have some sort of manifesto, write down what we commonly believe in?' We made a set of ten or fifteen points, got together in little buzz groups and spoke about education, state, politics, welfare, housing, what we thought a Christian view of those would be.

"For the first time, I met up with black and colored Christians who had been in jail for months and who were sitting with broken ribs kicked in by the police and were smiling and forgiving and talking to me as a white person. That was like heaping coals on somebody's head. It made a tremendous impression."

Botha said that before this experience, "Most of us never questioned." She'd always steered clear of people who challenged the system, such as South Africans whom she'd met years earlier at university in Holland, who'd left the country. At the time, she thought, "They're dangerous people, you don't want to associate with them." But at Koinonia, "Here was this fine Dutch Reformed colored minister sitting there and he says ja, he's got two ribs kicked in by the police and he was in jail for six months, he was never taken to trial, and suddenly you start thinking."

The group met for hours to hash out the statement and talked to each other on phones they later discovered were tapped by the police.

"Eventually we decided we would publish it in a Sunday newspaper on a weekend. Which for us was a very courageous thing because Calvinists aren't supposed to read Sunday newspapers. So if you go out in public on a Sunday, that's some statement. Then suddenly all kinds of horrible things happened. Steve Biko was killed. On the Sunday that our thing is published there's this [Dr. Robert] Smit and his wife murdered. Up to this day we still don't know who killed him."

Then Monday she got a taste of what it was like to be a "schoolgirl." Tjaart van der Walt, the newly appointed rector of Potchefstroom University, began to do to Koinonia signers what Vorster had done to him.

"I can vividly remember walking to my office Monday morning," Botha said. "Ten to eight, the telephone ringing and the principal saying something like, 'Did you participate in that document?' and I said yes. He said 'Well I just had a telephone call from the prime minister'—B. J. Vorster—'demanding that it be withdrawn, and you better see to it that it is done.'

"I got such a fright. I didn't know what hit me. I ran to the other guys. There's no way of withdrawing it, of retracting. What we then did was distance ourselves from the actions of the English group [who had carried out a public protest]. We did not retract anything that we had published in that specific document as such.* Strange things started happening. The theological seminary started pressuring [students], telling them things like 'if you participate in this group then you will never be allowed to become ministers of the church.'

"A week or so earlier van der Walt had said he was quite thrilled, this was a very great thing we had done. He's getting a lot of flak from all quarters, but he thinks it was a really good thing. About two weeks later

---

*The signatories seem to have expressed regret for the timing and public exposure of their document, while claiming to stand by their document.

he calls and now he says this is really a terrible thing. By about three weeks later he invited us over to his house one evening. We have a very friendly evening, and at the end he says he wants to give us friendly advice not to associate with one another anymore. This group of people is a bad influence on one another. Why don't we spread our wings out and find other friends?

"A month or so later the executive council [of the university] decided to call us to appear before the board. That was bad. We met with three members of the board and they said that we had caused stir, we caused embarrassment and did we know what we were doing?

"Theuns Eloff, he must've been about a second- or third-year student at the time, the courage that kid had! The three old gentlemen sitting there were in their late sixties already so they must've all been part and parcel of the 1938 Voortrekker thing* and Ossewabrandwag. Theuns said, 'Now suppose that your university principal was against the Ossewabrandwag at the time and you had been working toward some goal of the Ossewabrandwag, would you have accepted their criticism?' No answer. Because, I mean, it was just a parallel situation."

Then two of Botha's Dutch Reformed Church dominees visited her to express their concern. She realized her phone was bugged. "We were being watched by all kinds of odd little men sitting in cars at odd times and places. Now I find it a joke"—but then it was her first direct exposure to the police state. "Of course if I'd been shoved in jail and my ribs kicked to pieces, that would've been far worse. But for me as an establishment-like person, it was bad enough."

When she noticed her apartment was being watched, she went to the police. After three weeks of silence, she tried again. A policeman "with a big mustache, who still uses snuff" told her, " 'Miss, you know, my men say it must be something up here [she pointed to her head]. My men say they see your light burning at night until two, three o'clock—you must be working too hard.' Hallucinations, you see," Botha said sarcastically.

"So this lasts a couple of months and I'm too scared to talk about it." Gathering her courage, she told her story to Potchefstroom's member of Parliament, Louis le Grange. He "gives me this knowing look" and said nothing for weeks. Then one evening when she was visiting her mother, which only police who were watching her would have known, le Grange phoned her there and told her not to worry, the police weren't interested in her, just her contacts with others.

*   *   *

*The Broederbond-led Great Trek centenary reenactment.

Pieter Potgieter, by 1992 an influential Broederbonder, indicated that Tjaart van der Walt's failure in 1977 to resist the university council pressure against the Koinonia participants left a sour taste.

"If he had had the courage to stand up for his own convictions, he would have," Potgieter said. "It turned out that Tjaart became somewhat dull once he was appointed rector. He was a lively and provocative kind of intellectual, but the moment he became rector it was all gone."

Potgieter said he himself had signed an "apology" but then "distanced" himself from it when a reporter phoned him for clarification on his views. He wasn't sure that his "distancing" ever made it into the papers.

Louwrens du Plessis, a law professor at Stellenbosch and a prominent member of the ANC in 1992, recalled, "Van der Walt had just become rector of the university and we thought we had this more broad-minded liberal rector now. We were so naive that I was in the office on a Monday after we drafted the declaration, taking it to him, asking Tjaart, 'Would you sign?'"

Du Plessis laughed merrily at the memory.

"Of course he wouldn't. He's an opportunist and he wasn't committing himself right from the outset. And the 'apology' statement was as politically naive as everything else we did. I don't regard it as a retraction. We stood with everything we said. But we just took a step or two back, which was a mistake." Van der Walt "used our 'apology' against us. He said, 'If even you can't stick to what you're saying, how can you expect me to support you?' I must say, knowing Tjaart better now, I also wouldn't go to war with him on my side."

For du Plessis, the meeting with members of the university board was particularly enlightening. "The council people thought that they would convey to us their decision, which was actually very arrogant because they were telling us 'You're Methodists' and all the things that were swearwords at Potchefstroom."

After the board members officially ended the meeting, the Koinonia people individually buttonholed them.

"We simply went for them," du Plessis recalled. "Each one of us grabbed one of the members of the council and we continued the discussion. Some of them just dwindled. It was actually tragic to see, these people were so self-assured when they came in. One of the guys told me, 'Ag, man, I was also young you know, and I also did some irresponsible things.' I learned a lot from it."

The coercion didn't end with the prime minister and university board. Du Plessis recalled that another cabinet minister, Connie Mulder, the Minister of Information and a Dopper, executed a little black-mail to get the Koinonia people to cave in: "Mulder phoned the rector of the university and he told him that the *Citizen* was going to publish a story that Koinonia was actually inspired by Beyers Naudé," du Plessis said. "That was the kiss of death." The *Citizen* was the right-wing news-paper that later, in the 1978 Information Scandal, was revealed to be secretly and illicitly funded by taxpayers' money.

"With the knowledge I have now, I wouldn't even have signed the Koinonia Declaration," du Plessis said. "I would have done much more. The murder of Biko—we still thought, 'Well, at least just have a fair trial on the matter, but perhaps there is still the possibility the Security Police didn't kill him.' We were too shortsighted to really realize what it was all about. More unqualifiedly identifying with Steve Biko at the time would have been a more appropriate thing to do. Although we would have lost our jobs then because I think we pushed them about as far as we could at the time."

In 1992 Tjaart van der Walt announced that he was quitting as head of the government-funded think tank, the Human Sciences Research Council (HSRC), located in a mauve and pink building in Pretoria, with a modern, undulating facade and an immaculate parking garage. A big man with curly hair and eyes that matched his gray suit, he was soft-spoken to the point of inaudibility and frequently cited the religious nature of his convictions. It appeared to him that he was slated to be the next head of the FAK.

He spoke wistfully of wishing he were back translating the Bible into Afrikaans, a "great part of my life," he described it. Trained as a dominee, he said he sometimes longed again to have a quiet little congregation that believed in what he said. Van der Walt was leaving the HSRC just as a financial scandal was blowing in, and the political winds were radically shifting.

"I knew the people well," van der Walt said of the Koinonia group. "And I knew they meant well. I differed from the way of approach.

"I became principal [rector] May the first, '77. And when the council met in June [more than six months after the Koinonia Declaration], they wanted to censure these people. I said, 'I can't do that,' and I had to ask my name to be minuted with the minority. 'I'll speak to them, in the sense that they could have phrased some things differently.' "

What about assertions by Potgieter that he, Tjaart, had agreed with 99 percent of the Koinonia Declaration, that the Potch group had checked its statement with him before they went public with it, and even after publication he said he thought it was a good idea?

Van der Walt didn't disagree.

And what about Elaine Botha's charge that after pressure was applied, van der Walt reversed position, said Koinonia was a terrible idea, and urged the group to disband because they were a bad influence on each other?

"I wouldn't agree," he responded. "Quite frankly, I can't remember all the details. I had extensive contact with them. And there were quite a number of drafts of the declaration. And that's why I said with the contents, say for ninety-nine percent or something, I could agree. But there was something about the way it was launched, I can't remember quite exactly how that worked.

"It's not that easy for a young principal to stand up to the council, but I felt an obligation, that's why I invited them to my house to give them patronistic, fraternal advice. I said I think the way the thing has been launched has been so counterproductive."

It was the manner that was wrong, not the substance.

Van der Walt said that he couldn't remember a call from Prime Minister Vorster demanding that Koinonia be withdrawn. He agreed that when he became rector, Vorster was already suspicious of him because of the 1976 conference on "Justice in South African Society" for which Van der Walt and Johan Heyns had been called on the carpet.

"I can remember my director of public affairs said, 'There's a file that thick about you in the security offices.' I wish I'd kept some of the fan mail I got. I still remember one letter I got that was written in red. I'll translate, it was in Afrikaans. 'Professor I'm writing in red because you love red, you Communist. You ought to see a psychiatrist.' "

Van der Walt was still smarting from being called a Communist and being "warned when I was a theological professor not to speak so unwisely at synod.

"I don't want to just damn John Vorster," van der Walt said. "He was something of an ambivalent kind of character. Like so many Afrikaners are."

Ambivalent about what?

"Many things."

Had he just described himself, too? He had wedded himself to the classic Broederbond arguments used to squelch dissent: work within the system; it was the manner, not the substance, that was not productive; the time was not ripe. These arguments savaged idealisms, such as Koinonia, and sucked the substance from men.

"I can understand if people would say that this looked like coercion," van der Walt said. "All I can say is, it wasn't meant as coercion."

CHAPTER TWENTY-ONE

DID F. W. HEAR THE VOICE OF POTCHEFSTROOM?

There are two reasons why the small Dopper church is important. First, Doppers are sometimes portrayed among the Afrikaners as the conscience of the *volk*. Second, F. W. got his law degree at Potchefstroom, the "Dopper university," and has become the most famous Dopper around. He had forgone an academic career at Potch to pursue a political career. Did his religious upbringing lie behind his political about-face?

The cliché used by Theuns Eloff about the Doppers is that they are morally conservative but politically liberal. "Morally conservative" makes them sound more moral than others, but it should rather be "socially conservative." What it means is that they disapprove of dancing, reading newspapers on Sunday, and similar manifestations of libertinism.

UNISA history professor Albert Grundlingh argued that the 1978 Information Scandal, a misuse of taxpayers' money to fund secret projects, "blew the bubble off the Calvinist, upright solid citizenry." Because the scandal centered on a Dopper, the Information minister Connie Mulder—destroying his career—and brought down Prime Minister John Vorster's government, it made a particular mockery of Dopper incorruptibility.

Another Afrikaner belief, Theuns Eloff said, is that Doppers are "Christian first, Afrikaner second." He said that Potchefstroom University, after a thirty-year fight, finally persuaded Parliament in 1951 to declare it a Christian university, a unique status. Eloff claimed that because F. W. was a Christian first, he could more easily become president of all the people, not just the Afrikaners; he could make that emotional leap away from apartheid more easily than could a non-Dopper.

Grundlingh didn't see Potch the same way, arguing that it was so Afrikaner to begin with that its Nationalist nature was a given. Other universities had undergone wrenching processes of Afrikanerization after 1948, in which history departments were forced to adopt *volks-*

geskiedenis (*volk* history). At Potchefstroom University, this wasn't necessary because the institution "grew out of an exclusively Afrikaans nineteenth-century theological seminary" that was Afrikaner nationalist to the core, with a "chosen people" gloss.

Still, something *is* odd about Potch. Some *verligtes* at Potch pecked at apartheid, irritated the authorities, and gained reputations for being contrary and prophetic. Perhaps they were striving for a religiously informed ideal. But often their politically progressive righteousness shone only because the entire Afrikaner political spectrum was shifted so far to the right.

Potchefstroom professor Pieter Potgieter, a Broeder, asserted that "from the early fifties there used to be always this small body of personnel who were progressively thinking. It was referred to as 'die stem van Potchefstroom,' 'the voice of Potchefstroom.' By that was meant this rather small but very clear and convincing voice coming from a few people at Potch.

"The first one that was associated with this voice was the poet, Totius," Potgieter said. Detractors see Totius as an ideological progenitor of apartheid theology. "Afterwards it was Professor Snyman at the theological seminary. But the most well-known Potchefstroomer that articulated these ideas was Professor L. J. du Plessis."

Du Plessis, chairman of the Broederbond from 1930 to 1932 and a National Party intellectual who became a critic of Verwoerd's race policies, is mostly remembered for his contributions to the Afrikaners' efforts to capture economic power. He is also the subject of Potgieter's unpublished book.

After L. J. du Plessis, the voice was articulated by Professor Hennie Coetzee, who used to be the head of the anthropology department, Potgieter said. Coetzee gathered around him a group of young people who started publishing the magazine *Woord en Daad* (*Word and Deed*).

Coetzee at times challenged the official apartheid line and was then summoned by Verwoerd and Vorster to explain himself. Elaine Botha views him as proof that "We've at least had a minimal culture of criticism here in Potch."

Wimpie de Klerk and law professor Louwrens du Plessis succeeded Coetzee as editors of *Woord en Daad*, and the magazine gained a reputation for reformist Christian commentaries. "The journal was often referred to in Parliament," Potgieter said. "John Vorster always asked, 'What do the Potchefstroomers say about this?' " It was a "small group of people thinking very fundamentally and critically: you won't be reflecting Afrikaner thinking accurately if you don't go into this whole business of the voice of Potchefstroom."

Broederbonder Potgieter saw himself as part of the Potchefstroom tradition. "I personally in many, many speeches countrywide and in articles in papers, I took this line, that quite apart from the moral merits of the [apartheid] policy, it is just not practical. Not a single policy in the world that I know of could move ten million people against their will from point A to point B." The voice, it seemed, was a level, unemotional, pragmatic one.

A central Dopper tenet, and one that Potgieter said F. W. "got with his mother's milk," was "reformational thinking," the Dopper Calvinist doctrine of "sphere sovereignty."

"Reformational people view society as an intricate set of human life spheres," explained Potgieter. "The family, the university, church, government, business, sport communities, they are interlocking but, in their authority structure, very definitely separate or unique. The authority of one sphere of life, like that of the state, may not interfere with another life sphere. In South Africa that principle was transgressed many, many, many times. For instance, the act on the prohibition of mixed marriages, that interfered with personal choice. That's a most fundamental individual sphere issue which the government transgressed for many years." A good Dopper would see that the government was intruding on the personal sphere and oppose the law.

Kobus van Rooyen, a lawyer and the former head of the Publications Appeal Board (the top state censorship authority), claimed that a government-hands-off attitude, which was similar to "sphere sovereignty," informed his own thinking when he liberalized state censorship (apart from security matters). The old notion had been that South Africa was a Christian state and its government should preserve Christian values, necessitating heavy censorship. Van Rooyen thought the idea of "sphere sovereignty" must have affected F. W. too. For example, van Rooyen said, when F. W. as Transvaal National Party leader dealt with the question of stores being open on Sunday, he argued for the state not to intervene.

Journalist Dries van Heerden supposed that "sphere sovereignty" might have affected F. W.'s ability to undergo his political flip-flop from apartheid conservative to reformer. But he also noted that F. W. in the 1990s was "preaching *regstaat*—the state based on the rule of law. That thinking in Afrikaner circles has come out of Potchefstroom University." The *regstaat* idea had particularly been espoused by Louwrens du Plessis at Stellenbosch, after he left Potch.

"Eventually, when he got elected as president, he had a very clear religious understanding of what his calling was," Potgieter said. "I know it because I know him very well. The dominee that conducted the service [where F. W. was installed as president in 1989] took a section out of the Bible which plays on this thing [a calling]. He made his sermon from a verse in Jeremiah. The Latin words that he referred to are *coram dei*, 'I am called upon by God to act now.' This was the whole atmosphere in which the sermon was conducted.

"Even before that, I think that F. W. would have experienced this whole business of him becoming president in a very religious manner," Potgieter said. "Justice. I think that F. W. said to himself that 'I must take it seriously. There is only one way in which we can pull through in God's eyes, and that is to administer justice.' That's a very fundamental religious approach." All those years of enthusiastic support for apartheid were because F. W. had to "toe the caucus line" to get ahead in National Party politics. Once in power, de Klerk implemented his religious convictions, Potgieter argued.

Dominee Willem Saayman was dubious, if not cynical, about F. W. and the National Party and their use of religion to mobilize support. It didn't look like lofty moral commitments to him. De Klerk had to be more subtle about theology than Verwoerd and others, because as apartheid crumbled, a "new" National Party would have to include people of all colors in order to maximize its electoral power, and that would include Asians and coloreds, many of whom were Muslims.

"What de Klerk does very cleverly is he brings his own minister along," Saayman said, "a man by the name of Dr. Bingle of the Dopper church. He's his personal minister. Very often Bingle is the man who preaches or prays or makes the religious noise, and F. W. himself, not so much. He presents more of a secularized Afrikaner. But in moments of great emotional depth he will make some kind of reference of thanking God or something like that."

Were the people running the "new" National Party genuinely religious?

"Depends on how you define that term," Saayman said. "Whatever is useful is in the end admissible because the one thing that must endure in Africa is the Afrikaner."

There's a popular South African phrase that succinctly captures a feeling of confusion or ambivalence: "Ja, no, well maybe." Frequently used in describing South African politics, it could well apply to the raging debate over whether or not F. W. had a moral conversion, a genuine change of heart, an experience like Saul's on the road to Damascus—in a flash of light he was struck blind, converted to Christianity, and became Paul.

H. W. van der Merwe, a sociologist and mediator, was certain morality played a role in F. W.'s political actions in 1990. "I am convinced that there was a strong moral element in de Klerk's conversion," van der Merwe said. "And I found it very meaningful that he went out of his way repeatedly to deny that he had a Damascus experience. Political leaders feared that if the Afrikaners suspected that our leaders have Christian conversions, they will let us down."

But since the historical argument was that the Afrikaner was an outstanding moral, Christian, and honest person, why would such a conversion be suspect? "A moral conversion is an emotional experience," van der Merwe said. "That's not to be trusted. It's like a reborn Christian. You can't trust them. We always say, 'Look here, these reborn Christians, it doesn't last.' And de Klerk was very worried that people might think he's now a reborn Christian. That's not a good thing for a politician. I think de Klerk's own moral base had been eroded. He could not carry on defending apartheid on moral grounds, and that's what he spelled out." So van der Merwe believed de Klerk had shifted on moral grounds but couldn't publicly admit to it.

André Louw, professor of political science at UNISA, disagreed. He saw the shift as primarily pragmatic. "The Afrikaners are never sentimentally moral," he said. "They are Calvinist. To them, what happens has got more to do with Divine Providence than whether you are good or bad. Apartheid was wrong in the sense that they tried to do the impossible. In trying to make it work, you become immoral. There's nothing wrong in nations having self-determination, but if you insist on self-determination that denies the self-determination of others, then it becomes immoral. Most ideologies are immoral in that sense. I mean, all of them can say, 'Look, the intention was good.'"

His analysis fit snugly with the Dopper reputation for pragmatism—apartheid didn't work, therefore it was not God's will, and it would be wrong to continue trying to make it work. But because the intent was pure, there is no need to apologize for trying.

Willie Jonker said, "One of my colleagues here [at Stellenbosch seminary] was a member of the Dopper Kerk. He gave me a clipping from a Dutch newspaper reporting on what de Klerk had said in the Netherlands. And my colleague said, 'I can tell you, for a Dopper, that is equivalent to another person sobbing of heartbreak because he's sorry. If a Dopper says that, it's equivalent to a real apology.'"

What did de Klerk say?

"It was a wrong policy."

Did that mean F. W. was "sobbing of heartbreak" because the policy didn't work (if it had, the Afrikaners would still be in power)? Or was he "sobbing" for the killing and hardship apartheid caused? Will the real F. W. stand up?

Ja, no, well maybe.

CHAPTER TWENTY-TWO

CHANGING GOD'S WILL

Molecule by molecule, hint by wink, nuance by insinuation, the Dutch Reformed Church, the biggest Afrikaner church, is being dragged toward change. The pace of change is killing—both too slow and too fast. For its more *verligte*, usually urbanized, educated members, the church's rate of change has been slow as a trilobite's, causing many to seek faith, or no faith, in more relevant places. But for the *verkrampte*, usually less-educated church members, any deviation at all from the old apartheid theology causes heart murmurs and schismatic itchings.

Shifting the *volk*'s thinking about apartheid was the task some *verligtes* set for themselves in the early 1980s. "Making ripe of the Afrikaners for change" is what Broederbond head Piet de Lange called it in 1992. And according to de Lange, they succeeded: the move away from apartheid that culminated in de Klerk's February 1990 speech "was effected to a large extent through the Broederbond's innovative and change-orientated attitudes." During the presidency of P. W. Botha, 1979–89, the Broeders were eclipsed in the government and National Party by Botha's security apparatus and party machinery. In the Dutch Reformed Church, however, the Broeders' influence dominated.

The Broederbond's point man in the church was Moderator Johan Heyns. Under his leadership in 1986 a church commission issued a report, *Kerk en Samelewing* (*Church and Society*) that argued, somewhat fuzzily, that humanity's unity under God was prior to racial distinctions and thus there was no basis in Scripture for racial separation. In 1990 a slightly revised *Church and Society* document made the argument more explicitly. In 1992 Heyns said that the change in church doctrine "was the work of the Holy Spirit," but that "surely He works through you and He wants you to do something. We tried to prepare the spirit and the minds of the people to make '86 possible, so that we could eventually adopt that report."

The *Church and Society* report was a watershed. "I think that is the most important document that was published in the last century as far as the DRC [Dutch Reformed Church] is concerned," Heyns said. It caused the first schism in the white church since 1859.

How the white church came to this pass is mostly a history of outside pressure, from the "daughter" churches, from the "mother" churches in Holland, from the other churches that belonged to the South African Council of Churches, and from outside South Africa, especially the World Association of Reformed Churches (WARC) and the Reformed Ecumenical Synod.

But "outside pressure" is a nasty term to traditional Afrikaners who, in contradiction to their belief in Calvinistic predetermination, are fanatically defensive about controlling their own destinies. "One of the problems in our country was the fact that due to apartheid we ended up on different islands, not only ethnic islands but also ecclesiastic islands," Heyns said. "Now we have to start building bridges from one island to another." But the bridges Heyns and other Afrikaners had in mind were to extend outward from the Afrikaners, built to their specifications. The islands weren't to be pushed together, nor were the Afrikaners to be moved to some common mainland. "We would like Afrikaners to bring about reformation primarily in our hearts—that is, where we live on our own little small island," Heyns said. For an Afrikaner to confess that someone "outside" had caused him to change would, in the common view, emasculate him. Those from among the *volk* who had tried to change the church's course—like Ben Marais and Beyers Naudé—had been pushed off the island.

Before World War II, ties were strong between the Dutch Reformed churches in South Africa and the Reformed (Gereformeerde) Church in the Netherlands. The theologian Abraham Kuyper's fascination with the Afrikaners at the turn of the century had developed into close contact between the Dutch Christian-National movement and its Afrikaner counterparts in the Dopper church. These bonds lasted until the Nazis conquered Holland in May 1940. Although some of Kuyper's Dutch followers supported Hitler, the majority of Gereformeerdes fought in the resistance, taking high casualties. Thus ended the warm relations between the Dutch church and Afrikaner Nationalists, many of whom supported nazism. Some church ties remained after the war, but in the 1960s the Dutch church swung to a pronounced antiracist position.

After the great Cottesloe eruption in 1960, when the South African Dutch Reformed Church suppressed or cast out the few dominees willing to stand publicly against apartheid, the church sank into slamming anti-apartheid Christians as liberals, humanists, and Communists. Beyers Naudé led the list.

231

Naudé reached back into German history to seek theological comfort and found Dietrich Bonhoeffer's concept of a "Confessing Church" (die Bekennende Kirche), an anti-Nazi position for which Bonhoeffer ultimately died. Its principal tenet was that the church must remain faithful to—or return to—its original confession of faith rather than accept political ideologies that violated it. Naudé resurrected the idea of the "Confessing Church" in 1965 in *Pro Veritate*, causing a stormy debate in Dutch Reformed Church circles. The idea reverberated down through the next two decades, to varying degrees in almost all of South Africa's churches.

As early as 1968 a top theologian from the Free University in Amsterdam, where many South African Dutch Reformed ministers had been educated, shocked Afrikaner theologians when he told them disparagingly: "You worship a different God." By the seventies the Dutch church stood completely opposed to apartheid and in 1974 it signified its position by awarding an honorary doctorate to Beyers Naudé.

Theological terminology provided ammunition for intraparty disputes between conservative Nationalists and those who gradually began chipping away at apartheid's more impractical aspects. When in 1969 Prime Minister John Vorster's government for the first time permitted "nonwhite" foreign sports teams to compete in South Africa, Andries Treurnicht, then editor of the Pretoria daily newspaper *Hoofstad (Capital City)*, charged that the *verligtes* were not "standing by God and His Word," and accused them of "rejecting the Christian-National basis of our whole social, educational and political way of life." It was the first time that National Party leaders had accused each other of subverting Christianity. A Dutch Reformed dominee and chairman of the Broederbond in the years 1972–74, Treurnicht remained a theological dinosaur. His 1975 book *Credo of an Afrikaner* revived all the old Kuyperian themes, and in 1982 he led Conservatives out of the National Party.

Studies show that during the 1970s, the most diligent churchgoers were those with the greatest prejudice. Still, a microscopic wording shift took place in the seventies, as the church hierarchy explained its support for apartheid less on biblical grounds and more on "practical" grounds (e.g., the "practical" problems of white prejudice toward interracial mixing).

In the "family" of Dutch Reformed churches, opposition to apartheid surfaced in the 1970s.* The African Dutch Reformed Church, with a

---

*The white Dutch Reformed Church has three "sister" churches (formerly "daughter" churches). These are the Nederduitse Gereformeerde Sendingkerk, or Dutch

membership of 900,000, led the way in 1974 when its leaders encouraged Beyers Naudé and the Christian Institute in its actions. They helped form the Broederkring, Brother Ring, a group of radical ministers including whites who worked in black churches. In 1975 the African Dutch Reformed Church joined the South African Council of Churches (SACC), from which the (white) Dutch Reformed Church had withdrawn after Cottesloe. Then, with the coming of the Black Consciousness movement in the 1970s, many young coloreds started to identify themselves as blacks and sided politically with the majority Africans. Discontent erupted in the Sendingkerk, which has 500,000 members, or about 28 percent of the colored population.

Sendingkerk minister Reverend Allan Boesak, who was educated in Holland and supported Black Liberation Theology, returned home to the Cape in the late seventies and was appointed chaplain for students at the University of the Western Cape, where he extended his political reach. He has said it was Beyers Naudé who turned his anger against whites in constructive directions. With fellow ministers, Boesak repeatedly called for the government to repeal apartheid legislation. He rejected the government's 1982 tricameral parliamentary reform proposals because they excluded Africans.

In 1981, under Boesak's leadership, African and colored ministers launched the Alliance of Black Reformed Christians in Southern Africa (ABRESCA). Resurrecting the "Confessing Church" argument, ABRESCA declared apartheid a sin and heresy. This position paved the way for the biggest crisis in the white Dutch Reformed churches since Cottesloe. It occurred in the World Alliance of Reformed Churches (WARC) where the Dutch Reformed Church and the NHK had remained members. Led by Boesak and the Sendingkerk, WARC proclaimed apartheid to be theological heresy and suspended both the NHK and the Dutch Reformed Church at its convocation in Ottawa in 1982. Furthermore, Boesak was elected WARC's president. Just as it had quickly dissociated itself from the Cottesloe report, the NHK promptly resigned from WARC. The Dutch Reformed Church at its 1982 synod waffled, voting by a majority to quit WARC, but not by the necessary two thirds. Thus the DRC "rejected" the WARC suspension.

*   *   *

Reformed Mission Church, for coloreds; the Nederduitse Gereformeerde Kerk in Afrika, which is predominantly African; and the Reformed Church in Africa for Asians, with only one thousand members.

The political backdrop for all this church activity was turmoil. In response to black resistance and looming international sanctions, Prime Minister P. W. Botha clamped down with military and police might, while setting about rewriting the constitution. His long-range objective appeared to be an easing of apartheid.

This was more than the conservatives could stomach. Many observers think the NP/CP split so appalled Botha that it caused him to pull back permanently from the course of reform being charted by Broederbond *verligtes*. The Dutch Reformed Church wouldn't touch the party split with a ten-foot sermon.

While the white church leaders refused to budge from support of apartheid, the ecumenical opposition to apartheid intensified, with liberation theology spreading like a veld fire. Black clergy of all denominations, including Dutch Reformed, were in the forefront of protests and boycotts. In 1983 Allan Boesak helped found the anti-apartheid United Democratic Front of six hundred community organizations and was elected one of its "patrons," along with Beyers Naudé. Black theologians within the Dutch Reformed churches intensified pressure on the white churches. The Anglican Church, which had both white and black congregations, declared apartheid a heresy. And then, in 1985, 185 clergy of all denominations and races published a commentary called Kairos, a Greek word meaning "moment of truth." The Kairos document was the boldest, most comprehensive exposition yet of the new liberation theology. It said that the Christian-Nationalism behind apartheid

> is as mischievous, sinister and evil as any of the idols that the prophets of Israel had to contend with. Here we have a god who is historically on the side of the white settlers, who dispossesses black people of their land and who gives the major part of the land to his "chosen people." . . . The god of the South African State is not merely an idol or a false god, it is the devil disguised as Almighty God—the antiChrist.

In 1986, with *Church and Society*, the Afrikaans Dutch Reformed Church began officially to enunciate its new theological analysis of racial separation. Compiled by a commission, *Church and Society* looked like a typical authoritarian, though *verligte*, Broederbond-steered operation. "It was a small body of only fourteen people [not all Broeders] who worked out the draft," Heyns said. "That is how it works." It then was adopted by the general and regional synods.

Heyns pointed out what he considered the pertinent paragraph in the document, as it was revised in 1990. Paragraph 285 said: "Any system which in practice functions this way [favoring one group], is unacceptable in the light of Scripture and the Christian conscience and must be rejected as sinful." It was a theological turnabout and a direct affront to the conservatives. And it was applied retroactively, Heyns said: "This is acting from [in effect since] 1948."

The hard-line ministers dug in their heels. On June 27, 1987, according to Heyns a "very cold and wet day," they left the Dutch Reformed Church. In a meeting with 715 Dutch Reformed Church members and dominees present, 17 percent voted to stay and 83 percent voted to establish the new Afrikaanse Protestante Kerk (APK), led by Dominee Willie Lubbe. Among the 17 percent, the former Broederbond chairman Carel Boshoff voted to stay and help form a conservative lobby within the Dutch Reformed Church.

Schism.

"That came as a shock," Heyns said. "Being the moderator at the time, I can tell you, that was a traumatic experience. I will never in my life forget the year of 1987 and especially June, the end of June, when this church [the APK] was established. We were aware that some would leave the church, but surely we never ever had in mind that that amount would leave," Heyns said, still stunned. "And I was the one who so much liked to unite the church." About fourteen thousand Dutch Reformed Church members initially left for the APK.

"One would not wish this to your most bitter enemy," said Beyers Naudé, sympathizing with Johan Heyns. "Political schisms yield easier, but the religious ones go much deeper."

The APK head Willie Lubbe, he who spoke of antelope apartheid and wore a macadam-colored suit, remembered a Heyns who wasn't so liberal and didn't seek a unified church. Lubbe and Heyns had studied in Holland at the same time. "At that time there was no one more conservative than Professor Heyns. How can a man make an about-turn of one hundred eighty degrees?" Lubbe asked. He himself had been consistently right-wing, joining the Herstigte Nasionale Party after vehemently opposing Prime Minister John Vorster's sports policy and quitting the Broederbond in 1970 because of the rising influence of the *verligte*, whom Lubbe criticized as bringing politics into the Broederbond.

Heyns and other *verligte* church leaders argued in 1986 that the change in church doctrine was the result of rethinking theology. Lubbe didn't buy it. "They're telling you this, but that's not the reason," Lubbe said. He was convinced that there was some sort of [Broederbond] conspiracy that "infiltrated the church and succeeded in taking over the church for that policy of integration." *Church and Society*, he said, was developed secretly, undemocratically. "When that document was laid before the General Synod, not one percent of the members knew what was in it."

Ina van der Linde, a religion reporter for *Vrye Weekblad*, said that judging by what she had heard at a very secret APK meeting that she attended in disguise, the reason for the schism was political and personal, not theological. "I do believe it was politics," she said. "They just couldn't tolerate the church now saying that apartheid is sin." And she claimed that many of the dominees who defected to the APK were already unhappy as members of the Dutch Reformed Church, people who "had cases against them in the presbytery because they were incompatible, a lot of difficult people."

The discontent of the malcontents threatened the Dutch Reformed Church centrists. After the walkout, church leaders halted reform cold in its tracks, fearing more defections. They replaced Johan Heyns with a moderator less identified with change. "You simply do not want to lose so many members," Heyns said.

The church was caught between the threat of further defections on its conservative side, and increasingly strident demands from the daughter churches to establish unity across racial lines. In an attempt to stave off the hemorrhage of members to the right, the church fudged the issue of unity. In 1992 Heyns claimed, deadpan, that there already was unity. "We said it even in the first document, essentially these four churches are one. Now we are looking for structures to express that essential unity. We are working very hard on that, trying to accommodate the differences that we have."

But the black daughter churches demanded that the Dutch Reformed Church declare apartheid a heresy (not just a deviation, a mistake, or a sin), affirm this as *status confessionis*, or confession of faith, and break its ties with the Broederbond. They saw a lack of commitment to a new egalitarian ethos in the white church's reluctance to condemn as heretics its dead members who, the *Church and Society* document said, supported apartheid with "honest and noble intentions." Meanwhile, by 1992 the APK claimed a membership of about thirty-three thousand adults and twelve thousand children in 229 congregations with 120 dominees. Its theological seminary in Pretoria had four professors, six students, and sixteen students doing preparatory undergraduate studies. Lubbe predicted the seminary would grow.

*　　*　　*

Theologian Willie Jonker said he'd never known a church to confess.

"I haven't heard the Roman Catholic church say, 'We're sorry, Martin Luther, you had a point.' No, they didn't do that."

He chuckled. He was sitting in a big meeting room in the sheet-white Stellenbosch seminary building. The seminary was founded in 1859 to counter the liberal theology that Dutch Reformed Church dominees had been getting in Holland. A giant polished table and the cold winter air seeping through the unheated building lent a hair-shirt atmosphere.

"A church cannot confess as a body," Jonker said. "So I was the only one that could do it. I was the only one that *had* to do it."

In November 1990, a multiracial meeting of 230 leaders from eighty religious denominations was held in the southwestern Transvaal town of Rustenburg. The town's name became a synecdoche for both the meeting itself and Jonker's electrifying confession.

Jonker is a Dutch Reformed dominee sidelined in the sixties when he defended Naudé. He had refused to join the Broederbond. He wrote a booklet in 1962 that espoused unity for all the Dutch Reformed family of churches and was roasted for that in *Kerkbode* magazine by a Professor Hanekom of Stellenbosch, who accused him of "liberalism." During the ensuing ostracism and his stint as a professor at UNISA, Jonker decided he'd had "too high self-esteem." He seems a meek and mild man, perhaps suffering from what the religion reporter Ina van der Linde described as the Afrikaners' psychosis of forever wondering if they are "chosen," and never feeling adequate. One could imagine Jonker murmuring *mea culpa, mea culpa* as he strolled around the beautiful, whitewashed town of Stellenbosch searching for a hint of pride in his thoughts.

He said that when he arrived in Stellenbosch twenty-one years ago, "In the beginning people were afraid that I would do strange things, but I didn't do strange things." When he came to the Rustenburg meeting, he "had a burden on my heart" over apartheid. But he'd learned a thing or two over the years. This time he stuck his toe in the water to see if the "time was ripe.

"When I prepared myself for that meeting, I read a lot about, and the works of, Dietrich Bonhoeffer, the German theologian; you know about him?" Jonker asked. "Bonhoeffer said that the church must make a confession of its guilt, but you'll never get a whole church to make confession," Jonker said. "That's impossible. So some people must do that vicariously, on behalf of and in the place of."

Beyers Naudé's mid-sixties resurrection of Bonhoeffer and the "Confessing Church" had finally seeped into the Dutch Reformed Church. For although Jonker stressed he was not a church official—"I was just there in my own name"—the story he told about his actions at Rustenburg made clear that the church gave him a wink and a nod for his "confession."

Jonker had decided that "something existential must happen" between the Dutch Reformed Church white Afrikaners and the rest of the population. Rather than just producing words on a synod document—like *Church and Society*—someone had to confess guilt, and "the others will have to forgive us. Just like children. [Or] you'll never get to the point where you can move ahead."

On the morning of his speech, Jonker was sitting at his desk in the room he shared with the moderator of the Cape Synod of the Dutch Reformed Church, drafting a possible confession. Although Jonker portrayed himself as a beleaguered outsider, he was a member of the DRC commission that wrote the 1986 and 1990 *Church and Society* documents, and so was his roommate. As his roommate had his hand on the doorknob to leave for a prayer meeting, Jonker recalled, "He turned and said, 'Willie, sometime we'll have to tell these people that we're sorry.' I said, 'I'm just sitting here and writing that.' "

Jonker told his roommate he was thinking of saying in his confession that he had no permission from the church, but the man told him to leave that out, just make a confession.

Jonker vividly remembered the inadvertent drama of the moment in his speech where he had decided to insert his apology. "I said, 'Well, I have something else that I would like to tell you.' Then I looked for that little paper and I couldn't find it. It was written in pencil. I looked on the floor. After a while I found it just beneath another piece of paper. But during that moment I caught the attention of everybody in that whole audience. I read it in complete silence."

The confession was published in a book of conference proceedings:

> I confess before you and before the Lord, not only my own sin and guilt, and my personal responsibility for the political, social, economical and structural wrongs that have been done to many of you . . . , but vicariously I dare also to do that in the name of the DRC of which I am a member, and for the Afrikaans people as a whole. I have the liberty to do just that, because the DRC at its latest synod has declared apartheid a sin and confessed its own guilt of negligence in not warning against it and distancing itself from it long ago.

"Nobody said anything," Jonker recalled. "Nothing happened. And I just went on."

But at the end of his address a bustling beset the hall. One of the first to leap forward and shake his hand was the Anglican Archbishop Desmond Tutu, who asked to talk at the podium. In his impromptu speech, Tutu forgave Jonker.

But what about the black and colored Dutch Reformed ministers? When the entire rest of the audience rose to its feet after Tutu's response to Jonker, they sat like rocks in their chairs. Only they knew the arcane DRC relationships and the abstruse religious lingo. They knew Jonker was only one churchman, not the church, and they still sought a confession of heresy, which in technical terms would be an admission of a far deeper guilt than was implied by a mere confession of sin.

Jonker's and Tutu's statements ricocheted throughout both black and Afrikaner church circles. What standing did Tutu have to accept Jonker's apology? Whom did Jonker represent? Tutu delivered an eloquent speech the day after Jonker's confession in which he conceded he had no mandate for his acceptance. The DRC, sidestepping the actual apology, issued a statement saying that Jonker's version of the *Church and Society* document was accurate and the Dutch Reformed Church wanted the document to be the basis for reconciliation.

The white church would not go so far as to proclaim apartheid a heresy (as had been done by WARC in 1982) because to do so would mean that apartheid's supporters' intentions had been evil, deliberately against God's law. One of the few things that National Party and Conservative Party supporters could agree on was that they and their forefathers had only the best intentions. Good intentions, even gone awry, were the pure, noble tatters covering their guilt.

From what Jonker said, the establishment patted him on the head for his confession. "I know that really a substantial part of the Dutch Reformed Church identified themselves with what I had said. I know the right-wing Afrikaners detested it."

Jonker had not gone further than the church in admitting guilt. He had not admitted heresy. But this fine theological point was lost on the average right-wing Afrikaner, who thought that admitting any sin connected with apartheid meant that he and his ancestors were going to rot in hell. Other Afrikaners were disgusted with Jonker's confession in front of those despicable English speakers, whose hands and hearts were just as bloody as the Afrikaners'. To them it was like confessing to a murder before murderers.

Jonker also "received reaction from government personalities in the cabinet, who were very glad about it. Some of them spoke to the state president also," he said. "His position has been that it could have legal repercussions if he as a head of a state would make such a confession. So you'll always hear him say, 'Many things have been done wrongly' and so on, but he cannot do it in the same way.

"Johan Heyns told me a week or two ago [in mid-1992] that he still was of the opinion that it has had a mighty effect," Jonker said. "If I had thought about it beforehand, maybe I wouldn't have done it, because any sensible person would perhaps not have done it. But I am still of the opinion that it was the correct thing to do and the only place where it could've been done. I've never seen another place yet where it could've been done."

One churchman's apology, no matter how much condoned by church leaders, does not solve the problem of church disunity. The white Dutch Reformed Church faces in the religious realm the same conundrum confronting the National Party in the political. To guarantee its electoral future, the NP must attract African voters, but courting them drives right-wing whites into splinter parties. In the church, unity with black denominations is necessary for survival, but pursuing unity risks igniting further defections to the APK. The fatuity of Johan Heyns's assertion that unity already existed was shown by his comment that structures were still needed to make it a fact.

In 1993 two of the black Dutch Reformed churches, the African and the colored, joined to form the United Reformed Church. Its representatives successfully lobbied the South African Council of Churches (SACC) to reject the white Dutch Reformed Church's application for observer status in the ecumenical SACC. The unified black church leadership knew better than anyone else the duplicity of the white church's assertion of unity.

Meanwhile, in preparation for the white church's October 1994 synod, Broederbond dominees of the Dutch Reformed Church worked the grass roots of the church, guiding numerous committees in local congregations to support a merger with the black church. At the synod merger plans were endorsed, but they entailed a gradual, two-year process. From the blacks' standpoint, reform crawls forward at a snail's pace.

Johan Heyns continued to play a prominent role in both the church and the Broederbond. In 1993 he became a vice chairman of the new, mixed-race Afrikanerbond that purportedly replaced the Broederbond. In February 1994, he announced, to the distress of hard-line right-wingers, that he was trying to mediate differences between the National Party, the ANC, and the right-wing Afrikaner Volksfront. A main mover in the mid-October 1994 synod merger plans, Heyns also engineered President Mandela's address to the synod and organized a standing ovation for him from the dominees. Three weeks later he was assassinated. Heyns's murder may breed even further caution in church leaders, retarding the merger process and delaying the Afrikaners' departure from their *volk* island, enabling them to worship their "different God" awhile longer.

CHAPTER TWENTY-THREE

LAMENTATIONS

Caught between defecting conservatives and the black churches' demands for an admission of heresy, the church is rotting from within. It makes some people shrug, but others are piteously sad.

"The dominees don't have influence any longer," said the religion reporter Ina van der Linde. "There was a wonderful story on the deep *platteland* about this dominee who tried to apply the new document [*Church and Society*] of the Dutch Reformed Church, and his own congregation threw him out. The press, everybody just kept quiet. That's how powerless they are. There are many stories like that on the *platteland*."

Theuns Eloff, who left the Dopper ministry to work for the Consultative Business Movement, said, "It's very frustrating in the church today. They are definitely behind. I think I am doing better work here than I would there."

Historian André du Toit said, "The time when the church gave any lead is very distant—I would say about fifty to sixty years [ago]. The church adjusts: I mean, de Klerk gives the lead, Heyns will give him his support."

Some young Afrikaners, especially educated, urban ones, just float quietly away from the church.

The investigative journalist Jacques Pauw, whose great-grandfather came to South Africa in 1857 as a missionary and founded the Dutch Reformed (colored) Mission Church in Wellington, resigned from the church in 1987.

"I just decided one day I don't want to go to church anymore," Pauw said. "As a child I had to go to the NG [Dutch Reformed] Church every Sunday. But I never listened to the sermons, I thought about other things, so it never played that important a role in my life."

For his first job did he have to have the traditional reference letter from his dominee before he could be employed?

"Yes, absolutely," he said, highlighting one of the historical great powers of the churches. "I think I still have it today, my letter from my dominee. I must say, I'm not sure whether the church plays that important a role anymore. You know, although the right wing will always talk about Christianity and God's chosen people and whatever, I think it's more the idea of the *swart gevaar* [black peril] and losing power" that drives them.

Another journalist, Dries van Heerden, who was raised in a Dutch Reformed parsonage and whose brother is a dominee, said, "To a very large degree the church is the architect of its own undoing—because it has a ritualistic, formal setting which doesn't attract young people anymore. The church has a habit of giving answers to questions that nobody asked."

Such as?

"The church is still debating, you know, whether people should live together before they are married. Young people of this country resolved the question ten years ago. They don't care a shit what the church says about it, they just do it.

"It's the same with gambling. That is one of the best examples of the breakdown of traditional Afrikaner values. There is this wonderful story of a deacon in the APK church who won a million rand [gambling]. Suddenly he's a millionaire and the church says, 'No, no, no, gambling is strictly against the church teachings, you'll have to give the money back.' He said, 'Screw the church.' He's definitely no longer a deacon and I doubt very much whether he's still a member of the Conservative Party. He's probably turned Nationalist overnight because he's got the money now to buy his own apartheid. [He's rich enough to afford to live away from most blacks.]

"What disillusioned me about the church is its absolute inability to act as the conscience of the Afrikaner nation. They did not call for a single political change in this country before the government did. They were behind in every move. And even in the climate which de Klerk opened up for anybody to say almost anything, the church is still waiting for the damn government to make a move. And then it puts a stamp on it. It's a spineless organization."

Another young man, Kobus van Loggerenberg, who had been in training to be a dominee at the University of Bloemfontein, "became aware of the role the church played to sustain this [apartheid] system. That made me question the basis of the church, the Scripture, the whole theology. I was brought up in this tradition that the role between the church and state was never questioned."

In the end he left the white church and joined the Sendingkerk.

"I'm not religious in the traditional sense of the word, but I still see a role for religion and the church to play in South Africa," he said. As for the white Dutch Reformed Church, "There's no theological leadership because the church has become what people wanted it to be. It's to comfort their social way of living and not to question it. In that sense I was disappointed because I believed the church was of God."

The church is not toothless. It can still make members toe the line, at least in public. One man who asked to remain anonymous said he could not openly express his religious doubts because his "sins" would be visited on his children, perhaps preventing them from getting the jobs they wanted.

This man came to political consciousness on the right of the spectrum, in his case in the far-right Herstigte Nasionale Party (HNP). In 1966 he thought "we were a chosen people and this [Verwoerd] was our messiah. I felt the world was decadent, that liberal values were the beginning of anti-Christian influence."

A teacher taught him how to think from different perspectives, how to question.

"I started to question religion because I see that churches are indoctrinating and not educating. I believe in some force up in heaven, but I don't want to identify it or define it because I believe it's beyond humans to really understand the gods, if I may call it that. But I dare not say this at work. I would be marginalized.

"I don't like to be double-faced. I find it very difficult to live with hypocrisy. In terms of my religion, I'm really liberal. In politics, I'm moderate to liberal. But in terms of the relationship of my daughter with men, I think I'm basically conservative. I wouldn't like her to have premarital sex; it would really be a problem to me. Although I've educated them [my children] to make their own decisions.

"In our house we have many debates on religion. I'm open with my kids on that. They know where Dad stands. But I'm also causing a problem for them: if they apply for initial jobs they have to have references and one of them normally is the dominee." If the dominee doesn't say the applicant is a churchgoing person, it raises doubts in the prospective employers.

Piet Muller, who writes for *Insig* (*Insight*) magazine and the Sunday newspaper *Rapport*, was "reared by the Calvinists in the Orange Free State," he said. A few "very, very staunch" members in his Dutch Reformed Church wanted to send him to Holland to mold him into a professor of philosophy.

"Then the dear Lord played a prank on me," Muller said, with a twinkle in his voice. "One December holiday, He brought me into contact with the words of the new generation of Jewish philosophers, [Martin] Buber, Franz Rosenzweig. After I'd read them, I realized that I could never become a Calvinist. Not even one of these new Calvinists."

Why not?

"The whole dehumanization, the strictness, the authoritarianism, the patriarchal traits of them didn't fit my character," Muller said.

How right he was. Muller's personality is bubbly, but not frivolous.

"A work that made a tremendous impact on my life was Franz Rosenzweig's *The Star of Redemption*. Rosenzweig [1886–1929] was paralyzed, he could only move his eyelids. He wrote, he completed his philosophical works, he had a weekly column for a Berlin newspaper, and a tremendous correspondence. His wife had to hold up the alphabet and from the blink of the eyes deduct which letter he wanted to use. But that man, like Buber, had such a tremendous impact on me. That is where I went wrong, you see, I read the wrong books."

Muller became a journalist for seven years, went to university to acquire a Ph.D. in philosophy, then swung back to journalism. In 1992 he worked in the heart of the establishment. Muller was effervescent, a man for whom the phrase "serious fun" seemed invented.

"Coming from a family where everybody is very tense, I never found real silence," he said. "Everybody was always busy, always shouting, always doing things. I became a Quaker because of the thirst and quest for quiet." He became a member of the Wider Quaker Fellowship and because of his longing for quietude, started meditating with Buddhists. "They are very friendly people," he said, but added, "I don't like the chanting: when they start chanting, I get up and go out because that really disturbs me.

"Now I find I'm looking for a church in between the Quakers and the Buddhists, if I could ever find that one. I don't mind living on the fringes of ecclesiastical society, that doesn't bother me at all. We have quite a small community of like-minded Afrikaans-speaking people in Pretoria."

Muller had not withdrawn from official membership in the Dutch Reformed church, believing that "it's not morally right to leave the church if you attack it. I think the problem with the church is that it cannot adapt to modern circumstances. It is a tragic thing. They cannot reject the Synod of Dort because that is their declaration of faith, their Calvinism, which is permeated with the old seventeenth-century rationalism.

"You know, the church was never with the Afrikaner in significant moments," he said. "The church refused to join the Great Trek. They refused to send a dominee for the trekkers for political reasons. Many times in significant periods in history, the church was behind the times." He thought it still was: "This time the Afrikaner is trekking to the heart of Africa," Muller said. "I think it is a trek of the mind, an acceptance of what this continent means to all of us. That for ninety years, from 1900 to 1990, we regarded Africa as the enemy."

In contrast to Piet Muller, who cajoles the establishment but is not vastly distressed, Dominee Jan van Rooyen is totally despairing. He attributes his five heart attacks and heart-bypass surgery to the stress of trying to reform the church from within. His lamentation is a wail for the lost soul of the church.

"Until 1960 there was a genuine conviction that the Lord put us here with a specific purpose, to serve and to help and to uplift. Then all of a sudden it became introverted, the whole thing, after Cottesloe. Everything that smacked of moving out [associating with blacks] was called 'social gospel.' We've been 'yes' people for so many years. We've been 'yes' people ever since 1948, when the Nationalist Party took over."

Van Rooyen became a "no" person after 1960, when he read a British Council pamphlet telling what apartheid really meant. Not believing what he read, he carried out his own investigation and concluded the pamphlet was right. He admitted he did not always have the courage to speak out, yet was often an aggravation to the church establishment. He became what another dissenter called 'n klippie in die skoen, a pebble in the shoe.

Dissension over "social gospel," a concept imported from the United States in the 1960s, immobilized the church, van Rooyen said. Pietism, withdrawal from social involvement, especially from helping blacks, swept through the Dutch Reformed churches. "Social gospel became an absolute swearword," he said. "Ministers in the DRC became introverts. Church became a place where you put your head in the sand, where you were free from this life. Everything was spiritualized."

Van Rooyen was born in 1928 in Doris, in Namaqualand, South Africa, "the most beautiful flower country in the world." He followed his father into the ministry and studied at Pretoria University with Johan Heyns, Willie Jonker, and Carel Boshoff—it's such a small, small society. Then that pesky British Council pamphlet pricked his conscience.

He visited the United States in 1966, on a State Department tour, and decided to research the American right wing. (Little-known American right-wingers frequently appear in South Africa and are well received in some circles.) In the U.S. van Rooyen interviewed "members of the lunatic fringe," including Edgar Bundy, an American who had been visiting South Africa to lecture on the dangers of communism and the virtues of apartheid. Upon van Rooyen's return to South Africa, he published excerpts from his interview with Bundy that were critical of apartheid. The *verkramptes* went crazy. The secretary of anticommunism in the Dutch Reformed Church charged van Rooyen with lying. "They had no proof that I lied. In questioning, I said, 'How can you say I lied, how do you know that Bundy didn't lie?' 'No, Bundy would never tell a lie,' " was the reply.

Van Rooyen published a brochure entitled *Communism in the Church?* that attacked carpetbagging American anticommunists such as Bundy. "At my own expense I had it printed and sent out to every minister in South Africa and to all the newspapers." It caused an uproar. "Fortunately, [the editor of *Beeld*] Schalk Pienaar gave me very near to a full center page of the Sunday newspaper in which *Beeld* defended me, took up my cause, and that was the end of the Americans coming in preaching on communism."

One of van Rooyen's later pamphlets described the devastating consequences of the pass laws on Africans, how in a few seconds in pass court hearings people were "processed out"—declared illegal in the cities and remanded to forcible transfer to the desolate homelands.

"He had quite a number of brochures," van Rooyen's wife, Joupie, said. An articulate, graceful woman, she had gone out to work soon after her marriage precisely so her husband would feel free to speak out, even if his job was imperiled.

Van Rooyen laughed bitterly at the absurdity of it all in 1992. But he was the victim of much harassment for his stands within the church. At a church circuit meeting soon after the assassination of Prime Minister Verwoerd, a motion of condolence was proposed that included thanks to God for Verwoerd's apartheid policy. Van Rooyen successfully argued for removal of the part of the motion that indicated God approved of apartheid.

On a Sunday morning following the meeting he read in his newspaper, he said, " 'Dutch Reform Minister Shocks Community. Such Procedure Not Known Even in Holland.' I thought, 'Who is this clod?' I started reading, and it's myself. And they said that I objected to the motion of condolence. But I didn't, I objected to that certain phrase of the condolence. It took many meetings to get that sorted out."

In another instance, Minister of Native Affairs M. C. Botha decided to remove blacks from Alexandra township in Johannesburg to remake it into a white area. The laws stated that if blacks were living in an area redesignated for whites, they had to get permission to stay. The authorities started splitting up families, shipping people out, demolishing homes.

"I saw it with my own eyes. Say, for instance, the house had ten rooms and you have ten families staying in the house—they would send away the first family, and break out that room. I saw a house where the roof was balancing on two rooms. I stepped in, and with the cooperation of the local minister there, I said, 'Sorry I can't take this anymore.' The Africans couldn't do a thing because the machine guns were pointed at them the whole time.

"So I got a history of every family. And I went to the court where these people were summoned to appear. One morning I came in in such a hurry that the presiding magistrate stopped the proceedings. And I said, 'These people who you want to send away now, they were born here. I have proof of it.' The whole thing was changed there.

"I was given hell by the native affairs commissioner and the whole thing boiled over in the newspapers and I was the Negrophilist."

Joupie van Rooyen remembered: "The children were seen as *kaffir-boetiekinder*, children of a *kaffirboetie* [kaffir brother]." They were tormented in school by children and teachers alike. One schoolteacher, when she saw the name of a popular song by a black singer written on the van Rooyens' daughter's notebook, spent the class period telling the students that the girl was a *kaffirboetie* and wanted to marry a *kaffir*. Another time the teacher told the daughter she'd make sure that she failed the all-important matriculation exams.

Were there people outside his congregation who supported van Rooyen, questioned the system?

"They were absolutely in a small, small, small minority. As far as the church is concerned, I had very, very, very little sympathy. I remember one evening it was dusk, the phone rang and the person on the other side only said, 'Well, brother Jan, it is a colleague speaking.' He spoke in a whispering voice. Then he sympathized with me and told me that he is continually praying for me, and put the phone down. When my family asked who was it and I told them, my little daughter said, 'Dear Dad, wouldn't it have helped if he only said it was so-and-so speaking, and I support you?' "

Now, with the astonishing political changes in 1990, does the church have a role to play?

"No, I firmly believe that the Dutch Reformed Church has no role to play," van Rooyen replied unhesitatingly.

The mission is lost, the church had long been too self-absorbed.

"From our well-known ministers came all sorts of excuses: 'I have nothing against missionary work, please, please don't misunderstand me, but honestly, we haven't got the money.' And then moments after that he would receive an enormous increase in his salary," van Rooyen said. "The missionary work, I wouldn't say came to a standstill, but it became a relatively small section of the church's work. With the result that the church lost more and more and more of its influence."

The Afrikaner is scarcely even sending missionaries off its *volk* island anymore.

"We spiritualize everything. That's why I don't see the Dutch Reformed Church in any sense as a factor in the future of South Africa. I was in church the day before yesterday. On Sunday I must go, I can't stop myself, I've been going for so many years, I was born in the church. But I have a problem that you go and you waste your time. You really waste your time. It's a horrible thing to say."

Braam and Constand Viljoen, identical twins with similar farmer tans, laser-blue eyes, and white hair receding at the same rate, symbolize the great political divides that run through so many Afrikaner families. Politically, they share a concern about a potential Communist tyranny. But Braam would compare that tyranny to the National Party's apartheid rule—not an analogy Constand would likely make.

Constand, the South African Defense Force chief of staff under P. W. Botha, entered politics in 1993 to lead the right-wing Volksfront (People's Front). When the Volksfront decided to boycott the 1994 election, he quit, formed the Vryheidsfront (Freedom Front), and was elected to Parliament.

His twin, Braam Viljoen, taught church history at the relatively secular UNISA for twenty-three years, then quit to campaign for Parliament with the liberal Progressive Federal Party in 1987. When he lost, he took up farming on rented land near the Ndebele homeland, joined a political party in the homeland, and worked for the liberal Institute for a Democratic Alternative for South Africa (IDASA) in Pretoria. In a bizarre twist, Braam Viljoen became highly trusted by conservative Afrikaner farmers in the Transvaal who loathed the National Party and the Broederbond. For his political activities in exposing government killings of Ndebele opponents, Braam's name was on a death-squad list, along with that of the academic David Webster, who was killed in May 1989.

"The church not only does not have a strategy, but one often gets the feeling that it has no pastoral care or concern about its members," said Braam. "So often I have seen in the past a member simply moving away in frustration from the Dutch Reformed Church into the APK, and the Dutch Reformed Church will not do a thing about it. In fact some of them feel it's good riddance. The religious dream of the Afrikaner is shattered. We have nothing left. So many Afrikaners, and I'm one of them, simply let go of the church. I've become almost a de-Christianized person. I know how dangerous it is because you get to a position where there are just no anchors left anymore. I think this is going to be a general phenomenon in Afrikaner society."

Does anything give him any hope at all?

"My main source of hope comes from the black community. The way they are ready to forgive. They do not look for revenge. I think we still have a reservoir of goodwill amongst the blacks. But I'm also frightened by the anger in the youth I see coming."

What does Braam personally hold on to?

"At present I am drifting. Perhaps the most meaningful thing to me is activity. Feeling your way. With no support of systems, with the basic disregard and disbelief in systems.

"The Afrikaner put himself almost in touch with God and he considers himself to be a being called by God, determined by God, with a destination, by God," he said. "When that doesn't work out in reality, then it's a comedown. I believe that the Afrikaner is facing a far greater existential crisis than Vietnam was for the Americans."

In fact, it "may be comparable to what happened in Europe after the Second World War, when the shattering experience simply made people go into existentialist thinking. With nothing, really, in the way of an anchor."

PART V

THE AFRIKAANS LANGUAGE

O sorrowful land, Africa. Will there never be a resounding voice coming from your vast country? Will there never be a blinkingly white cloud, climbing up on your horizon to speak of hope?

—N. P. VAN WYK LOUW,
  "Die Dieper Reg" ("Deeper Justice"), 1938,
  translated by Marianne de Jong

CHAPTER TWENTY-FOUR

ROMANCING THE LANGUAGE

The Afrikaans word *taal* means language, but *die taal*, the language, refers specifically to Afrikaans. Novelist J. M. Coetzee wrote of exploring "the wondrous alien territory" of a foreign language "at the risk of misreading the lay of the land." South Africa's language geography is endlessly convoluted, but in it lie major clues to Afrikaners' nationalism and to the apartheid mentality.

Perhaps the two most familiar Afrikaans words in the international lexicon are "trek" and "apartheid," the one meaning an arduous trip, the other denoting an execrable social order.

Dominee Jan van Rooyen sneered at the prissy attitude of outsiders who reacted to the word "apartheid," when in reality it was merely a linguistic innovation used to take the sting out of a preexisting situation.

"We all [whites] practiced apartheid for centuries, but the word that we used was 'segregation.' In Afrikaans they said *segregasie*. In English, 'segregation.' General [Jan] Smuts said, 'Our policy is a policy of segregation.' Then the blacks started taking offense. They didn't like this word.

"The Dutch Reformed Church, my church, had an enormous missionary program. Our missionaries' reports said, 'The black people don't like this word.' At a missionary congress at Kroonstad in the Free State on the twenty-eighth of June, I think it was, 1928, a certain Dominee Strydom coined the word *apartheid*. He suggested that for the sake of the feelings of the black people, let's rather get a different word, because this word [*segregasie*] hurts them. Then *apartheid* took over [among Afrikaners]. The English section of the South African community kept on talking about segregation. Then all of a sudden, after 1948, they started talking about apartheid.

"This word was sent out to all the corners of the earth, as though it is a word that cannot be transferred, translated into any language, so low a situation it describes. It belongs to the Afrikaners: only in Afrikaans is there such a filthy word. Which is not true, it is part of politics, it is a game."

But while the world learned to hate apartheid and, by association, the language from which it came, Afrikaners remained fervently proud of their young, beautiful language. They are delighted when outsiders make the effort to learn and to appreciate what they consider to be their greatest invention.

One of the youngest languages in the world, Afrikaans is today spoken as a mother tongue by 6.1 million people, 2.5 million of them white, or 16 percent of the South African population. Another 6 million or 7 million can speak or understand Afrikaans as a second language. (Worldwide, approximately 38 million people speak Dutch or related languages—Flemish [spoken in Belgium], the dialect spoken in Surinam, and Afrikaans.)

English is the home language in South Africa for 3.4 million people, only 8.7 percent of the total. But as it is identified as an international language, it has become the language of education for many blacks.

The two main African language groups are Nguni (which includes Zulu, Xhosa, Swazi, and Ndebele), spoken by 17 million people, and Sotho (North Sotho, South Sotho, and Tswana), spoken by about 10 million people. In addition there are Shangaan/Tsonga and Venda in the northeast of the country, spoken by 2 million people.

It was one of those fixed-in-amber moments, a confluence that pleases. Susan van Rensburg sedately carried the tea and miniature sausage rolls into her husband's book-walled study in Auckland Park under the towering needle of the SABC television antenna. Reflecting the tidy, tree-lined suburb, with Johannesburg's ubiquitous droopy eucalyptus, the conversation for more than an hour had been utterly cultured, striving for erudition. All about Afrikaans, the language of the *volk*. Few topics are as emotion-laden to a committed Afrikaner.

The retired professor's wife poured the tea. Milk first? Or the tea? Whites in South Africa have preferences on this and on whether a man or woman should pour.

Professor Frans van Rensburg examined the poem he'd just been handed, a poem about learning Afrikaans back in the States.

"May I read it aloud?" he asked.

Spoons clinked musically in the china teacups. He began a grandiloquent rendering, impressive considering he hadn't read the poem before. He had only a hint of those lovely Afrikaans r's, sneered at by some English speakers, r's that roll on and on like a Scottish burr.

The Charm of Wortels: or Learning Afrikaans

> I steep in a language
>> where carrots are *wortels*,
>> pronounced vortels.
>> Verbs tint me from inside,
>> eager to obliterate my pallor,
>> quivering like tea leaves
>> vibrating along in a watery way.
>
> I feel words clamoring
> to lure a stray human to dye.
>
> In a stupor I oblige,
> become a warm *amber-kleur*.

"Well, well, well," the professor of Afrikaans said in a voice like a knell. And then, *"Baie, baie mooi"* [very, very beautiful].

The author sat delighted, not least by the felicitous conjunction of tea words and tea water.

Learning two thousand words of Afrikaans had been *baie, baie mooi* and relatively easy. It is a language stripped of most verb tenses and all gender endings.

Naas Steenkamp, a director of the Afrikaans-owned mining conglomerate Gencor, a man who produced exquisite metaphors even in English, said of his mother tongue: "It is a virile and natural language born in a setting essentially of illiteracy and therefore freed of the shackles of formalistic Dutch grammar.

"The influence of German, French, and then of course this infusion of vigor from Malay and Portuguese slaves produced a language that is to me so expressive and beautiful that I rile at my Afrikaans-speaking colleagues wherever I'm in contact with them, be it in the business world or wherever, at the way Afrikaans is being banalized, at the way the alien invasive weeds are moving into Afrikaans."

Steenkamp spoke quickly, like a sleek passenger train clicking along a track.

"If you consider the way Afrikaans developed, the speakers of Afrikaans had only one individual in the great covered-wagon trek who could read the Bible to them, and maybe the odd dominee and maybe one or two leading lights. The rest of them were uneducated, simple people who spoke the language as they heard and understood. They also

255

simplified it for communication purposes. We don't have 'I am, you are, he is, she is, we are.' We have simply 'ek is, jy is, hy is, sy is, ons is' [using the same verb form for all personal pronouns].

"It's very often mistakenly seen as a pidgin Dutch or as just a patois. The Afrikaners are greatly discursive and chatty people. The language lends itself beautifully to that," Steenkamp said.

Anton Goosen, a forty-something rock musician, agreed with Steenkamp. A counterculture icon who is frowned upon by the Afrikaner establishment, he speaks a more hippie English than the mining magnate, but similarly waxed rhapsodic about the language he loves best.

"It has very expressive poetry. It's guttural. Three tenses.'Was, is, will.' Without the word 'be.' Three. It's very, very, very easy, it's very descriptive. You can swear better in Afrikaans than in any other language I know of, because of the German guttural thing. Ja, the word *kak* is much stronger than 'shit.' In normal conversation, polite conversation I'll use the word 'shit.' Not *kak*, you know. The word *lekker*, you must have heard. It doesn't mean 'nice,' I mean, 'nice' has become like 'Have a nice day.' Whereas *lekker* is just— Ag, there are many examples," he said, suddenly inarticulate.

Does he think *lekker* sounds edible?

"Yes, ja, beautiful. And 'sweet' in Afrikaans is *lekkergoed*. 'Nice stuff.' The poetry flows off this language, it's a language that dances on the tongue, really, from the tongue to the ear.

"Breyten Breytenbach our poet did great work in Afrikaans. Ja, he's the most acclaimed writer in Flemish Dutch Afrikaans. Poetically, as far as the usage of this language, this guy is probably the biggest master that this language has ever come up with.

"When Breytenbach writes something like 'Good morning thorn tree, are you already licking your thorns clean this morning?' Or, 'Hello,' oh God, you know . . ." Goosen waved his hand as if calling the forgotten phrases from the air. " 'Hello foetus of the day.' It's a voice everybody in the world can understand. It's just that Zen way of thinking."

For even fully bilingual Afrikaners, Afrikaans is the language they use to express the core of their being. Two Afrikaans journalists sat in an apartment in Johannesburg musing about their language. Marichen Waldner, a reporter for the Afrikaans weekly *Rapport*, in Pretoria, is physically delicate, with fine, strawberry-blond hair. She talked sweetly and softly, but urgently. "The Afrikaans literature and the Afrikaans poetry that we know and we love makes wonderful use of the Afrikaans language. Also, when I sit down in front of the word processor and want to write something from my heart, I don't write it in English. I write it in Afrikaans. None of us are comfortable [working] at English-language newspapers."

Ina van der Linde, an imposing, dynamic woman who wrote for *Vrye Weekblad*, tried to pin it down: "There is something, the whole thing of basic honesty with yourself and with who you are."

Loving their language, the two women chafe against the restrictions clamped on Afrikaans by Broederbond-engineered organizations and education seeking to consolidate the *volk*: their language is part of the battleground of Afrikaner nationalism.

Other Afrikaner journalists had leapt the abyss to work for English-language papers. Marietjie Myburg, a tall, graceful woman who had dust-blue eyes, wore a loose, long skirt as she sat in her large office in the liberal *Daily Dispatch*'s East London Victorian-style building. An editorial writer, she is just over thirty, and unexpectedly mellow for someone married to a Dopper dominee. Her job represented a political position: she would rather have reported in her own language, but the Afrikaans papers all supported the government, which she refused to do.

Historically the *Daily Dispatch* was one of the English newspapers most hated by establishment Afrikaners. Donald Woods, known overseas as the friend of the Black Consciousness leader Steve Biko, was editor in the seventies. He launched vigorous anti-apartheid broadsides from these offices before he left the country, in 1977, his departure triggered by an incident where his daughter donned a T-shirt that had been powdered with an acid-based powder Ninhydrin that had been mailed to him by the security police. The girl had a painful reaction for several days but no lasting effects.

Myburg, who mixes English and Afrikaans in speaking ("My generation of Afrikaners speak that way"), said, "I feel quite strongly about language. I love to speak Afrikaans and I love to mingle with my Afrikaans friends. But my husband doesn't," she added. "He has a little logo saying 'Nationalism'—what is that saying? Who said it? Oscar Wilde or someone—'Nationalism is a disease, it's the measles of mankind' or something like that."

She gave a *lekker* laugh, deliciously relaxed.

"He says you communicate through language. I feel a bit more emotional about my mother tongue. A lot of my friends today are atheists or agnostics, and we often laugh about it, that you still have this something: you can't swear in Afrikaans. It's all right to swear in English. You can say fuck and God and Jesus Christ and everything in English. But in Afrikaans, no."

Myburg said she and her husband have thought about emigrating abroad. "I have respect and admiration for people who do, because it's not just a question of packing your things and go. There are so many things to consider. I feel quite strongly about language. I love to speak Afrikaans and to mingle with my Afrikaans friends."

"The word 'volk' is a powerful word for which there is no English equivalent," said Marichen Waldner. "This word 'volk' is what caused all the trouble in our history, our exclusive Afrikaner volk. The English translate it as 'people,' but it carries an emotional value which is untranslatable."

Agreeing with her, Professor of Education Martin Trümpelmann of Rand Afrikaans University said, "The Afrikaners make very much about volk and nasie, which you do not have in English—you only have 'nation.' The difference is that volk is a closer ethnic thing: the Afrikaner volk but the South African nation. The terms 'group' and 'volk' are seen more or less as synonyms. The Afrikaner didn't emphasize nation. The nation was just nonexistent." The nation would have included all whites.

The taalstryd, or language struggle, bubbles at the hot core of Afrikaner nationalism, with the historical "enemy" being English speakers. Afrikaans has slowly evolved into a spoken language since 1652, when Jan van Riebeeck landed and tried to communicate with the Khoi and the San, who possessed dazzling languages comprised of many clicking sounds.

"There are very few people who could master something like Khoi or Bushman because it's got seven clicks and each one's got three"—the linguist Hans du Plessis paused to think and continued—"each one's got an aspirated click, a guttural click, and a [he made a clunking sound like wood hitting wood] click.

"The only thing you hear are clicks," he said in his spacious office at the University of Potchefstroom.

"It's not the clicks that Afrikaans has taken over, it's the grammar, the structure. Also verbs, adjectives, and adverbs. That is why it's part of Africa."

Professor du Plessis's gentle smile, fuzzy sweater, and gentle mocking humor made him seem teddy-bear-like. It was a dry, cold June day on the platteland around Potchefstroom, the very bottom of winter. The veld here is similar to the land in Oklahoma or Iowa, states that du Plessis favored when he visited in 1976. He didn't like Cambridge, Massachusetts, because he found the people were snooty.

He searched for words to show that Afrikaans could "name" Africa better than English or any other European language. English names for natural objects, for trees, for animals were really Afrikaans, he said. "Afrikaans was here before English; it was here in pioneer days between 1652 and 1806. Afrikaans became part of the continent, became everything that the Boers on the Great Trek met on the way north, trees, whatever, which were then named in Afrikaans. Africa cannot really be said in English.

"For instance, when one goes into the veld and experiences the wind blowing over these plains, Afrikaans uses the word *huppel*. That's the sound the game makes in Africa when they go over the grass. It was Khoi originally and it means something that goes on and on and on. Afrikaans has taken these kinds of morphemes from African-based languages," du Plessis said. The dictionary translates *huppel* as 'frisk', 'hop', or 'gambol'.

"There are for instance Afrikaans verbs: if you're just sort of loitering around, you are doing things, just standing there, in Afrikaans we can say you do it *stan-stan*. Or *sit-sit*. That double thing is a Khoi construction."

Du Plessis gave a more modern example of influence by African languages. His children say, "Ek soek botter," which means literally "I'm looking for butter"—or "I want butter"—a syntactical construction which comes from Zulu, Tswana, or northern Sotho. In northern Sotho, "Kin yaka botoro," that *yaka* means exactly *soek*, or 'seek'. Those languages haven't got the construction "I want to have." But as far as his children knew, "Ek soek botter" was pure Afrikaans.

Professor du Plessis was careful not to say that Afrikaans was better than African languages at naming Africa. Other Afrikaners are not so meticulous. J. M. Coetzee wrote in *Doubling the Point* that Afrikaners unconsciously mimicked German Romantics, who thought that only they could experience their "passionate intimacy" with the landscape. The sinister corollary, Coetzee wrote, was that "closeness of fit between land and language is—so the reasoning goes—proof of the Afrikaner's *natural* ownership of the land." It was a small step from that claim of natural ownership to the actions that stripped millions of Africans of their lands.

Afrikaans grew slowly among the often illiterate Dutch settlers, the Africans, and the slaves from other parts of Africa, from Malaya, Indonesia, Ceylon, and India. Educated Dutch people and British settlers derided it as a *kombuistaal*—a "kitchen language." The pioneers who forged north away from Cape British rule took their creole language with them.

Not until 1815 did someone try to write in Afrikaans. And then it was

Cape Malays writing the Koran in Afrikaans with Arabic script, a fact ignored until recently by white Christians. Afrikaans was not written in the Roman alphabet until 1860, and not until 1875 did a formal effort begin to develop the embryonic language. In that year an organization called the Society of True Afrikaners (Genootskap van Regte Afrikaners, GRA), was founded in Paarl in the Western Cape. The society's manifesto proclaimed: "There are Afrikaners with English hearts and Afrikaners with Dutch hearts. There are Afrikaners with Afrikaans hearts. These last we call true Afrikaners and call out to them to come and stand with us."

In 1876 S. J. du Toit published a small book called *The First Principles of the Afrikaans Language*, marking the start of what came to be called the First Language Movement. But it was slow going. By the 1890s, educated Afrikaners still favored Dutch over Afrikaans and were increasingly using English.

At the end of the century an Afrikaans newspaper had been founded, and books and poems began to appear in Afrikaans. In 1890, advocates of a simplified Dutch instead of English or Afrikaans formed the Taalbond (Language Union). Transvaal journalist Gustav Preller argued for Afrikaans over Dutch in a series of articles called "Laat 'T Ons Toch Ernst Wezen" ("Let's Take This Matter Seriously"), and thus began the Second Language Movement. It really took off with the publication in 1908 of two books of Boer War poems, one by Jan Celliers and one by S. J. du Toit's son, J. D., better known as Totius. The Second Language Movement, unlike the first one, which had been supported by more liberal people, centered on Potchefstroom and the conservative Dopper church, of which Totius was a member.

Totius, along with others, found in the Afrikaners' language evidence of their separateness as a group, and the basis for the religious legitimization of what became apartheid. Preller's call to develop Afrikaans appealed to the Doppers' desire to be a unique "nation" of people, especially distinct from the British society that had rejected Calvinism. Biblical exegeses, particularly of the Tower of Babel story, contended that God wanted mankind divided according to language. This infused passion and holiness into the expansion and propagation of *die taal*.

In reaction to heavy-handed British attempts to stamp out Afrikaans, these new Afrikaners, united by the bitter memory of their defeat in the Anglo-Boer War, rallied around their infant language. Afrikaner anomie intensified as largely illiterate Afrikaner farmers from drought-stricken areas migrated in their tens of thousands from the *platteland* to the cities seeking jobs. They were a superstitious peasant people, ripe for political and cultural manipulation. The Broederbond made the *taalstryd*, the language struggle, one of its major vehicles for mobilizing Afrikaner nationalism while also helping to *ophef*, uplift, the people by developing their language skills.

The ground had been tilled by the Second Language Movement's institutions, which set up newspapers and magazines such as *Die Huisgenoot* (*The House Companion*) that were aimed at the barely literate and disseminated the myths of the *volk*, and idolized and subsidized authors who romanticized the sufferings of the people in their struggles with the British imperialists.

This was the time when the words *trek* and *trekker* gained legendary status. Though they entered the language in the 1880s, only after 1910 were they widely substituted for the words *emigrante* or *landverhuisers*, as the migrant farmers had generally been known. Many writers imitated Gustav Preller's emotional newspaper series on the pioneer Piet Retief by manufacturing other trekker heroes. Thus the *Groot Trek* was institutionalized and glorified in every Afrikaans school. The historian Isabel Hofmeyer remarked on "a sediment of 'Afrikanerness' which had settled in many households," as the *volk* was maneuvered into a burgeoning romance with its own language.

The Broederbond's cultural arm, the FAK, coordinated a growing welter of Afrikaner organizations, including some whose task was to manage dispersion of the language. The Afrikaans Language and Culture Organization (Afrikaanse Taal en Kultuurvereniging, ATKV) was founded in 1932 to raise the cultural level of the many thousands of Afrikaner railway workers. A similar society, the ATKB, founded in 1953, catered to Afrikaner postal workers.

Revisionist historians later argued that in addition to idealistic nationalism, urban middle-class Afrikaners had material interests in consolidating the *volk* and extending its literacy because this would create demand for services such as newspapers and education, that the middle class could provide—in Afrikaans.

The illiterate Afrikaans-speaking peasants' children flooded into new educational institutions beginning in the 1930s, and young Afrikaners acquired academic credentials in ever growing numbers. With a new literature, degreed leaders, and articulate spokesmen, the Afrikaners could be proud of their language, their burgeoning literature and educational achievements. At last they knew they were a "civilized" people possessing their own culture.

Ironically, it was the English speakers who set the stage for Afrikaner ascendancy in South Africa when they mandated in 1912 that civil servants be bilingual in English and Afrikaans. While English speakers didn't deign to learn Afrikaans, upwardly mobile Afrikaners eagerly studied English. Since many of the founders of the Broederbond were junior civil servants, it's no surprise they looked to take over the civil service. Public service became the Afrikaners' career goal, while the English concentrated on the much more lucrative business of business. In 1925 the Union of South Africa government declared Afrikaans an official language alongside English.

After the Nats' electoral triumph in 1948, the Afrikaners made the civil service their kingdom, their power, and their glory. Public-service jobs proliferated with the octopus of apartheid, that great duplicator of laws and bureaucracies, until, by the late 1980s, an estimated 43 percent of economically active Afrikaners were employed in the public sector.

What began as an effort to protect Afrikaans from English predations evolved into an ideology applied to all of South Africa's "groups." Since Afrikaans made the Afrikaners a "nation," the reasoning went, black Africans too were defined by their languages. To fulfil God's will, the apartheid system divided them up. Each "group"—Zulus, Xhosas, Swazis, Ndebeles, North Sothos, South Sothos, Tswanas, Shangaans, and Vendas—was assigned to a "homeland" or "Bantustan." But another motivation must have been at work. Xhosa-speaking people were divided into two homelands instead of one. Meanwhile, white people were lumped together as a unit despite their various mother tongues. This inconsistency exposed the system's racist underpinnings.

Piet van der Merwe, probably a Broederbond *vriend*, became chairman of the Commission for Administration—the civil service—in 1989. A soft-spoken, gracious former professor of labor economics and former Manpower Department official, he sat in his giant office on the twelfth floor of a building in downtown Pretoria. "The language question is always an emotional one," he mused. Although he was himself sanguine about the future of Afrikaans under a new government, "I think one must be practical," he said. "Tampering with language is like tampering with one's religion. There must be freedom of choice."

The lesson about freedom of choice had only recently been learned. While reveling in their own Christian National Education, the Afrikaners had sought to engineer the language and cultural development of others. In 1953 the government established its Division of Bantu Education. The division, which evolved into a department, mandated the use of African languages beyond grade four, displacing English. The department claimed its intent was to preserve black culture, when in fact the effect, and intention, was to keep blacks in low status.

In 1958 the department decreed that half of the subjects in secondary schools not taught in mother tongues should be taught in Afrikaans, the other half in English. There was a shortage of teachers and textbooks, and as it was difficult for students to follow instruction in three languages simultaneously, the policy was not enforced. Schools generally chose Afrikaans or English, mostly English, in addition to the local tongue. Then in 1974, the new, more conservative minister and the deputy minister of Bantu education, M. C. Botha and Andries Treurnicht, decided to enforce the 1958 decree in the Transvaal. Implementation began in 1975 over the objections of school boards, opposition Parliament members, parents, and students and despite a shortage of teachers and books.

On June 16, 1976, angry students in Soweto marched across their grim, coal-smoke-clogged township to confront government authorities, denouncing the policy. They wanted to learn in English. The language issue was the spark, but deeper grievances nationwide caused the country to flare up like tinder. Hundreds of students were shot, many were tortured and died, and Soweto became a global symbol for revolt against racism.

Afrikaners were puzzled by the revolt: Afrikaans was a wonderful language. Why would blacks be so violently allergic to its use but accept the equally foreign colonial language of English? It took the Afrikaners years to understand—partly because apartheid worked so efficiently. People of different races were so distanced that they could barely hear each other screaming, let alone empathize or comprehend meanings. The students were labeled "terrorists" and "Communists" by the establishment.

"I think it's highly debatable that people have to be taught in their mother tongue," said Martin Trümpelmann, a professor of education at Rand Afrikaans University. "It doesn't make sense for the blacks at all because they have to compete in the white man's language in the end. You're actually keeping them inferior by keeping them with their mother tongues. If I as an Afrikaner wanted to send my kid to an English school, nobody would've complained. But the black couldn't send his kid to my school [or an English school]. All in all the system was seen in terms of racial and language criteria."

The Afrikaans professor Frans van Rensburg, retired from the university where Trümpelmann taught, disagreed. "One of the main reasons for the large school dropout [rate of the blacks] is the difficulty with English. That is one of the reasons to advocate the use of indigenous languages in any case up to a certain point."

Up to what point?

263

"Well, you know the educational field is in flux. In 1976 that was one of the main reasons," he said, elliptically referring to the Soweto uprisings.

"Dr. Treurnicht insisted upon the rather rigid application of the constitution's language provisions, without taking account that there were not enough books in Afrikaans available or in the black languages. That was one of the main factors for 1976. It was not really the principle of the whole thing, but the mechanism. How can you expect teachers to teach a language without the availability of books?"

The sanctity of their own language is so embedded in most white Afrikaners' psyches that few could believe that blacks really resented *die taal*. Even with Afrikaners' experience of belittlement by the English, many of them could not see, as van Rensburg showed, that they had meted out analogous, if not worse, treatment to Africans.

Other Afrikaners inside the establishment, such as Hans du Plessis, gradually came to understand the political liabilities of Afrikaans. The Potch professor seemed much less programmed in his responses to questions relating to *die taal* than most establishment academics. He was learning flexibility, actually changing his thinking, not just saying that he was changing.

"At first I think we didn't believe that the whole thing [Soweto] had anything to do with Afrikaans," he sighed. "The average Afrikaner, and that includes the Afrikaner cultural organizations, did not realize there was a problem. They ignored the whole thing and said, 'Well, that's nonsense.'

"The first time I heard that the whole apartheid system was designed to retard black people, to keep them down educationally, I thought that's absolute nonsense because we did everything we could. Then one realizes, well, you didn't, you forced them down on their own language. What Verwoerd said at the time was 'Keep them in their own languages, then it's very difficult to move up the social ladder.'

"Among ourselves the linguists started a discussion. We tried to think, how can a language be oppressive? And then we realized it's not the language, it's the user of the language that's the oppressor. The moment we realized that, it was kind of easier.

"But Afrikaans is not just the language of the oppressor, it's the language of the oppressed as well. It's the language of the liberation movement of the Western Cape. In the Western Cape, actually in the Karoo, there was the Cape Professional Teachers' Association, which is a brown [colored] association. It advocated something called alternative Afrikaans, which we originally thought meant something different in structure. But when we met these people it became clear that they meant a new content. It didn't mean a new dialect: it meant Afrikaans with a new cognitive concept."

Meaning without politics?

"Yes, without politics, without apartheid built into the whole language. There was a meeting that was one of the most important seminars on Afrikaans in Durban. It was called 'Power, State, Language and Struggle.' That was in '89. I'm not sure who they were, but it was, for instance, people from the alternative Afrikaans movement and people from IDASA who brought everybody together, everybody meaning linguists from these different points of view. That was the first time I realized it's not easy to understand this whole thing of Afrikaans. We met people from the ANC. One person who had recently returned to South Africa stood up and said that when he came back, he got into a South African Airways plane in New York and they were talking Afrikaans. He thought, 'Oh shit, here are the police again.' " To that man, du Plessis realized, Afrikaans was the language of apartheid's enforcers. "That made the difference in my way of thinking.

"Then we had a conference where everyone was invited. Before, you invited all the whites to an FAK congress and then you invited the brown people to a teachers' organization. Since then we've had a range of seminars on Afrikaans, and realized we're talking about eleven languages, eleven equal languages, and every language has got the right to say, 'Well, I want to be official.' The moment we realized that, the whole debate shifted from a debate of Afrikaans must be *the* language, as it is at the moment, to a more tolerable opinion."

It took thirteen years, from 1976 to 1989, for du Plessis and many of his fellow Afrikaans linguists to realize how blacks felt about the language of the oppressor. They were not on the cutting edge of change. But one of the verbs du Plessis used most often was "realize." An artist crafting a cartoon of this genial, if slightly naive, man would draw a light bulb floating in the air ahead of him, with the man running to catch up to the bulb so it would be over his head.

In 1992, a few days before du Plessis talked about his coming to awareness, more than forty people were killed in night raids, possibly at police instigation, in ANC-Inkatha violence in the black township of Boipatong between Potchefstroom and Johannesburg. Two days after the massacre, President de Klerk visited the township to convey his condolences but was greeted with fury and signs saying GET OUT. Threatening throngs surrounded his limousine. A black commentator in the *Star* newspaper said the white establishment's shock at de Klerk's hostile reception "revealed an astounding failure to fathom the level of anger engendered by violence in Boipatong and other townships across the land."

The furious mood of the blacks in South Africa was quite obvious to outside observers. But du Plessis was taken aback by the black reaction. "I was shocked at the way de Klerk was called a murderer," he said. "If there was one person that really tried to get out of this pile it is de Klerk. Whether he's moving fast enough that's another question. If you looked at his face when his car passed the camera, I thought he was so shocked, he didn't expect it either."

"Better late than never" could be the motto for du Plessis and other members of his generation who are finally abolishing statutory apartheid. However, their continuing ignorance of their own country and their sheltered political judgments remain unfortunately reminiscent of their attitudes in 1976 and Soweto.

To retain an accurate perspective, remember that Professor du Plessis is on the moderate left of the Afrikaner spectrum. Compared to most Afrikaners he looks tolerant and flexible. The philosophy that language determines identity/*volk* cannot be unlearned overnight.

According to the former head of the Security Police, General Johan Coetzee, right-wing Afrikaners simply cannot fathom any reasoning about language other than their own. "If you say to the Afrikaner that the campaigning for democratic rights by the black people follows the same lines as what the Afrikaners went through, you know what he counters with? 'If that's the case, why don't they fight for their own language rights? Why aren't they fighting for Shakespeare in Xhosa or Zulu?' "

Right-wingers, imbued with their own nationalistic myths, believe that "part and parcel of their fight was a language one," Coetzee explained. They cannot comprehend the liberation of a "nation" unless it is defined largely by language, as is their own. The multinational nature of the ANC is beyond their ken. Some believe that the ANC is in fact the ethnic movement of the Xhosa people (Nelson Mandela is a Xhosa) and that members are dishonest in portraying it as a multiethnic political party.

As if to prove Coetzee's contention, Jan Grobbelaar, the Conservative Party mayor of Phalaborwa, a copper-mining town in Northern Transvaal, said, "To me the ANC is not actually a nationalist group. I think they are too mixed up with the Communists. If you look at Inkatha [Gatsha Buthelezi's Zulu party], if you look at Venda [the "homeland" of the Venda people] political parties, I would say those are nationalist parties. Because it's a party for a people in a specific country. And I've got a lot of admiration for that. But looking at the ANC, they've got whites, Indians, coloreds, blacks, from all over the place. They must have a language, they must have a culture and so on. And the ANC is a mixed-up group, to me."

Also in Phalaborwa, the CP member and former AWB leader Fritz Meyer enthused over a map drawn up by Jan Groenewald, the brother of Major General Tienie Groenewald, a leader of the Afrikaner Volksfront and a former Military Intelligence head. "It's a very logical division of the country," Meyer said, "because it's based on language differences."

Koos "Bomber" Botha, the CP member of Parliament who helped bomb an empty white school rather than let children of returning ANC exiles use it, also argued that language and nation must go together. "We are the only people in recent history that developed their own language. That's why I'm so cross with you, you the Americans, the strongest country in the world, the leader of the world, you speak the English language of Margaret Thatcher. You've got a couple of hamburgers in your mouth when you speak, but the point is you didn't develop your own language. This I can't understand. I feel so cross when I think about an American and I listen to him and he speaks English."

The more conservative Afrikaners just can't comprehend the American melting pot. Ethnicity is the only realpolitik to them, and language is both its proof and symbol. Language is their flag.

CHAPTER TWENTY-FIVE

ROOINEKE

"We Afrikaners called them *rooineke* and they would call us *japies*," said Dries Struwig, referring to English speakers.

Struwig is a retired Security Police interrogator who until 1990 worked at the infamous John Vorster Square police headquarters in Johannesburg, where, according to various accusations in court, he tortured prisoners. Struwig was sitting in his living room with his wife, Leana, in the suburb of Brackenhurst, south of Johannesburg proper. Their two little girls watched television in a nearby room.

Rooineke, a taunting term for English speakers, originally referred to the red-collared, formal British uniforms used at the beginning of the Boer War. But what did *japies* mean? "*Plaasjapie*, a young person who comes from the farm," Leana helped. A *japie* is a dolt.

"Ag, but I think that's all gone, forgotten," said Struwig, positively expansive. "Now sometimes you find English- and Afrikaans-speaking guys talking in the pub about the Anglo-Boer War. It'll be a laugh. Because I think the whites in South Africa have come a long way and I think that we are great friends. The Anglo-Boer War, that's gone and forgotten."

John Horak is a former police spy who reported to the Security Branch chief, Johan Coetzee. A journalist by profession, he began spying in 1958 for the National Party government because he hated English speakers.

"I come from a poor Afrikaner home in Kimberley. I subsequently got academic qualifications, but those days, coming right from school, the Afrikaans press wouldn't employ you unless you were a graduate. That was for very simple reasons, because it was usually at university that you got recruited into these exclusive Afrikaner organizations. So there was no option open, I had to go to the English-language press. Which made my mother cry. She prayed and fasted for a week for the Lord to deliver me of these English-speaking people. He didn't answer the prayers."

Horak, a short, graying man, sat in a sparsely furnished, unheated, cold office at the headquarters of the Apostolic Faith Mission in Johannesburg

268

for which he was the public relations officer. "Now, I one afternoon went to maybe eight shops in Kimberley to buy an undershirt. My mother would have given me a hiding to find out I went into an English shop.

"I would say '*Gee my 'n frok*' [Give me an undershirt] and the lady behind the counter would say, 'Excuse me?' And I would look up and say 'Afrikaans?' And she would say, 'I can't speak Afrikaans,' and then you would say 'It's high time that you learned,' and you turn around and you walk out, you see. She doesn't want to say it in your language, you tell her to go to hell."

Horak may not have been aware of it, but he was acting in tune with Broederbond campaigns to boycott English businesses. A typical directive in 1936 was "Never shop where you are not served in Afrikaans . . . and tell the trader why."

"The English-language press actually made me hate them," Horak said. "The better I was doing there, the more I got to hate them. Because they were actually more anti-Afrikaner than Afrikaners were anti-English at that stage. The rift was deep in this country."

"My father at the beginning of this century had to carry a board. When he spoke Afrikaans this board was put on his chest, around his neck. It said, 'I'm a donkey.' "

Jan van Rooyen, a retired Dutch Reformed Church dominee, still felt the old wounds.

"Basically South Africa was an English colony," he said. "General Smuts was an adherent of the old empire idea. You had many Afrikaans-speaking people who spoke English and sent their children to English schools, who even took English as their home language.

"I remember distinctly when we came here [to Johannesburg] in August 1939, before the outbreak of the Second World War. When you went into the OK [OK Bazaar department store] in town, you would speak to the girl behind the counter, Afrikaans-speaking girl, and she'd refuse to serve you in Afrikaans. She used English.

"In '48 the Afrikaans-speaking group took over, then the pendulum was swinging. We all became Nationalists and the Nationalists' vote grew with every election. We don't like to be part of a minority. Definitely. You want to be part of the group."

Van Rooyen's dynamic wife, Joupie, elaborated: "I think we both grew up in homes where there was a tremendous feeling against the English."

"That's right. There were reasons for it, absolutely reasons for it," Jan van Rooyen said bitterly. "You don't do that sort of thing to people. England just decided that they did not want us here. Shortly after the discovery of diamonds, England annexed the diamond fields. The gold mines, poor old [President] Paul Kruger had an enormous time with the so-called *uitlanders*, the [English-speaking] outlanders, in Johannesburg who absolutely refused to cooperate with the [Boer Transvaal] Republic. And Cecil Rhodes did his utmost best to have the Transvaal taken as a British colony also. Really the Afrikaner had an enormous lot of horrible experiences at the hands of the English. And especially Natal. Natal is an absolutely English province."

"The last outpost," his wife murmured.

"Ja, it was the last outpost. After 1948 they wanted to remain a colony of England. The Afrikaner developed an inferiority complex," he insisted. "That's why my people are shy."

Professor Elaine Botha agreed that there was a strong sense of cultural inferiority among the Afrikaners. The language slights cut deeply. When asked why language is such an "obsession" with Afrikaners, this woman, extremely articulate in English, gasped as if punched in the stomach. She didn't like being called obsessed. "Language represents one's whole identity," she said, "which I don't think people living in the Anglo-Saxon world can even understand. If you said to me, 'You're not allowed to be Elaine Botha because we don't like people looking like you,' that's just unacceptable to me. And I think that was the message that a whole couple of generations of Afrikaners got in this country.

"I recall going to school in a little Afrikaans school in Krugersdorp, getting on the bus with the English kids and the English schoolteacher on the same bus would say, 'Oh here the dirty East School children come again,' and it's the Afrikaans children, you know. I think we were as clean as any other kids. But the whole notion, they couldn't stand the sight of Afrikaners. And then you respond in a very strong way, and that picks up momentum."

Naas Steenkamp, that most urbane of industrialists, remembers his shock at discovering at Potchefstroom University the gulf between the Afrikaners and the English. He'd gone to high school at a dual-language school in the Cape and his father was a "detribalized, footloose, irreligious Dutch Reformed" man, so the rude introduction to "what it meant to be an Afrikaner" came late. "On the very first day I heard English being spoken at the notice board and here were two English girls whose parents in Johannesburg had decided it was a smart idea to send them down to a unilingual Afrikaans university. I spoke to them in English and that stigmatized me from that moment onwards. 'This guy speaks English. What weird phenomenon is this? An Afrikaner who speaks English?' Bear in mind that this was in the early fifties and Potchefstroom University was a tribal college in virtually its purest form. Christian National Education and the rest of it. I became a bit of a marginal figure from the word go."

In his office at the law school in the citadel of Afrikaner learning, Stellenbosch University, Louwrens du Plessis was surprised to hear praise of the rolling r's of the Afrikaans accent.

"Perhaps that's the American view," he said, smiling. "Because I phoned someplace in the States, those who answered on the other side said, 'Where do you come from? You've got such a lovely accent.' I felt so good about it.

"Now it may seem to be a small thing, but we Afrikaners were laughed at when we couldn't speak English properly and when we used wrong words. I have appreciation for English speakers who speak Afrikaans and do it with their accent and make mistakes. I had an experience of teaching at the University of Cape Town. The real English-speaking students don't accept you. If you pronounce a word incorrectly, you know, or say something wrong, they will go for you." Their hostility implied that they viewed him, because of his slight mistakes, as a less educated, less civilized person, one still bearing the mark of the *kombuistaal*, kitchen language, instead of the Queen's English.

Elsabe Brink, a historian who was on the Johannesburg City Council, thinks Afrikaner defensiveness over the language reflects a class conflict.

In the thirties and forties, "You had a very large working-class component linked up with the whole poor white question," she said. "Then you had a very small section of Afrikaner intellectuals who studied in Germany, who moved into political positions, moved into the SANLAMs and so on. They had struggled very hard to achieve any positions of power vis-à-vis English language power, against the Oppenheimers of the world, mining houses, which was all in the hands of English capital. It was very difficult in the forties and fifties to progress in any professional areas if you weren't English."

Brink, a member of the Democratic Party in 1992, sports impeccable Afrikaans credentials that go back six generations in the Cape—a long tradition of ministers and schoolteachers and school inspectors. She sat primly and somewhat warily in her genteelly seedy old house in Auckland Park, the same suburb where Afrikaans professor Frans van Rensburg lives, but miles away in attitude. Occasionally Brink's phone rang and she crossed the room to activate her fax machine.

"Having grown up in a house where Afrikaans language and culture is very important, my going over and, say, voting for the Progressive Federal Party, was basically also making a choice for English. Politics was very largely run on language and culture lines rather than the liberal/conservative values."

Nevertheless, she insists that Afrikaners are more British than Dutch.

"I lived in Holland for two years. We're not Dutch. Afrikaners are more British in their whole social structure, their way of living and of socialization, of thinking, of communicating, everything. I mean, we'd been a British colony since 1800. People seem to forget that. I find it very ironical that the primary school I went to, which is very Afrikaans, in the late fifties, early sixties, had turned so conservative that rather than open their doors to fellow brown Afrikaners, they decided to amalgamate with the English.

"I remember a time when I couldn't speak English, first of all, and secondly, our big sport was to go and have fights with the little English children, you know, on the golf course. Go and punch up the local English kids, boys and girls, both of us together. Not that it happened often, but that was the kind of a level of integration that you had with English-speaking people. I think we've always been part of their culture."

Philosophy professor Zach de Beer Postma, sitting in one of those cubicle offices at UNISA, said, "When my mother was at school in the thirties, you still had dual-medium [English and Afrikaans] education. One of the first things the Nats did when they came to power was split the English from the Afrikaans schools. And it worked so effectively. South Africa is a lot of countries. There is not really a common nationality.

"I must say it is one of the things in America, you land in an airplane and immediately you are in an American atmosphere. You don't get that sense of unity in this country. There are pockets of it, but in America your Negroes speak with American accents.

"In the rural communities here so many white Afrikaners rarely even go outside their province. I thought when TV came in Afrikaans and English, people would learn to speak both languages. But I frequently travel to the north still and there people switch off the TV when an English program comes on. Even English news. I can't get over that."

Aren't there any Afrikaners who actually like English?

Sampie Terreblanche, the dynamic bête noire of the Broederbond and an economics professor at Stellenbosch University, slumped in a meditative way and expatiated.

"We had this booming sixties," he said. "The roaring sixties, as America had its roaring twenties. Our roaring sixties with a high growth rate. A very interesting thing that has developed since the sixties is the rapprochement between the English and Afrikaners. The relationship between the English and Afrikaners is as good as never before.

"Afrikaners became prominent in the business world. There was this very quick embourgeoisement of the Afrikaner, perhaps too quick. They start to understand the language, more than one sense of the word, of the English speakers, and the English speakers, the business community, became aware of all kinds of favors, all kinds of patronage from Pretoria."

A man who was perhaps the very incarnation of the type of Afrikaner businessman that Sampie Terreblanche meant was P. J. T. Oosthuizen, a lawyer for South Africa's giant state electric company ESCOM and the general in charge of the tanks that moved to the outskirts of Luanda, Angola, in 1975–76.

Oosthuizen is rich. He owns houses in Johannesburg and on the ocean in Cape Town, and his Johannesburg house is decorated with lovely antique furniture. He's well traveled and, a former Olympic target shooter, is a member of the U.S. National Rifle Association. He visits the United States regularly and is fluent in English. He sent his children to school in Germany. "I am very fond of the British system because I am very closely associated with their military system," Oosthuizen said. "Our system is really the British system adapted. Whenever I go to Europe and I end up in England, at least I feel at home because I start off with a breakfast that I understand.

"The English language is so eloquent and I find myself very attracted to the British sense of humor. For example, I understand the wit that you find in the law courts.

"My co–South Africans, Afrikaans-speaking South Africans, will want to crucify me for this, in fact I've said this openly already, that I think that South Africa should have only one language and that is English.

"In fact, in ESCOM I recommended that English be made the official language of ESCOM, full stop. Now, not even later. For very practical reasons. Firstly, it is an international language. Secondly, then you escape the necessity of creating more than one. Why use Afrikaans and not Xhosa, Sotho, Zulu, and so forth? Which makes it an impossibility to run a business. So make it one language—English."

A small holstered pistol hung from his belt.

"I call it in Afrikaans a 'Smit and Wessels,'" he said, smiling, "because those are Afrikaans names. But it is a Smith and Wesson."

*   *   *

Annie Gagiano could be called a Stellenbosch brat since she grew up in the architecturally and environmentally romantic Afrikaans town and then became a professor of English literature married to a professor of political science, both at Stellenbosch University. She was one of the four or five faculty members who, by 1992, had joined the ANC. She folded herself gracefully onto a bean-bag chair in a corner of her small office, unlike what one would expect of a mother of four with gray threading delicately through her pulled-back hair.

"A big influence in my life was English literature," she said. "At school and also when I came here. The sort of values that I thought were important and healthy were here in the things I read." She waved to the stacks of books on the shelves behind and above her head. "Also I almost made for myself a spiritual home in this subject. There's very few of these classics that wouldn't convey something of what I was looking for."

Can't she find it in Afrikaans literature?

"At the time I was a student, there was a lot less of Afrikaans literature and there wasn't the kind of poet like Breyten [Breytenbach] that there is now. I think that Afrikaans has made a very interesting development. I know very well a number of examples like [novelist] Jeanne Goosen. It's just that liberating zaniness of their attitudes. Because of people like that it is possible to hang on to Afrikaans. But that's partly because it developed a freedom of expression. Afrikaans to me is just a language and Afrikaners are people like other kinds of people."

English superciliousness grated on Professor van Rensburg's Afrikaner sensitivities. Ken Owen, much-despised editor of the mass circulation *Sunday Times* newspaper, wrote that the language of the "new South Africa" was English and that the Parliament, which conducted business in Afrikaans, was a dying factor. "I have seldom seen a much more imperialistic thing said," the professor exploded.

"I think the English are a bit stupid. If they'd only recognize the Afrikaans language without a grudge, they will see how many tensions disappear. Language lies at the heart of many of these things. I say the Anglo-Boer War in many respects still lingers on."

CHAPTER TWENTY-SIX

WHOSE AFRIKAANS?

Professor Hans du Plessis heaved a big sigh, thinking of the big picture.

"You know 'control' is one of the key words in this whole thing," he said. "Who wants to control what. The Afrikaans mentality is: 'I want to control and that's the only way I can live.' It's changing, quite rapidly I think. I hope. You can change the laws quite easy, but to change the heart's not that easy."

Professor Frans van Rensburg said several times that he was not being prescriptive about language. But he had a plan that he "showed to people in places where important decisions are taken." Under his plan English and Afrikaans would remain official languages and a third African language could be chosen by blacks. He called it "A Language Policy for a Unified South Africa."

His plan fed into that great maw of Afrikaner plans, and eventually in 1993 the Broederbond-controlled Academy for Science and Art (Akademie vir Wetenskap en Kuns) issued "A Language Plan for South Africa," under which Afrikaans and English would continue as the "countrywide official languages," while nine African "principal" languages could "acquire official status in a prescribed constitutional manner." But not immediately, apparently.

"I think that people have been learning these past years that you can't be prescriptive," van Rensburg said. "So I proposed that if the black community as a whole feels like it, then they amongst themselves should decide which one [of their languages should be official]. Let's get the indigenous languages going."

"How superimposing," responded Achmat Davids with exquisite sarcasm, when told of Professor van Rensburg's plan.

Under apartheid classifications, Davids is a colored of Malay origin. He trained as a social worker at the University of Cape Town and at Ohio State University. He pursues historical and linguistic studies about Cape

Malay Afrikaans and received a master's degree in linguistics from the University of Cape Town. He was awarded a fellowship at Yale University in 1992 to pursue his linguistic studies but only recently has gained recognition for his work at home in South Africa.

"How totally out of touch with reality," he added of van Rensburg and his plan. "No longer can people be dictated to as to what language they ought to speak. This is why I said that the ANC came with what I would regard as a fairest language policy ever."

The ANC at first proposed to divide the country into several language regions with each region having three official languages, which Davids said would leave Afrikaans an official language in most of the country. But this too was a hot potato. As the constitutional negotiations ground on, the ANC's proposal shifted to a call for all of South Africa's eleven major languages to have equal status, agreeing to constitutional measures that give the nine provinces considerable autonomy in language policies. But because that's going to be impossible to implement, the language issue is still unresolved.

Up a fairly steep hill from Cape Town's business district is some prime real estate close to the ocean. This few square miles of low, old pastel-colored houses is the Malay quarter. A muezzin can be heard blaring the call to Muslim prayers from a small mosque. Achmat Davids and his wife, Karima, live in one of these quaint, cramped houses. Karima did not say she was Achmat Davids's wife, that her business was sewing, that she wrote poetry and worked with street children, but she let the hints seep out like spices that wafted into the room where she was sewing party dresses made of chiffon and other diaphanous cloth. Confections of dresses suspended on hangers frosted the walls.

When Davids appeared, called from the recesses, he shuffled in, in a disheveled outfit. He was fleshy with a pleasant face and a few teeth. Perhaps this was the wrong house, the wrong man? But his appearance belied his erudition.

"Money went from taxes to the FAK, to the Akademie vir Wetenskap en Kuns. They were only promoting Afrikaans as a white man's language. Who says that Afrikaans is in fact a language of Europe? Who says that it was made only by white Afrikaners? Were they ever part of its formation?

"My answers to those questions are all no. The language came about as a result of the contact of the slaves and the indigenous Khoi people with Dutch. Afrikaans is first noticed in the mouths of black speakers, not white speakers; white speakers called it a 'kitchen language' or a 'Hotnot's language' and gave it all its negative names."

Davids paused to plunge back through the house's hallway, full of playing children, to bring back his 340-page master's thesis about the Malay, Arabic, colored origins of Afrikaans.

Under apartheid coloreds were divided into seven groups, including Malay, Griqua, and Cape Colored, which was again a heterogeneous lot. Davids speaks a variety of Afrikaans called Bo-Kaap (Upper Cape). The name refers specifically to the Malay quarter of Cape Town.

"It's an Afrikaans that is different in many ways from Standard Afrikaans," he said. "It's different in terms of its pronunciation, its vocabulary, its philology as well as phonology. Sometimes even in terms of its syntax. My Afrikaans is in fact greatly influenced by the languages of the slaves. We use words in Afrikaans which are not used in any other part of the country.

"But my Afrikaans is not regarded as the standard form. I say that is absolutely nonsense, it's the oldest form of Afrikaans. The charm of the words we created as a community existed long before the standardization of Afrikaans."

Is there any dictionary for his Afrikaans?

"Zero. Zilch. There is a noticeable tendency amongst Cape Muslim Afrikaans speakers to pronounce the Afrikaans diphthong 'ooi' as 'ay' or at times to use the 'ha' instead of the standard 'ge' for the past tense of the verb, or to change the pronunciation of the double 'd' or a 't' in the middle of a word to an 'r.' Like 'middag' or 'bottel' tends to be pronounced as 'mirrag' and 'borrel.' This pronunciation is already known to have existed in the nineteenth century."

Davids said that white Afrikaners do not realize that even as they view Afrikaans as their language of liberation vis-a-vis the British, so coloreds in the Cape and *platteland* consider *their* Afrikaans a language of liberation against apartheid.

"The future Afrikaans is going to be one that is accommodating and more reflective of the other languages in the country as well. One sees this already in what's known as *fly-taal*, which is Afrikaans spoken by the African people."

The mining executive Naas Steenkamp agrees. "The true virility of Afrikaans is no longer to be found in white cultural circles. The speakers of Afrikaans that speak the most exquisite Afrikaans are mostly coloreds stretching from the Cape up along the northwestern parts. These are people who grow the language organically."

Davids complains that the Society of True Afrikaners in 1875 was the beginning of the "Dutchification" of Afrikaans. Once the Nats came to power they set up organizations to entrench the language and make it "whiter." According to Professor Marianne de Jong, Afrikaans is easy for a Dutch person to read, but speaking it is more difficult. Davids said that when he spoke his Bo-Kaap Afrikaans in the Netherlands, he could scarcely be understood.

Hans du Plessis, who recommends Davids as an expert linguist and "a very good thinker," was on the language commission that revised the blue-covered *Woordeboek*, dictionary, which sets out the spelling of Standard Afrikaans. He admits that, as Davids charged, this is a "white" production.

From its founding, one of the main aims of the Academy for Science and Art had been to promote Afrikaans by "scientifically" planning its structure and by establishing major literary prizes, du Plessis said. Other cultural organizations such as the ATKV (Afrikaanse Taal en Kul-turvereniging), FAK, and the Rapportryers fought to maintain Afrikaans as an official language, and the ATKV provided prizes for popular writing.

He explained that the Academy for Science and Art appointed a language commission to codify Standard Afrikaans. Its *Woordeboek*, which he compared to the *Oxford English Dictionary*, has only made it up to the k's so far. Du Plessis admitted there were thousands and thousands of Afrikaans words that were not in the blue-covered Standard Afrikaans dictionary.

"We used the term 'general civilized,' that was the term for Standard Afrikaans. That meant all the others must be uncivilized," du Plessis admitted with chagrin. He hopes that attitudes will change and that the "white" dictionary will be redone by a democratically formed language commission.

"I have some rude things to say about this blue-covered thing," Achmat Davids said, chuckling, referring to the Standard Afrikaans spelling dictionary. "I wrote a review of the blue-covered thing and it was issued by the Akademie vir Wetenskap en Kuns. I attacked the thing because it ignored other varieties of Afrikaans, especially Bo-Kaap Afrikaans, and it had a tendency to go back to spelling forms that have been discarded in Dutch.

"It failed to give recognition to the fact that the greatest numbers of speakers of Afrikaans happen to be colored people living in the Western Cape who speak a different variety of Afrikaans. Or different varieties of Afrikaans, which need to be recognized, like Griqua Afrikaans, which is spoken by the people living in the Northern Cape who are the descendants of the Khoisan people."

When Hans du Plessis and other linguists started work on Afrikaans dialects in the 1960s, their work was controversial. Du Plessis studied a community of black people in northern Namibia called the van der Merwes.

"What happened was they went on one of these silly Boer treks, then they were left behind and didn't have contact with Standard Afrikaans. We taped them about three or four years ago: it was Afrikaans as spoken in 1900." He remembered that after addressing an FAK meeting a man approached him. "He didn't say thank you at all. He just said, 'Well how the hell can you give our language away?' And that's the thinking—we are giving our language to the brown people now.

"But how on earth could we give it away?" du Plessis asked rhetorically, "because they had it before we did."

Marianne de Jong said, "Afrikaans cannot define a tribe anymore. I think people also know this means your language is not your ethnicity anymore. If you switch on your TV, there are black people speaking Afrikaans in the commercials, and people don't complain."

But Klaus Steytler, an author and the husband of the novelist Elsa Joubert, did complain: "Bad language drives out good language, bad books drive out good books, bad civilization drives out good civilization," he said. "Language must be a precise tool. I must be able to say exactly what I mean. I would like people to speak properly on paper. They can talk as they wish. But I'm sure this question of precise language is also a very serious problem in America. As elsewhere where the language is softening up."

When told that his fellow Cape Towner Achmat Davids, whom Steytler did not know, argued that standardization should be inclusive rather than exclusive and that there were thousands of Afrikaans words that were not in the dictionaries, Steytler said: "Well I couldn't believe."

Because he doesn't know the words?

"I would know them, seeing that I live here," he replied. "I think it's overstressing a point. Now the inclusion for instance of colored people in the Akademie is slowly happening. It should have happened previously, but that was the whole walk in the darkness since 1948."

Many younger Afrikaners strenuously disagreed with Steytler on the issue of standardization. It is in fact a major reason for young people's disenchantment with the establishment. Ina van der Linde, for example, who was raised to speak *suiwer*, pure, Afrikaans, despises the "Standard Afrikaans that was pressed down on us at school. It took away all the originality and creativity in language. It was a way of suppressing spontaneous expression."

Van der Linde worked for *Vrye Weekblad*, a newspaper popular with young Afrikaners in part because it was more readable than other Afrikaans papers. English speakers who hadn't read Afrikaans since school also were attracted to it. The Witwatersrand history professor

Cynthia Kros said, "It's wonderfully written in a very beautiful Afrikaans. Very good, vivid, and idiomatic as well." Within the *volk*, the paper epitomized the fight between Standard and a new Afrikaans, the front lines of a modern *taalstryd*.

"We use informal language; we try to write the way people speak, and that is influenced by a lot of English words and very un-Standard words," van der Linde explained. "We're trying to say f. you, we aren't going to do it that way any longer. I'm critical of the way the youngsters do it [use the language] because sometimes it's bloody laziness. It's diffi-cult to think original Afrikaans because the English just pops up. We live in an English culture. I never listen to Afrikaans because it makes me sick the way they still impose Standard thoughts. The unoriginality of that is just boring." She advocates a middle way—neither the rigidity of Standard Afrikaans, nor the sloppiness of using English indiscriminately.

Van der Linde disagrees with Klaus Steytler's lamentation over the softening of the language. "Standardization was a stiffening that hap-pened to Afrikaans. It made for thinking in structures, thinking in con-ventional ways and it's typical of our society, of this patriarchal society."

The issue of Standard versus colloquial Afrikaans mirrors issues of class conflict and mobility, according to Ina van der Linde. "For instance, if you speak to brown people, the moment they start thinking they are moving up in society, they start speaking this [Standard] Afrikaans I'm talking about."

Van der Linde's friend and fellow journalist Marichen Waldner elabo-rated: "The Afrikaans of the street is a harsh language and has harsh sounds, but you go to a meeting of the Akademie vir Wetenskap en Kuns and you will hear soft-spoken language." She called this "cultural" Afrikaans—not the language she speaks to her colleagues.

The editor of *Vrye Weekblad*, Max du Preez, explained the emotional importance of this, the first left-wing dissident newspaper in Afrikaans. "In the last five, six, seven years we became dissidents in Afrikaans. We remain culturally Afrikaners, classified ourselves as *boere* and Afrikaans. Before my generation, people who rejected Afrikaner nationalism, who jumped out of the *laager* [camp], became Anglicized and started speak-ing English. It was really one or two individuals before my generation like [van Zyl] Slabbert, like [Breyten] Breytenbach, that remained cul-turally Afrikaans, ethnically even Afrikaans.

"We said screw this, there are enough of us, let's form a separate lobby and they can't claim that we're not Afrikaners. So that was a very impor-tant change.

"Also we write a people's Afrikaans and that irritates the shit out of them," he said. "For example, *swartbuurt* means 'black neighborhood,' but it's not a township." In *Vrye Weekblad*, when reference was made to apartheid black "townships," such as Soweto, the English word "township" was used, not the Afrikaans *swartbuurt*, which did not reflect the deprived status of black residential areas under apartheid laws. "If a lot of black people were to move into Sandton [a white suburb of Johannesburg], you would call that a black neighborhood, but a township is a township is a township," du Preez said. "We talk about the townships and township violence."

Although *Vrye Weekblad* could be spotted on the desks of staunch Broederbond members such as the politics professor Pieter Potgieter of Potchefstroom University, it was the bane of the establishment. The concept of loyal opposition was not a popular one in Afrikaner society. For instance, *Vrye Weekblad* cut across one goal that tended to unify left- and right-wing Afrikaners, their desire that Afrikaans would retain its official status. "We are running a campaign that Afrikaans should lose its special status," du Preez said. "That's ugly stuff. This is a real war brewing here."

Du Preez carried on his war by taking potshots at one of Afrikanerdom's cherished shrines, the Taal Monument.

The white granite and concrete monument soars on a magnificent hill overlooking the Cape town of Paarl. Erected in the late 1960s, its creation was inspired by two men. The first, C. J. Langenhoven, who wrote the poem that became the national anthem, "Die Stem van Said-Afrika" ("The Call of South Africa"), in 1914 compared the potential growth of Afrikaans to a steep curve, or hyperbola. The most spectacular element of the monument is a spire that sweeps up in a hyperbolic curve on one side, with a sheer vertical face on the other. The second, the poet N. P. van Wyk Louw, who said in 1959 that Afrikaans "forms a bridge between the enlightened West and magical Africa," is alluded to with representations in the monument of the languages that contribute to Afrikaans. Perhaps the monument was a waste of taxpayers' money, as one man said. Certainly it insulted blacks with its three rounded nubbins representing African languages, but it occupies an exquisite site and is one of the less ponderous of Afrikaner monuments.

Max du Preez attacked the Taal Monument, using the genital imagery and generic crudity fondly adopted by Afrikaner men when they are being insulting. "I went to this thing," du Preez said. "I'd never been there before. I wrote how I felt. I said it looks like a huge Boer lying on his back. These are his phallus and his testicles. These big balls you know. And I said it's trying to penetrate the sky. God, people thought it was blasphemy."

* * *

Klaus Steytler may bemoan the decline of Afrikaans civilization, but a younger generation welcomes it, tongue in cheek. The codirector of the new small publisher Hond—'Hound' or, most probably, 'Cur'—Ryk Hattingh, was quoted in the liberal *Weekly Mail & Guardian* in 1993 as saying, "There is a lot to be said for bad literature. We want to be there when Afrikaans literature disintegrates. With a bit of luck we can all experience the decline of a 'civilization.'"

Hond happened to be howling at the moon for joy, having just published the latest Breyten Breytenbach book to rave reviews. European-style angst and surrealism has long had a niche in sophisticated Afrikaans literary circles, tiny though those circles are.

Some Afrikaners were educating themselves out of their language and in the process becoming, if not Anglicized, at least internationalized. Stellenbosch professor Annie Gagiano's refuge in English and American literature was an obvious case. Aside from a small amount of fine poetry and a few good novels written in the past thirty years, there was not a vast array of Afrikaans titles for omnivorous readers.

Marichen Waldner said, "The philosophies of value and the theologies of value and the literatures of value are not in Afrikaans; it's in English."

"There are two poles [in Afrikaans fiction]," Ina van der Linde commented. "What they call middlebrow, these sentimental, marshmallow-type stories on the one side and, on the other, literature which is unreadable and ununderstandable unless you know mythology and that sort of thing. It's boring."

Freelance journalist Dries van Heerden pointed out a breakdown, especially in middle- and upper-class homes, in the traditional *volk* obsession to send children to Afrikaans schools.

"It's not any more a matter of big debate over the family table, where to send them to an English school means you'll be ostracized from society. Now it's a question of which school is closest. On the other hand, if you go to the *platteland*, or to the western suburbs of Pretoria, which is very sort of lower class, the only schools available are Afrikaans schools.

"If people are so concerned about the Afrikaans language, why don't they buy Afrikaans poetry and language books? I mean, they'd rather read Louis L'Amour," van Heerden added with a laugh.

Corporate magnate Naas Steenkamp noted that Afrikaans had lost the battle in the marketplace. "I've been party to numerous efforts in the business world to bring Afrikaans up to an operational level alongside English, where it could be regarded as a language of economic value. That's been in vain because Afrikaans has got no economic value whatsoever.

"It isn't used. You don't advertise in it. You don't conduct business in it. Even if you are an Afrikaner, you don't conclude deals in it. You don't speak it across the counter, partly due to the fact that so very many immigrants from the U.K. and elsewhere went into the commercial and retail trade. The characteristic of the English immigrant is not to say, 'I'm sorry, I don't speak Afrikaans, do you mind speaking English?' It is simply to remain stony-faced and to respond in English. For a lively and expansive people like the Afrikaners this comes like a very rude, cold shock. Now at that elementary level I find myself irritated," he chuckled, possibly at his resemblance to more right-wing Afrikaners.

As to the economic activity of colored communities, Steenkamp continued, "That's why I said [Afrikaans has] no commercial or economic value at the urban level or in the level of corporate business. But at the hawkers' level, and certainly if I include agriculture in 'commercial,' then obviously it still has significance. But it's not the language of written commerce or of electronic communication."

The erosion of the language occurs not just where it rubs shoulders with the "other." It happens in the hallowed halls of Afrikaner institutions. Johann Rissik, an agricultural-developmental expert who worked for the Operation Hunger charity in Lebowa homeland north of Pretoria, said that the number of English speakers who were students at Stellenbosch University was high, 30 or 40 percent, he said. (It's 20 percent, according to Rector Andreas van Wyk.)

"You learned to become quite bilingual. And afterwards you don't realize whether you are speaking English or Afrikaans," Rissik said. "People ask you, is that guy, that friend of yours, English- or Afrikaans-speaking? You have to think about it. It was a nice environment to study in, really it was."

That would not warm Professor Frans van Rensburg's heart. He constantly fretted about the future of Afrikaans. And he had found a most unlikely ally—a writer named Dan Roodt, an enfant terrible of the establishment, who wrote an alarmist article in a Dutch magazine in 1992 that trumpeted the achievements of Afrikaans and panicked about those who would try to get rid of it.

Contradicting Naas Steenkamp, Roodt claimed: "Afrikaners are not even aware of it, but they have successfully completed the Third Language Movement and have firmly established Afrikaans in commerce, the media, the civil service, and the arts to such an extent that the language and its speakers will only vanish from South Africa in the event of a Pol Pot–type revolution. Unfortunately South Africa has no lack of revolutionaries at the moment, some of whom would like to wage a campaign against Afrikaans."

Roodt argued: "The interpretation that Afrikaans was the spark of the [1976 Soweto] riots was sent into the world by the English press" and "no scientific study has ever been undertaken to ascertain if the use of Afrikaans in schools was really the main reason" for the black protests. His use of the word "scientific" conjured up the "objective-scientific" jargon that was all the craze in Afrikaans universities that had produced voluminous research supporting apartheid.

Roodt's article sounds like a war cry. The Afrikaner is a victim again. The *taal* is imperiled. Raise the flag.

CHAPTER TWENTY-SEVEN

THE FRIENDLY LANGUAGE

In March 1992, an article in *Rapport* newspaper quoted Nelson Mandela as saying he hoped Afrikaans would be transformed from a language of the police and jail to a "language of friendship and democracy." Mandela taught himself Afrikaans in prison.

Two months later Afrikaans newspapers announced that a new organization would be set up called the Stigting vir Afrikaans (Foundation for Afrikaans) and its motto, curiously, was *"die vriendelike taal,"* the friendly language. One imagines the real *vriende*, the Broederbonders, jabbing each other in the ribs down at the Dorsbult Bar and joshing, "Ja, die vriendelike taal."

"The Afrikaner Broederbond has over the years taken a series of deliberate and conscious decisions as to what initiatives are necessary to ensure continued Afrikaans hegemony or grip," said a person who asked to remain anonymous. "I am not privy to what goes into their thinking, but I do know that this is an Afrikaner Broederbond decision that we need a Stigting vir Afrikaans. I think it's a joke. You don't establish *stigtings* or academies for a language that has disqualified itself as the language of political discourse, because previously its political discourse was conducted from a purely restrictive, ideological position, making it the oppressor from others' point of view. Also there simply isn't the willingness on the part of the Afrikaner yuppie to insist on Afrikaans being used. You don't achieve that with your *stigtings*. But most important, Afrikaans is not a language of white people. There are more nonwhite, if you'll pardon that odious term, nonwhite speakers of Afrikaans than white. What the Stigting vir Afrikaans is going to achieve, I don't know. They probably have smart answers to what I just said."

They do. Ton Vosloo, whose publishing company Nasionale Pers is both midwife and sugardaddy of the Stigting vir Afrikaans, is also chairman of M-Net, South Africa's only cable-TV entertainment channel. M-Net broadcasts mostly U.S. movies and serials. Talking about the economic future of Afrikaans publishing, Vosloo said, "I will just give you one statistic. *Die Burger* [Nasionale Pers's Western Cape paper], which is the National government-supporting [paper], just over fifty percent of its readership is colored. The sole growth of the *Burger* in the last fifteen years was in the colored community. The white community is going pffft and you've got to cultivate across the color line."

Vosloo's strategy, cultivating the colored Afrikaans readership, sounds very much like that of the journalist Gustav Preller, whose work early in the twentieth century built the foundation for Afrikaner nationalism and enlarged the market for Afrikaans writing. Vosloo said that Nasionale Pers "depends a lot on Afrikaans. A lot of people use it as a tool to earn a living. For us, as an Afrikaans publishing house, the paradox is now that we are publishing more and more in English. English will now begin to subsidize Afrikaans. You have to do it to stay in business."

Stellenbosch economics professor Servaas van der Berg chuckled at the notion that Vosloo and the people at M-Net might be feeling guilty because they were destroying the Afrikaners' culture with all the American movies broadcast on cable TV, so they started the Stigting. He said that there had been little success with efforts to raise funds for it. *Die Burger* had run a series of articles appealing for individual donations, but the response was so pitiful that they stopped the articles.

The Stigting, said van der Berg, "is a top-down process. It doesn't come from within the Afrikaans community. I don't know whether that means that Afrikaans has become less important to people. I think to an extent it has. I think that is inevitable in the sort of changes we are making."

Nationalist pride is a major motivating element in setting up the Stigting. "My first prize is to keep the official status [of Afrikaans] because a lot of things go with that," Vosloo said. "Some people equate Afrikaans with an old order that has died. One thing de Klerk did in 1990 was to liberate Afrikaans, to unshackle us. One must be very careful not to recreate and reenergize Afrikaner nationalism in the chauvinistic sense, because then you'd get a negative reaction not only from the Treurnicht-type Afrikaner. You'll get a lot of good liberal Afrikanerdom on their hind legs."

The Stigting vir Afrikaans seeks to draw the broadest range of Afrikaans speakers into their project. "We canvassed the idea, I even went to see [the late Conservative Party leader Andries] Treurnicht," Vosloo said. "I said, 'Look, we are in favor of Afrikaans, full stop. Are you willing to be associated?' And I said, 'But we have no color, we are color-blind. Our trustees are going to be comprised of all the people. I've got the only Asian woman in the country with a master's degree in Afrikaans, she's on the board. We've got blacks, we've got coloreds.' Treurnicht said, 'I'm sorry, we draw the line. You have people of color involved, we are out of it.' Now the Stigting is being shot at from the left and from the right."

Another supporter of the Stigting, Wimpie de Klerk, said, "Afrikaans must be depoliticized, that's very true and we're on our way to doing that. Two years or three years ago a black man would have been offended when you address him in Afrikaans. That's getting more relaxed."

De Klerk, an ex-*vriend* but still obviously in the halls of Nationalist power, said he didn't think Afrikaans would be an official language in the future, and that doesn't particularly bother him. "But we must create a huge trust fund for Afrikaner literature and Afrikaner theater," he said.

Hans du Plessis, who was present at the launch of the Stigting, is optimistic. "What I fear is that some cultural organization is going to try to manipulate this whole thing. But at the moment it's not happening," he said, apparently oblivious to what others found obvious—that the Stigting is a classic Broederbond operation.

Stellenbosch law professor Louwrens du Plessis wasn't fooled, but he wonders why the FAK and the Broederbond always have to be on the defensive. Afrikaans has been becoming less of a political issue with blacks and coloreds, but the Stigting has unfortunately dragged it back into the political crossfire, he asserted.

Frederick van Zyl Slabbert said of the Stigting, "Oh, that's a lot of crap. They want to promote Afrikaans, preserve Afrikaans, it's the old thing again. That won't work one bit. Afrikaans is going to survive despite that, not because of that."

"What someone like me sees them doing is marketing the language," said Stellenbosch English professor Annie Gagiano. "It's making the language a power base."

And that great lover of her language, Marietjie Myburg, groaned, "Ooh, I think it's just an FAK in disguise. I just wish they would leave Afrikaans. I get so tired when I hear all these actions to promote Afrikaans. It doesn't need all these things. I get very irritated by it actually."

Henning Myburgh, at the IDASA office in Bloemfontein, said in his soft, cultured voice, "The more cynical view is that the preservation of two dominant languages is a way of dominating the rest of society, in the sense that access to those languages is the opening or closing of opportunities."

His colleague Kobus van Loggerenberg agreed: "It's an example of arrogance and insensitivity, an example of the way they're thinking about the 'new South Africa.' If they had started a fund now for assistance to victims of the violence and they had used the Afrikaans paper to do that, then I would say these people understand what this is about."

Max du Preez said, "I was invited to be one of the keynote speakers at this Stigting vir Afrikaans. They wanted me so badly, I had all kinds of pressure on me. Promising ads, your ticket back into the bosom of the *volk* and all kinds of things. And this is apolitical [they said], 'We don't want you to change your politics, but come and make a speech. Say you support us and how much you love Afrikaans.' I nearly did it until I found out exactly who they were."

Who were they? Ton Vosloo?

"Ja, Nasionale Pers, Broederbond, FAK, National Party, Dutch Reformed Church. This is an ugly, ugly thing. What binds Afrikaners together from extreme right to extreme left, virtually, is the agreement that Afrikaans should remain an official language. And we have been saying from the word go, 'bullshit.' If we want this language to survive, unshackle it now. Make it free now. Our point of view is that resentment against Afrikaans will not disappear as long as it has artificial legal protection. It has no moral right beyond that of Zulu, Xhosa, Sotho, Pedi, Tswana as an indigenous language. We say it is an indigenous African language. They [Africans] see it as a colonial language. As a Dutch.

"Look at the colored population," du Preez said. "They stopped speaking Afrikaans. It's their home language, they're the first Afrikaans speakers. They don't want to speak it anymore. They want to speak English."

When du Preez said the Stigting was a nasty development, he was referring to the authoritarian cast of the plan's advocates. The lengths to which they'd go to discredit critics of their idea—like him—lent credence to his evaluation. Ton Vosloo, smooth and sophisticated Stigting advocate, worked hard to discredit *Vrye Weekblad's* editor. "You know, we called him 'Mad Max' whilst he was in Namibia. He was on a plane with a U.N. delegation and the plane crashed and he was badly concussed. After that accident they called him 'Mad Max' because he was very erratic in his personal life and in journalism too," Vosloo said.

"He wrote the weirdest pieces. He was our Nasionale Pers representative there. Then he left us. And some of our newspapers wouldn't use his copy. Those that didn't use it said he was unbalanced in his reporting. He was leaning over so much to SWAPO [the black liberation movement elected to power in 1990] that his judgment was colored. I also thought that he became very erratic. You see, his wife left him and started working for an American. She went on trips with guys doing television things and then she became a journalist and ditched him. I think she earned more than he did at that time. And it became a great personal crisis for him to handle it."

Asked what he thought about *Vrye Weekblad*'s role in Afrikaner society, Vosloo said, "I don't respect its journalism that much. I think if you look at it and also at the makeup and the writing, some of it is very turgid. They've done a few bold things."

Vrye Weekblad's crusade against government death squads had resulted in multimillion-rand suits by police officials against the paper. Nasionale Pers would never have so seriously challenged the establishment. Vosloo conceded that having *Vrye Weekblad* at the forefront of investigative journalism did enable mainstream journalists to be a bit more aggressive too. "Yes. So in that sense, give him the credit for shifting the barriers." But he still caviled at the small paper's claims to significance.

A similar nastiness, the reaction of the powerful to challenge, was aimed at Theunis Englebrecht, the music critic for *Beeld*, a Nasionale Pers newspaper in Johannesburg. Englebrecht described how a little bit of satire of the Stigting cost him a lot.

"I interviewed this band Indecent Obsession from Australia, a teeny-bopper band. And I decided I'm going to write a very funny story about it because they're really a bunch of wimps. I wrote parts of the interview in English. In brackets afterwards I wrote, 'I'm writing this in English because the members of the band are speaking English, so the Foundation for Afrikaans doesn't get worried because a column in an Afrikaans newspaper is using English expressions.'

"The next day when I got in to work"—Englebrecht paused and gave a whistle that sounded like a guillotine blade falling—"they came down on me with force and I lost the Pop Column. I mean, it was tongue-in-cheek. But they pulled out everything they could get. So I lost the Pop Column."

Englebrecht's housemate, Ansie Kamffer, an agent for alternative Afrikaans musicians, said that the Stigting organizers had phoned her and pressured her to let her clients, Anton Goosen and Johannes Kerkorrel, the latter known for his wildly popular satirical attacks on the government of P. W. Botha, be associated with the Stigting and let it pay for a nationwide music tour for them.

"It's a political weapon for them," Kamffer explained. "Then they will say the Stigting is progressive and relevant in the new South Africa. They got a lot of credible artists at their first function. They wanted Johannes Kerkorrel to perform at the launch of this thing. So I said fax me your directors and I saw the names and I just laughed—Ton Vosloo, Stellenbosch Farmers' Wineries, Professor Elize Botha." Elize Botha was the then foreign minister's sister-in-law and a leading academic defender of the establishment.

Perhaps the overriding intent of the Stigting was to reunite the "tribe" of Afrikaners, the coloreds with the whites, so viciously sliced in two by the Nats in 1956 when the coloreds were expelled from the voters' rolls in the Cape. Even some Conservative Party members, such as Koos "Bomber" Botha, saw this. "I think within the next couple of years we will have a rethink. We will have to have another deal with the coloreds. At the end I think they belong with the Afrikaner."

The Broederbond was there first, already trying to make a deal with their colored relatives. Would it work? Would the coloreds vote for the National Party?

"Yes, I think they will," said Achmat Davids, sitting amid flouncy crinolines and tutu-stiff prom dresses that his wife was sewing. "They voted very strongly Nat in 1923."

That was quite a while ago!

"This tradition lingers on," he said dryly. "The same sort of ploy that Hertzog used in 1923—the cultural sort of identity with the colored people—de Klerk is using at present. You see, the colored community is a very prejudiced community. They still look upon the [white] Afrikaner as the natural leader. The bulk of the colored community are members of the Dutch Reformed Church. The colored community in the Western Cape is suspicious of the ability of the ANC to keep the country in a stable condition. De Klerk has been very effective in maintaining that image by virtue of the way that the unrest has been perpetuated.* In that way he has convinced the colored community on the whole that the African is too unstable, vicious, brutal. They kill their own people, how the heck are they going to rule the country?"

But what about the fact that coloreds joined the Black Consciousness movement and the United Democratic Front in the 1970s and '80s?

"That was an intellectual movement. It has not filtered very much down to grass roots," Davids said.

Davids was right. In the 1994 elections, the only province where the National Party won was in the heavily colored and Asian Western Cape. And in the largely colored Northern Cape Province, the race was close, with the ANC winning 50 percent to the NP's 41 percent of the vote.

As for the Stigting, Davids said he would have no compunction about accepting money from the foundation for his projects. "But I think their general direction is wrong. I think the only way in which Afrikaans is going to survive is, to use a famous word created by the Nats themselves,

---

*Davids was referring to Inkatha/ANC violence, which many observers believe was being provoked by government agents.

toenadering, to be accommodating, to reach out to other people. They should in fact be *toenadering* to the African languages." His idea is to fund dictionaries between Afrikaans and the African languages, such as a Zulu-Afrikaans dictionary or a Xhosa-Afrikaans dictionary.

"There's more sense in trying to promote the language to the twenty-seven million nonspeakers of the language or the second-language speakers. So Afrikaans has equal partners to compete with and in the process of competition it will survive.

"Ja, 'die vriendelike taal,' " muttered Davids, with a sour smile. "And I say fine, I'm also an Afrikaner and it's cheek for other Afrikaners to say they want to promote my language as a friendly language. We've always called ourselves Afrikaners, long before the whites could object to that."

CHAPTER TWENTY-EIGHT

WRITING WRONGS?

A Labrador retriever named Beaumont provided the running gag on a late summer night in March in Melville, a whitish suburb of Johannesburg, as the temperature sank from a dry-hot 83 degrees Fahrenheit to a tooth-chattering, desert chill at ten P.M. Beaumont knew that Marianne de Jong, a fearsome feminist literary critic to some, was actually a pushover.

As de Jong delved into nuanced and searching analyses of Afrikaner authors and politics, Beaumont fudged his stolid body under the professor's white plastic table, with its detachable (broken) leg.

"Beau-mont," she entoned like a foghorn in her deep, resonant voice. "Beau-mont, come outside." That meant moving beyond a low iron grating that was really only a symbol of outside.

De Jong is professor in the Theory of Literature Department at UNISA. A sophisticated intellectual in the European sense, she is up-to-date with international trends in literary theory and is passionately gripped by Afrikaans.

Less than a week after the 68 percent "yes" vote in the March 17, 1992, all-white referendum that asked voters to approve or disapprove the negotiations being conducted by F. W. de Klerk with the ANC, de Jong said, "I'll tell you something, we all burst into tears. I've never in my life voted for the Nationalist Party, and all my friends have never done so. We did so now because of the issue. When the results came out, all my friends here, we just burst into tears. And when F. W. de Klerk recited this poem by the man one could say is the T. S. Eliot of Afrikaner writing, you know, I just, whooooo, there I go!"

She gulped back new tears, as she recalled F. W. reading a few lines of the poem "Deeper Justice" by N. P. van Wyk Louw—one she translated into English on the spot:

> O sorrowful land, Africa. Will there never be a resounding voice coming from your vast country? Will there never be a blinkingly white cloud, climbing up on your horizon to speak of hope?

The implication was that the "yes" vote for negotiations was that white cloud, that sign of hope for Africa.

"Now I must just tell you that I'm speaking as somebody who has been working together with quite a few people to make it clear that N. P. van Wyk Louw was an ultimate racist and possibly a Nazist, okay?" de Jong said.

N. P. van Wyk Louw, who died in 1970, who made Afrikaans a recognized literature, who was disturbed when the Nats stripped the coloreds of their right to vote in 1956, is the poet and essayist for all seasons and all political sides among Afrikaners.

"Don't read him. It's nonsense," said the novelist Jeanne Goosen, an ANC member. "The AWB [Eugene Terreblanche's neo-Nazi organization] have worked their slogans out of van Wyk Louw's work," Goosen said. "You can use him for anything you want. He was a brilliant man, a very Afrikaner nationalist. But actually a loner. He didn't mix with the government."

A freelance journalist, a liberal professor of Afrikaans at the University of the Witwatersrand, an English-speaking mining executive, the former head of Security Police, the head of the Broederbond, the poet's former publisher, a member of the censorship board, and the retired Afrikaans literature professor Frans van Rensburg—all saw the poet in diverse guises.

Van Rensburg, who wrote several books about van Wyk Louw, said, "This man, had he written in another language, he would have won the Nobel Prize. I regard him as the best writer this country has produced, not only in Afrikaans but in all the literatures, including the Nadine Gordimers, the Alan Patons." He described how as a young man in Paris the poet sat in a café pondering the "Moroccans and all the people from the East with something unique they had" and wondered what made his own people unique. Van Rensburg described van Wyk Louw's *Klipwerk* (*Stonework*) as "little folk poems that have sprung spontaneously from farms in the remote areas, little glittering things, ahead of modern European, international art movements like surrealism, expressionism." His epic poem *Raka* tells how a "tight-knit black community goes aground. It was intended as a warning for a culture to be on its guard for the slackening of norms."

Rena Pretorius, the only woman on the Publications Appeal (censorship) Board, wrote her doctorate on the concept of being an intellectual, one of van Wyk Louw's major concerns. "I don't think he would have supported the whole idea of apartheid," she said. "He warned against the problems, you know." Pretorius noted that van Wyk Louw lived eight years in the Netherlands and when he returned in 1957, he became professor of Afrikaans at the University of the Witwatersrand, a traditional bastion of English liberalism, rather than at one of the Afrikaans institutions linked to the Broederbond and thus to the NP and the government.

Piet Muller, the *Rapport* editorial writer and *Insig* magazine editor, "worked very closely" as a young man with van Wyk Louw at Human-Rousseau publishers. He explained a great shift that took place in van Wyk Louw's politics. "The thirties were a period when all intellectuals were either National Socialists [Nazis] or Communists. He was certainly a National Socialist, but there is nothing of that in his works after 1950," Muller said. "Van Wyk Louw was a great prophet. I only wish he could have lived to see what happened after the [1992] referendum. He and Verwoerd were absolutely two opposing poles. Verwoerd tried to destroy him by all means because he had such influence through theoretical works and his poetry, while Verwoerd had the political influence.

"There was a famous event in 1965 at the first five-year festival of the new republic when van Wyk Louw was commissioned to write a play. Verwoerd was so furious [at the play] that he got up and walked out. Because the Afrikaner was portrayed in all his frailties and all his uneasiness with certain things. I was there. I watched it. Then Verwoerd attacked van Wyk Louw at his speech, his great speech, his public-event speech, in an oblique way but in no uncertain terms. Van Wyk Louw didn't want to have the play staged again after that. Although it is a deeply moving play."

Has anybody staged it since then?

"No, because his widow still controls the copyright," Muller said. "While Verwoerd lived, people were too scared to quote him [van Wyk Louw], but I think his *Liberale Nasionalisme* [a book of essays] is the most quoted book in Afrikaans at the moment."

According to Bobby Godsell, an English-speaking Anglo American Corporation executive who read all of Prime Minister Hendrik Verwoerd's speeches, to gain an understanding of the Afrikaner, *Liberale Nasionalisme* is useful in interpreting what the nationalist Afrikaner means by the often-used word "group," a word at the center of apartheid rhetoric. In the 1950s when the Nats were stripping the coloreds of their right to vote, van Wyk Louw carried on a correspondence with an English liberal friend in *Liberale Nasionalisme*, published in 1958.

"Van Wyk Louw argues that groups are fundamentally important," Godsell said. "I think probably all minority groups would agree with him. I suspect if you talk to Korean Americans they would say that

Korean identity was very important. If you talk to white Anglo-Saxon Protestants, they would say, 'What's identity?' But if they were to suddenly land in a society where the prevailing language was Korean, they might feel differently. And it's very strong in van Wyk Louw that it's easy for people from a dominant culture to wish away issues of group identity. He insists group identity is central, but it never can be used as an excuse to deny people individual rights. People have individual rights first. Then you add group identity on top of that."

Professor of Afrikaans Gerrit Olivier of Witwatersrand University is less sanguine about van Wyk Louw's reaction to the coloreds' loss of the vote. "He's the most important authority who established nationalism as a discourse in this country and gave it intellectual credibility," Olivier said. "I think he also defined the role of the intellectual within the Afrikaner society."

As what?

"Well, there's a bit of ambivalence there. Initially he took the view that the intellectual should criticize the nation but ultimately remain loyal. Which is a difficult concept to analyze. I think it means that all criticism has to be given within the framework of the nation and not outside of it. Remain within the law but be critical within it.

"Later on he launched quite a different concept, saying that the intellectual even in a great crisis should go on doing his or her own work. He said, should there be a crisis, and he's talking about the colored vote, what does an intellectual then do? He simply said you go on doing your own work. I think that is evading the issue. His position was influential in the circle of Afrikaner intellectuals."

More than influential—profoundly influential. Piet de Lange, the head of the Broederbond 1983–93, contended that he had opposed what the government was doing in the 1950s. "We have an Afrikaans poet, van Wyk Louw, who in the thirties spoke about loyal dissent. It's within that framework that my personal dissent took place," de Lange said.

Professor Olivier, whose dissent against Afrikaner hegemony went much farther outside the *volk* than de Lange's, felt a certain sympathy for the fact that van Wyk Louw preceded him as professor of Afrikaans at the English-speaking University of the Witwatersrand. "I think he was at Wits for the same reason that I decided to go there. He didn't want to be bothered with all the old Nationalists. You could do your own thing there and function in more freedom than he probably could have had at an Afrikaans-language university."

Since van Wyk Louw was one of the theoreticians behind the Afrikaner *volksgeist*, it was assumed that he would have certain atti-

295

tudes. But he could confound those expectations. A former head of South Africa's Security Police, Johan Coetzee, admitted that he was shocked by an encounter he had with van Wyk Louw, whom he expected to be Afrikaans down to his toenails.

"I knew N. P. van Wyk Louw very well," Coetzee said. "As a matter of fact, when he came back from Holland, he came from the airport to the town on a bus. Something happened on this bus, someone jumped off the bus and ran away, and I had to interview him. I was then a police lieutenant in Johannesburg. I asked him what happened when he was now off this bus. He said, well, he took a taxi. You know, he was speaking in Afrikaans. And I said, 'But why do you say "taxi"?' Because in Afrikaans we say *huurmotor*. He says, 'No, but this word "taxi" has got a right of existence in South Africa, in Afrikaans, because it is an international word, and you can say it in German,' and so on. I was very astonished."

In traditional Afrikaner society N. P. van Wyk Louw is elevated to the status of a literary monument and his writings can be construed to support many positions. His political beliefs were murky, like a crime committed before many observers, where what happened depends on who's telling the story.

Daylight was fading on Marianne de Jong's patio, tingeing the topmost pink flowers on the kopeck tree. Three droopy weaverbird nests were slung in the low, fat palm tree like heavy shoulder pouches. Beaumont struck again and the table caved over.

"Beau-mont," de Jong groaned, with a plangent equality given to both syllables. De Jong was trying to describe whether Afrikaans authors helped cause the erosion of apartheid.

She said N. P. van Wyk Louw and another poet, D. J. Opperman, "belong to another era when Afrikaans didn't even exist yet and the Afrikaner had no political power. That was before the 1950s."

Then the sixties came: the ANC was declared illegal; Nelson Mandela was jailed for life; black writers were censored, tortured, and exiled; and a few Afrikaner writers launched a literary rebellion. They were called the Sestigers (the Sixties). Reflecting the Europeanness of the movement, the novelist André Brink—actually born in 1935—said, "I was born on a bench in the Luxembourg Gardens in Paris in the early spring of 1960."

"Certainly the Sestigers, who were avant-garde in the European sense, kept a public intelligence alive," de Jong mused. "André Brink never stopped causing a stir. But whether this changed anything—I would still be tempted to say no. The structures would not have allowed literature to make a substantial difference, especially in the time of the State of Emergency [in the eighties]."

What about the novelist and essayist J. M. Coetzee?

"Coetzee, it's so difficult to say anything, because he is surely the best living or dead South African author," de Jong said. "Totally amazing. But I don't think he has a political impact at all. In fact, a lot of people find him elitist. Especially black readers would find him elitist. Not political enough, not relevant enough, which one could contest, but that is a feeling amongst informed black readers. I don't think he's got any political influence although he does take a political stand. When there was a conference and Salman Rushdie was invited and then disinvited because of Islamic influence in COSAW [Congress of South African Writers], Coetzee attacked the disinvitation because of the infringement on aesthetic freedom. He really outdid [Nadine] Gordimer totally in that little debate."

Gordimer defended the disinvitation?

"Yes, it was very difficult because you know Islam has always been ANC-aligned, so it is very difficult to now make the comrades [militant ANC supporters] angry. I mean, they've done so much for you."

What about the blatant love-hate relationship the Afrikaners have for one of the original Sestigers, their best-known poet and literary bad boy Breyten Breytenbach, who was jailed for seven years for his political activities?

"That's a million-dollar question," de Jong replied. "It's one on which one has to speculate, because it is a psychological issue. Having said that, may I light a cigarette and then try to answer?"

Sure. She stepped into her cottage and turned on a light inside that suffused part of the patio, returned, lit her cigarette, and took a sip of Shiraz wine.

"Since the Afrikaans language was co-opted by the National Party as part of their ethno-myth, and since any literary achievement was to belong to the *volk*, once you've got a Breytenbach, who achieved so much, you cannot do without him. Not even if you are a Nationalist. Same with Brink. They would ban them, they would censor them, they would jail them, and they would still love them. As soon as Breytenbach was unjailed, he got a prize."

What does she think of his writing?

"You know it's a lifetime of writing, so you have to say a lot about it. He is the only surrealist Afrikaans author and certainly one of the three, four really important authors who have written Afrikaans. Certainly his writing is international class. It has been inspired by a revolutionary instinct which is more than just political. Lately, I think, his role has waned. It is very difficult to explain why, but left Afrikaners, including me, are getting very irritated because he begins to repeat all the jargon. 'Let us not be Eurocentric,' he says, while living in Paris. We think, 'Okay, we're over the debate between Afrocentrism and Eurocentrism. You stay in Paris, buy yourself a villa in Spain, just don't take us for fools.' This is very recent.

"The fact he never stopped writing in Afrikaans has made a difference [in the erosion of apartheid]. Whether it has caused the change, I would say no. But that there's a certain impact and that it has created something like an open debate, perhaps an ambiguous area from which the sensibility for the reform comes: it's a daring thesis, because what has caused the reform, if not that? If there wasn't somewhere an area of debate going on?"

Professors of Afrikaans literature always include Breytenbach and Brink in undergraduate courses, de Jong said, with the possible exception of two professors, Frans van Rensburg at Rand Afrikaans University and Rena Pretorius at the University of Pretoria.

Certainly van Rensburg did not want to talk about Breytenbach. Twice he was asked what he thought about the poet, but he slid off the subject, as if it were lubricated. He did complain about the Sestigers, "who stuffed English words in their Afrikaans sentences, [and then] the smaller type of people too who run away with the idea and it's such a mess of language."

He admitted, "They did a very important job by writing the country open, bringing into literature themes previously shunned."

But. The buts are big with van Rensburg.

"It went overboard for some of them. I think they have gone too far in connection with morality. There is a definite amoral and immoral aspect in the writings of some of the Sestigers."

Political morality, sexual morality or family, or what?

"The whole thing, but inter alia, sexual morality too. It's a bit too narrow to narrow it down to sexuality as such. It is a much broader thing, but it is inter alia that."

The third time was a charm: What about Breytenbach, his poetry, and *Confessions of an Albino Terrorist*, a book he wrote about his years in prison? Outside of the country his prestige is enormous.

"Yes, much prestige, I think a bit on dubious grounds." Van Rensburg finally took on the poet. He wanted to appear polite. It was his nature. But, as frequently happens in this tiny elite of a small minority, venom will out. Especially perhaps because Breytenbach himself goaded the establishment Afrikaners beyond their endurance. "You know, Breyten-bach participated in politics when he was a student at the University of Cape Town in the early sixties, and he joined the radicals there. He comes from a poor family. He went abroad and there he met this Viet-namese woman, whose family holds high political jobs. She had a father I think who was an ambassador in Paris. But in any case, he got caught up in radical movements in Paris, you know, it was the sixties."

What does he mean when he says Breytenbach is from a poor family?

"Very modest family in Bonnyvale, southwest of the Cape in the wine country."

It isn't a prestigious family at all?

"No, not at all. So to marry this golden lotus, his parents had to give evidence that he was of pure blood before he could marry her. I person-ally thought, well, he is throwing everything at the government on account of its racial policy, and then he does exactly the same thing. He allows his parents to submit that evidence to her people. His mother told me on the occasion when I was the speaker as chairman of the commit-tee who awarded him the Central News Agency prize. I had great admi-ration for his work until a certain stage. But he got into such radical politics. His last volume of poetry, it's, you know, he is excreting on his country. He's going out of bounds. And I personally feel I do not accept advice on my country's future from a person like that.

"He is one of our finest poets in a certain part of his work," van Rens-burg explained. "But he has written some of the worst things in Afrikaans too. He is able to deliver potboilers too, because he sometimes experiences financial trouble and difficulties. That is what I was trying to say about his background. His wife has a sister in very high places, and the comparison with that strikes his wife as, 'oh, why this, why can't I have a better . . . like my sister?'

"That is my dual approach to Breytenbach. One of our finest love poets, but on the other hand, a man who has written a lot of pure non-sense."

Hans du Plessis of Potchefstroom University agrees with the love part. "I think he's one of the very, very best handlers of Afrikaans that we've ever had. Very good, especially when he doesn't write politics. His love poems, his nonpolitical verse is to my mind better poetry. His emotion, especially when he writes about his wife, that's absolutely fascinating."

Gerrit Olivier sat in his 1920s house, a former white miner's house in Brixton, near Johannesburg. Yellow and salmon-pink flowers cascaded over the high wall into the minuscule front garden. Olivier is thin, blond, and handsome, and wears a small earring, the latter connoting his distance from the straitlaced Afrikaner establishment. In the eighties he helped start the publishing firm Taurus, which printed books by Breytenbach and Brink and others who were likely to be banned, selling the books by mail rather than through bookstores.

Can he describe Breytenbach's poetry for people who do not read Afrikaans?

"Well I can try," Olivier said, sipping cranberry juice. "His poetry draws on surrealism and on Zen Buddhism. On a linguistic level it is extremely complicated poetry. So many hidden meanings come to the surface that the reader feels quite baffled. Breyten's an excessively gifted poet. He introduced free verse into the Afrikaans literary system. It had a main impact.

"Within Afrikaans literary discourse there is this belief that poetry and literature dealt with universal things and shouldn't get stuck into everyday matters," Olivier said. "Among establishment critics there was a tendency to see the poems that dealt directly with politics as inferior. Breytenbach's poetry came across as too blunt, occasionally offensive."

Breytenbach long ago addressed the ambiguity of the anti-apartheid Afrikaner artist's position. In 1971 he said, "If you write or paint or film as an Afrikaner you have to compromise the only raw material you have, yourself . . . you become fodder for the tribe."

To Olivier, Breytenbach is the antithesis of N. P. van Wyk Louw, who advocated continuing quietly with work in the face of political crises, and D. J. Opperman, who put pressure on authorities behind the scenes.

"I think what Breyten did was considered to be rather an unseemly thing to be seen doing: open association and involvement with a political group."

Heavy rain pummeled the tin roof of Olivier's house, the last of the rain in 1992 in this semidesert land. A small calico cat settled onto laps and licked any guests' hands for extended periods of time.

Olivier thinks some Afrikaners identify with Breytenbach's "strong emotional need to actually do something" to oppose the authorities. "Although I'm a good friend of Breytenbach and though I've never really discussed it with him fully, I think there was a lot that was very naive [about his infiltrating back into South Africa to recruit people to work against apartheid].

"I realized that especially when I studied in Holland and met other members of Okhela, which was the organization on behalf of which he came to this country. Okhela was a very romantic branch of the ANC. It was actually a way of moving back on the sentimental level to the supposed democracy we'd seen in the old Boer republics."

Olivier remembered how Taurus decided to publish Breytenbach's *Confessions of an Albino Terrorist*, his book written in English on his seven years in prison.

"We decided that we would ignore the fact that [publishing] it was a transgression of the Prisons Act and the Police Act as well. But we couldn't ignore the fact that it probably was defamatory of a few individuals. So we got legal advice on that. They made a few amendments. Then there was a wager and my wager was that nothing would happen because they would not touch Breytenbach after all that happened. It would be too damaging even to ban a book of Breytenbach. And the same went for us as his publisher. I'm sure it was considered. I think the argument must've been, look, even though we'd love to, we'd have the Afrikaner establishment against us. In a way the Afrikaner establishment got some credibility through us."

The journalist Jacques Pauw recalled that when Breytenbach returned to South Africa to receive the *Rapport* prize for literature, Willem (Wimpie) de Klerk, then editor of *Die Transvaler*, promised Breytenbach he would publish the poet's speech in full, no deletions. "Breytenbach got very emotional as he went back into Pretoria for the first time again, and I think he was driven past the Pretoria Central Prison where he was kept for seven years," Pauw said. (In fact, Breytenbach was two years in solitary confinement in Pretoria Central, then five years in Pollsmoor Prison in the Cape.) "He became very emotional, very upset, changed his speech. That's when he said that the Afrikaner is shifting God around as though he was a Casspir armored vehicle. I was there that night and I remember people leaving the auditorium because they were so upset by Breyten's speech. De Klerk published the speech unchanged to the end, with all the swearwords and whatever. And that was one of the major reasons why he was fired in the end, because he did that."

The singer and musician Anton Goosen, who thought Breytenbach wrote exquisite poetry, also said, "He's pissing on our country at the moment. He married a very rich Vietnamese girl and it's all very well to sit there in Paris painting the river. Us okes that didn't run away and are sitting here encountering it and trying to help, that's a different thing." (Breytenbach became a French citizen in 1983 after his release from prison in South Africa.)

Jeanne Goosen said, "I think he's the most fantastic poet Afrikaans ever had and will ever have. He's a very sensitive man. But a few things are not kosher. He's a bit of an elitistic snob. You see, those who landed up in jail for more than a year at a time in the struggle, they became elitist. I don't even think he ever met one ordinary black, only intellectuals."

Frederick van Zyl Slabbert is a liberal Afrikaner politician who when he was in Parliament for the Progressive Federal Party helped get Breytenbach out of jail and is a very close friend of the poet's. He said "Ja, that's good stuff" of the prison book. Slabbert said he didn't read a lot of Afrikaans literature. "I'm not crazy about André Brink and I cannot stand Gordimer. They are apartheid novelists."

He hastened to say that doesn't mean he dislikes the people. But Gordimer's work "just bores me to tears." He clearly respected Breytenbach, though he'd had rancorous fights in print with the poet over his attitudes in coming back to South Africa and for badmouthing Afrikaans.

Will Breytenbach come back to live in South Africa?

"No, he won't come back. His wife would come back," Slabbert said.

Why?

"Oh, Breyten has become a European. He's a Parisian. I mean, he loves the language and he loves coming here now, well, I'm not sure he loves coming. He gets very worked up about it."

The establishment loves and hates him, the left-wingers are irritated at his long-distance lectures. And what about the right-wing Afrikaners, who are two thirds of Afrikaners? Well, *they* prefer Breyten's brother Jan Breytenbach, founder of the 32 Battalion of counterinsurgency— "reconnaissance" or "recce" soldiers—the Breytenbach who halted Angolan tanks by digging a trench, jumping in it, and shooting missiles up into their bellies.

Steve Booyens, an ex-recce who served under Jan Breytenbach, said of Breyten: "If he is twenty-five percent of his brother, he is an absolute giant. It doesn't matter what he's gonna do, he's gonna do it well. It's just that he's not my kind of person."

Not his kind of politics?

"No, definitely not. But do yourself a favor: to follow the history of South Africa read Wilbur Smith's books."

But Smith is not even an Afrikaner.

"No, but honestly if you read this it will give you insight into the origins of all the problems in South Africa. That, in a not unpleasant way, will explain a lot of things to you, You know I don't speak very well. I'm not a politician. I know what I feel."

Booyens continued with encomiums to Wilbur Smith, who writes popular and romantic historical sagas about South Africa that are not exactly up-market literature, but are best-sellers in South Africa.

Other Afrikaners disliked Breytenbach even more intensely—hated him. Prime Minister John Vorster had Breytenbach arrested and jailed. "Vorster hated him with a passion," said van Zyl Slabbert. "They tell the story that when Vorster at a National Party rally was slipped a note by [then Justice Minister] Jimmy Kruger saying 'We've caught him and arrested him,' Vorster said to Jimmy Kruger, 'Don't make this public, just give me a day to enjoy this on my own.'"

"It blew me away in 1980," Theunis Englebrecht said of Elsa Joubert's novel *Die Swerfjare van Poppie Nongena* (*The Long Travels of Poppie Nongena*). "I was at a very impressionable age [fifteen years old]. I think it did the same thing for a lot of people. It really influenced my political consciousness."

Published in 1978, *Poppie Nongena* tells the story of a Xhosa woman in the Cape whose life, like most blacks' lives, was devastated by the apartheid pass laws. Those laws required constant monitoring of the travels of Africans, who were until the late 1980s banned from being in so-called white areas without job-related permission. Over the years millions of Africans, often seeking work in "white" areas, were jailed for violating the laws.

The music critic and rock musician Theunis Englebrecht was by 1992 politically far to the left of Elsa Joubert, in fact on the edge of advocating anarchy. Back in the early eighties his staid Nationalist upbringing and outlook on the *platteland* had been changed by reading Joubert's book.

"It was two worlds in one, you know, black and white, and we didn't know what the black people were living like," said Englebrecht.

Why wasn't the book banned?

"There is no overt political propaganda. It's just this plain simple story about the black woman and her life, the problems of her children, how her life was influenced by apartheid. It was a very human story.

"I was brought up by a black woman, you know," Englebrecht said. "She is still working for my parents. So I think that is why I could relate to the book." After reading *Poppie Nongena*, Englebrecht looked at this woman differently. "I started asking questions about her life, her family, about the way she feels. The book definitely made me aware that black people are human beings too and they've also got emotions, they've also got children they love, they've got aspirations and ideals. They're not just out there, you know, people making your food in the mornings or just working for you like a slave. They're human beings as well."

National Party supporters found Elsa Joubert's *Poppie* quite acceptable. For example, while that stickler for propriety Professor van Rensburg was trying to avoid discussing Breytenbach's influence, his wife Susan walked over to the professor's floor-to-ceiling bookcase and plucked out a book.

"I want to ask whether you know this book because I think it was much more of an influence," she said, holding up *Poppie Nongena.* "Because this wasn't intended to be an onslaught on the government."

"That sympathetic light on black experience is much more real than Alan Paton's work," Professor van Rensburg added, referring to Paton's 1948 *Cry the Beloved Country.* "This was a woman having come across another woman and hearing her out."

Poppie was serialized on the radio, and since the government controlled the airwaves, that meant it had National Party approval, or at least that the *verligte* wing of the Broederbond approved.

Another indication of acceptance was that Kontak, a *verligte* Afrikaner women's organization started in 1976, immediately adopted the book for use in educating its membership to the need for improving race relations. The then Broederbond chairman Gerrit Viljoen was on Kontak's advisory board.

Annemarie Nutt, chairman of Kontak in 1992, said, "Kontak had a series of meetings in different branches on this book because it was a very good way of introducing better relations, and you know bringing in the plight of the blacks to the notice of people who really were not unsympathetic."

The *verligte* Broederbonders used *Poppie* to reeducate their *volk,* approving of the book's message and its gentle style of hinting that laws were unjust. Eight years after the novel's publication the pass laws that controlled blacks' movements were abolished.

Marianne de Jong noted that *Poppie's* publication caused a spate of letters to the Afrikaans newspapers, part of a tradition of public debate. One letter by the Stellenbosch University philosopher Johan Degenaar noted that Joubert's book explained the structural violence of apartheid, a concept foreign to most Afrikaners. De Jong nonetheless had mixed feelings about *Poppie.* "Elsa Joubert's book is very paternalistic," she said. "It states what happened to a black woman [under the pass laws] and the main character was saying that although she doesn't like violence, she understands why the children do this [protest and die]." De Jong thought the portrayal of the black woman was Joubert's view of a black woman, not an authentic black voice.

"This book was a barometer, an indicator of a public mood, a public sensibility which was still a Nationalist sensibility, a Nationalist self-critique. There was room for it.

"You know it's a difficult thing to answer the question about the possible role of literature [in changing apartheid]," de Jong said. "*Poppie Nongena* rocked the boat but it didn't change the government. It was very far from doing that." However, de Jong argued that *Poppie* remarkably sparked "debate about structural violence in the Nationalist press while the government was at the same time putting people under one hundred eighty days' banning orders on the same front page."

Why did the novel have such a strong impact?

"Because it was written by an Afrikaans woman whose Afrikanership was above doubt," de Jong said. "I think the critique against the government was there for much longer than we knew, but in a subtle way. The people who criticized the government were not prepared to topple it. They still voted for the Nats although they critiqued them."

Elsa Joubert's married name is Mrs. Klaus Steytler. She is descended from the Murrays, a Scots Presbyterian missionary family headed by Andrew Murray, who came over in the early nineteenth century and reinvigorated the Dutch Reformed Church, not least of all because five of his six sons were ordained and four of his five daughters married influential ministers.

"I said Murrays, but my forebears were mostly French Huguenots, straight line through from 1688," Elsa Joubert said.

Descendants of the Huguenots claim a longer tradition of education than, and hence an intellectual superiority to, many parvenu Afrikaners. Born in 1922, Elsabe Antoinette Murray Joubert Steytler was elite before the National Party came to office to empower and elevate the Afrikaner: impeccable pedigree, undergraduate degree from Stellenbosch in 1942, and a master's from the University of Cape Town in 1945.

In Joubert's gracious, oldish home on the beautiful slopes of Table Mountain, her servant served tea and she said, "Thank you, sweetness." To her interlocutors she was less polite, gradually revealing herself as a crotchety curmudgeon, no matter how many nice things were said about her book. Her corrugated, croaky voice fit her prickly attitude.

Why wasn't her book banned?

"Probably because it was the truth and because it was so convincing, I think," Joubert said.

But a lot of books that are the truth were banned.

"Yes, not always though. Very many of them have been slanted that have been banned. Also, I think they felt that I was honest in my approach. And I wasn't using apartheid for my benefit. I think the important thing was that my bona fides were good. I am Afrikaans-speaking. My own work is done in Afrikaans."

Many Afrikaners, when asked whether they've thought about what it felt like to be black in South Africa, are stopped cold, thinking the question quite odd.

"It doesn't stop me cold," Joubert said, nastily.

Isn't that the point of *Poppie Nongena*, to put the reader in somebody else's shoes? The question was meant as a compliment.

"No, it's because it's a very stupid question, actually," she sputtered, as if insulted. "You are what you are. And you must make the best of what you are. If I was a pygmy, I'd try to be a worthy pygmy. I think it's quite a futile question. I can only try to be as good a white as I can, as good a white female as I can. Of course we empathize. Do you think we haven't been trying? I come from a family of missionaries. Some of them died, and their children died in the mission field. My aunt was a doctor. Her husband was an educator. This is sacrifice, hey? Their children from the age of three or four were sent to my mother's parents to be reared till they were about seven or eight in South Africa because malaria hadn't been conquered.

"I was in Nyasaland myself, Malawi, and I saw in their little church the whole list of little babies of missionary children, mostly Steytler, my husband's name. His people were there. My people were Murrays. We did a lot and we empathized and we worked ourselves to the bone because we wanted to put ourselves in the place of the black people for feeding and educating and treating and healing."

But the motivation behind that was to convert them wasn't it?

"It wasn't to convert them at all," she exploded. "It was healing. This aunt of mine was a medical doctor. She wasn't a preacher. She was a nutritionist. My son is devoting his life to training lawyers. My son-in-law is working with housing. It's been our way of life to make sense out of Africa. Not to make them black white people, black Westerners, but because there are such numbers of them to give them a livable life.

"So there's no such thing as we were apart. We were apart in the sense that our children went to different schools. But we saw that our maid's children went to school and that they had books and they had clothes.

"Every word I've ever written has been to try to bring together the two races. To come and tell me that I haven't got empathy, or the Afrikaners haven't got empathy is just rubbish. What's getting us, especially from the outside world, is uninformed prejudice."

Maybe another attempt to compliment her book *Poppie Nongena* would be useful. She was told that many people were favorably influenced, that they say things like 'Until I had read *Poppie Nongena*, I never thought of my maid as a real person.'

"Well that's their business, not mine," Elsa Joubert said.

Novelist Jeanne Goosen strolled in her garden through the drizzly rain with her calm, six-year-old Doberman.

"My dog has four names," Goosen said. "Spier Oskar Rosamando van Spandau.

"That's the fanciest thing about me," she added.

It seems appropriate that words are the fanciest thing about this writer who published a novel in 1991 that upended Afrikaans literary trends and captivated the imagination of the *volk*. Almost 100,000 people bought *Ons Is Nie Almal So Nie* (*We Are Not All Like That*), tremendous sales for a book in Afrikaans.

Goosen's rented cottage in the Auckland Park suburb of Johannesburg, next to the Rand Afrikaans University campus, was comfortably messy, quite unlike the usual neat-as-a-pin, middle- and upper-class Afrikaner homes. She seemed not to have a servant, a highly unusual condition for a white in South Africa.

But then Goosen is an odd Afrikaner woman. She joined the anti-apartheid United Democratic Front in the late eighties and the ANC in 1989, while it was still a banned organization. But long before that, in the seventies, she worked with Quakers in building churches and schools in black townships. In her fifty years she had been a radiographer, a journalist, a street hawker selling everything from chamber pots to her own books, a fisherwoman in Plettenberg Bay, and a clown in a Pretoria circus. Describing the clown act, she jumped up from her wicker chair, flapped her imaginary clown feet, and swatted her bottom as if she were wearing gigantic butt padding.

Also unusual for an Afrikaner woman, Goosen speaks at a high volume, one that escalates as she sips her whiskey-laced tea. She has the sturdy face of a Breughel peasant. "I was raised very quietly, come to think of it," she said. "They say, 'Oh you've behaved badly' if you are Afrikaans and you make a noise. It is all very, very quiet."

She said she'd like to live in Holland again for a while. "I like them because they open their mouths very wide when they speak and they're very loud. And they can make a lot of noise. Paraguayans I also like. If you sit with them, everybody speaks, a lot of children playing around. Italians, they cry and laugh and make music, everything at the same time. Blacks [in South Africa] are nice too, they make a helluva noise and they tell nice stories."

Goosen's preferences are extraordinary, since white South Africans almost universally complain about blacks being noisy and raucous.

Annemarie Nutt is more the norm for an elite Afrikaner woman. She lives in the plush Johannesburg suburb of Northcliff and is so seemly that one was tickled to spy, literally, a very white slip showing. Although she is the opposite of the vociferous, bohemian Jeanne Goosen, she loved her latest book.

Jeanne Goosen's *We Are Not All Like That* is lowbrow, or at least non-avant-garde; it paints the Afrikaner as crude, bigoted, and speaking a most un-Standard Afrikaans, a portrayal that the establishment would have rejected before 1990.

"The language [of the novel] was wonderful because it was the way people spoke then," said Nutt. "I went to an Afrikaans school which just started up before the war and was still trying to improve the environment of students. It's Groote Schuur, now one of the best Afrikaans schools. I had a very wide collection of children at this school. I could place some of my friends in this context by the way they spoke. I found it [the novel] to be excellent."

"She's brilliant," raved Theunis Englebrecht of Goosen. "She's writing unlike anything else in Afrikaans. It's not very academic. It's very streetwise sort of stuff. Raunchy Afrikaans. Full of compassion but not in a sentimental way. Very controlled."

"I love her," said the *Vrye Weekblad* journalist Ina van der Linde of Jeanne Goosen. "She uses the language the way she talks. She's always been rather low-class and she's got a good head on her shoulders. She comes from sort of a railway background, poor people, and she speaks language that way, I love it. The way she uses the language is so creative."

Marichen Waldner chimed in: "Jeanne Goosen used to write highbrow poetry that was almost unreadable and we didn't like it much. Then she sat down for fun and wrote this thing. It became immediately loved in this country."

Henno Cronje, the head of the FAK, said he'd read Goosen's book and thought it excellent.

Is it a new kind of writing, new language?

"Ja, but that's not actually very new," Cronje said. He recalled an Afrikaans author who years ago wrote stories about an Afrikaner named Ampie. "Ampie was a very poor young boy. He said funny things and many people didn't like it. They said, Ag, how can this person write about an Afrikaner scene this way: it's humiliating us. That's fifty years ago."

That was before the FAK?

"I don't think the FAK was a factor at that time."

What had happened? Can Jeanne Goosen explain why the Broederbond approved of her book that depicts Afrikaners unfavorably?

Goosen said her novel would not have been accepted for publication by the big Afrikaans publisher Haum before President de Klerk unbanned the ANC and took the lid off the society on February 2, 1990.

"I gave the manuscript [to the publisher] on January fifth. Then February the second came. Then his [de Klerk's] statement and then every-body had guts," Goosen said. "I actually thought, now everybody's going to kick me out as a writer, going to tell me that I'm too, that I became middle class, no?"

Instead of elitist?

"Yes, because although my other books are complicated and against the establishment, they were highbrow literature.

"Ah, writers of the sixties could identify with the romantic agony," she said. "In fact the first anti-apartheid books were in the sixties, but it became elitistic, very intellectual. I've got nothing against intellectual-ism. But actually those books still feed Afrikaner nationalism in litera-ture. 'Die Afrikaner het gearriveer,' the Afrikaner arrived, you know, we're intellectual, we know about everything. It lost the reader com-pletely. Because nobody read anymore. [Goosen wasn't a Sestiger but she had followed in that movement's footsteps of intellectual and surre-alistic fiction.]

"I decided to get out with a big publisher, an ordinary publisher. No provincialistic thing because Taurus, also in the struggle, became very elitistic. I wanted to give my book out very cheaply, I told them. It must be under twenty rands. It sells for 16.95 [about six dollars]. The cheapest book here in Afrikaans is about thirty rands. I wanted it in paper, soft cover, and I wanted a movie idol on the cover. I wanted it in the fascistic colors, red, black, and white."

She got all those things and a CNA literary prize to boot. The prize hangs ludicrously high on the wall of her tiny bathroom.

We Are Not All Like That is set in Cape Town, where her father was an engineer back when the railway network, manned mostly by Afrikaners, stretched north to Zambia. Is it about her own family?

"Partly," she said. "I think it's emotional biography. It's more or less all the people I ever met in my life. It's the streets in the Cape, in the sub-urbs, then this upcoming of the National Party, this 'Ons moet vooruit—We must progress, we must get learned.' The book is a comedy. But it is not paternalistic, it's not sympathetic, it is as it is. All the groups. And they're all labeled with names, *kaffir, houtkop, koelie* [nigger, wooden-head, coolie], it's all in there because they spoke like that. There were no other names for it. It's very harsh now to look at it, it's true. It's quite amazing because the Academy [for Science and Art] appointed a com-mittee about five years ago to take all these words out of books that were being reprinted. And here's a modern writer bringing them back."

Goosen served more tea from the set she took from the top of her refrigerator in her jammed cottage. The rain began to plonk on the corrugated metal roof. She collected three bright pink cushions from the garden chair on a patio outside the front door. "Spier, asseblief, man [Spier, please, man]," she cajoled her restive Doberman into a sitting position. "I toured this country with that book, got invitations from libraries, and all these aunties and uncles they sit and ask questions. They want to know, 'What's going to happen now, and it's true, what you wrote, and it's very sad, but what can we do?' Especially old people, it's quite sad, here we all sit, everybody did such a lot of harm. Tremendous harm."

Goosen is a dynamic and angry person, who is proud of her fury and uses it for creative energy.

"I experienced anger as a form of freedom. It leads to a free flow of words. When I was a child we still had mixed schools, with Portuguese and everybody. Everybody used to play together and the evictions of other colors only came in the late fifties. So we all grew up together. But later on the language changed of course. In Afrikaans, they wiped out this whole creolic influence of the Bushmen, the Zulus, Sotho, Xhosa. They sterilized it. And of course all the English words, or most of them. They changed the grammar. The verb we used to use like the English-speaking person in the middle of the sentence. Then it came at the back of the sentence," she said chuckling.

Does she actually remember that when she was a child the verb was in the middle of the sentence?

"Hmmm," she affirmed. "Today it's back in [the middle]. Yes, nobody speaks pure, or standard, Afrikaans anymore. All of a sudden after February 2 everybody just, in a hell of a slang, because everybody kept on speaking like that at their homes, an Afrikaans with Malay words and you know, all these languages."

What does she mean, after February 2, everybody—

"Relaxed!" she said. "Psychologically too, in their language. Never after that a pure or Standard Afrikaans book ever came out in this country. I made a study of it."

A bit later she said, "So that's more or less the background and I'm definitely exaggerating."

It was anybody's guess as to exactly what she exaggerated. Was that a tincture of the theater-of-the-absurd, or the "decadence, a hysterical thing" Goosen talked about as a source for creativity in her latest medium, the cabaret? At the end of the meeting Goosen gave away a mounted photograph of a child, with tousled brown hair and aged about seven, wearing the AWB's swastikalike insignia, whose shouting face is contorted in hate.

Spier, the Doberman, ought to meet Beau-mont, the Lab, because both were mellow and had laid-back attachments to two exceptionally independent and eloquent women. Maybe they *had* met. Marianne de Jong and Jeanne Goosen are friends, and it was de Jong who suggested talking with Goosen. Beaumont slunk from out of the dark night, seeped under the table away from Marianne de Jong, and lay his sweet jaws on a guest's foot.

"Goosen is interesting because she's beginning to write about the crude racism," de Jong said. "She's broken this almost self-imposed ban of the writer on the crudeness of racism in this country. Brink was not prepared to be crude enough, you know. He attacked in a moralistic sense, because they didn't want to know, they didn't see it as racism."

Are colored Afrikaans authors affecting white writers?

"Oh yes, very much so recently. Since the last two, three years. One guy, Patrick Peterson in the Cape, and some other people who are just coming up. In Afrikaans there have been colored writers, but few of them. They were used as examples of the broadness, so they were actually being co-opted. But these new guys like Peterson and Hein Willemse are not co-optable. They are not very good at this stage, but I am sure that is going to come in a very strong way, very soon.

"You know one of the nicest things I've heard was when Jeanne Goosen said, 'Afrikaans is a creole language,' " de Jong said. "It is per definition a total mixture. Tomorrow it can be anything and if you don't like what you hear, sorry for you, but that is the reality."

That "colored" future for Afrikaans and Afrikaners is what Jeanne Goosen's colloquial novel points to. She resurrects the sympathies of Afrikaners for their colored neighbors in pre-apartheid days, and glories in the return of the earthy language that the "cultural" establishment had tried to purge.

"I still can't believe I wrote the book," Goosen said. "That I actually had the guts. I knew that this is what writing is really about. This time I laughed myself to pieces and I cried myself to pieces and I became practically hysterical.

"I'm not worried about Afrikaans. I don't think it'll die, because it is the language of poor people in this country. But I'm very worried about cultural poverty in the name of the language. Because again they are starting now with this whole damn standardization of Afrikaans. The FAK, the ATKV. In the name of preservation. Afrikaans will survive on its own now. We don't need the establishment or academics to tell us we must do our little bit."

PART VI

POLICE STATE

In general, the degree of responsibility increases as we draw further away from the man who uses the fatal instrument with his own hands.

—HANNAH ARENDT,
Eichmann in Jerusalem:
A Report on the Banality of Evil

They hope to bleed South Africa so dry that in the end whoever comes into power will have to share it with them. That is what I call the "Samson complex." The biblical reference, Samson: in the end if I can do nothing else, I can pull out the pillars and we shall all perish together. It's nurtured in the Special Forces. They are the people I am really afraid of.

—DOMINEE WILLEM SAAYMAN,
ANC member

CHAPTER TWENTY-NINE

UGLY THINGS HAPPENED

By 1977, Verwoerdian apartheid had fizzled and sputtered out as a useful ideology for rallying the *volk,* while black protest flared around the country. So Afrikaner planners slapped more ideology on top of the old. The newly identified problem was "total onslaught" from monolithic communism. The solution, developed by the defense minister, P. W. Botha, was "total strategy," or police-state terror as carried out by the Security Police, military forces, and Military Intelligence. God was called upon to approve, and He did, since the enemy was communism, alias the antichrist.

The new ideology was really an expansion of the anticommunism that was already enshrined in law. In 1950 Parliament had passed the Suppression of Communism Act, which defined communism as "any doctrine or scheme which aims at bringing about any political, industrial, social or economic change . . . by the promotion of disturbance or disorder" or "which aims at the encouragement of feelings of hostility between the European and non-European races."

Under the new rallying cry of "total onslaught," the Nationalists' thinking went like this: the Soviet Union was manipulating other states to oppose South Africa and thus weaken Western civilization. Theories of class hostility and a program for race mixing aimed to destroy the Afrikaner bastion of pure Christian belief. Humanism, "forcing everything together and saying that's new age," as Dominee Pieter Nel said, was communism. Even the desire for church unity was communistic.

Church and Broederbond eminence Johan Heyns said in 1992, "P. W. Botha made out of every problem a communistic problem. Apartheid was the strongest weapon against communism. It wasn't possible [for the church] to touch [oppose] this very effective weapon."

Apartheid's planners had transmogrified the vague specter of communism into a bogey that caused flesh to crawl, that gnawed the nerves, that wrecked men's sleep and made them torture, kill, and go mad. Only with the collapse of the Soviet empire and the resultant diminution of the Communist threat did the NP initiate its 1990 reform program.

*   *   *

"Total strategy" was first applied, secretly, beginning in 1975, to the postcolonial war in Angola. In Operation Savannah the South African Defense Force (SADF)* lined up with the American CIA and the People's Republic of China to support Jonas Savimbi's UNITA (National Union for the Total Independence of Angola) movement against the Soviet-backed Marxist MPLA (Popular Movement for the Liberation of Angola) government. The SADF aimed to drive north into Angola's capital of Luanda, conquer the MPLA army, and hand power to Savimbi.

Max du Preez was there as a conscript in 1975–76, but he didn't know it at first. His surprise was typical. "Called me up for a three-month camp," he remembered. "I'm regiment Boomspruit, which is a Bloemfontein regiment. I was infantry. Put us in trucks, said we are going to fight SWAPO [South West African People's Organization] in Ovambo. You travel for days. And you wonder, but you're not allowed to ask questions. The first time we knew that we were deep into Angola was when we started seeing these funny black soldiers who were deployed with us. So who are these guys? And then they said, 'Um, UNITA.' And I said, 'What the hell is UNITA doing in Namibia? This is wrong, how can we have UNITA in Namibia? This is breaking international law.' "

As du Preez sat with his platoon of more than thirty men looking at the lights of Luanda, Defense Minister P. W. Botha denied in Parliament that South Africa had anything to do with Angola. The troops got more information about their own movements from BBC radio than from their commanders. Then, in a reversal of American policy, the United States failed to back the South African offensive and the SADF had to withdraw.

With du Preez and some others, SADF "total strategy" indoctrination of defending Christianity against communism failed. He refused to fight. "I'm the worst soldier that the world has ever seen. I am incredibly scared of large noise and blood and dying people." He was court-martialed and sent home. His whole platoon joined with him, and, he

---

*The South African Defense Force, the most powerful in Africa, was expanded by Defense Minister and later Prime Minister P. W. Botha. Except for the Israeli and Swiss armies, it is the most reliant on reserve forces in the world. In the early eighties it consisted of 40,000 permanent force troops, 60,000 national servicemen, and 380,000 reserves. There are two operational sections of the army—a conventional force and a counterinsurgency (COIN) force. COIN was, in the eighties, by far the larger of the two. In addition, the security establishment includes Military Intelligence, Counter-Intelligence, National Intelligence Service, and Security Police, according to Mark Phillips in *War and Society: The Militarisation of South Africa.* The research and production network includes the Armaments Corporation (Armscor) and about 1,500 private contractors.

said, their case was not unique. "There were lots of platoons and sections and individuals who refused to fight."

The government faced a quandary, according to du Preez. "They couldn't punish us because then they had to admit that this kind of thing was happening. It was a major embarrassment to them. It hasn't been written anywhere" in South Africa. To do so, he said, would have violated the Defense Act of 1952, as amended. "Ja, you can't even write about Operation Savannah, still not to this day [1992]."

Du Preez's war record didn't hinder his career. In 1978 he was sent to Namibia as a reporter for Nasionale Pers, and then became bureau chief there. His disaffection with the "total onslaught" ideology was deepened by his experiences in Namibia, where he was friendly with both sides in the war.

"I was quite a good friend of Jannie Geldenhuys, who was then the chief of the Defense Force in Namibia. We used to go drinking on a Saturday morning together. The whole German custom. Wonderful thing, called *Frühschoppen,* where at about eleven you start drinking beer and eating raw meat and you know, all these savage customs of the Germans. Used to love that. And Jannie Geldenhuys, who is a remarkable man, used to come with us, some of his officers and most of the journalists. Anton Lubowski used to go with us.* Lubowski was one of my best friends. I [also] had very strong personal friendships with senior members of SWAPO and with senior members of the Defense Force. We would go drinking together. And the chances were, ten kilometers away they would wage a war against each other. It was a very artificial kind of situation in Namibia."

The Namibian/Angolan military strategy was also used in Rhodesia and Mozambique. In Rhodesia, South African police helped support Ian Smith's white government and its army against Zimbabwean nationalist movements until independence came in 1980. In Mozambique, South Africa escalated a devastating war, taking over support of the RENAMO (Mozambique National Resistance) guerrilla movement initiated by Ian Smith's government against President Samora Machel's marxist government. The states neighboring South Africa trembled at attacks carried out by the South African army and police, watching helplessly as South

---

*Lubowski, a civil rights lawyer who joined the Namibian independence movement, SWAPO, was killed by a South African death squad on September 12, 1989. In a June 1994 inquest the Namibian judge Harold Levy found that the Civil Cooperation Bureau head, Joe Verster, arranged the murder. The CCB, a secret branch of the military, was under the State Security Council, which is discussed later in this chapter. Verster has said he never undertook a mission without approval from the highest level of government.

Africa targeted the camps, installations, and personnel of the ANC based in their countries. Also, all across southern Africa young South African whites in the military were being killed and becoming brutalized and shell-shocked, while their government often denied any military involvement.

For years the police and Security Police, dominated by Afrikaners, were the primary defenders of white rule against waves of black resistance. Successive parliaments expanded police powers, and protests met with increasing state-sponsored violence.

From 1963 on, police could detain people for ninety days in isolation for interrogation, without charge, and the detention period could be renewed. In 1965 the ninety-day limit was doubled. In 1966, short-term "preventive" detention for fourteen days was added to the police's panoply of tools, followed in 1967 by Section 6 of the Terrorism Act, which provided for indefinite detention without trial for purposes of interrogation. Long-term "preventive" detention was introduced in 1976, under which political activists could be detained for twelve-month renewable periods. Anyone could be detained for six months in solitary confinement. These fragmentary pieces of legislation were rationalized in 1982 under the Internal Security Act, which was further streamlined in 1986.

In addition to these laws, security forces gained further powers if the government declared an area to be under a state of emergency. Under emergency legislation dating from 1953, the head of state could declare twelve-month states of emergency. In such situations, members of the security forces (including police, SADF, and Prison Services) could detain and interrogate anyone for the duration of the emergency. Detained people had no right of access to lawyers, family, or friends, and states of emergency could be (and were) renewed, thus indefinitely extending the detentions. Estimates are that under regular and emergency regulations approximately 73,000 people were officially detained from 1960 to 1990.

Torture as reported by detainees and their families was commonplace, police denials routine. Common forms of reported torture included sleep deprivation, enforced standing for long periods, enforced physical exercise and exertion, being kept naked during interrogation, suspension in midair, beating, slapping, kicking, electric shocks, attacks on the genitals, hooding, food deprivation, strangulation, dousing in cold water, water deprivation, application of lit cigarettes and chemicals to the skin, bright light, being exposed to excessive cold and heat, being made to walk barefoot over broken glass or stones. In a 1987 study, 83 percent of 175 detainees surveyed reported some form of torture.

Another study showed that claims of injury were consistent with observed physical symptoms in 97 percent of cases surveyed.

At least sixty-nine people who were political activists are known to have died in detention from 1963 to 1990. Reported forms of death included injuries to head or body, slipping in a shower or on soap, falling down stairs, hitting the head against a desk while fainting, and being shot while trying to escape. "Suicide" was the most frequently reported cause of death, with detainees found hanged, strangled, fallen from windows or down stairwells. Many more died outside formal detention, in unknown and unexplained circumstances.

The police-state culture remained after 1990 because the same police remained in their jobs. In 1992, the pathologist Dr. Jonathan Gluckman claimed that of two hundred cases of deaths during police custody (not necessarily under detention rules, but for any reason) that he examined, a large proportion had been murdered by "out-of-control" policemen. Gluckman said that almost every week people died in the custody of those whose duty it was to protect life. In 1992 alone, more than 119 people died in prisons.

P. W. Botha rose to power through the National Party and was an avid fan of the military. First as defense minister, then as prime minister and state president, he transferred power from civilian to military and police authorities. The security establishment grew rapidly after Soweto, and by the early 1980s Botha had set up the National Security Management System (NSMS), headed by the State Security Council (SSC) and organized down to grassroots joint management committees (JMCs). The NSMS and the joint management committees became a parallel government, usurping civilian structures. The church leader Johan Heyns saw the militarization of society as an extension of Botha's own bullying response to an underlying inferiority complex. "He was only one year [at] university; he had that sort of academic inferiority complex," Heyns said.

The newspaper columnist and editor Piet Muller said, "The [black] uprising of 1984 gave the military the opportunity of taking hold of the whole country. That was an absolute military coup. Even the tiniest district or segment of a district was under immediate military control. They took precedence over the civilians, civil servants, and the politicians."

More meticulous analysts might not classify the policy as a military coup, since in 1989 Botha was replaced by de Klerk, and the civilians in the National Party appeared to take back much of their lost power. But from the late 1970s until Botha's ouster, the National Party and Parliament were eclipsed and state security apparatuses proliferated. Security

319

structures grew like roots in a mangrove swamp: partly exposed but largely invisible, they intertwined below the surface and extended their reach into every pool.

There were eleven police forces in South Africa and eleven police commissioners, including the homelands' supposedly independent police authorities; however, over them all was the South African Police commissioner, whose operations penetrated into surrounding countries and as far afield as Geneva and London. South African support for Ian Smith in Rhodesia was largely a police function. The South African Police Security Branch honed its skills in Rhodesia and then applied them at home, specializing in interrogation, torture, misinformation, and dirty tricks. The SADF had its Military Intelligence department, and National Intelligence operated separately, under the office of the president. The police, defense, and intelligence organizations all had clandestine operations.

The police were apparently the first to develop death squads. Starting in August 1981 in Vlakplaas near Pretoria,* "turned" ANC and Pan-Africanist Congress guerrillas under SAP control were trained to be killers of anti-apartheid activists and fighters. In 1986, the Civilian Cooperation Bureau (CCB) was set up to carry out the nastiest of dirty tricks. It recruited former criminals and notoriously violent policemen to harass and assassinate state enemies. Investigations in 1990 revealed the CCB was set up by, but was intended to become independent of, the SADF. A 1994 biography of P. W. Botha written by Daan Prinsloo said that in 1986, Law and Order Deputy Minister Adriaan Vlok in a report to Botha titled *Derde Mag* (Third Force) recommended setting up the CCB. Affidavits from former operatives in 1994 indicated the chain of command went to the top of the National Party government into the State Security Council. President Botha headed the SSC, and its cabinet-level members included Vlok, F. W. de Klerk, Magnus Malan, Pik Botha, and Kobie Coetsee.

Death-squad killings appear to have continued up to the election in 1994. But new revelations about connections with the police and SADF security apparatuses were hampered by the wholesale burning of documents by the government beginning in 1992 and by the separation of the official lines of command from the activities of the dirty-tricksters.

While the public was kept officially in the dark over many years, many Afrikaners knew that a secret war was going on and that there was a high

---

*Vlakplaas was first written about by journalist Jacques Pauw in *Vrye Weekblad*. His exposé relied on interviews with former head of Vlakplaas, Dirk Coetzee. The last Vlakplaas commander, Eugene de Kock, in mid-1995 was being tried in a Pretoria court on more than 120 charges, including eight for murder.

degree of cooperation (as well as competition) among the police, the defense, and intelligence forces.

"People were prepared to buy it," said the Stellenbosch University economist Sampie Terreblanche. "Internally it boiled down to a low-intensity war and very ugly things happened."

When Dirk Coetzee, the former police agent in charge at Vlakplaas, told journalist Jacques Pauw in 1984 that he'd helped in the killings of lawyer and anti-apartheid activist Griffiths Mxenge in 1981 and the student leader Siphiwo Mtimkulu in 1982, Pauw said of himself: "From there on I started learning the other side of Afrikaner politics and Afrikaner life. I wasn't shocked because we all knew it was going on."

When Pauw checked and found that Coetzee's descriptions tallied with the newspaper accounts, he decided to pursue the story. He met with the former policeman about once a month, from late 1984 to 1988, and compiled a file on his encounters. In November 1989 for three days in Mauritius, Pauw listened to Coetzee tell about murder missions in South Africa, Swaziland, Lesotho, and Botswana. From Coetzee Pauw heard: "People were shot, poisoned, harassed, burnt, stabbed, and blown to pieces. Cars were stolen, dogs poisoned, and houses bombed." The former Security policeman admitted he was involved in at least twenty-three serious crimes between January 1977 and December 1981. Coetzee implicated, among others, the Security Branch head and later police commissioner Johan Coetzee (whose response is in Chapter 30).

"[Dirk] Coetzee was telling everybody about what he did," Pauw said, including, among others, the National Party member of Parliament Wynand Malan; the then editor of *Die Vaderland*, Harald Pakendorf; and the Democratic Party national chairman, Tian van der Merwe. "Everybody knew it was happening and it was in a way accepted."

Pauw's stories on Dirk Coetzee and the death squads were published in November 1989 in *Vrye Weekblad*, after F. W. de Klerk became president. Pauw's 1991 book, *In the Heart of the Whore*, screamed the story into the public Afrikaner silence on death squads.

Jacques Pauw, with his naive demeanor, seemed an unlikely candidate for investigative journalist, particularly since he came from the heart of the compromised Afrikaans press. But scandalous stories fester all over South Africa, begging for brave journalists and editors to write and publish them. When he was a reporter at *Rapport* a few years before, Pauw too had been a tool of the police. "The Afrikaans mainstream press has been an evil instrument used by the military, by the security forces," he said. "To give you an example, Jeanette Schoon and

321

[her daughter] Katryn Schoon were blown up in August '84 by a parcel bomb in southern Angola. I was sent by my news editor to interview the commissioner of police, Johan Coetzee, about this parcel bomb. He gave me an interview about the internal strife in the ANC and how they kill each other and Jeanette Schoon was wiped out by another faction of the ANC. I wrote my story about the internal strife in the ANC, and [how] yet again the government was being blamed for ANC misdeeds. I totally forgot about this article. Then when I did the research for my book and got all the clippings from all of the years, I discovered my own article."

On top of what Pauw called the "utterly, utterly evil" editorial policy of the Afrikaans press, the overall news media were penetrated by Security Branch agents.

John Horak, an Afrikaner who rose to a top position in the English-language press—morning group editor of the South African Associated Newspapers (SAAN)—was in the pay of the Security Police for twenty-seven years. Of the English press he said, "You could divide an English-language newspaper into fifty percent state informers and fifty percent Communists." In 1985 Horak was given a job openly in the security establishment, but unhappy with his treatment, he publicly defected to the ANC in 1992. (His story is in Chapter 30.)

South Africa is a wounded country. Its victims and its torturers walk around each other, unhealed.

Jabu Ngwenya, the president of the South African Musicians Alliance and an ANC activist since the early eighties, said in April 1992 that he'd probably been tortured more than almost anybody else in the country. His friend, music entrepreneur Attie van Wyk, said that Ngwenya had told him in detail about his torture. "He was hanged from a tree in the nude in winter and had water thrown all over him," van Wyk said.

One of the Security policemen who interrogated Ngwenya was Dries Struwig, of John Vorster Square police headquarters. After retirement, Struwig often was a security guard for music concerts staged at Johannesburg's huge Ellis Park Stadium, and there he and Ngwenya met again. Many people claim to have suffered under Struwig's fists and the zealotry of his boss, Colonel Arthur Benoni Cronwright. (The views of Struwig and Cronwright appear in Chapter 30.)

One was a former Methodist minister, Cedric Mayson, the editor of the Christian Institute's magazine, *Pro Veritate*, in 1977. He testified in court in 1984 that when he was detained by the Security Police in late 1981, he was tortured by Cronwright, Struwig, and others. Then fifty-three years old, he was kept naked and handcuffed for four days. His feet swelled from standing through sixty hours of continuous questioning. A swatch of his hair was yanked out. "Lots of people were brought in and others peered in at me," he testified. "I realized a dehumanization process had begun. They began to criticize me and mock my claims to Christianity. They asked me how I could be a Christian if I was a terrorist, a member of the ANC, and a Communist. Captain Andries Struwig, a former police boxer, punched me in the chest."

Mayson explained to the judge why he wrote a statement admitting guilt. "Quite frankly, my lord, I was afraid of dying in detention."

Under "total strategy," police and army functions and personnel overlapped in the shadowy world of covert operations where, to maintain deniability, many covert operations structures had been officially divorced from the police and the military.

"The guys who went into the Civilian Cooperation Bureau had to resign from the SADF [and/or police force]," Pauw explained. They were promised huge sums of money if the CCB was exposed, and some received large pensions in the early 1990s as information leaked out in judicial inquiries.

"They were the thugs of apartheid," Max du Preez said. "Now they feel bitter. They say they did the dirty job for the government, now the government's turning against them. Some of them have extreme right-wing leanings, but I think they are mostly professional thugs and professional soldiers. All they want to do is kill people."

F. W. de Klerk and other Afrikaner leaders are "dead scared of them," du Preez said, because they "know all the dirty tricks, they have friends in high places [who] helped create them. You can't kill a monster like the CCB." Du Preez claimed that the CCB operatives continue to prosper under the government's "Blue Plan," which set up front businesses for them. They could finance themselves for twenty-five years on the money they stashed away, he said. Every CCB agent had his own private army. Du Preez said there were "six, seven thousand people, twenty, thirty, or forty agents with their freelance soldiers." Some of them functioned on their own, but, du Preez argued, "There is no way in the world that de Klerk does not know fully of the strategies in terms of township violence of the Military Intelligence and Security Branch, the KwaZulu Police (KZP), and Inkatha."*

*In April 1995, three convicted hit-squad murderers—two KZP police and an Inkatha Freedom Party zealot—testified in mitigation of their actions that they acted on orders of their superiors.

In 1994 Dirk Coetzee, back in South Africa, told a reporter from the British newspaper *The Independent* just before South Africa's first multiracial elections that Security Police agents were "a monster on the loose. De Klerk has always feared the police generals. He knows they are a monster on the loose, a huge mafia. They have the real power in the country."

At about the same time Dirk Coetzee was talking, just before the 1994 election, the outgoing Nationalist government secretly received and granted a blanket request for amnesty (called "indemnity" locally) for 3,500 people, many of them Security policemen and former high officials. It was a list of last names with initials. When the applications were discovered about a year later, President Mandela and his colleagues were furious. The ANC's position was that at the very least the deeds committed by these men should be detailed and made public. Three of the four Security policemen interviewed in the next chapter were on that secret list: Andries or A. A. Struwig, John Horak (who said he did not ask that his name be put on the list), and their boss, Johan Coetzee— that is, there were several "J. Coetzees," and Johan Coetzee never denied newspaper reports that he was one of them.

The September 12, 1977, death of Black Consciousness movement leader Steve Biko in Pretoria, after he had been brought there naked in the back of a Land Rover overnight from Port Elizabeth, remains one of the most notorious of many murders of anti-apartheid activists carried out under "total strategy." Biko was well known in South Africa and around the world as the vibrant, articulate, and charismatic leader of the BCM. His death aroused an international fury that shocked the NP government. In the subsequent inquest, the court found that no policeman could be directly blamed for the death. The magistrate's finding was that Biko's death was due to brain injury, that "head injuries were probably sustained on September 7 [1977] in a scuffle in the Security Police offices in Port Elizabeth," and that "the death cannot be attributed to any act or omission amounting to a criminal offense on the part of any person." For observers, the inquest publicly exposed the extreme methods and lack of accountability of the Security Police.

In 1995 former police spy John Horak and other police sources confirmed that there is a story widely told within the Security Police force attributing responsibility for Biko's death to someone other than Colonel Piet Goosen, the officer who, because he commanded the group in whose custody Biko died, was the one generally thought responsible. This other security policeman rose through the ranks after 1977, and recently retired from a top-ranking position in police intelligence. He was known by the nickname "Biko."*

This story was first reported by editor Max du Preez in the *Vrye Weekblad* of June 19, 1992, under the headline "Só Is Biko Doodges-laan" (Thus Was Biko Beaten to Death). The paper reported in Afrikaans and is here translated:

"The evidence before the judicial inquiry after the death of Steve Biko in 1977 was delayed and falsified . . . because the policemen who were involved in the Biko incident knew that his death was caused by the serious assault of a certain policeman.

"Horak provided the name of this policeman and full details to *Vrye Weekblad*, but after legal advice *VWB* decided preliminarily not to publish his name. He is well known by a nickname which he got precisely because he 'buggered' Biko up so badly, says Horak.

"Horak says that the policeman, today a colonel in the security police, was a young policeman in Port Elizabeth when Biko was arrested on 18 August, 1977. He was one of the investigating officers.

"The policeman was 'fiercely loyal' to the then head of the security police in Port Elizabeth, Colonel [Piet] Goosen, who later retired as a brigadier.

"Early one morning in September during interrogation Biko allegedly hurled insults at Goosen.

"Horak relates: 'That evening (the policeman's name) had a few drinks with his friends in the canteen, where they decided that it could not be tolerated that a black man should talk to their commander in such a fashion.

"'At the instigation of (the policeman's name) they went to Biko's cell where he and his friends beat Biko terribly. Biko died five or six days later, and all of us in the force (police) knew that he died as a result of injuries that he sustained in the assault.'"†

In 1995 Horak described the *Vrye Weekblad* story as the one "doing the rounds in the police." He said it "is the version the average run-of-the-mill person smiles about and accepts to be the story."

Asked his opinion, Horak said, "Do I think it's a credible story? Yes, very much so."

Horak credited du Preez's publication of his story with helping to

*At our publisher's request, we do not publish the man's name here.

†Shortly after giving the interviews to du Preez, Horak fled South Africa for Britain due to fears for his life. Horak returned to South Africa in October 1992, having gained a public promise from the police that, despite their earlier charges that he had lied, they had no case against him and would not investigate him.

keep him from meeting an untimely end. He said, "In order to preempt anything they could do to me, Max [du Preez] published that stuff, which I fully agree with. I thought he did a very brave act. Probably his articles are one of the reasons why I am still talking to you today."

Following up on the *Vrye Weekblad* article, a prominent reporter sought to contact the man Horak named at police headquarters in Pretoria.

"I phoned security headquarters," the reporter recalled. "I said, 'May I speak to Colonel [the name], please?' And the receptionist said, 'No, I'm sorry, we don't have a Colonel [the name].' I said, 'Do you have any Colonel [the last name]?' 'Ja,' she said, 'the only Colonel [the last name] here that we have is Colonel Biko [the last name].'

"That's how arrogant," the reporter said. "He is kind of a legend in the police force. He's a very senior man in Pretoria. Very senior man."

Some South African police sources consulted about Biko's death confirmed Horak's story. Others held to the more official line that Piet Goosen was responsible. Goosen, who died in the early 1990s, had testified extensively in the 1977 inquest into Biko's death. The other man did not appear at the inquest.

Asked his opinion as to why the other man didn't testify at the inquest, Horak said: "In those days everybody was protecting everybody. The original inquest and what went on there was purely a sort of dress show."

When head of the Police Academy and former Commissioner of Police Johan Coetzee was asked in 1992 what he thought of a report that the Security policeman named by Horak killed Steve Biko, he said: "I don't know anyone by that name. Ag, no, the man that was well known to have, was supposed to have killed Steve Biko was Colonel Goosen. First time I've heard it."

When it was pointed out that the man named by Horak was promoted to headquarters in Pretoria, Coetzee said: "I don't say it's impossible you know. It's a big organization and people get promoted, but I mean, I know all the senior blokes."

Many people involved in "ugly things" remain in South African society. The drive to expose their acts cuts against the wish for national reconciliation. In 1992 journalist Marietjie Myburg worried, "If we don't set proper rules now and do a proper purge, we will have this kind of thing in this country forever."

CHAPTER THIRTY

BEATING THE LIZARD

As front-line warriors of the "total strategy," Security Branch policemen gathered intelligence, interrogated detainees, planted misinformation, and directed and carried out counter terrorist operations. Under P. W. Botha the Security Branch was the equivalent of the U.S. CIA and FBI rolled into one, competing and cooperating with Military Intelligence. With approximately five thousand members, the Security Branch was a small but extremely important part of the sixty-thousand-member police force. As in many police states, police interrogation is often a euphemism for assault and torture.

The players in the police drama have their own views of the old battles and the current transition.

Dries Struwig was a captain in the Security Police when he interrogated the Methodist minister Cedric Mayson, Jabu Ngwenya, and others in the late seventies and early eighties. He retired in 1990.

When barrel-chested, six-foot-plus Struwig was a young police constable, he happened to be on duty in the black township of Sharpeville on the fateful day of March 21, 1960. Crowds of blacks, mostly women, gathered around the police station, protesting the extension of the pass law to women. The crowd was chanting, singing, and shoving up against the security fence surrounding the building.

In a burst of gunfire that was to launch international pressure against South Africa, the police killed 68 people and injured 178.

Struwig said there were between fifteen and twenty thousand people in front of the three-foot-high wire fence around the police station.

"They put the children and the women in front and then they started throwing stones and shooting from the back and we were only a few. We were standing in a line, about fifty, sixty of us, and someone [police] drove in two Saracens [large armored vehicles], and the allegation was that they shot out of the Saracens. There was nobody in those Saracens. It was only ordinary rifles that we used against them." The mass of people was enormous, according to Struwig. "You know, if you stand on top of the Saracen, you can't even see the back of the crowd.

"I was on the Flying Squad [that handled burglaries, robberies, and rapes], and as a driver I was generally allowed to have a revolver and six bullets. Nothing more. I fired three shots with a .38 revolver. Now, that was how long the shooting lasted.

"I think we were doing it to protect our own lives. When we got there that morning they said to us, 'This is Cato Manor.' Just prior to this nine policemen had been killed in Cato Manor [in Natal]. I was frightened because I thought, 'Well that's the same way we're all going to go.' "

Struwig said jets dived down at the police station, trying to scare off the crowds. "They tried to throw the rocks at the airplanes and where does it land? You were ducking and diving all the time."

Does he think his three shots killed somebody?

"Ja, well, you see, what happened is, somebody threw a rock at the bottom of my ribs here, and it was like someone hits you in the solar plexus, and I went down on my knees. And there was, they, the wire, they were pushing that over. And someone was trying to do me with these kerries [heavy sticks with knobs on the end], and I had to fire these shots."

Into one person?

"Ja, well ah, well, into, you can imagine, there are thousands of people there and what you see in front of you, you only see people. I still feel now that what we did that day was the only thing we could do," Struwig said. "Unfortunately, they put the kids in front. And the women."

Shortly after Sharpeville the young Struwig spent twelve years "in the operational area," which meant the "bush war" against Africans seeking independence from colonial rule in Rhodesia, Angola, Mozambique, and South West Africa (Namibia). Struwig said he was in Ovamboland (northern Namibia), the Caprivi Strip (a long finger of northern Namibia reaching out to the east, sandwiched between Botswana to the south and Angola and Zambia to the north), Benguela (Angola), and Rhodesia. "We did the same work as the Rhodesian Selous soldiers," he said. He didn't elaborate, but as Steven Ellis and Tsepo Sechaba put it in their 1992 book, *Comrades Against Apartheid*, the methods of the Selous Scouts counterinsurgency units were "unspeakably atrocious. They would torture any prisoner who they thought might have useful information," and were particularly interested in using poisons against their enemies. The Rhodesians developed a nerve gas that could be put on clothing, and they poisoned rivers and food supplies behind enemy lines.

When Struwig returned to Johannesburg after twelve years, he worked at Security Branch headquarters at John Vorster Square. He remained there until he retired in August 1990, six months after F. W.'s February 2 speech. "I went off medically unfit," he said. "But to tell you the truth, I couldn't see myself as a policeman being apolitical in a situation where the Communist Party and the ANC are disbanded. In '84 they were still the enemy and that was part of my life for thirty years. If things were as it was before the second of February, 1990, I think I would have stayed on in the police force. But it's very difficult to now adapt to different laws."

At home with his wife, Leana, and his two elementary school–aged daughters, Struwig dressed casually in sweatshirt and shoes with no socks. Phlegmatic, he looked to be in his sixties. Leana looked twenty years younger, pixielike with a short haircut. She was pert and loving toward their cute daughters, shuffling them to the back rooms. Strain lines around her mouth barely hinted at her rigidity. She turned out to be the more vituperative of the two, aggressively defending the beleaguered right-wing Afrikaner creed, derisive of liberals and left-wingers who, she thought, had forfeited the right to be called Boers.

Struwig said he'd been shaped, as he felt everyone was, by his upbringing. But different from some, he remains faithful to that background. His father had been a member of the Nazi-supporting Ossewabrandwag at the time of World War II, so Struwig was a lifelong conservative.

His wife went along with his logic. "You can't be one thing and another thing. You have to be one thing," she said. The two believed that if people were raised in a certain way, they had to always hold the same beliefs or else be liars or hypocrites. Struwig argued, for example, that President F. W. de Klerk's brother Willem, considered to be a liberal Afrikaner, was "bluffing himself, being a liberal. I was a kid and I knew him as well as his father. They did not believe in what he believes in." Struwig scorned liberal industrialists, such as "the mine groups, De Beers and Harry Oppenheimer. They exploited the blacks. I personally can say thank God I've never done that in my life. Honestly, I think I'm the last person in the world that will want to degrade a black or a colored or an Indian."

Most unbelievable, from his viewpoint, were Afrikaner left-wingers. He said, "It boggles my mind, honestly" that anybody could call themselves an Afrikaner and, for example, be a member of the ANC. "That's like calling a person an American and a Japanese at the same time," he said. When he was told about Willem Saayman, the Afrikaner Dutch Reformed dominee and ANC member, Struwig said, "I think he's a liar" because ANC meant SACP (South African Communist Party), and Com-

munists are the antichrist, and Afrikaners—or, as the Struwigs preferred, the Boers—were first and foremost a Christian people, so no one
could be a real Afrikaner, much less a dominee, and an ANC member.

Why is Christianity so important to him?

"I've had so many blessings being a policeman," Struwig said, "being
on the border so long and I never stopped a bullet. I think if you want to
be a policeman you must be a Christian for the simple reason, if you're
not a Christian, then you cannot be objective. If you do not believe in the
Bible, then you cannot enforce the law. Because all the laws that are
made come out of the Bible." The Bible says "that the antichrist should
be dealt with in any fashion as long as Christianity will survive."

Do the stories, such as those of Dirk Coetzee, about the death squads
strike him as plausible?

"Ag, I mean, anything's possible. Death squads meaning what? I was
in the Security Branch for many years and on the border for twelve years
and I never, why must we have a hit squad, for what? I can't see any reason for it. If anybody doesn't abide by the law, then you arrest him.

"For all the years that I've been in the police force, I haven't come
across a death squad or a hit squad. Whether they had in the army, I
couldn't say, but we definitely didn't have anything like that in the police
force."

As a policeman, to understand the people with whom he was dealing,
Struwig took courses in ethnology, "the study of different cultures, especially among the blacks." Examples of what he learned are that Sothos
won't eat pork but Xhosas are very fond of it; when blacks go into an elevator first, they don't mean to appear rude, but rather "go in first to tell
you that there is no danger" there. Blacks won't greet whites first
because "they respect you." Leana explained, "It is improper for the
inferior person to greet first."

"They are very easily intimidated," Struwig said.

"They cannot think a year ahead," Leana added. "And they scare very
easy. You know, when they're in a big group they're very strong, but you
get them alone and they're cowards."

Do you think Mandela is a coward?

"Well, he is not a hero," Struwig said. "He's anything but a hero, not
with me. F. W. de Klerk is not a hero."

Struwig's heroes are mostly back in Boer history. Meanwhile, he
admires Willie Lubbe, the head of the breakaway whites-only Afrikaans
Protestant Church (APK), of which the Struwigs are members. "I've got
very much respect for him. First, he's a very good Christian, he's a good
Protestant, and he's a very intelligent man and he's all against violence."

Another man he admires is Clive Derby-Lewis, a vociferous right-winger and member of the Conservative Party. It doesn't matter that Derby-Lewis isn't an Afrikaner by birth. His political commitments entitle him to join the front ranks of the Boers and be considered one of their genuine spokesmen. In October 1993, Derby-Lewis was convicted of conspiracy to murder in the April 1993 assassination of the ANC and SACP leader Chris Hani.*

Another man Struwig spoke highly of was his former superior, Arthur Benoni Cronwright, who was "in charge of our investigations" at John Vorster Square. "He's a very, very good Christian, and he knows the Bible very well. And I heard him say to a certain Cedric Mayson, who said he was a Methodist priest, he [Cronwright] quoted him out of the Bible, and he made a booboo out of him, honestly."

What was Mayson's case?

"He had money that belonged to the ANC and he also had a lot of connections with the ANC. And getting these guys safe houses and places to stay. Those were the allegations."

Does he think that this Methodist minister Cedric Mayson was the antichrist?

"Well he must be because he is a member of the Communist Party," Struwig said.

Was Struwig's job to interrogate?

"Ja, interrogate, that was part of it. Ag, there were allegations in the newspapers that I took off his clothes. It's absurd because there are brigadiers and colonels on the same floor and they could just walk into the office at any time and those are things that they do not tolerate.

"If you don't know Arthur Cronwright and you heard what all the newspapers say about him, you'd think he was the biggest horror in the world. But if you know him as a person, he's a very softhearted gentleman. When it comes to his work, he's apolitical and he looks at what the lawbook says and that's what he does. He's also retired now. He must have been a captain when you spoke to him [in 1978]. He went off as a lieutenant colonel. What happened to him, the ANC bumped him off at

*After Nelson Mandela, Hani was the most popular politician in the country. He was the former head of the ANC's guerrilla force and at the time of his assassination was secretary general of the Communist Party. Derby-Lewis was found guilty and sentenced to death, along with the Polish immigrant trigger man, Janusz Walus. Luckily for the two, South Africa's death penalty had been suspended under pressure from their ANC enemies, when the ANC was unbanned in 1990, and it remained so following the ANC's ascension to shared power after the 1994 election.

the Great Hall. That's at the Wits University in 1975–76. We were to get into the NUSAS [National Union of South African Students] office. There were only a few of us and they had one of these fire hoses and they squirted us with that. They grabbed him and threw him off [a stairway]; he's only a small guy, he fell one and a half stories on his back. He's had many back problems ever since. If you look at him you see he walks with a skew; he looks unbalanced when he walks."

Arthur Benoni Cronwright was Dries Struwig's boss in the Security Police. He was a captain when interviewed in 1978, a major in 1983, and he retired as a lieutenant colonel.

Cronwright was notorious for directing the "interrogation" of activists of the Soweto uprising during the late 1970s and early '80s, including Cedric Mayson in 1981–82, and Jabu Ngwenya. As a member of the Full Gospel evangelical church he was known to try to "convert" his prisoners to his brand of thinking. Human rights documents and court records, for example relating to the death of the black protester Elmon Malele in 1977, testify to his viciousness. He was one of hundreds of similar policemen, men who are still walking around South Africa with horrible deeds on their hands and in their brains that they justified as appropriate Christian defense against the "total onslaught."

Cronwright has a gigantic voice, an amazingly big voice. "He could shout all day" and not get tired, Jabu Ngwenya said in 1992. Ngwenya was detained many times, once to be interrogated about Cedric Mayson.

Slightly built, thin, and meticulous with close-cropped hair, Cronwright was interviewed in 1978 about his brand of Christianity. Cronwright barred use of a tape recorder or notebooks. He brusquely entered the sparsely furnished waiting room on the ninth floor of John Vorster Square, one floor below the interrogation rooms. He ordered tea for two, then he began screaming at the reporter to reveal who it was who had said he was a committed Christian. After a few minutes he settled down to drink tea and talk about how he had been "reborn" four years previously.

Captain Cronwright said that when people are born again they talk in tongues. You would think to look at them that they were drunkards, he said. They were "drunk with the glory of God." The big change in his life since he had been saved was that before he never talked about God, but now he did so constantly.

You can be saved twenty times a day, he said. You can be saved while you are walking down the street. You cannot describe how it feels, but it is the most wonderful thing. The best communication is with God, not with people, he said. In describing the first time he was born again,

Cronwright asked if the reporter had ever heard a choir of angels singing in full tone in a church where no people were singing. Cronwright said he did not believe what he read in the newspapers about police torture as it was publicized at the inquest into Steve Biko's death in 1977. He only believed what he heard from God.

When he was asked how Christians could justify killing when the Bible commands "Thou shalt not kill," Cronwright said, "The Bible says you can kill." Asked where, he replied that the Bible says you must drive Satan out by force, you must destroy Satan. When a person is saved he has freedom. Under God's law the other laws do not affect you, he said.

The similarities between Cronwright's and Struwig's Christianity were evident. Such beliefs were useful among the police (and others) to anesthetize their minds while they did what they were paid to do. By extension, it would be psychologically cataclysmic for them suddenly to question their past deeds and creeds. Cronwright's megaphonic, incantatory voice, giving orders, helped drown out his subordinates' vagrant doubts.

"He's a very, very good Christian," Struwig said in 1992.

John Horak was an intelligence agent, a police spy on English-language newspapers. He surfaced in 1985, taking a job as chairman of the Strategic Communications Committee of the State Security Council. That job didn't go well, and he was moved to another job; then in 1990 he took early retirement as a colonel. Lonely and disaffected, he defected to the ANC shortly after being interviewed in 1992.

"He's been for years not *lekker in die kop* [nice in the head]," said John Horak, speaking of A. B. Cronwright. "He makes Eugene Terreblanche [leader of the neo-Nazi AWB] look like a left-winger. The last I heard of A.B. he was some training officer in the AWB. There's something emotionally terribly wrong there. I don't know what it is. In my opinion, he's not okay."

Horak was a walking example of paranoia as he prepared for his defection to the ANC after twenty-seven years as a spy for the Security Branch. But maybe it was genuine persecution—he said that shots had been fired through his apartment window, and letters he'd mailed to himself had never arrived.

Horak was in his early fifties, about five foot seven, with bluish eyes, light-brown hair going gray, rusty-orange silk handkerchief in his jacket pocket that almost matched his tie, beige trousers, and no smile. Horak never smiled. His new job was as public relations man for the Apostolic Faith Mission, his mother's church and his since he was born.

Working for the Security Police, Horak recalled, was like a holy call-ing—serving the *volk* against its enemies. Even today, he said, "Eighty percent of Afrikaans pupils would see it as your God-given task to spy for your country."

Since he was working for the good of the *volk*, the means he used, such as character assassination and informing on fellow journalists, were justified. He was mystified as to why, after his long career of service, people seemed to mistrust and dislike him, and he could no longer find employment as a journalist. After all, "I'm a people man," he said. He did not smile.

Horak said he got into the spy business when "I joined the English-language press in 1958. I was then approached by the intelligence agen-cies and I became an agent." That same year he faced trumped-up diamond-smuggling charges in order to gain criminal credentials. "There's an organization worldwide which is part of intelligence and that is to keep the [De Beers] diamond industry intact. You infiltrate the diamond smugglers and then you buy back the stolen stuff in order to keep [up] the artificial market price."

He is very proud of his longevity as an agent undercover—a cover he claims was blown only in 1985 when he took a publicly visible job with the State Security Council. "Normally with an undercover man the operative life span for a Western agent is three and a half years, and I lasted twenty-seven years," he said. His career was so unusual that when he surfaced in 1985, he claimed, he was given psychological tests to see how he came to be the "longest-surviving agent." He said the tests indi-cated he would make a lousy agent.

His explanation for his longevity as a spy was "my faith, my belief. What makes agents crack over the years is the fact that they have noth-ing besides themselves. My base is in God," he said. "I saw communism as something that, well, Lenin said religion was the opium of the people, so you [Communists] are coming here to destroy my very fabric. Sharpeville came when I was twenty-one. Now in my mind Sharpeville was absolute proof of the Communist activity in this country. What was a Communist those days? It was basically somebody that said all the races should mix, and he was anti-God." Horak differentiated between his anticommunist duties and a pro-apartheid stance: "My record won't ever show one instance where I worked for apartheid."

He became an experienced practitioner in the business of "strategic communications." As an example of what that meant, he described how in the mid-1980s, bread prices had to be raised. "This would have caused a lot of resistance, so suddenly you heard in jingles on the radio about the longer bread, a longer loaf. It was going to have a longer shelf-life. So by the time the price actually goes up, everybody is looking forward to seeing this new loaf, rather than worrying about the price. That was part of strategic communications.

"On the other side, it would include blowing people, a guy, for argument's sake, making a fierce attack on this country say in the United Nations or somewhere else, you know, it would be very interesting if the *Washington Post* started a story about his homosexual activities. That's also strategic communications." From his position as an editor, and taking orders from his Security Branch handlers, Horak gained plenty of experience in his trade.

Horak probably did not directly, with his own hands, maim or kill anyone in the line of duty. But in addition to his involvement in "strategic communications," he collected information on anti-apartheid activists and left-wingers and placed himself to help destroy the reputations of those individuals his bosses deemed proper and useful targets for character assassination. In the 1970s, Horak said, "The character assassination that went on was incredible. I'll give you an example. If a guy was on his way up on a newspaper, it doesn't matter how professional he was, a quiet word that maybe he was seen with some Security Branch guy, and that was to be the end on the [liberal and anti-government] *Mail*. I could tell you of many people that's like that.

"I can also tell you that on an evening, I was on my way to Winnie Mandela's house, and at Orlando Bridge, by pure accident I ran into a roadblock, ordinary police roadblock. And I was detained for a few hours at the Orlando police station. Some newspaper picked it up and the next morning it appeared in the papers that I was detained. You see? Two days later, I don't know if this was coincidence, but two days later I became the deputy chief sub-editor of the *Rand Daily Mail*." He implies that such a detention would polish his anti-apartheid image and lead to promotion.

He said he became close to Winnie Mandela, whose children he regularly ferried to a private school they attended in Swaziland, and thus had credentials among anti-apartheid activists, which allowed him to learn about their activities and connections. "Basically at that stage it was of import for me to be seen in the company of people, not necessarily to infiltrate the ANC. You know once people form associations, it's like in any part of the world, they see you in a particular company, so they assume certain things. So they start using you. I can well remember once some people calling me into a church hall and showing me some petrol bombs they had made, with which they were going to burn down

335

the Afrikaans colored teacher's training college in Bosman. And asking me whether these bombs would be strong enough to do the job. And of course the next morning when they got to the school there was an iron ring around the school, preventing the school from being burnt down."

Horak claimed that under orders from his Security Branch superiors, he had attempted to smear a South African judge by leaking information from security files to newspapers about the judge's supposed left-wing connections. He told of incidents where the police planted bombs (at theaters showing Richard Attenborough's film about Steve Biko, *Cry Freedom*) and attacked people and then blamed it on right- or left-wing radicals.

Horak said that although he was both a full-time spy and a full-time journalist ("I was blessed with energy"), he was paid only for his intelligence work, and was required to turn over his journalist's salary to the state. "I was making very heavy financial sacrifices," he said. He became very lonely. In order to carry out his job, he had to be publicly associated with the left, which led to his rejection by those with whom he would normally be friends. His own brother, after reading about Horak's connections to Winnie Mandela, refused to speak to him.

He claimed that his extensive international travel, along with contacts in South Africa with liberal Afrikaners and English speakers, gradually undermined some of his dedication to the government's ideology.

By the early eighties, he had become disillusioned and wanted to defect, he said. First he tried the Americans. He went to Keith McCormick, an attaché in the U.S. consulate in Johannesburg, "who was probably more anti-red at that point than I was." The United States and South Africa had passed messages back and forth through Horak and McCormick, and Horak said he taught McCormick how to evaluate the South African press. In the early eighties Horak asked McCormick to arrange a job for him on a U.S. paper, but McCormick told him to try New Zealand instead. Then Horak tried Britain, but that didn't pan out either.

Having ascended by 1985 to quite a high position in the English-language press—morning group editor of the English South African Associated Newspapers (SAAN) group—Horak wanted to quit, "basically because the political situation started to bother me."

The only man he ever trusted was his police handler, Johan Coetzee. One of Coetzee's orders to Horak was to watch the journalist Benjamin Pogrund, who was later an editor with the *Rand Daily Mail*. He had watched Pogrund for ten years when he was suddenly yanked off the vigil. He believed it was because Coetzee decided he'd become too

friendly toward Pogrund. "I had crossed the line," Horak said. "We actually became very close friends. I believe that Benjamin Pogrund and
General Johan Coetzee were probably the two individuals who had the
most to do with my makeup and my character. They are at opposite ends
of the pole. But they're actually two of the few people that I've met in life
that believed in what they were doing."

Horak thinks that "General Coetzee is a brilliant man. He gave many
lectures to the CIA and the FBI and the Americans. He's been many
times to Fort Langley* to lecture there. He's got three or four master's
degrees and one or two doctorates from various fields. By 1978 General
Coetzee sent a paper to the government saying it was impossible for the
police to carry out the laws made anymore, these apartheid laws. They
must change, they must talk, he was the first."

When Horak had doubts about police operations, Coetzee soothed
him. "I remember when a guy jumped from John Vorster Square police
cells and was killed. I was very concerned about that. The next day my
handler gave me a book, the *Penkovsky Papers* [by Oleg Penkovsky].
There's a paragraph where it's written about the instruction of Russian
agents to commit suicide rather than hand them[selves] over." Another
time, Horak read that someone he knew had been assaulted while in
police custody. He said he told Coetzee, "This is not right." He said that
Coetzee reassured him: "We arrest people who do this."

Horak feels he was ultimately "compromised" by Coetzee, whom he
still reveres. "I think Coetzee in mid-1985 became scared, he realized I
was going. I think one of the reasons they allowed me to surface was to
prevent me from going." Coetzee had him appointed to the chair of the
strategic communications committee of the State Security Council.

Horak held the job for only a few months because, he claimed, his
heart wasn't in it. He wasn't ruthless enough in how he dealt with the
press. Removed from the committee, he became the chief of research
and media adviser at Security Branch headquarters, and during
1988–90, he was involved in training new Security Branch policemen.
He took early retirement in 1990.

In 1992, after three hours of interviews for this book and thirteen hours
with Max du Preez of *Vrye Weekblad*, Horak, who had retired with letters of high praise from his police bosses, defected to the ANC and fled
to London, where he apparently talked about his former contacts and
the government's strategies, while living in fear that some former col-

*The CIA's headquarters are in Langley, Virginia.

league might kill him. According to newspaper reports, he was hanging out with Dirk Coetzee.

Former reporter colleagues regard him with a mixture of pity, distaste, and humor. The *Star* newspaper reporter Peta Thorneycroft remembered that at the *Rand Daily Mail*, Horak had regularly stolen and kept her notebooks with names of her contacts in them. Horak's colleagues knew he was a spy all those years, she claimed, while Horak thought he had fooled them well.

"Alas poor Horak," some of his former colleagues wrote, "we knew you well." It emerged that the South African Society of Journalists had sent a delegation to his superiors voicing their concern when he was appointed SAAN morning group manager.

Johan Coetzee, a retired police general, was commissioner of police between 1983 and 1987 and before that was head of the police Security Branch. He is the epitome of the South African "securocrat," a bureaucrat of the national security structure. When he reached the top, Coetzee's direct boss was President P. W. Botha, with whom he sat on the State Security Council. Coetzee was ultimately responsible for the work of Struwig, Cronwright, and Horak. He was interviewed in 1992.

Time of year: July, a time when dust storms blow, obscuring the radio towers, driving grit into the eyes, depression into the brain.

Interview site: Above the Polly Arcade in downtown Pretoria. Security Police headquarters, a mundane-looking building.

Room: A spare office with a round, dark wood table, a white crocheted doily on it, an ordinary bureaucratic desk not in use, a potted plant with dark-green dagger leaves.

Johan Coetzee has cool gray-green eyes with fleshy lids that slice across the corneas. His brown, flat hair grays at the temples. His completely gray mustache splays downward from his nostrils like the outline of a jinrikisha driver's hat. He wore a black, shiny leather jacket over a blazing white shirt and executive tie, maroon with blue pin stripes. His physique is trim, his movements economical. He speaks quickly, straightforwardly when he wants. But sometimes for paragraphs at a time he swoops from one topic to the next till the meaning evaporates. His talk is then so stream-of-consciousness that it meanders, then fans out into a delta. It's not because he doesn't speak English well or think clearly: he says exactly what he wants to say, and never more than he intends. It is a style of evasion that defeats efforts to pin him down.

For example, Coetzee gave a circuitous answer to the question "Have religious themes been important in your life?" He said he was very

338

active in school councils and the Dutch Reformed Church for many years . . .

So you find my own mother was very, the Roman, we had very many Roman Catholic priests from Germany here. You know, the missionaries were very very, still today the Roman Catholic church, the missionaries in South Africa, in Molteno, a great friend of mine, Aliwal North, and so on. It's all German missionaries. And but at that stage they were all pro-Hitler. The Roman Catholic church in South Africa. No story about this Deutsche Evangelische Kirche, you know, that the Protestants were, the Catholics were also in South Africa, at least. And she visited them quite regularly you know, although my father was never in the Ossewabrandwag but my mother never joined but she was very interested in this development in the world that England was fighting for its very survival there. You know, America was completely out of the picture here. No one worried about the States, no one knew about the States. Even in history. At matric [matriculation], I think, it was at varsity [university] level that I first heard about Washington, George Washington, and even that wars of independence and things like that.

There was a lot more like that, especially when he was talking about Dirk Coetzee, the former policeman who exposed the Vlakplaas death squads.

Born and raised in the tiny town of Molteno in the Eastern Cape, Petrus Johannes Coetzee joined the Mounted Police straight out of high school in 1946, when he was sixteen. He learned stenography and was so fast that he was assigned to take notes at political meetings and trials in the fifties. He was seconded to the German police during the Verwoerd era, a time when Britain refused to take South Africans for advanced police training. Under Prime Minister John Vorster, Coetzee, then a high-ranking Security Police officer, ferried letters back and forth from Vorster to Zambia's president Kenneth Kaunda, promoting the stillborn policy of detente with other African states. At the time, Hendrick van den Bergh was the head of the Bureau of State Security (BOSS), the predecessor of the South African Police Security Branch. Coetzee survived the vicious and perpetual inter-intelligence-agency rivalries, and when P. W. Botha ousted Vorster and BOSS collapsed, a vast reshuffle occurred that brought Coetzee into prominence. He thrived under Botha, from 1979 as head of the Security Branch, then from 1983 until July 1987 as commissioner of police. Newspapers claimed that his retirement in 1987 came because hard-liners in the government found his strategies too subtle, not hard-edged enough to counter the Communist onslaught. His were strategies of subversion, demoralization, and disorientation, rather than frontal attack.

But his methods included physical attacks, bombings, and killings, as well as subtler subversion by penetration, information manipulation, and character assassination. It was clear that some newspaper reporters were under his thumb, so nauseatingly laudatory were their stories about him—especially those praising his intellectual brilliance, his vaunted scholarly interest in Marxism, his master's thesis written on the Congress of Democrats (the white branch of the ANC), his working on a Ph.D. thesis on Trotskyism in South Africa, and his role as lecturer in political science at Rand Afrikaans University (where the former Broederbond chairman Gerrit Viljoen got him the job—"I think he is a scrupulously honest man," Coetzee said).

Coetzee presented himself as a cold professional, expert in the mentality and means of his adversaries in the low-intensity warfare of the "total onslaught": "Unfortunately in the story of the African National Congress, there is this history of [Communists'] involvement: they are the people with the plans. If you read [Albert] Luthuli's book *Let My People Go*, he talks about cooperation with the white Communists. He says they are so intelligent, they've got such good plans, and they've got the nice printing presses."

Did Coetzee accept P. W. Botha's "total onslaught" and "total strategy" vision?

"I never used it in any of my speeches," Coetzee said. "I said it was a serious onslaught and I said it many times and I've said that you should gear yourself and you should mobilize your energy. I also said unless we remain the children of the law, quoting Cicero, unless we can, there's something above all these things, and as I see it, it must be the law. Unless we remain the children of the law, we are doomed. We can have special legislation, that was my attitude."

But special security legislation in South Africa went very far.

"Yes, yes, yes, yes, yes," Coetzee said.

Was it needed?

"I think, my attitude was that interrogation was very necessary—I'm just going to order us some tea now—very necessary because it is the only way that you could get a broad picture of what is planned against you."

But Coetzee revealed his hand on "total onslaught" when he told about an old Afrikaans saying. "There is a story with intelligence organizations all over the world," he began. "They tell their governments what their governments want to hear. If you think your boss wants to talk about Marxism, [that] he preens himself because of his knowledge and

340

his expertise, I mean, you make a point to make sure that you know. There's a saying in Afrikaans, 'You take a small lizard and you beat it until it's a crocodile for him.' "

That's what Coetzee did for P. W. Botha. He took the anti-apartheid lizard and beat it into a Communist "total onslaught" crocodile. Not because he believed in what he was doing—unlike Struwig, Cronwright, and Horak—but because "that's my job. This is what a security, intelligence organization, this is what the CIA is about."

Vrye Weekblad's Max du Preez laughed when he heard about Johan Coetzee's comment. Du Preez said actually the saying had a different slant: it was *about* police techniques: "How do the police catch a crocodile? They catch a lizard and beat it until it admits it's a crocodile."

Urbane, complimented as brilliant, Johan Coetzee resided at the top of an establishment that compiled an impressive record against its enemies during the period 1979–87. The South African Police was enthusiastic and murderous, both in its clandestine war and in its response to unrest in black townships. Observers generally agree that the ANC's military efforts were largely thwarted by the government's countermeasures. The ANC military was capable only of symbolic physical damage to the state.

General Coetzee, according to a fawning article by Bruce Loudon in the *Sunday Times* of June 5, 1983, was the SAP's "masterspy." Under his stewardship, the SAP's Vlakplaas base came to be the residence of a later, increasingly well-documented death squad. For example, the former Vlakplaas head Dirk Coetzee claimed that in 1980 his team bombed ANC transit houses in Swaziland; in October 1981 they killed an activist named Sizwe Kondile, burning his body to cover their tracks, and then killed two more ANC men, one of whom had turned himself over to them but was useless, another of whom they captured but could not turn to their own use. The lawyer Griffiths Mxenge was stabbed to death in 1981; his wife, Victoria, also a lawyer, was assassinated in 1985. Johan Coetzee claimed that ANC infighting was probably responsible for the murder.

Dirk Coetzee told Jacques Pauw that Johan Coetzee's most famous agent, Major Craig Williamson—who had penetrated anti-apartheid organizations in South Africa and Geneva—told him (Dirk Coetzee) that Johan Coetzee's police were responsible for a 1982 bomb blast at the ANC's European headquarters in London. According to Jacques Pauw's *In the Heart of the Whore*, "The London operation was regarded as an enormous success and a private medal parade was held in General Johan Coetzee's office, where he awarded decorations to the men involved."

The attacks and killings continued throughout Johan Coetzee's tenure at the Security Branch and as commissioner of police, although the general was quoted as calling the death-squad accusations "unadulterated nonsense."

Major Dirk Coetzee was General Johan Coetzee's least favorite topic— except in the sense that the general wanted to make sure that Dirk's character, record, sanity, and story were totally besmirched. And Dirk was a fairly easy target. Increasingly upset with his treatment within the police force beginning in 1981, he became involved in many shady deals. Johan Coetzee first pressured Dirk out of his Vlakplaas command, then increasingly isolated him, eventually subjecting him to a court-martial for his indiscretions. He was accused of revealing information to a high political figure about an ongoing police investigation of that figure.

But the hard nub of the problem was that Dirk Coetzee's claims about the Vlakplaas death squad rang true and were corroborated by steadily accumulating evidence.

The general hated the major, and by indirection discredited him: "Ask yourself a few questions. He [Dirk Coetzee] came [to Vlakplaas] in the beginning of '81. In October '81, just go read that, he's told that he's transferred from the Security Police, he's going to a desk job. But in November–December, "Please now, before you go, go and kill someone for us." We're not so stupid. If I wanted to kill someone, I can tell you, I think I've got enough intelligence and organizational abilities to do it by people that no one would ever find out. And, as a policeman, I know that you cannot do it. It leaks out. There's no way that you can in any type of open situation, you can't take the whole police force with you. You can't take, it's impossible. So you can't go and kill people."

That is, the general urges you to believe that he's too smart to leave loose cannons lying around.

In contrast to his vituperation against Dirk Coetzee, the general is mellow about his former agent John Horak. "He was a very lonely man. I've got great respect for him," Coetzee said. "As a matter of fact, my wife and he were great pals. You know, they had lunches together and so on. He had a mother that was suffering from cancer in Bloemfontein at some stage and he always befriended a few people and he went out of his way to sort of influence them. He was also a great Mason. I don't know if he told you that.

"He felt, that's what he told me, that subsequent to me leaving [retiring in 1987], he felt that he was no longer anyone's protégé. I think in his life, no wife, no children, eventually one needs a walking stick to operate from. To know there's someone that one can talk confidentially to and I think that was one of the influences, many influences, the other one obviously in the present situation in South Africa, there are people like him who would feel that in a new South Africa they would be tarnished with the brush of the old South Africa and it would be best to cut your links completely and visibly with that, you know.

"He was basically never an infiltrator of anything. I think it was also well known that he was a good friend of the police."

Horak is convinced he was underground all those years.

"No, no," Coetzee chuckled patronizingly. "Unfortunately he's dramatizing it a bit. I don't think he wants to lie about it, that's not in his nature. He was a kingpin amongst journalists. It's termed 'overt intelligence.' "

Coetzee denied Horak's assertion that as early as 1980 Coetzee had told the government their apartheid laws were unenforceable. Rather, he had told the Rabie Commission* that "any security organizations can only have a holding action for politics."

As for Horak's claim that he had to turn his journalist's salary over to the state, Coetzee said: "Ag, please. I'm telling you that he's misleading you. The fact is that until he resigned and his boss was my good friend, Mr. Myburgh, and now, Myburgh, now, don't from that infer at all that Myburgh was a police agent. He was just a South African editor [of the *Sunday Times*] that I as a senior bloke would go and talk to, which doesn't make you agents, does it?"

It was curious that Coetzee had brought up Myburgh's name. Horak had explicitly said that Myburgh was such a high-level agent that he would have succeeded Hendrick van den Bergh, the head of BOSS, if the latter had died.

"Ooh, no, no, Tertius Myburgh never ever worked for the Security Police or the Commissioner of Police," Coetzee said emphatically.

But Horak said he'd been told by Coetzee's secretary that he, Horak, must protect Myburgh's cover "at all costs," even if it meant blowing his own. To that assertion Coetzee said, "I remember that very vaguely."

Coetzee insisted that he believed in a free press and then he said Horak—who was paid by the Security Branch to subvert newspapers—was a "good journalist."

---

*The Rabie Commission reported in 1982 on its investigation of security legislation, recommending that in all major aspects the legislation be retained.

What about Horak's claim that Coetzee had given speeches many times to the CIA in their Langley headquarters?

"It's not completely true, what he says," Coetzee replied. "Our association, mine with the CIA, was concerned with the Arab threat. As a matter of fact I was instrumental in getting a closer relationship between the Israeli security police and the South African police. Because our ANC at that stage was being trained by the Arab terrorist organizations. Israel and South Africa, there was the story that they were cooperating in many fields.

"I was very involved in my own life in very many pro-Jewish projects," Coetzee said. "We had, for instance, in South Africa, [an] organization, the Eighty-eights. The eighth letter of the alphabet being H, Heil Hitler, they were the people that came from Hungary. After the war a lot of these Hungarians came to South Africa. They were very anti-Semitic. With the Jewish Board of Deputies at that stage we worked out a plan to weed them out."

Coetzee said he wrote an honors thesis in history on the Palestinian Question. "I wrote a chapter about that strange affinity between the Jews and the Afrikaners," he said. "They're both basically the [same] philosophy, the thrust of the church, even if you sit in the sermons and listen: the Old Testament, the thrust of that, you know, wanderings and the reverend would read all these old stories about so-and-so begot so-and-so begot so-and-so, and they went on ad nauseam."

What did Coetzee think of another man who was in his Security Police Force, A. B. Cronwright?

"Ah yes, but you shouldn't have [interviewed Cronwright] because he was a right-winger, complete right-winger," Coetzee said. "Besides that he was a maladjusted man."

He beat people and killed them.

"Yes, and that's why he was eventually taken out of the Security Police."

He was promoted.

"He was promoted but he was transferred to another branch where he couldn't do it. Cronwright left the police and he joined the AWB," Coetzee said.

Did Coetzee know anything about Dries Struwig?

"Struwig? Who is he? A big bloke?" Coetzee asked.

Pretty big.

"How do you get involved, with respect, with all these maladjusted chaps? This chap, this chap was thrown out of the police force because of assaults on his wife, dear lady."

But Struwig said he retired in 1990.

"He retired as a captain or something, he should have retired as a brigadier. He was eventually, so many times was his promotion retarded.

"There are people in Johannesburg that I can recommend [for interviews], a hundred Security Branch guys, ordinary guys that worked there and never, that are in churches and on school committees. There's Colonel Jordan who was attached to security in a senior position; there's a Colonel van Wyk in Aukland Park, living there in retirement and with his children at universities, one daughter is with me here at UNISA and so on. I mean, you're getting all the bad eggs, it seems to me."

But informed people say things are a bit out of control and there's a rift to the right in the police which may be very hard to keep track of.

"Ah, let me just order some tea quickly," Coetzee said.

This time tea came forth.

In July 1987 Coetzee officially retired as police commissioner, drew his pension, and went to work for the Foreign Affairs Department. Presumably he could claim "foreign affairs" credentials because his turf had covered setting up spies in foreign countries, and he also said he was the architect of the (ultimately failed) Nkomati Accord of March 1984, a nonaggression treaty between Mozambique and South Africa.

Upon Coetzee's retirement as Commissioner of Police in June 1987, according to Coetzee, Foreign Minister Pik Botha asked him to negotiate peace between the two Xhosa homelands of Transkei and Ciskei, torn by power struggles between their leaders. A *Star* newspaper report noted on January 25, 1990, that the purpose of Coetzee's vehicle for those negotiations, the Regional Commission for Security Cooperation, which was closed in 1990, "was probably to provide a convenient base for Coetzee to coordinate security activities in the region."

Was that the hardest job of all?

"Yes. How did you know that? You must be clairvoyant! For three years I worked at that, except for the period that I investigated the foreign lobbying system, how does that affect South Africa. Ja, I won't comment on that. I spoke to [Kansas Senator] Nancy Kassebaum a lot and a lot of other people in Washington for a few months to investigate who influences who about what," Coetzee said. "And is this democracy or is this an abuse of democracy?"

In 1992 Coetzee was still not thoroughly retired. He was the head of the South African Police Academy in Graaff Reinet, in the Great Karoo, which gives a three-year B.A. degree developed at UNISA specifically for policemen. "Unless we can train people academically, it's no use training them in a routine way, you know, like parade ground work and routine. You've got to broaden their mind. Mine is a long-term thing. Young people, their minds, it's a good Roman Catholic concept also, their minds are still more open, you can still condition it, you know."

A police officer who must remain anonymous said in 1992 that under General Johan Coetzee corruption was rampant at the academy. Coetzee, this source said, had appointed low-ranking, ill-qualified police officers to high-paying senior professor positions. The informant was afraid to speak out in public.

On July 29, 1994, the *Weekly Mail & Guardian* reported that, in a report to the International Training Committee, set up to evaluate the training of South African policemen, British professor of criminal justice Mike Brogden had attacked the police academy's degree as being "like a dinosaur—all body and little brain. It reflects the thinking of a different era."

What does Coetzee think about apartheid all those years? Does he think apartheid was a mistake?

"Ahhhh, I think they should never have given it a judicial process," he said. He noted that in the U.S. youngsters who walked down the street together were generally sticking with their same race of people. "That's apartheid," he said. "It's not judicial apartheid."

In the postapartheid environment, Coetzee flowed with the political currents. "I think democracy is better equipped to withstand the ravages of time, you know, than what you have with a very dogmatic thing, which cannot, uh, the economic, and even the climatic things destroy it eventually. That is your problem. I mean, even nazism, if you look at what Hitler did in Germany in 1934 to 1939. Pulled up a nation that was going through to the dogs by its bootstraps, made it into a strong, virile nation. But is that what we want?"

For a bit there, in Coetzee's expounding the rationale and necessity of democracy, it looked as if he was "beating the lizard" for a new boss—supporting F. W.'s new political stance of advocating one-person one-vote democracy.

But Coetzee claimed, "I've got no allegiance to anyone anymore."

As head of South Africa's police academy, is that possible?

CHAPTER THIRTY-ONE

A SOLDIER BETRAYED

Almost all white, male South Africans have gone through military training and national service. Most own guns. Following years of "border wars" and service in townships, thousands of them are psychological time bombs. Many simply endure, memories gnawing at their minds. Others quietly join underground commando units. Add to them the Afrikaner police, who are usually less educated and more right-wing than South Africa Defense Force officers, and the sum is a society of violence, trained but uncontrolled.

"My cousin was a dog handler," said Johann Rissik, a rural development worker for Operation Hunger. "He had experience [in the SADF] on the Mozambique border chasing refugees [fleeing into South Africa to avoid starvation and war]. And he can't yet quite come to grips with the whole issue. Every now and then he'd say, 'Oh, poor bloody refugees, you know, what have they done? All they are trying to do is get food.' The SADF used to shoot at them if they didn't stop. The dog squad was brought in to try to catch them instead, because it cost the SADF less to stitch up the refugees [with dog bites] than to patch them up after they'd been shot with a high-velocity rifle.

"Stories of rape and assaults [by SADF against refugees] were common," he said. He told of another relative who was "very active in chasing, shooting, and probably killing people, and he certainly can't accept what he did there. He was quite brutalized by the whole thing. I was at university when he came back, and . . ." Rissik's voice softened and he mumbled. Then he said, "He was wild, put it that way. They have a good term for it in Afrikaans, *bosbefok*, bushmad. Those guys came back and they had a totally different set of values. If they don't like somebody, they beat them up."

"We're moving into a Vietnam syndrome you know, where you have people who fought a hard war and came back and never really got the adulation that they probably deserved for their military exploits," said Dries van Heerden, a freelance journalist.

347

"Joe Verster was a very good friend of mine," said van Heerden. "He was the head of the CCB."

The Civil Cooperation Bureau was South Africa's version of Oliver North's off-the-shelf, stand-alone, independently funded special operations unit, replete with professional killers. It was set up as a secret unit of the SADF.

"Excellent soldier, brilliant guy," said van Heerden of Verster. "But this guy is sitting nursing a grudge. No political problems with what's happening in the country, but he was ridiculed in newspapers for one or two operations that went wrong. He will never get the just accolades he deserves for the many operations, most of them outside the country, which were massive successes from a security point of [view of] a government convinced of the 'total onslaught.'"

Quite a few of these men may nurse grudges that they risked their lives and are now derided, van Heerden said. "There are a number of these guys, I'm talking brigadiers thirty-nine, forty years old, still got twenty years of service left in them."

Van Heerden, who was researching a book on right-wing groups, believed that these and other former Special Forces men are the real threat to South Africa's long-term transition to democracy. "Those are the guys one should fear more than the potbellied guys in brown khaki uniforms. Because these are highly trained, professional guys with a certain economic status they could lose." By "the potbellied guys" van Heerden meant the neo-Nazi members of Eugene Terreblanche's AWB.

In March 1992, just before the all-white referendum that F. W. called to measure support for his policy of negotiation with the ANC, an ad appeared in South African newspapers signed by Colonel Jan Breytenbach. Addressing "fellow veterans of recent African wars," he called for a "no" vote to reject de Klerk's reform process. "You did not lose in Angola. You were betrayed by politicians acting under foreign pressure. You did not lose in SWA/Namibia. A No vote is a vote against the anti-Christ who would destroy all hope and launch us into spiritual slavery," the ad read.

Colonel Breytenbach, brother of poet Breyten Breytenbach and of the SADF general Wynand Breytenbach, is the founder of the SADF's 32 (Three-two) Battalion, the most famous of the five mercenary reconnaissance commando units, or recces (pronounced "rekkies") that carried out unconventional warfare on South Africa's borders and in neighboring states. Three-two's members wore unmarked uniforms, used nonregulation equipment such as Soviet-made AKs, and were allegedly paid bounties based on the number of people killed. A racially integrated unit, its original black members were Angolans from the FNLA (National Front for the Liberation of Angola), which was supported by the CIA. The recce units' command structure was outside that of the regular SADF; they were answerable only to the head of the Defense Force.*

Three-two Battalion was born during Operation Savannah, South Africa's 1976 invasion of Angola. Poised to take Luanda, the South African forces were forced to withdraw when Secretary of State Henry Kissinger decided that expanded military aid would compromise U.S. international interests. The South African soldiers won the campaign, only to be deprived of conquest by the politicians. The war ground on for thirteen more years.

In 1989, having lost air superiority to the Angolan government's Cuban allies, South Africa began experiencing high casualty rates and gave up on the Angola war. The six-thousand-member 32 Battalion, mainly black mercenaries paid by South Africa, trained and run by whites, relocated to Pomfret in the Northern Cape. Known for their ferocity in the Angolan war, its troops soon began showing up in townships in Natal and east of Johannesburg where they gained reputations for being hired killers, murderers, and rapists.

In a July 1992 letter to the *Sunday Times*, Colonel Breytenbach scathingly attributed the 1976 Luanda retreat to "politicians with cold feet." He excoriated de Klerk and his team for negotiating with the Communists and disbanding 32 Battalion. He was convinced that, because of the fear and loathing the ANC and its allies maintained toward 32 Battalion's men, the heroic soldiers would become permanent targets of retribution.

"They will be forced to hack their individual ways away from the group protection and comradeship of the most exceptional unit that ever existed in the SADF," Colonel Breytenbach wrote in the newspaper.

When recces return to civilian life, "there's a lot of damage there," said retired General P. J. T. Oosthuizen, who was overall commander of the ground forces in the Savannah Campaign. "A man who serves in the

---

*During the eighties there were four recce regiments in addition to 32 Battalion that specialized in unconventional warfare; they were based in Durban, Pretoria, Phalaborwa, and Langebaan, according to Mark Phillips in *War and Society: The Militarisation of South Africa*, edited by Jacklyn Cock and Laurie Nathan. They allegedly carried out many of the attacks into South Africa's neighboring states, and trained and deployed proxy forces such as Renamo in Mozambique. A 32 Battalion defector in 1981 said the battalion worked with UNITA in Angola. In addition to the recce units there were other specialist units, the more notorious being the Koevoet, 'crowbar', unit in Namibia. All of these units were called Special Forces.

reconnaissance units is really off-beat to start off. He does not have the normal cultivated values system, that values system that has become holy generally to white people of this country. What is right could also be wrong, that's the sort of person."

Oosthuizen, who was Jan Breytenbach's superior until the recce units gained independence from the standard chain of command, had been a member of the citizen force or reserve military since his training as a tank expert shortly after World War Two. A lawyer working for the electricity monopoly ESCOM in 1992, he had tried to help several recces returning from the services, men who couldn't readjust to civilian society.

"They are killing machines," Oosthuizen said. "I mean this is the guy you send in and forget about him. He comes back months later, smelling to high heaven and half dead, but he's performed a task. They come back and are disorientated." Unlike most soldiers, for whom the reentry counseling was successful, "These chaps you really have to spend much more time on. This is being done and mostly I think with success. But unfortunately, also very often, not with some success."

"We have a saying in Afrikaans, 'Soort soek soort'," said the musician and concert organizer Attie van Wyk. Type seeks type.

Attie and Isa van Wyk met Steve and Joeleen Booyens on a skiing tour of thirty-eight South Africans in the Austrian mountains. The four were the only Afrikaners in the group. Their skiing vacation took place the week of the whites-only referendum in mid-March 1992.

"South Africans could actually vote during that week," van Wyk recalled. So he and Isa and the rest of the group, including the Booyenses, took time off from skiing to vote. "We voted in Innsbruck and they were the only two that voted 'no.' I couldn't believe it, as intelligent, educated people.

"Their standpoint was—my mouth hung open when I heard this—their standpoint was that we should have a revolution now and we should kill ten million blacks, at least. This guy's a bit crazy. He spent five years in the mercenary 'recces' after university. He admitted that he killed a lot of people, a lot of black people, at the border, and I suppose it's still in his blood," van Wyk said.

Van Wyk, a laid-back, left-wing rock music producer and entrepreneur who promoted Paul Simon's Graceland concert in South Africa, razzed Booyens. "I said to him, 'Do you know what AWB means?' It means Afrikaners Wifout Brains." Van Wyk explained that Afrikaners who speak English poorly use "f" instead of the "th" sound.

"I told him I belong to the ANC and that the sooner Mr. Mandela comes into power, the better. His wife had a photograph taken with me and I made the *amandla* [power] salute [raised fist]. It made them absolutely furious. I thought they were going to kill me. But I was just having a bit of fun, you know, I was just having them on.

"He was an outcast among the group of South Africans. When they arrived in the pub later that night, nobody was interested in talking to them. I asked the woman, 'Why are you so antiblack?' And she said she works in town and when she walks out in the streets the blacks touch her where she doesn't want to be touched. I said, 'Come on, I've been working in town for years and years, my wife works there also, I've got many female staff and it never happens. Come on, don't talk absolute nonsense.' Anyway, very old-fashioned theories."

"You're most welcome [to come]," Steve Booyens said on the phone when he agreed to be interviewed. "Honderd persent. You can put your own opinion, I don't care, but I ask that you listen to our case."

A placard that leaned against the walled compound of the Booyens' spiffy, newish house in Sunward Park, a suburb southeast of Johannesburg, warned: BEWARE AMERICAN PIT BULL.

When the bell was rung, Duku-Duku came bounding out, his lips pulled taut. The black-on-white dog was bouncing like a boxer ecstatic with anticipation as his master pushed a button and rolled open the fifteen-foot-long black security gate. Duku-Duku lived for his master. His master called him his son.

"I've got a dog like myself," said Steve, poker-faced. "You know, he's the most peace-loving creature in the whole world, and I adore him. But he's broken his canines on that gate when somebody irritated him, ja. I will love peace, my normal self, but when there's really trouble, I go nuts," said Steve.

"You do, you go nuts," Joeleen affirmed.

"Ja, I do. Ja. Unfortunately."

Since Steve was a dentist, did he think about replacing Duku-Duku's broken teeth?

"I couldn't fix them," he said.

A few ferns and other greenery nestled cozily in the crook of the house's entrance corridor. It was the last color seen in the house, except for Joeleen's jacket with a harlequin diamond design in chartreuse, yolk yellow, orange, and black. She is thin and tall and wore spike heels. Her hair had a pouf on top. She wore dangly black earrings and her lips were glossy orange with a dark rim that resembled the kohl around her eyes, which made them seem like sockets. Her glowering mood contrasted

351

starkly with her bright clothes. Steve wanted her to keep her mouth mostly closed and decorative.

He is handsome, barrel-chested, with a full head of brown hair down to his collar and a mustache coiled over his top lip, obscuring it. He wore a classy, blousy white shirt that was loose at the neck and tan pants. Well over six feet, he is 220 pounds of fitness, as one would expect of a thirty-something ex-recce.

"I look at Duku-Duku quite often and I can't understand how he keeps control there all day," Steve said. "People irritate him, dogs bark outside, but he will focus on something like Joeleen and myself sitting inside, and all he wants to do is to come and sit with us and have fun with us. Then suddenly something will push him too hard and he will change in a minute."

Where'd his name come from?

"Duku-Duku. It's a place in northern Natal where I did my selection for my military course. It's the prettiest place in the whole world and the most dangerous place in the whole world."

What is the translation of Duku-Duku?

"Plaas van swart," Steve said.

"Place of dark," Joeleen translated.

"It's a Zulu name for a dark place. I can't translate it for you," he said. (In fact, it's an Nguni ideophone meaning "later" or "in a little while.")

The mangrove swamps around the Duku-Duku Forest Reserve in northeast Natal along the coast north of Richards Bay were the site of Steve's selection for Colonel Jan Breytenbach's battalion. Steve became interested in joining the 32 Battalion when, during his national service stint in Angola, he was bumped from a helicopter full of wounded soldiers and forced to stay behind in the bush with members of a half-white, half-black 32 Battalion regiment. He admired what he saw.

"They did everything the way the book says, down to the T. I just loved the discipline in the unit. You always knew where you were. You always knew who was in charge, and it's just functional *honderd persent*, that's why I joined it."

After he signed up, one of two thousand, he survived thirteen weeks of training in Duku-Duku and was one of only fourteen men who made it into 32 Battalion, serving 1981–85, attaining captain's rank.

Steve grew up in a soldiering family and said he had "always been a militant kind of guy, a good physical fighter." At one point he said he was always capable of "sorting out" any blacks when he walked into a room, but then he said, "I never had a real quarrel with blacks; they were never really anti-me."

Whom then did he fight?

"The area I grew up in [in Pretoria] had a lot of immigrants, a lot of Portuguese that always had all these weird ways, you know, to us weird. We were brought up that you never look very flashy, you never do anything to encourage other people to dislike you. You did the right thing, you were polite, you would never encourage a fight. You would always try and be humble up to a certain point. These Portuguese were very loud people.

"You must remember that Afrikaans boys were taught to be men, almost in the same fashion as blacks are. We've lived with them for several generations and it rubs off. I think that's why they still in some way respect a white with power. A weakling that talks and talks but does nothing will never, never become anything in their eyes."

Joeleen said Steve had been many places in Africa as a recce. Steve frowned; he didn't want to discuss that. She suggested he tell about when he had to survive for days and days without a bath or shower during his training. Steve tapped her on her arm as a clear directive to hush. She shriveled to reticence.

A spotlight glared over a small swimming pool and through one window of the living room. The ultramodern furnishings, sterile as a dentist's office, were the two colors of Duku-Duku, plus chrome. The chairs were black leather. An abstract painting on one wall was splattered with black paint. There was not a book or magazine in sight. While Joeleen served pastry-swathed sausage rolls, Steve uncorked the wine.

Steve said there were Afrikaners, some of whom were colored, and then there were *Boere*. He was a Boer. The *Boere* fled the British in the Great Trek and fought them in the Anglo-Boer War. The *Boere* didn't like F. W.'s reforms and would not accept black rule. De Klerk, the Conservative Party and Eugene Terreblanche of the AWB, none of them represented the *Boere*, according to Steve. In fact, he sneered at the AWB's amateur soldiering.

"*Boere* are people that would really put their head down and go for the fight. *Boere* may fight like dogs," Steve said.

In the background Duku-Duku bobbed up and down as if on a pogo stick, first in front of one living room window, then the other.

"You know, that creature is so loyal to me. If I don't like someone, he'll dislike them." Menace evanesced so lightly through his words that one wondered if one had imagined it.

How does Duku-Duku know when Steve dislikes someone?

"He feels it," Steve said, then added, "I don't know, you know, I'm not a dog psychologist."

If that was a joke, Steve didn't let on. His expression remained as smooth as the span between his pit bull's eyes. In fact, Steve and Joeleen, generally, were as glum as South Africa's newspaper headlines in 1992. They were so pessimistic about the future that they had decided not to have children.

"If you look at the whole educational system they are introducing at the moment, it threatens traditional standards," Steve said. "There's a colored community next to us, Vosloorus, and they're most definitely coming [into the white Afrikaners' schools]. I don't know how well you know the coloreds and their social behavior. I'd never let my kids go to the same school as them. Never. Just look at the teenage pregnancy."

"They are vulgar people," Joeleen said.

"They really are," Steve agreed. "I don't want my children to be exposed to them."

Referring to black violence ("Look at Zimbabwe where seventy thousand Matabele were killed, simply because they were Matabele") and malnutrition in Mozambique ("All those people are rushing here"), Steve said, "Would any logical person like to see an African government in South Africa, judging by the track record of the rest of Africa?"

He described the apartheid government of several years ago as "normal."

"You know, for Africa, control is normal. The first law of the jungle—and Africa, believe me, is jungle—is a strong man running the country."

"I used to be very liberal, very open," Joeleen said. "When I started prosecuting [as a lawyer] in the branch courts in Sandton [a white suburb which included the black township of Alexandra], it radically changed me. They [blacks] would breast-feed in the courtroom. While testifying, they would pick up their dresses and show the magistrate where they were raped."

Joeleen also recounted the story Attie van Wyk said she told on the Austrian ski trip, about being approached by three black men in downtown Johannesburg. She said she "just stood there and let them talk." She didn't use the pistol she carried in her purse and that Steve had taught her how to use. Fortunately, after a while they got bored and left her alone, she said.

Steve had firm opinions about Africans. "It's unnatural for them to work. The normal black person, man, would sit underneath the tree, his wife would be doing the gardening and providing out of that. He'll be a beer drinker. And they will have more than one wife. They are so different from us.

"I know lots and lots of blacks. I grew up with them during school holidays on the farm [belonging to his family, on the outskirts of Pretoria]. I was brought up by a black nanny. I knew her children very well. Anna still comes to visit me when we are back in Pretoria.

"The bloke that taught me stick-fighting was a guy named Phineas Mawi who was a Shangaan who would fill this whole doorway. You must remember, fighting to them is what is a man. It is something you have to do."

Phineas, who was quite a bit older than Steve and who died several years ago, taught Steve to bike-ride and to fix bikes, as well as stick-fight. "I virtually grew up under the same sort of education I would have gotten as his son. That's something that very few people understand, that most Afrikaners are brought up by black people. We learn a lot about them because they teach us about them."

But Phineas's "son" certainly would have learned the Shangaan language.

"He wouldn't teach me, it wasn't allowed," Steve insisted.

But some Afrikaners do learn African languages.

"Because they work with the workers," Steve said. "But to the black, for a white to start speaking his language is very bad. Phineas put the maximum effort into us, he neglected his children to teach us. He would take the blame for things we did, such as digging a hole and causing people to fall into it. He went between us and dogs attacking us."

Did Phineas call Steve *kleinbaas*, little boss?

"Yes, of course," Steve said.

"One thing you must understand is we are pushing them into a foreign environment and this is irritating them," he added. "These people are much more animal than we are. And by animal, I don't mean it in a bad way. I mean that they really feel the experience. When they want to express themselves, they *do* that. They're the same with fighting. They go all out. Most of these people come from rural areas and their education will take you half a lifetime to pick up. Their [Western] educated layer is incredibly thin. They're not going to get their education like this," Steve said, snapping his fingers to indicate how fast. "In one generation. It's going to take a long, long time."

In Steve's family, higher education took two generations. After the Boer War his grandfather was a construction worker on a dam where accommodation and food were the only pay. He then went to work for the railways for the rest of his life. Steve's own father, one of thirteen children, was a civil servant who studied at night, finally qualifying as an advocate when he was sixty-five years old. Steve graduated from the University of Pretoria as a dentist. His older brother is a neurosurgeon.

"We've been here for a couple of generations, three hundred years. I'm from French Huguenot stock," he said. "That Boschendal we're drinking now is French Huguenot wine down in the Cape. We civilized this country, we tried to educate them.

"You must remember in South Africa in the thirties and forties they had nothing here that was worthwhile looking at. Where would we have been without that system [of apartheid]? We wouldn't have industry in this country, if we didn't come here and start forcing them to work in the mines. They would still be farming out there somewhere. For us to build up something we needed to control the environment. We had to keep the blacks out of the cities to prevent the crime that you have at the moment. Since control has gone by the wayside, crime has escalated in the white suburbs like you can't believe. Every open yard at the moment is occupied by a couple of squatters. This control had to happen to create some wealth in the country."

Steve adores control and discipline. Africa, he said, needs more of them both, but Steve's claims that he has control and discipline grew so persistent that alarm bells of skepticism clanged with each mention. The words recurred like movie theme music heralding a character on the verge of hurtling out of control.

"Without outside intervention, we would have kept control of this country completely," he said.

Is control the mission?

"I think so. Because in the old days we kept things going, five, ten, twenty years or so ago. We would have made a lot more progress if we didn't have to fight the Angolan wars. I think we possibly could have incorporated Rhodesia, Mozambique, whatever. I mean, even up in Zambia they had these car dealers selling cars effectively. Things were going pretty well, everybody was reaping the benefits, although some guys weren't reaping as much as others. If it had kept on going like that, the whole thing would have followed through at a much better pace."

Is the mission also wealth?

"How do you measure success in the First World?" Steve asked, as if the answer was obvious. "You know, if you go into a country with no material wealth and just Christian missionaries, I promise you will have a lot of resistance and if you go with a lot [of wealth] you will do very well. People can see what success has done for us, they will soon follow our religion as well."

But Jesus didn't bring money.

"That was two thousand years ago, okay, and it was very different then," Steve said.

He and Joeleen are very religious, he said. But they don't go to church because the church's policy now allows coloreds and blacks to attend services. He feels he can commune well with God in his car on the way to work.

"I think that I have a very good relationship with God and I'm not going to have that influenced again by anybody's opinion."

Steve readily admits he is guided by the way he was educated. That training is his strength, he believes.

"You know, when you take a little boy and you teach him something that's right, you mustn't change it thirty years down the line. I go by what I think is right. My upbringing has always taken me through difficult situations. Through fear and violence in the African jungle. But when you talk about the way that you were brought up, think back into your childhood years, a loving mother, a good strong father, everything is nice and cozy, your room, this is part of my upbringing. This is the way I was put together. This is me that will never cheat anybody for one cent in his whole life, I don't do things like that. That created me. That's the mold I was cast in. That's me.

"My feeling for what we are here is something that can't be changed within me. You see, those are my foundations. That is what I built my whole life on. It's like a building moving its foundations: it's not possible."

But can't flexibility be a healthy alternative? In earthquake zones buildings are designed to sway on their foundations. Steve countered with a dentist's analogy.

"If I cap a cavity, I prepare somebody's teeth by making sure that everything underneath what I am doing is one hundred percent solid. I've looked at a lot of things in my life that have flexible foundations. Some colleagues of mine. You can't build with that. And by covering too much you actually destroy the whole thing."

After building a life on the foundations of Afrikaner orthodoxies, Booyens feels he has been betrayed by his people's leaders. Like an enormous number of Afrikaners, Booyens bitterly nurses his hatred of F. W. and the Nats. *Verraaier*, traitor, is a word in common and constant usage among right-wingers, even as previously it was used by the Nats against the few anti-apartheid Afrikaners. A deep sense of victimization pervades the right wing, with self-pity its sour underside.

As for Nelson Mandela, who was jailed in 1960, when Booyens was a very small boy, "I would have hanged him because in black society of that day he was a terrorist. If Mandela wanted to die for his honor, then he would have stood up for the fight and done something, killed a guard or whatever. But he didn't. He wanted to play the political game and he's still doing it."

Unlike his brother the neurosurgeon, Steve proudly voted "*nee*" in the March 1992 referendum. His brother voted "*ja*," and Steve said he derogatorily called him a *ja-broeder*, yes-brother.

"He's not as militant as I am," Steve said. "I actually am much more militant than I am trying to show you."

How militant is he?

"I could kill the shits," Steve responded matter-of-factly and as if he and his buddies said it often.

Which shits?

"All of them, including F. W."

A presentiment of cataclysm was in the air. It was as if the African *tokoloshes*, dwarflike part-human evil spirits, were loose in the land, preying on the Boers. (Actually, some Boers, with vestigial peasant superstition, were known occasionally to visit African *sangomas*, spirit doctors.)

"I think serious anarchy is not too far off," Steve said. "The moment we lose control of our police and our military there is going to be anarchy. Our Special Forces are unfortunately completely disassembled now. National Intelligence, which is F. W.'s baby, has grown enormous. He's got an incredible covert-action network, possibly the best we've ever had. He's completely taken out the right wing. He's broken it up in pieces. He's a very methodical, brilliant man when it comes to that. Then you've got the nice U.S.A. building special forces camps—one hell of a big base outside Gaberone—in Botswana to deal with the right wing in the northern Transvaal."

Steve said one of his friends was "on the official tap list," with his phone being bugged, but he figured he himself was not important.

"You know I haven't been in this kind of cloak-and-dagger game, never in my life. I was a normal soldier in the bush. But when push comes to shove, my people . . ."

Steve paused as if the rest should be clear.

If his people call, he will serve?

"Ja, I will do that, yes," he said.

So he claimed to be ready, again, to die. But something even more apocalyptic seized him.

"You must remember that we Afrikaners are sitting with the nuclear possibility. If they see they are going down the tubes, somebody I think has got to push the right button. It would be the honorable way out. It's making a statement. It will end the chapter of the Boer nation in the right way."

PART VII

FACING
BLACK RULE

.

And as ye would that men should do to you, do ye also to them likewise.

—LUKE 6:31

We enter into a covenant that we shall build a society in which all South Africans, both black and white, will be able to walk tall, without any fear in their hearts, assured of their inalienable right to human dignity—a rainbow nation at peace with itself and the world.

—PRESIDENT NELSON MANDELA,
in his inaugural speech
at the Union Buildings
on May 10, 1994

CHAPTER THIRTY-TWO

DOWN AND DIRTY IN PHALABORWA

Plummeting down the Drakensberg mountain range east toward Mozambique, one melts into the lowveld heat. Scruffy, cantankerous trees, thorny bushes, and tough grasses grasp furiously to life. Here, shoved into a very large corner, are the wild animals that signify Africa: the giraffes, elephants, lions, wildebeests, the antelopes, the baboons, and the hippos in the few rivers that are more creeks than rivers. Most of the animals roam in the granddaddy of southern Africa's nature reserves, Kruger National Park.

Slap up against the park, and about halfway up its western border, lies the "white" town of Phalaborwa. Two giant statues of elephant tusks curve over the town entrance and exit signs. It's a nice town, town fathers think, which means tidy, with watered islands of flowers and bushes, paved streets, and several inns. It's a company town of 7,500. Two companies, actually. Palabora Mining Company (PMC) in tandem with Foscor, a phosphate mining company, owns most of the simple, ranch-style houses. The town lies next to a two-billion-year-old volcanic pipe rich in metals and minerals.

Phalaborwa's open-pit mine is as methodically sectioned as a spider's web. For nearly fifty years men have scraped its mammoth gray crater, terraced the earth down a quarter of a mile from the rim. They load rocks containing low-grade copper and phosphorus onto specially built vehicles that spray water to flatten the fine dust as they go, lugging ore back up the web to be processed.

"My job is to make big stones smaller, eighty thousand tons of them every day, from that size [cantaloupe size] down to bug dust," said Johann Steynberg, head of PMC's Department of Concentrator. He tried to smile because that's the closest he ever got to making a joke. But his mouth, like a theatrical mask transfixed with mild gloom, refuses to curve up at the edges.

Steynberg is a workaholic. In his spare time he supervises laborers on

361

a little gold mine that he owns twelve miles outside of Phalaborwa. "It's fine gold," his wife, Annette, says of his private mine. Dust? "Ja, it's quite tricky to get it out," she says.

Steynberg's gravity makes his rather straitlaced wife seem downright jolly, and his serious, college-age daughter, positively raucous. His driving adage is, "My philosophy has always been that you should never become a controversial person." Variations include: "My point of view has always been not to be extreme," and "You should always count your words when you talk."

The worst things he said about Manie Kriel, a National Party candidate for the city council, were that Kriel was "running the town down" and "contributing to bad publicity." He said Kriel was "outspoken" and "a real liberal." For Steynberg, those are harsh condemnations. Manie Kriel is a local real estate agent and a "new Nat"—a National Party member extolling multiracialism and "power sharing." Divorced, he has lived with his English-speaking girlfriend for three years. Manie likes to socialize at the Hans Merensky Club, Phalaborwa's country club named after the mine's developer. He resents that during the campaign for city council the Conservative Party circulated a newspaper photo of him sitting at home barefoot with what looked like a cocktail in his hand. Manie prides himself on his golf game and on being one of the guys. He is an expert at hanging out.

Steynberg does not hang out. He never goes to the Hans Merensky Club to chat and drink on Friday after the week's work is done. He doesn't chat. He pontificates, except when he is being spare with words. Now a CP member, he has been "Mister Civic" in Phalaborwa since 1968, when he moved there with a metallurgy degree in hand from the University of Pretoria. Name the office, Steynberg has held it—mayor; deputy mayor; elder in the Dutch Reformed Church; chairman of the management committee, the inner circle of the council; local chairman of the National Party until he decided to switch in 1983 and fought the Nats as local chairman of the Conservative Party; member of the Phalaborwa Commando, etc.

Steynberg is so studiously respectable—and there are many Afrikaners like him all across the Transvaal—that it is hard to square with the National Party's demonization of the Conservatives. They mostly aren't law-breaking, racist monsters. The main difference between the Nats and the Conservatives is that the Conservatives are more honest about still speaking the old apartheid language. Many of them realized early on that the Nats had started down a slippery slope: if you give the coloreds and the Indians the vote, the blacks are going to want it too. Aside from disliking the National Party's reform politics, many Conservatives loathe

the party because it is the political arm of the Broederbond. The Broederbond promotes NP policies behind the scenes. Steynberg had been a member of the Broederbond, but resigned in the early eighties.

Steynberg's opinions consist of the usual Afrikaner Christian National political orthodoxy: all Afrikaners want is their own freedom and self-determination. Apartheid is only formalized self-determination. Afrikaners aren't materialistic. They were sent to Africa by God to promote Christianity. Blacks are "different": "If I place a high emphasis on electricity and TV and a car, and he says 'Live in a hut, eat maize meal, and it's the women's duty to work,' why should I say it's wrong?" And as for servants, "Ninety percent of us today would prefer to do without them, but we've also got a social responsibility. We've had two blacks here working for us for the last twenty-four years. My gardener is living here in the back; he would kiss the ground that I'm walking because I'm strict but I'm fair." Under majority rule there will be a civil war because Zulus won't accept the ANC. International sanctions against South Africa weren't adopted to abolish apartheid but to get blacks in power, so the West can get its hands on South Africa's wealth.

Most of all, Steynberg dislikes F. W. "It's a criminal offense to intimidate people, to threaten them," he said. "That's what de Klerk and his crowd did. They made it very clear that unless we vote 'yes' [in the 1992 referendum], there's going to be a war in South Africa. There are a lot of Afrikaner graves on the road, on our path. It's a sad story that the outside world is trying to kill South Africa. You just have to look further north and see what has happened. Zambia, they're not even self-sufficient anymore. They used to be one of the richest countries agriculturally in Africa."

Karl Sullwald, another CP city councilor and a construction magnate, provides much of the financial backing for Phalaborwa's right wing. A German who immigrated after World War II, Sullwald's uncompromising pro-apartheid position and limited education make him a delightful target for Nats characterizing CP members as lowlifes and thugs. Sitting in his company's office on Mansfeld Street, near Phalaborwa's small shopping center, Sullwald spoke a very limited English with mushy diction, as if he had cotton balls in his mouth. As translated by his friend and employee, Mr. Bloem, Sullwald said he came to South Africa from Germany in 1952 when he was eighteen to work in construction in Cape Town. He was promised then, he said, that South Africa would forever remain a white-run land. The Nats broke that promise. His two refrains were that "north of the Limpopo" (in Africa not ruled by whites) all was chaos, and that the "outside world" and the *geldmanne* (capitalists) wanted to break the whites' economy so they could control it through the more pliable blacks.

The Nats claim that the Phalaborwa CP is Sullwald's tool and is populated by racist AWB members. Their portrayal is partly accurate—Sullwald is a local leader, and there are active AWB people in the CP in Phalaborwa. But most CP people in the northern Transvaal are middle-to-lower-class Afrikaners who feel marginalized by the autocratic NP and yearn for respectability, peace, and decorum. They are churchgoing people who were never direct beneficiaries of the Broederbond-Nat gravy train and who resent being railroaded by them.

Phalaborwa's soft-spoken, uninflammatory CP mayor, Jan Grobbelaar, owns a metal-fabrication business that is increasingly receiving contracts from PMC. He pays his black and white employees the same wages for the same work and can back up his claim with bookkeeper's accounts. He finds his black employees more stable than the white ones, because they need the jobs more desperately. He is happy to train any employee to carry out skilled metalworking jobs.

About the same age as Manie Kriel, Grobbelaar seems gentle and credible. He says that it has been traumatic for him to change membership from the Dutch Reformed Church to the Afrikaanse Protestante Kerk. He left because "all the [Dutch Reformed] dominees belong to the Broederbond. It's not easy to listen to that dominee because you can see the political agenda coming through."

The struggle between the NP and the CP for Afrikaners' support was especially vitriolic in towns across the Transvaal. While the CP and NP fought for position among the 7,500 whites in Phalaborwa, a political stormcloud was gathering just over the horizon. With impending transition to majority rule and the end of apartheid homelands, the town's governance structures will somehow be integrated with those of the two giant neighboring black townships.

Phalaborwa's struggle, as with other Transvaal towns, focused in late 1991 on a consumer boycott of white businesses by blacks who did not live in the white town but worked there and did most of their shopping there. The blacks lived mostly in two nearby townships, which were still run in 1992 under national apartheid laws. That is, the Phalaborwa city council did not control the townships. In a sense the Nats sided with the black boycotters, and Manie Kriel, under the guise of mediating, accused the CP city council of being obstreperous foot-draggers. The NP was positioning itself for the new structures, while the CP was hoping to stave off change.

Manie Kriel's version of local events is that he worked with the ANC from the huge townships of Namakgale and Lulekani (combined population more than 128,000) to resolve the black consumer boycotts. Grobbelaar's rather different analysis is that the boycotts were initiated and exploited by the Nats. Starting in Pietersburg, the ANC, encouraged by the NP, had targeted various CP-run towns in the Transvaal and finally hit Phalaborwa. Most of the boycotters' demands were issues over which the local councils had no authority. For example, Grobbelaar said, the blacks demanded that the army camp just outside Phalaborwa be removed—something that only the central government could decide to do. They also wanted national taxes reduced and local police and magistrates removed. None of these could be effected by the municipal government. In addition, although the town councils in the Transvaal were mostly controlled by the Conservative Party, the Nats forced these councils by means of national laws to do what the NP wanted; thus the CP was accused of intransigence for measures over which it had no authority.

As for truly local issues that had sparked black protest, such as the relocation of a taxi waiting area from the center of town to a more peripheral location, and the construction of a toilet block that was said to be inconveniently far from the bus stop, Grobbelaar said Manie Kriel turned those into emotional battles to discredit the CP council, putting forth the NP as the party able to make deals with the blacks. "In the middle," Grobbelaar said, "the people of Phalaborwa were actually the losers."

Squatting on Grobbelaar's desk was the pinkish ceramic figure of a naked, bearded man with his head thrown back, huge teeth in a wide-open mouth. He looked as though he was screaming, but Grobbelaar said he was really laughing uproariously. The figure's ambiguity evoked the terrible edginess of whites, living amid the vast population of Africa, who had subscribed to a theory of superiority and avoided contemplating *swart gevaar*. As they faced the imminence of black rule, they still played the old white political power games.

Manie Kriel, under the guidance of Danie Botha of the Pietersburg National Party office, thinks he has come to terms with the continent.

"I love black people," Kriel said. "I think we are fortunate to have them in South Africa. We give them jobs. They make life much easier for us, let's be honest. You don't have this kind of luxury in America. A friend of mine is Jim Palmer, he's a golfer. He said, 'Man, I live in London and you know who washes the underpants for Jim Palmer?' He says, 'Jim Palmer.' We are so spoiled in this country, it is unbelievable."

Citing the hundreds of thousands of rands lost by Phalaborwa businesses during the recent boycott by blacks, Kriel said, "The buying is lying with [depends on] the black people. We must bring these people into council." Of course, Kriel and the Nats were making a virtue out of the inevitable. The black majority in South Africa is going to rewrite the entire setup, but Kriel and the Nats were acting as if they were the engine causing the change.

"I've always accepted a man for what he is, not for the color of his skin, so it was easy for me to adapt to that, it wasn't a problem," Kriel said. "I've got very good, in fact, it amazes me that the chairman of the boycott committee still calls me *baas*. I said to him, 'Call me Manie.' He says, 'No, I got too much respect for you, I can't just call you Manie.' I don't mind. But you know, what I'm saying is, in our household there is no apartheid. I realized years ago, the moment I leave my house, I cannot give the black lady an old tin to drink coffee in. She's gonna use my Noritake in the house because I would have done the same, hey? They use the same things that I use, the same plates, they don't sit at the table when I'm eating, but they use the same plates, the same cups, the same saucers, they get the same food. I've got an outside toilet, I don't know if she's using it, I've got no problem with that, if she wants to use the inside toilet, she's welcome to use it. I'm not going to jump over the roof. I've gone over that rubicon in my life."

According to Kriel, the CP candidate for city council, Fritz Meyer, is "a radical. He's fanatic. I don't think you can change, you won't change Eugene Terreblanche. He believes that he's right and he can quote you from the Bible that we're on the wrong way. They feel good when they've got their uniforms on, when they're in a group together, specially those guys with the balaclavas.* I laugh at them. We call them the Ninjas, the Ninja Turtles, say, 'Hey, where's your Ninja suit today?' You know. I'm not scared of those people. They get very cross because I'm not supposed to know that they are Ninjas, but I know they're the Ystergarde [AWB's Iron Guard]. I get death threats at home."

Kriel turned Fritz Meyer into Eugene Terreblanche in the second sentence. It is a technique well used by the Nats generally, to characterize the entire CP as the neanderthal bigots, violent quasi-militarists of the AWB. The Nats' most effective campaign poster against the CP in the March 1992 referendum was a photo of an AWB man in a balaclava mask and wielding a gun. The caption read: YOU CAN STOP THIS MAN. VOTE YES.

Meyer was in the AWB, but he quit it after the referendum, when two thirds of the whites voted to support de Klerk's negotiations with the

---

*Head coverings with slits for eyes and mouth.

ANC. "If you see yourself as a democrat, then you must accept that," he said. He opposes the illegal actions AWB members favored. "So now our political leaders must come with a plan," Meyer said. At the time he was pinning his hopes on some kind of a *volkstaat* where like-minded people could form a homeland.

A decade younger than Manie Kriel, Fritz Meyer is dark, handsome, and fit. For eighteen months he lived in a yellow brick house supplied by Karl Sullwald's son, the only house on the street with a high wall around it. It came that way, Meyer said, because Sullwald Junior had a lot of bricks. Meyer is married to gentle and earnest Germien, a crafts artist who ran Phalaborwa's monthly flea market. They have two small daughters whom Meyer dotes on. He was trained as a computer programmer but veered into CP politics, following a family tradition. Years before, his farmer father was an unsuccessful HNP candidate in Natal. Typical of many politically split Afrikaner families, a brother supports the more liberal Democratic Party.

The old-fashioned cordiality of the Afrikaner blossomed in Fritz and Germien. Without servants (a point of pride to Fritz but a burden to his wife), Germien prepared a *braai* as Fritz put the babies to bed. Fritz had built an impressive barbecue in the small backyard. It was a drought year and the yard was mostly dirt, with chickens walking pigeon-toed all around.

Germien said that when they arrived at this house, ants were everywhere. Finally some chickens solved the problem, eating the food the ants liked, and, as Germien said, "The ants trekked." Over the *braai* pit on a scaffold stood a sign that the CP had used in the referendum: NEE spelled out in light bulbs, though some of the bulbs were missing. During the evening, as the sun faded, Fritz went into the house and returned to plug a few more bulbs into empty sockets. Over *vleis* (meat), *roosterkoek* (grilled cake), and beer, Fritz talked politics, propounding the usual CP positions. "The ANC will bring a civil war because the Zulus will never accept the Xhosas governing them." And "The Boer people will also never accept being governed by anyone else. Democracy in South Africa will not work with our huge Third World component. The blacks are not really Christian. The moment the blacks take over, standards start dropping, and we won't accept that."

Fritz and Germien have lively senses of humor and were surprised that Americans derided their own politicians and laughed about them. Their perception of the United States is of a country full of people sanctimoniously and hypocritically condemning South Africa, while maintaining their own racist society. Throughout the evening, when Fritz made what he felt was a particularly telling point, he asked, "What do you say about that, *perfesser*?" At the end when he was pleasantly tipsy and talking about *kaffirs* this and *kaffirs* that, Germien said she hoped the guests realized that Fritz was kidding about the use of the term *kaffirs*. When it was pointed out that Fritz exploded *"perfesser"* from his mouth in the exact same tone as *kaffir*, he and Germien laughed merrily.

It was July, winter. As the temperature plunged with nightfall, and more and more clothes were borrowed and donned, Germien and Fritz told their tale of the city council campaign for Ward Seven. They lost by thirty-two votes, which they considered a great defeat, given the CP majority in town. Fritz believed that the main reason for his defeat was the Nat threat that if the CP won, there would be more business boycotts. More direct, however, was the campaign of character assassination mounted against him, including a tactic that white employers had often used against striking black workers: trumped-up charges in court.

The day after he was nominated as a candidate for the council, Fritz received an anonymous phone call "saying they were looking for somebody to make a court case against me." Five days later "I got a call from the same person saying that they now found somebody," Fritz said. And sure enough, he was charged in court with intimidation. He was never told who brought the charge. Three days before the election the local paper ran a prominent article about the charges, which were said to stem from Fritz's actions at an AWB rally several months earlier.

The case was postponed twice. Fritz said, "It's a lot of hogwash. Intimidation." He expected the charges to be dropped eventually. Germien ran out and bought up as many papers containing the story as she could, but Manie Kriel also scooped them up and then redistributed them to Ward Seven voters. Fritz claimed that somebody threw a rock, smashing and breaking a window of his car, when he was out campaigning, and that he had seen Manie Kriel and some of his colleagues in the area shortly beforehand.

"They must be cleverer than we are," Fritz said. "We're not devil enough. They are booting us, outmaneuvering us, really. I don't think the people know what they voted for. I think a lot of them are very naive. We are going to get a black, most probably ANC, government and they refuse to admit that. There's not one National Party supporter who said, 'Yes I agree we are going to get an ANC government.' They all believe F. W.'s got a hare in the hat, a rabbit that he's going to pull out [to prevent majority rule]."

Fritz and Germien were relieved that the Phalaborwa election was over. Germien particularly detested the politician's life, the way that strangers insulted her and treated her as if she were a leper. The couple was leaving town. Fritz had been accepted for law school at the University of Pretoria, and Germien hoped to support the family with her arts and crafts work. Fritz grinned as he said he was going to learn "how to keep myself out of jail."

With Manie Kriel's victory, noncontroversial Johann Steynberg became the pivotal vote on the Phalaborwa city council. The nine-man council had four Nats and four CP members, with Steynberg, by then a declared independent, in the middle. Kriel had some down-and-dirty plans for Steynberg. Right after his victory, Kriel and his NP colleagues cooked up an honorary medal for Steynberg, for his long and loyal service to the town, because, Kriel said, "We realized that we need his vote to take over the council." But the strategy didn't work. Steynberg, whom the Nats called "the untouchable," voted with the Conservatives on several issues.

Kriel hoped to force Steynberg to resign from the council. "I'm going to put all kinds of pressure on that man really," he said. "We're going to make it uncomfortable for him. If Johann Steynberg goes, then the whole thing will collapse because then we will take over power. Then Sullwald will have no more power. That man thrives on it, his whole life is to manipulate people."

Kriel was in the thick of scheming, while Fritz Meyer waxed philosophical as he contemplated his departure from Phalaborwa's political scene. "You know politics is a mud game and it doesn't matter if you've got a white suit," he mused. "If you get into politics, you get into mud. If you're not willing to do that, then you lose. I'm not willing to do that."

CHAPTER THIRTY-THREE

CAN THE VOLK CHANGE?

Elna Trautmann wonders why. As a little girl, why did she receive "so much flak, resistance, problems, etcetera, whilst trying to assert my beliefs? Why was I ostracized for my opposition?"

An outside observer wonders rather, how? How could a gangly young girl have such nerve, when grown men quaked and dared not oppose the apartheid regime? How did she become so determined in the face of such power, such brainwashing, such peer pressure to conform?

Elna Trautmann, nee Strauss, in her early thirties, is tall, lithe, thin like an l. Her dark-blond hair falls straight to her shoulders like water. Her words explore in searingly cleansing ways. Her search for truth borders on the obsessive. For her, politics is inescapable. She is an Afrikaner. The system is her responsibility.

She picked the lunch site: the tea room beneath the tall pines directly behind the Rhodes Memorial in Cape Town. The grandiose monument on the side of Devil's Peak, with eight bronze lions guarding the bust of Cecil Rhodes—the personification of British imperialism—overlooks the University of Cape Town and, farther down, the often smog-wrapped plain that stretches toward False Bay on the Atlantic Ocean.

For Elna the Rhodes Memorial symbolizes a pivotal moment in her young life: "That was where I formulated my mission statement years ago. I reflected over the years of revolt, asked why I continued my thoughts despite the resistance and hurt, and then realized I was driven by this whole vision: 'To make a difference to but one who has been disadvantaged.' "

Her family left the town of Despatch in the Eastern Cape in the sixties for Otjiwarongo, a town in South West Africa (Namibia), about 180 miles north of the capital, Windhoek. There her father, Peet Strauss, became interested in mission work. "Every holiday we went to one of these mission stations," she said. "Dad would take the car and just drive into the bush for two or three weeks and later say he'd met the most wonderful people. He became so involved that he was chosen to be the mission secretary of the Dutch Reformed Church in Namibia and we moved to Windhoek. That was in 1971–72. We children started moving with him throughout the country and were exposed to cultural groups that very few Afrikaners get exposed to.

"Then the war started. My dad said from the beginning, 'You have to negotiate.' SWAPO was then fighting on the so-called northern border. He warned the farmers, if they weren't going to negotiate, they'd soon have SWAPO on their doorsteps. They got very angry about that speech.

"We never feared these SWAPO 'terrorists.' There was a big prison between Windhoek and Mariental where most of the SWAPO 'terrorists' were imprisoned. Whenever we passed there, he would point it out to us and say, 'Look, you see that, just remember a lot of people are being tortured there.'

"We would be exposed to those things and he never made a value judgment. He always let us know the other side to every situation without forcing us to agree with his or anyone else's point of view. It was the late 1970s when I became very politically aware. I didn't know what to do with that information, some clearly 'classified.' And apart from having to keep it secret, I also had adult teachers who would never believe half of it should I tell them what I knew. I was immensely frustrated and became a total rebel at school.

"The teachers didn't know how to handle me. I didn't know how to handle myself. My parents didn't quite know what to do with me. Dad decided the best would be for me to get out of that situation and get me back to my Afrikaner roots.

"I was sent to this institution that was something totally different. If there are two schools in South Africa where the real Afrikaner is bred, then it's Meisieshoër and Seunshoër [Girls' High and Boys' High] in Pretoria," Trautmann said. "I went to Meisieshoër with all the National Party leaders' children. For the first time I had to share a room with four other children. I remember the very first day, walking and staring for the first time through windows that had the most terrible burglar bars, with chicken wire. The air was gray. I hated it from the time I walked in there. I was always in trouble. It was more important for me to be me. No one else that I can ever recall from my school days took that route.

"On Tuesdays we had a class called *jeugweerbaarheid*, which is 'self-protection' class, but it's much more than that. During that time the boys were taught how to shoot and parade and the girls did first aid. This class was used for something else. All of us had to stand on our knees and they would measure the length of our dress from the ground. You have to pick up your dress to show that you are wearing the prescribed school panties. These checks weren't just on Tuesday. They could be anytime so that we couldn't jump the system.

"There were such a lot of things that we had to do. If you walked from one class to another you had to carry your case always away from the wall. I remember thinking, 'Where are we going? We're all just sardines.' I remember querying everything. I remember the boys' school coming in to 'kidnap' our head girl, you know just as part of a game. But they were dressed like robbers. I remember them running past with these guns and balaclavas while we were in German class. We were trained in Namibia for these situations. I ran to the door, locked it, dived under the table with my hands over my head and said, 'Down, down.' Everyone started laughing and thought, 'This one is quite crazy.' That happened within the first two weeks that I was there.

"I was the first girl to get a motorbike. I used to have a fifty cc. But then I moved out [of the dormitory] to live with friends twelve kilometers away from school and I had to come in on the big highway. You weren't allowed to drive with a fifty cc. So my dad bought me a hundred cc. He loved me to bits. I got away with murder because he loved me so much."

Her motorcycle, which the school tried unsuccessfully to bar her from riding, figured in a confrontation with school authorities. In an article she wrote for the school newspaper, which ironically was named *Stroom Op* (*Against the Current*), she argued that girls should not have to conform to stereotypes, but should be able, for instance, to ride big motorbikes. The article was not published. When she was thrown out of *Stroom Op*'s editorial board for protesting the lack of freedom of speech, she sat for two days in front of the office of Principal Blits, insisting on being seen, but failing.

Junior Rapportryers is the prime organization for forming young Afrikaner minds. "I remember we had to prepare a speech for the [Rapportryers] debate. We had this stupid topic, 'The Baggage That You Carry with You.' My baggage became the political crisis of the Afrikaner in Namibia. I couldn't tell my teacher what I was going to say because I knew she wouldn't allow it. So I wrote two speeches and that night when I stood on the platform, I had the speech about what is the future of the Afrikaner in Namibia. Halfway through my speech I remember one of the judges showed me that I had to stop. I refused. When I was finished, I walked out and everyone was dead quiet. No hand clapping. A man appeared from somewhere and said, 'Can I please have a copy of that speech?' and I said, 'This is the only one I have, take it.' I looked him in the eye and I said, 'I'm so glad at the end of the year I will be shaking the dust of conservative Pretoria off my feet forever and ever.' It was such a pity because I think I should have kept that speech. I would love to get this speech because I think it was so immature, so naive and probably not even dangerous at all. But unacceptable for a child of my age. You were there to be taught. You weren't there to have your own opinions." Her Afrikaans teacher warned ominously, "Just remember, rebels will never pass at university."

At Stellenbosch University, Trautmann found the freedom she'd always wanted. She did nothing but study furiously for four years, majoring in economics and industrial psychology. She turned into one of Stellenbosch's best students, "cum-lauding" everything, as she said, and winning the prestigious Stellenbosch Farmers' Wineries medal.

After her honors year, she left to work for De Beers in Namibia. That's the De Beers of Cecil Rhodes. De Beers Consolidated Mines, Inc., the diamond cartel for the entire world.

"I walked into De Beers and within exactly one month realized that all this must've been for a purpose," Trautmann said. "I've got a role to play in the independent Namibia. The years of not having had friends, the years of having annoyed everyone around me was for a purpose.

"I refused to say I was part of De Beers management, but management insisted that I was part of them," Trautmann said, reflecting on the dilemma that confronted her. She loved being a manager, but was dedicated to the workers' cause. She supported the labor union, trained members in computerization and techniques of negotiating, rejected her antiunion training, and joined SWAPO, Namibia's liberation movement. "I went along like that for five years, but it was quite clear that I had to choose—you know, do I get somewhere in De Beers or do I want to get somewhere in the political party?"

She tried to negotiate a community-development job for herself within the company, but when De Beers gave the job to someone else, she resigned. By then she had a South African husband, an electronic engineer for De Beers. Her "four or five months of absolute turmoil" while trying to decide what to do was set against a vicious political scene. Most alarming was the September 12, 1989, murder of Anton Lubowski, the most prominent Afrikaner member of SWAPO. Lubowski's murder hit Trautmann hard.

"Ja, the night we heard of Anton Lubowski's death, that was the first night when I was really scared," she said. "The next day in the bus an artisan said that all white SWAPOs were going to be the next to go. Now that was just small talk in a mining town, but that was the first point when I really became scared."

In deciding her future she tried a traditional Afrikaner tactic—she headed for the bush. "I went home and my dad rented a big Mercedes. We drove to the north. Ovamboland. It was very important that we go to Ovamboland and Etosha because that's been the link [the family's refuge] for all these years. For the first time we could sit down and reflect on what happened in the past few years. 'Dad, why did you send me to Meisieshoër? Do you realize what I went through in Meisieshoër?' He said, 'Did you realize the chaos that we were in to decide, what do we have to do for this child? We had created this child that didn't fit in with anyone else's thinking.'"

While seeking guidance from her father, Elna finally discussed with him the evidence she'd uncovered about his own secret clash of loyalties. Once when she was in high school, when she came home for vacation, "I was looking for paper to write on and I opened one of his drawers and I saw his resignation letter to the Broederbond. I was beside myself because I never knew he was part of the Broederbond. I was so angry with him. I wouldn't speak with him. I wouldn't tell him that I saw it, that I didn't want to come home. I was very angry with him.

"Only in those two weeks in 1991 did we talk about those things. I was so disappointed because I thought my dad, you know, different. I was also very disappointed when he didn't want to take a political role. He was between two fires because P. W. Botha, at one stage, and F. W. de Klerk at another both offered him political positions. At one stage they were thinking of splitting Namibia into a north and a south part and then just keep the southern part into South Africa and not the northern part. They asked my father to become the administrator general for the northern part. He'd always been involved in politics, but not openly."

Her father had contact with SWAPO too. "I never knew Anton Lubowski, but he was a personal friend of my dad's. And now my dad told me that Anton very much wanted him to walk over, to make a clear stand and say, 'I'm walking over to SWAPO's side.' But my dad was quite clear that he wanted to stay within the religion and to play a mediator role."

After the trip into the bush and with her father's encouragement, Trautmann returned to South Africa, to Cape Town, where her husband enrolled for further studies at the University of Cape Town. She went to work as Operation Hunger's regional manager. Her job gave her a way to be useful but stay out of South African party politics. She "hit the Afrikaans *taal* [language] hard," using it to the hilt, talking to white farmers and their black workers in the semidesert area called the Karoo north of Cape Town. She worked with Philip Davids, a politically savvy colored man who had been in prison for his anti-apartheid politics. Trautmann dealt with the Afrikaner men and Davids with the women who "had never seen such a clever *kaffirtjie*," little *kaffir*, she said, smiling sardonically at the memory of her and Davids's dealings. "It's been a real education to listen to white people justify things," Trautmann said. "I mean they speak with absolute certainty about the fundamental qualities of these black people, what they want, what they don't want, what their mental limitations are."

As a result of her travels and observations, Trautmann's assessment of South Africa's immediate future is grim. "I actually believe the ANC did the wrong thing to start negotiating," she said. "This was not the right time because we are creating expectations that are not going to be met. The only thing that's going to make the difference is violence. The people are saying Mandela is not delivering the goods so I can only see this thing flaring up into one hell of a violent solution."

And then in that pitifully small but quite moving tradition of Afrikaners who have, with deep agony, shucked off the Broederbond's blinders, Trautmann said that the only way the Afrikaners can guarantee their continued existence will be to become aware that there are great reservoirs of compassion among South Africa's blacks.

"One thing about the black man is that in essence he's not aggressive. I don't believe at all that Africa hasn't got compassion. Here they call it *ubuntu* [a belief that a person exists through other people]. I don't believe that any black wants to do to the Afrikaner what the Afrikaner has done to him. I have never in a discussion with anyone found any black who said he wanted to do that."

But she despairs of the Afrikaners' ability to change. The Afrikaners in the Karoo, for example, are not educating themselves or their children for the fact they are going to lose power. Change will come only when these people die out, she thinks. It could take a couple of generations.

CHAPTER THIRTY-FOUR

HOPE AND ITS SHADOW, DOUBT

In 1999 the half century of Afrikaner supremacy will close. That's when the five-year transitional government, a coalition including the ANC and the Nats, is due to end. Only the reckless would predict the Afrikaners' future. The breadth of the Afrikaner political spectrum mirrors the broad palette of possible futures for them.

The year 1999: 87 years after the ANC was founded; 81 years after the Broederbond was founded; 51 years after the Nationalists won power and ensconced themselves as apartheid theologians and overlords; 39 years after the Cottesloe church conference; 35 years after Nelson Mandela was imprisoned for life for treason; 24 years after the first photographs and names of blacks were allowed to be published in an Afrikaans newspaper (and Marichen Waldner called them *Meneer*, mister, in her story); 23 years after Soweto students exploded in protest over the enforced use of Afrikaans in their schools; 22 years after Steve Biko was murdered in jail by police; 14 years after Chase Manhattan refused to renew bank loans for South Africa, causing the value of the rand to plunge 50 percent against the dollar; 9 years after F. W. gave his astonishing speech that turned the ship of state around; 6 years after charismatic Communist Party leader Chris Hani was assassinated; 5 years after the first universal, multiracial election.

That's also 47 years after H. W. van der Merwe was shocked to hear the word *vrou*, woman, applied to an African.

It was an important but not widely known moment in South African history. The ripple across Hendrik Willem van der Merwe's consciousness caused by that one word spread gentle waves across Afrikaner history.

Friends call him by his first two initials, which in Afrikaans are pronounced Hah-Veeh. In 1949, as a nineteen-year-old Dutch Reformed Church missionary in Mashonaland (now in Zimbabwe), H. W. was appointed to be a school superintendent supervising black teachers. One of the "top ten regrets" of his life, he says now, is that "the teachers for whom I was the superintendent offered me their hand and I refused to shake it. I believed God willed me not to shake the hand of a black person."

Also while in Mashonaland, H. W. heard a British school superintendent refer to African women as "ladies." He and the other Afrikaner missionaries chortled at the Englishman's social faux pas. African women were never ladies—they were always *meide*, maids.

In 1952, when he went home to South Africa, his twenty-year-old brother returned from studying in Holland. And what did his brother do but call an African woman a *vrou*, woman, instead of a *meid*! H. W. recalled the conversation. "I said, 'You mean, *die meid*?' And he said, 'No, *die vrou*.' I frowned and I didn't argue. And African, black women became *vrou* for me. I don't think it was a Damascus experience, but I think the seeds were sown that evening. Maybe during my sleep it worked. I became opened for other views. I started reading and questioning. Through that word *vrou* I, as an Afrikaner, became an African." H. W.'s world had changed. "I farmed for one year, and in that year I started wondering whether I shouldn't perhaps shake a black man's hand. And then I went to Stellenbosch [University]."

As chairman of the university's sociological society, he invited black and English speakers from the University of Cape Town to meetings at Stellenbosch. In an organization called the Contact Study Group, he and two colleagues invited the first colored speakers. "I remember the first person we brought in was a very close friend of mine, a man with a doctorate, an old man, an academic who nobody knew because there were no jobs for such people. As he walked into the room, I shook his hand. There was a 'shhhhh' going through the whole audience of about twenty or thirty. They'd never seen a white man shake the hands of a colored person. Nineteen fifty-six. If I meet these people today, they say what a shock, what an emotional experience it was that night when they saw me shaking hands with this man."

Even as H. W. could only be reached by another Afrikaner in the depths of his inherited racism, so he began working to open other Afrikaners' ears. They weren't inclined to hear outsiders' words, living on the *volkse* island, but H. W., and a very few others like him, made them squirm. He also developed another trick: he made them shake hands with blacks.

At first H. W. van der Merwe looks as though he'd blend into any background. But gradually he grows forceful, like the warming sun that persuades a man to shed his coat. H. W. believes that experience, rather than argument, moves people to change. Experience, not exhortation or punishment, will move Afrikaners to abandon racism. He has been pressing Afrikaners into new experiences for a long time.

H. W. doesn't buy the common wisdom of the adage "*Boer maak 'n plan*" and of the claims that "Blacks can't plan, that's why they need whites." He doesn't believe in designing outcomes, he believes in starting processes. He has spent most of his life trying to replace Afrikaners' penchant for making plans with commitment to engage in process, which can undermine convictions that society can be forced into permanent, God-ordained slots. He chose an arduous task.

H. W. doesn't sound at all like the common notion of an Afrikaner. He is a self-described humanist, a pacifist, a Quaker, a sociology professor at the University of Cape Town, the founder of the Centre for Intergroup Studies, an optimist. A non-Broeder, an Afrikaner who publicly opposed apartheid, quit the Dutch Reformed Church, developed friendships with exiled ANC leaders as early as 1963, sponsored a public forum where the white media discovered Steve Biko in 1971, befriended Winnie Mandela in 1982, first met Nelson Mandela in 1984 and was asked by Nelson to help look after his children—H. W. has performed brave acts. He has done them quietly but not secretly: his rule of operation is honesty and openness. As a consequence, he's trusted by *volkstaaters*, by the Nats, by the homeland politicians, and by the ANC. He is one of the missing links in the search for how and why the Afrikaner leadership finally negotiated itself out of formal power.

Since the late 1950s, H. W. and his late wife, Marietjie, a well-known potter, held dinners where they invited blacks and whites together, sometimes to the guests' shock and chagrin. "We've had over the years at my home, on very many occasions brought together people who had never even shaken hands with black people," he said. "On some occasions we warned them and some others we didn't. And we had some very tense moments. We just had a rule, an unwritten rule. Every dinner party, we made sure that it was not one color."

H. W. became a Quaker in 1974 after he'd tried mightily, over many years, to change his Rondebosch (Cape Town) Dutch Reformed Church's policies. As a member of the church council in the mid-sixties he'd refused to quit the Christian Institute when the DRC synod ruled that no one could serve on a church council and remain an institute member. The elders couldn't show him how it was unbiblical, though, so they let him keep serving. For a year in 1958, H. W. and his wife had worked for a Quaker committee that ran the international student center at the University of California at Los Angeles. (He received his Ph.D. in sociology from UCLA.) "But because the Quakers don't proselytize, they didn't try to convert us. It was only in '71 that I got to know them in South Africa through their service arm. I was so impressed with the quality of the people. That's how the Quakers recruit people, through character, behavior. I just discovered here were people whom I admire and like, so it was a natural thing for me to leave the Dutch Reformed Church. Also I was never quite comfortable with the dogma and the doctrine of the church with its rigid prescriptions about heaven and hell and the devil. The Quakers have a good expression, they believe in 'varieties of religious experience.' That's my view. I respect different experiences, churches."*

Someday the entire story about how Afrikaner leaders reversed political direction will come out. Allister Sparks has told part of the story in his enthralling book *Tomorrow Is Another Country*, and Nelson Mandela's autobiography, *Long Walk to Freedom*, contains some tidbits. Mandela describes how he and other imprisoned ANC leaders were moved from Robben Island prison to Pollsmoor Prison near Cape Town in 1982. From there, he began trying to contact the government and initiate negotiations.

According to Sparks, after Kobie Coetsee became Minister of Justice, Police and Prisons in 1980, he was gradually convinced by Winnie Mandela's lawyer, Piet de Waal, that the policies of banning Winnie and jailing Nelson Mandela were counterproductive. Coetsee claims that Mandela's move to Pollsmoor was intended to make discreet communication between the ANC leaders and the government possible.

In November 1985 Mandela had surgery in Cape Town for an enlarged prostate gland. Winnie traveled on the same plane to Cape Town as Kobie Coetsee, approached him and convinced Coetsee to visit Mandela in the hospital. Somewhere in the background to this drama, H. W. van der Merwe was working on getting the two sides together.

On his own initiative, H. W. went to visit Winnie in 1981 in the town of Brandfort, to which she had been restricted under her banning orders. His first effort failed when Pretoria refused him permission to see her, "because I was on the Security Police blacklist," he said. In 1982 he was allowed to visit her. She was under house arrest, "So we spoke,

---

*Afrikaners in the Dutch Reformed churches have little of the antipathy toward Quakers that they do toward most other denominations. This may be partly because during the Anglo-Boer War the Quakers sympathized with the plight of Boer civilians. After the war they helped return many family Bibles to their Boer owners.

we stood at the gatepost, she on the inside and I on the outside and after half an hour we hugged and kissed each other," H. W. said. "Then she broke the rules. She walked out and went to meet my wife and she gave me a confidential message for Gatsha Buthelezi. And well, eventually she stayed in my home [in Cape Town] when she came to visit Nelson. At first without permission, defying the orders she had, and later on she got permission. And then Nelson asked to see me. So I saw him in '84.

"He was still behind glass [in the prison visiting room]. Also in '84, before I saw him, I was invited to meet the ANC executive committee in Lusaka; I met Thabo Mbeki and Alfred Nzo, and that started the first meetings. So when I saw Nelson, I gave him greetings from Alfred Nzo, from all his old colleagues. He got so excited, he clapped his hands.

"It's in my nature to look for what's positive and what's good," H. W. said. "So in '84 when Thabo Mbeki and Alfred Nzo talked to me for an hour and a half, asking me, 'What is going on in the government?' I told them the positive things. Thabo said, 'But if this is true,' and I don't think he really believed me, 'if this is true, they must be willing to talk to us.' I said, 'Yes they are.' And then Alfred Nzo said, 'Will you help us to meet them?' And that started the process."

How did H. W. know the government leaders were willing to talk?

"Cabinet ministers told me," he said. "I've known several of the cabinet ministers for years, we were students, we went to university together, and so on. They trust me, I think. I've gone out of my way over all these years not to embarrass any party. And so even the police. After my visits to the ANC I go and tell Johan van der Merwe, he was then Chief of Security, I'd go and tell him what I found and whom I talked to and what they said. They always frowned and said, 'Ag, they take you for a ride.' But I think I sowed a little seed."

H. W. isn't sure how he did these things, but he said two American mediators he knew, who were Quakers as well, had observed him in operation and decided it is his personality, that he makes people feel comfortable: "I lower the emotion." That is a typical H. W. van der Merwe understatement. Recognizing that a mediator, or, as he preferred to say, a facilitator, doesn't change things, and being sometimes frustrated by that role, H. W. said his task is to get people to communicate. He doesn't care what they say, he doesn't have a goal himself, he just wants them to talk to each other.

It might sound wishy-washy, but it isn't: there's something quite steely about H. W. "One thing I've found is that over the years, my impressions were usually very accurate," he said. "Partly because I find that when I talk to political leaders, and I'm on fairly good terms with all of them, if I look in a man's eyes, I can see whether he's honest or not. And so I believe that there is, on the highest level, a great measure of trust and understanding and there is some posturing. Which I don't see in a bad sense, because if you have no posturing, you'll never have a following."

H. W.'s eyes are not as soft as one might expect of such a peace-loving man. They are edged at first, as he takes measure, checks words against eyes, scrutinizes. He is about five foot ten and trim. His suitcase in the hotel room was of old, beat-up leather and had a makeshift rope handle. He wore funky, old plastic frame glasses and his bushy eyebrows brushed against the lenses. His regular glasses had been stolen when he was mugged several days previously in downtown Johannesburg. "I still have a stiff neck. I lost my watch, my wallet, even my glasses. Fortunately I had old glasses in my car which I carry because I'm on a long trip." He was unfazed, as only someone quite unmaterialistic could be. Slowly, as he takes one's gauge, he thaws, laughs occasionally.

When the Afrikaner establishment began to look for ways to communicate with the ANC, van der Merwe helped move the process along. In 1984 he took Afrikaans newspaper journalist Piet Muller to meet the exiled ANC leadership in Lusaka. Muller wrote positively about his experience. Then a group of businessmen went to Lusaka, and in 1986 a meeting in Dakar, Senegal, brought a range of Afrikaners together with the ANC's top leadership.

From 1986 to 1989, a committee set up by Kobie Coetsee met forty-seven times with Nelson Mandela and still remained secret, according to Allister Sparks. The Broederbond set up other secret meetings with the ANC outside South Africa. By the time P. W. Botha was ousted and F. W. stood up to change the world, few people knew what the top Broeders were planning for the future, but the plans were well under way. H. W. had helped blaze the route from Afrikanerdom to the ANC leaders.

Ultimate responsibility for the system of apartheid and the evil it wrought lies at the top, H. W. said.

Does that mean virtually all the former Nationalist cabinet leaders should be charged for their roles in apartheid crimes?

"It looks to me," he replied. "I find it very difficult to find anything wrong with black people who want these people to be punished. To have a Nuremberg trial and to have them either jailed or killed, or executed. I would have no personal resentment towards blacks who ask this, because after what they have suffered I think it is fair for them to say, 'We must charge these people.'

"I personally would object to it," he cautioned, "I will state so, because I oppose capital punishment. Especially as a Quaker, I should be very forgiving and very understanding and should have no feeling for revenge. I'm starting to switch in my academic work to looking at forgiveness, conciliation, restitution. The more I think of the work in this field, the more I feel the need that these atrocities be exposed. My stand now is that while I will not insist on punishment, because I think punishment is a wrong concept anyway, I do want these people to be identified and to be exposed. To be charged. They must come before a court or a tribunal or something. And it must be pointed out how they have exploited people, killed people, deprived them of their land. I don't think there can be any forgiveness on the part of the black people until these things have been publicized, made known."

When H. W. drove to Johannesburg from Cape Town in August of 1992, he picked up hitchhikers all along the way and in the process got a feeling for the political pulse of the country. His main worries are that the white security forces would sabotage the peace process and that the African masses had not caught up with their leaders' recognition they had to compromise. H. W., however, retains his faith in people's ability to learn from their experiences. The experience of working together, of moving into the transition, will, he believes, lead to a reduction of tensions rather than their exacerbation. "To sum it all up, I'm still much more optimistic than almost all the people I've talked to."

After five hours of talking with H. W. van der Merwe, it's hard to put into words the effect he leaves. He makes people feel better because he thinks they are better. He brings people together and warms them. He permits them their interests and delusions but is not fooled. He personifies process and hope.

Doubt, like a shadow, clings to hope's heels. Can the process work? Do the Nats mean it when they say they want democracy? Will they sabotage the ANC in future elections? Are Dutch Reformed Church moves toward unification genuine, or are they a ploy for co-opting coloreds to vote Nat? Do Afrikaners think they are going to maintain control of South Africa by other means, say, through controlling the economy?

Naas Steenkamp, an extraordinarily articulate and well-connected Afrikaner industrialist, but not a Broederbonder, worked for years at the axis of cooperation between English business and Afrikanerdom. As the director of corporate affairs at the giant mining company Gencor, Steenkamp closely watched the transition to black rule. He is as gloomy as H. W. is optimistic. He spoke in 1992 with an enticing eloquence and sweep of passion.

"I don't want to be too facile about this, but I suspect that there is a

deep-seated awareness [among Afrikaners] that the so-called grand philosophy for which God had planted us in southern Africa was in fact a
selfish, acquisitive motive, self-aggrandizing at the expense of other people. It was an inability to come to terms with the fact that this vast hin-
terland was not empty, but was a place in which you've got to bargain
and find for yourself a little niche. Which could have been done historically several times over but wasn't done.

"Instead the Afrikaner emulated British imperialism, saying, '*I want
all of it!*' " Steenkamp said, raising his volume. " 'I want the whole dang
shooting match. I want that power.' He superimposed himself on a completely unmanageable body politic. And he's been doing his damnedest
over four and a half decades to try and run that show to the certain
knowledge of people like myself, and forgive me for being arrogant
about this, but to the certain knowledge of people like myself that it is
unsustainable. One could just see it crumbling around you all the time
and as it crumbled you could see it being band-aided together into this
horrific edifice that had to be kept going ultimately through a philosophy
of a 'total onslaught,' and therefore everything goes.

"One would see the victims of that notion, especially the level of honesty in ordinary Afrikaans discourse, in his cultural life, in his political
life and everywhere. That gave the Afrikaner self-esteem a kind of knock
that I associate with tragedy, with the destruction of what could have
been a wonderful people."

Steenkamp remembered when he attended Potchefstroom Univer-
sity and first became aware of the Afrikaner *volk* island, in contrast to his
dual-language high school. He studied under L. J. du Plessis, the
National Party Transvaal chief, who became entirely disenchanted at the
"spurious nationalism that was being woven into a doctrine and sold to
Afrikaners with very obvious political intent . . . allied always to religious, chosen people echoes."

Steenkamp said he started visiting the library and reading and "I was
just aghast at the size of the lie that was being told."

He developed several friendships at Potch, including with the novelist André Brink. Another friend became "an abiding presence" in
Steenkamp's life. He was a bit younger than Steenkamp.

"The fellow student in my law class that I'm talking about was the son
of a cabinet minister and he was a hail-fellow-well-met. He had a girlfriend who was rather attractive whom I subsequently married. He was
the local political luminary. Highly intelligent. Very smart. He was
always a pace or two ahead of us in the law class. Very small law class of
six people, five people. And this lad was always ahead of the rest of us

and he and I also became good friends. Except that he came from a true blue Afrikaner tradition. Dutch Reformed, Dopper, father a cabinet minister. His father's sister married to the prime minister and he himself destined to become state president. It's F. W. de Klerk I'm talking about.

"I recall a conversation with him in which he said, 'Ah, come on Naas, you're not really United Party are you?' And I said 'No, I'm not really.' I remember saying something to him on the lines, 'I just don't believe this doctrine that you guys are pursuing.' And he passionately defended the whole line and I said, 'No,' and I must've said something that stuck with him along the lines of a classic definition of liberal values. That's what I felt myself responding to rather than this contrived and highly structured notion that you could engineer your way to a future where the Afrikaner would be safeguarded.

"We had long discussions over years on this subject and I claim a far greater degree of consistency in my political views than I can claim for him, although the sentiments remain friendly and warm, positive, especially because I relieved him of a girlfriend who wasn't going to be a suitable *volksmoeder*. They like one another still but she would not have been able to play that role."

In Steenkamp's view, the Nationalists' apartheid policy created a tragic legacy for the Afrikaners.

"This is the tragedy, that something that had such a colossal potential for good—there is so much about the Afrikaner that is attractive—that all of that had to be dissipated into living a lie that has changed the Afrikaner's personality. To see the destruction of a people is to me a major tragedy."

Steenkamp said that after de Klerk's February 2, 1990, speech, he congratulated his friend and said he now seemed aligned with those values he, Steenkamp, had advocated thirty years earlier in Potchefstroom.

"'I hope you are genuinely aligned with them,'" he said he told de Klerk, "'and this isn't just another tactic.' De Klerk said no. These classic liberal concepts of democracy and regular elections and all that sort of thing, these are, he believes, the only abiding values whereby the Afrikaner himself can survive, and in a fiercely competitive way perhaps prevail. So I said, 'Well great. As long as we are sure that in trying to prevail we are consistently faithful to those values themselves. Then we're okay.'

"But," Steenkamp added, "that's where I have my doubts. The only real major progress that we've made is that we've jettisoned a false doctrine and we are now preaching what I believe to be a valid doctrine," he said.

But is the preaching honest?

"I don't know," Steenkamp said, and laughed a large laugh. "I'm afraid I'm a bit despairing, and I wonder whether the Afrikaner nation isn't rapidly being destroyed."

Then he described an experience he had, a bad portent, a sign that many Afrikaner Nationalists don't understand or accept the liberal values.

"I had the agony of traveling with a cabinet minister the other day in a motor vehicle which I was driving. We sat in that vehicle for six hours and we drove a long distance and I nearly wept at the end of it. This guy was speaking Botha-speak [P. W. Botha] to me all the time in a confiding and brotherly fashion."

No matter how much the Afrikaners would like to think they can concoct a definitive plan for their survival, their futures depend on a process increasingly controlled by the people they long oppressed. Ton Vosloo, head of the Broeder-run M-Net television and the media company of Nasionale Pers, put it plainly: "We've come unshackled. We should now go for recourse to law [write a constitution to protect human rights]. The Afrikaners' future lies in that. But there are too many people now who are already saying, colleagues of mine, encouraging their kids to go [leave South Africa]. I think it's frightening.

"But, you know, you mustn't trust too much in a constitution and laws. Because we manipulated laws ourselves. Hopefully we would have learned a lesson.

"If they [the majority] act like we did, we'll end up in serious trouble. Hopefully they have leaders of wisdom who will say, 'We must pull together.' "

LAST WORDS

Whom should we believe, the judicious optimist H. W. van der Merwe, the sensible pessimist Naas Steenkamp, or the pragmatic Broeder Ton Vosloo?

We found promising seeds of peaceful change among Afrikaners, but also deep roots of violence. During the year following the 1994 elections, pragmatism appeared dominant and cooperation with the *volk*'s former enemies burgeoned. As Afrikaners lose control of the state apparatus, however, their insecurities will grow. Those who cannot tolerate uncertainty and have the means to leave the country may do so. Their less wealthy compatriots may yet rise against the new order. Much depends on the course of day-to-day events. The longer the Government of National Unity maintains political stability, the better are the chances that the new constitution, due to be completed in 1996, will be implemented in the 1999 elections, and that Afrikaners will ease into black-ruled South Africa. If major shocks occur—downturns in the economy, intolerable increases in crime, natural disasters—the new political order may fracture.

From outside South Africa, transition looked increasingly rosy during 1994. In March, just before the election, the armed right wing suffered a humiliating defeat when three AWB members were shot to death in front of TV cameras by black homeland police whom they claimed to be helping.* (The three were from Naboomspruit, where we interviewed Ben Steenkamp and Henry Rauch.) The right-wing hotheads cooled to icy stillness. The AWB fiasco caused a rupture in the umbrella Volksfront, with Constand Viljoen resigning to form the Vryheidsfront (Freedom Front), which eventually campaigned in the election. If one effect was to sideline

---

*With the Bophuthatswana homeland's civil service on strike and protests rising against President Lucas Mangope's refusal to accept reincorporation into South Africa, Mangope called upon the Volksfront coalition for help, apparently believing that the SADF could not be trusted. According to Allister Sparks, in *Tomorrow Is Another Country*, Mangope specifically asked Volksfront leader Constand Viljoen to prevent AWB units from joining the action, but they went anyway. When AWB men began careening in cars around the capital of Mmabatho, indiscriminately shooting at civilians (an estimated

the bumbling gun-toters, another was to drive the more professional military right-wingers, the Special Forces types, farther underground.

At the beginning of 1995, the Western press was celebrating the peaceful and constructive operation of the national unity government, and in particular the talents of President Mandela, as he assuaged the fears of his erstwhile enemies and promised further cooperation in the construction of a new South Africa. On a note of dissonance, the January 1995 National Party congress heard challenges to the NP leadership, charges that it was too close to the ANC-SACP alliance and was selling out Afrikaner interests. About fifty SACP members are members of Parliament under ANC auspices, and others are in prominent government positions. But the NP leadership, rather than cutting relations with the ANC, began seeking to entrench the idea of "power sharing" in the new constitution, thus staking out their position against full majority rule.

We hope things will continue smoothly but we can't quite quell the nagging awareness that South Africa's new government has yet to challenge white Nationalist industrial and financial interests. It will be impossible for the ANC to retain support without directly confronting issues of land redistribution, welfare equalization, and Africanization of the heavily Afrikaner civil service and shifting governmental priorities to the housing and economic development of the long-impoverished majority population. The special advantages of whites in general and Afrikaners in particular have only barely begun to erode. When they crumble, reaction could be swift and harsh.

As an example, despite great fanfare in the Western press over the integration of black and white schools in early 1995, education for blacks remains a flash point. Each white student still receives on average two and a half times as much government support as each black child. About 60 percent of black teachers are not fully qualified and 48 percent of black pupils in 1994 did not pass matriculation exams. Afrikaners' schools are still protected by the fact that largely segregated residential areas serve as the basis for school attendance.

Insecurity still grips the leadership at the very top of the NP, which so far has at least publicly cooperated with the ANC. The apartheid past is

---

sixty Africans were killed by the rampaging right-wingers), the homeland defense force mutinied. A Mercedes was stopped by return gunfire when one of its three AWB occupants fired upon soldiers at a roadblock outside of Mmabatho. One of the AWB men was apparently dead by the time the car stopped. The other two, one seriously wounded, pleaded for medical assistance but were executed by a homeland policeman while TV cameras recorded the scene.

not dead. While the AWB's gunslingers have been squashed, the National Party government death squad legacy remains. The men responsible for killing anti-apartheid activists during "total strategy" and as recently as 1994 have yet to be exposed and charged. Revelations are pouring out from the testimonies being heard in trials of police and former CCB men who, now that they have been abandoned by their superiors, are willing to implicate them. Culpability in political murders may extend upward to Deputy President F. W. de Klerk and Minister of Mineral and Energy Affairs Pik Botha, both of whom served on the old State Security Council under P. W. Botha.

If de Klerk and Botha are shown to have approved the assassinations and dirty tricks of the 1980s and 1990s, what will happen? Will the old establishment allow the process of revelation to continue? Will it permit removal from public life of its most prominent leaders? Or will an effort be undertaken to reexert control, pitting fearful Afrikaners against a now vastly more powerful majority? Afrikaners who supported apartheid and "total strategy" hold this horror in their hearts. It is yet to be exorcised.

We hope a genuinely democratic future is possible in which the Afrikaners will participate; however, given the lack of experience the *volk* have with free speech and open, democratic systems, we doubt that they can easily overcome the religious, political, and cultural brainwashing they have undergone. We are especially dubious about the purported demise of the Broederbond, not because we are conspiratorialists ourselves, but because Afrikaners' penchant toward authoritarian planning is as ingrained as is their victim consciousness.

It seems to us that the Broederbond now has a decidedly more *verligte* and younger leadership than before, and it is leading the *volk*'s adjustment to new circumstances. We believe it will continue to operate, with a new public front, the Afrikanerbond. But behind the benign front, still in the dark, the real string pullers will continue to manipulate, trying to retain as much wealth and power for themselves as they can. They will continue to press for advantage through regional and provincial politics and they'll seek to control privatized state assets such as the arms industry.

In the more distant future the fortunes of the *volk* will be determined less by the Broederbond and more by individual political and business entrepreneurs who go out on their own and deal with the new power in the land. But this will happen only as the old generation of authoritarian planners dies out.

Analysts who argue that the Afrikaners' pragmatism is winning out over their traditional ideology are partly right. But for years they were pragmatic when clinging to apartheid, amassing wealth but causing the *volk* to suffer tremendous moral deterioration. If more of those profess-edly egalitarian Afrikaners who say they quietly opposed apartheid long ago had loudly done so earlier, not only would many lives have been spared, but the Afrikaners would not have sold their souls and destroyed their self-respect. The tragedy to which Naas Steenkamp refers will take generations to overcome.

We should not feel too smug about the long road the Afrikaners still must travel. Afrikaners have not been total strangers to whites in the West. During the 1980s, Americans clasped South Africa to their bosoms and campaigned for and against economic sanctions, their voices reach-ing into corporate boardrooms, city and state legislatures, colleges, churches, high schools, and eventually the U.S. Congress. U.S. action against apartheid came late and it obscured, for some, a persistent truth: apartheid and its residual racism still reverberate in our own society.

If, as we know, our race problems are not solved, then surely South Africa's aren't either. The abolition of slavery in the United States was only the beginning of the struggle; similarly, the abolition of statutory apartheid only begins South Africa's healing. The two countries share many of the same bigotries, reinforced by religion and sometimes ame-liorated by it. Certainly, the changed circumstances will force more pragmatic changes in the NP's political approach, but most whites have yet to relate to the black population in any deep and empathetic way.

In the end, we are hopeful for South Africa, not so much because Afrikaners have finally faced reality, but because the majority population is richly supplied with thoughtful, talented leaders and empathetic, for-giving people. We believe, along with H. W. van der Merwe and Braam Viljoen, that the experience Afrikaners now face, of living closely with blacks, holds within it the greatest promise for development of a humane, egalitarian, and democratic South Africa. We are convinced that Afrikaners will continue to astonish the world and themselves as they learn from their fellow South Africans.

GLOSSARY

Afrikaanse Handelsinstituut   A commerce institute set up by the Broederbond in 1942.

Akademie vir Wetenskap en Kuns   Academy for Science and Art, a Broederbond-controlled scholarly organization.

ANC   African National Congress, a political movement founded in 1912. It followed a nonviolent policy until 1961, when it established the uMkhonto we Sizwe (MK), or Spear of the Nation, guerrilla army. The ANC was banned for thirty years, from 1960 to 1990.

apartheid   The system instituted by the National Party after 1948 whereby segregation of whites and blacks and total regulation of the latter were buttressed by an extensive system of laws such as the Group Areas Act and the Influx Control and Racial Classification laws.

APK (Afrikaanse Protestante Kerk)   Afrikaans Protestant Church, a schismatic, whites-only church that split off from the Dutch Reformed Church (NGK) in 1987.

ATKV (Afrikaanse Taal en Kultuurvereniging)   Afrikaans Language and Cultural Organization, a Broederbond organization founded to promote the Afrikaans language.

AWB (Afrikaner Weerstandsbeweging)   Afrikaner Resistance Movement, the militant right-wing movement led by Eugene Terreblanche. Many of its members admire nazism and fascism.

bakkie   Pickup truck.

ban   To outlaw. Both people and movements were banned under various laws.

Bantu   A language group. The word came to be viewed as derogatory by Africans because "bantu" services for Africans were inferior under apartheid.

Bantu education   The underfunded, inferior educational system for Africans set up under Prime Minister Hendrik Verwoerd deliberately to prevent Africans from being educated too far beyond a servant status. Bantu education was a main cause of student protest that set off the 1976 Soweto riots and uprisings around the country.

Bantustan   See HOMELAND.

Beeld   *Image*, an Afrikaans newspaper in the Nasionale Pers group.

Black Consciousness movement   A political movement that was banned in 1977. Its philosophy was that the blacks (including coloreds and Asians) had to liberate themselves and could not rely on whites. Its best-known leader was Steve Biko.

Blood River   The location of a battle on December 16, 1838, in which more than three thousand Zulus were shot dead by 530 Boer marksmen in revenge for the massacre by Zulu chief Dingane of 281 whites and some 200 colored servants. The Battle of Blood River became a staple of Afrikaner Nationalist imagery.

Boer   Farmer, an earlier term for Afrikaner. Plural: *boere*.

Bophuthatswana   Under apartheid, a tribal homeland recognized as a country by South Africa consisting of several noncontiguous areas mostly north and west of Pretoria.

Braai, braaivleis   Barbecue, grilled meat.

Broeder   Brother, a member of the Broederbond.

Broederbond   The secretive, all-male Afrikaner organization established in 1918 to further the interests of Afrikaner nationalism.

Broederkring   "Brother Ring," an organization set up by Christians in the Reformed tradition to challenge the biblical justification of apartheid.

CCB   Civil Cooperation Bureau, a shadowy extralegal organization under the SADF, responsible for death-squad murders. Its activities were first exposed by articles written by Jacques Pauw in the newspaper *Vrye Weekblad*, then in judicial investigations.

Christian National Education   The nationalistic education instituted by the Broederbond in the entire educational system, but applied most strenuously in Afrikaans schools.

coloreds   The apartheid term for people who are partly white and partly something else, such as Malay, African, Khoisan.

Conservative Party (CP)   A right-wing political party formed by a major split of Afrikaners from the National Party in 1982 in protest over a liberalization of apartheid that allowed parliaments for coloreds and Asians as well as whites. Andries Treurnicht was the leader during the 1980s and '90s. The origins of the split went back to the sixties and the *verligte-verkrampte* divisions of the National Party.

Cottesloe conference   World Council of Churches conference in 1960, where a declaration was issued that condemned apartheid.

Democratic Party (DP)   An amalgamation of white liberal parties that included in 1988 the Progressive Federal Party, or Progs, and newly dissident Afrikaners. Wynand Malan and Wimpie de Klerk, both Broederbond members, were active in forming the party.

Die Burger   *The Citizen*, an Afrikaans daily newspaper in Cape Town.

Die Huisgenoot   *The House Companion*, a high-circulation Afrikaans women's magazine.

die Moot   Valley in Pretoria on the north side of the Magaliesberg Mountains.

Die Vaderland   *The Fatherland*, Afrikaans Johannesburg daily.

Die Transvaler   *The Transvaler*, Afrikaans Johannesburg daily.

difakane   See MFECANE.

dominee   Minister.

Dopper   The colloquial name for the smallest and reputedly most Calvinistic of the Dutch Reformed churches, the Gereformeerde Kerk, with its center at Potchefstroom. The name "Dopper" possibly comes from *domper*, a candle damper or extinguisher, which is a reference to the church's anti-Enlightenment views.

dorp, dorpie   Village or small town.

Dutch Reformed Church   The largest of three Dutch Reformed churches.

Eeufees   "Century," specifically the centennial celebrations of the Great Trek.

eGoli   "City of Gold," Johannesburg.

Engels   English speakers.

ESCOM   Giant state-owned electric company.

FAK (Federasie van Afrikaanse Kultuurverenigings)   Federation of Afrikaans Culture Organizations, the cultural front organization of the Broederbond. Nearly three thousand cultural, religious, educational, and other organizations are affiliated to the FAK.

fly-taal   Afrikaans dialect spoken in the black townships, sometimes spelled *flaai-taal*

Genootskap van Regte Afrikaners   Society of True Afrikaners, founded in 1875 as part of the First Language Movement to promote Afrikaans.

Gereformeerde Kerk   See DOPPER.

Het gearriveer   Has arrived.

HNP (Herstigte Nasionale Party)   Reconstituted National Party, a far-right party that advocates the reinstitution of apartheid as practiced under Prime Minister Hendrik Verwoerd. It was founded in 1969 by Albert Hertzog, the son of the first National Party General J. M. B. Hertzog. The second HNP leader has been Jaap Marais.

homeland/bantustan   Under apartheid, an area designated as the residence for members of a particular tribe, for example, Bophuthatswana was the homeland designated for members of Tswana tribe. In practice, people from other tribes ended up in most of the homelands designated for one tribe. Thirteen percent of South Africa's land was designated for ten homelands.

Hottentots   See KHOI, KHOIKHOI.

Houtstok   Woodstock, the alternative Afrikaans music festival.

HSRC (Human Sciences Research Council)   A government-funded think tank that is heavily influenced by the Broederbond.

IDASA   Institute for a Democratic Alternative for South Africa, a liberal think tank and activist body founded in 1986 by Frederick van Zyl Slabbert and Alex Boraine.

Inkatha Freedom Party   The political party established by Zulu chief Mangosuthu Gatsha Buthelezi.

Jan van Riebeeck   The first Dutchman to land in South Africa. He arrived with a party of ninety settlers in 1652.

kaffir   Derogatory term for blacks.

kaffirboetie   "Kaffir brothers," or white people who are seen to be "Kaffir lovers."

kaffirboetiekinder   Children of a "kaffirboetie."

Kairos Declaration   A 1985 document, released by a group of churches opposing apartheid, that expounded liberation theology.

Kapie   Someone from the Cape.

Khaki   A derogatory term for the British and English speakers.

Khoi, Khoikhoi (also called Hottentots)   A nomadic, pastoral people indigenous to southern Africa who predated the arrival of black Africans and whites. Related to the San or Bushmen, they live mostly in Namibia and the area that became the Northwest Cape Province. The white settlers took their land and enslaved and killed them. They speak a click language and now number about 39,000. The Khoikhoi were the first indigenous people encountered by the Dutch, who settled on the Cape and referred to them derogatorily as Hottentots.

Khoisan   Refers to both the Khoi and the San.

kombuistaal   "Kitchen language," a derogatory name for Afrikaans indicating its origin as a language used by servants.

koppie   Hillock.

kraal   Rural household of Africans.

KwaNdebele   Under apartheid, the designated homeland for the Ndebele people.

laager   A circle of wagons that Trekkers formed to protect themselves from hostile forces. A laager mentality is similar to a siege, circling-the-wagons mentality.

landverhuisers   Emigrants.

lekker   Sweet, delicious, enjoyable, fine, merry.

location   A generic term for a black residential area, used before the terms "township," "bantustan," and "homeland" came into use.

mass action   Term used for the ANC's mass marches and consumer boycotts. The biggest one was a march on August 5, 1992, of seventy thousand people to the Union Buildings in Pretoria to pressure the government to negotiate ANC demands. That same week three to four million people stayed away from work in a general strike.

mfecane (also difakane)   The devastation wrought, beginning in 1822, by Zulu chief Shaka, who led his soldiers in attacks on people in the plain between the Drakensberg Mountains and the coast of the Indian Ocean. Tens of thousands of people starved and millions roamed across the land plundering and being plundered. Into this maelstrom went the Voortrekkers in 1836.

mieliepap   Corn porridge, the staple diet of black South Africans.

mielie   Corn.

MK (uMkhonto we Sizwe)   "Spear of the Nation," a guerrilla army of the ANC, established in 1961.

GLOSSARY

Namibia The country that borders South Africa to the northwest. From 1885 to the First World War, it was a German colony called South West Africa. It was captured by forces of the Union of South Africa, which got a League of Nations mandate in 1919 to rule the territory. The mandate was declared terminated by the United Nations in 1966, after which South Africa continued to rule South West Africa illegally until the latter won independence as Namibia in March 1990.

Nasionale Pers Afrikaans publishing and media company founded in 1915 and associated with a faction of the National Party. The company went public in 1994 on the Johannesburg Stock Exchange.

Nat Member of the National Party.

National Party (NP) The party of F. W. de Klerk and his predecessors that invented and implemented apartheid. Established in 1915, the NP took over the government after its electoral victory 1948, in which it defeated Prime Minister Jan Smuts and General Barry Hertzog's United Party.

Ndebele An Nguni tribe that split off from the Zulus.

NGK (Nederduitse Gereformeerde Kerk) The Dutch Reformed Church, the largest of the three Dutch Reformed churches in South Africa.

Nguni A Bantu language group that includes Zulu, Xhosa, and Swazi.

NHK (Nederduitse Hervormde Kerk) The Dutch Reconstituted Church, the second-largest Dutch Reformed church, which still is restricted to white membership. The NHK was formed by schism in 1858 by Voortrekkers in the Transvaal.

Oom Uncle, often a term of respect.

oorbeligte "Overenlightened," a term invented by Broeders for more liberal Afrikaners at Stellenbosch University.

oorwinning Total victory.

Ossewabrandwag Ox Wagon Brigade, a paramilitary organization that sided with Nazi Germany during World War II. It grew out of the 1938 commemorative **Ossewatrek**, ox wagon trek, and had massive grassroots support.

parastatals Large state-owned corporations that control major industries, such as electricity (Electricity Supply Commission—ESCOM), iron and steel (Iron and Steel Corporation—ISCOR), military equipment (Armscor), etc.

Pedi A tribe from the present-day Northern Transvaal area.

Perskor Afrikaans publishing or press company tied to the Transvaal branch of the National Party.

platteland Rural areas.

Polstu (Political Students' Organization) *Verligte* student group started in 1980 by Afrikaans university students opposed to a rightward turn of the Afrikaner Studentebond.

Potchefstroom Town southwest of Johannesburg, known as the center of the Dopper church and the home of the Dopper university of Potchefstroom. "Potch" for short.

Progressive Federal Party (PFP) White liberal party that was folded into the Democratic Party in 1988. Helen Suzman was the most famous PFP member of Parliament.

protea South Africa's national flower, specifically the giant bulbous king protea.

Rapportryers "Dispatch Riders," an organization resembling American Rotary Clubs and a proving ground for potential Broederbonders. There are also Junior Rapportryers.

referendum An all-white vote on March 17, 1992, on whether to support President de Klerk's negotiations with the ANC. The result was 68 percent "yes."

rooineke Redneck, derogatory term for English speakers.

Ruiterwag "Rider Guard," the "breeder" organization for the Broederbond, of males up to age thirty-one.

Rustenburg Conference An ecumenical church conference in November 1990 in the Transvaal town of the same name. The resulting Rustenburg Declaration condemned apartheid as a sin. Dutch Reformed Church theologian Willie Jonker asked for forgiveness for his and his church's complicity with apartheid.

SABC South African Broadcasting Corporation, a state-owned corporation that controls most television and radio services. Under apartheid it was a propaganda tool of the Broederbond and the National Party.

SACP South African Communist Party, founded in 1921 by a group of white intellectuals.

SADF South African Defense Force, the South African military machine.

San Indigenous hunter-gatherer inhabitants of southern Africa. They have also been referred to as bushmen.

SANLAM South African National Life Insurance Company, an Afrikaner financial and insurance conglomerate.

SAP South African Police.

securocrats Term used to describe the military and police officials who were in ascendancy in determining policy under the former president P. W. Botha.

Sendingkerk Missionary Church, the colored Dutch Reformed Church under apartheid.

separate development Euphemistic term for apartheid.

Sestigers "Sixtiers," a rebel writers movement in the 1960s that was Eurocentric and opposed apartheid. André Brink and Breyten Breytenbach were leading lights.

Shangaan/Tsonga Tribe centered in northeastern South Africa and Mozambique.

slim Crafty, wily; **slimheid** is craftiness, wiliness.

Soweto The giant township southwest of Johannesburg with a population estimated at two to three million. The name, an acronym for *South West Townships*, came to stand for the countrywide black uprisings against apartheid in 1976.

SSC State Security Council, the body that in the seventies under Prime Minister P. W. Botha became more powerful than the cabinet. Its members included the defense minister, five other cabinet officers, and the heads of the Defense Force, the police, and the intelligence services.

standard Grade in school. There's a two-year difference with the U.S. grade system, so standard five is the equivalent of grade seven.

Stigting vir Afrikaans Foundation for Afrikaans, set up in 1992 by the Broederbond to carry out activities for furthering the Afrikaans language.

Stormjaers Stormtroopers, an elite unit of the Ossewabrandwag that used terrorist tactics to disrupt South African support for the Allies in World War II.

SWAPO South West African People's Organization, the liberation movement of Namibia (originally South West Africa), that became the ruling political party after elections in 1990. South Africa had been ruling the country in contravention of the United Nations.

swart gevaar Black peril.

Swazis A people centered on the country of Swaziland and speaking a Zulu dialect.

taal Language, often meaning Afrikaans itself (*die taal*).

taalstryd Language struggle, usually referring to Afrikaans vs. English.

Tannie Aunt.

Third Force Refers to elements, possibly people connected to the government or former security operatives, who were/are causing mayhem and violence, especially in black areas.

"total onslaught" The ideology formulated in the 1980s under P. W. Botha that South Africa was under comprehensive Communist threat.

"total strategy" The military and political response to "total onslaught."

township Apartheid term for a black urban living area that didn't have full city status—since blacks living there were considered temporary residents.

Transvaal An old Boer republic, then the northern province in the Republic of South Africa.

trekboers Boers or Afrikaners who trekked from the Cape Province inland in 1835 in what is called the Great Trek.

GLOSSARY

UDF United Democratic Front, an umbrella organization for the anti-apartheid movement inside South Africa in the eighties, when the ANC and the Pan-Africanist Congress were banned. It expanded to become the Mass Democratic movement and was sympathetic to the ANC.

uitlander Foreigner.

UNISA University of South Africa, a correspondence university in Pretoria set up in 1947 by the old examining body that accredited all the white universities.

UNITA National Union for the Total Independence of Angola.

veld The grasslands on a plateau in South Africa and Zimbabwe. There's the highveld and lowveld, the latter subtropical.

verkrampte Conservative hard-liners; literally, "cramped ones." The terms *verkrampte* and *verligte* were coined by Willem de Klerk in October 1966 to refer to two opposite extremes in the National Party: the ultraconservatives who opposed all change in apartheid, and those who supported small changes.

verligte Literally, "enlightened," but see VERKRAMPTE.

verraaier Traitor.

vertroulike "Confidential," the usual description of the Broederbond by its members.

volk A word for which there is no English equivalent, meaning a combination of "a people" and "a nation," and with profound romantic and nationalistic overtones.

Volksfront Umbrella grouping of right-wing Afrikaners started in 1993.

volksgeskiedenis National history, a people's history.

volkstaat A state envisioned by right-wingers where Afrikaners could still hold power.

Volkswag "*Volk* Guard," the Conservative Party's culture organization, equivalent to the FAK.

Voortrek Adjective derived from Voortrekkers, the Afrikaners who left Cape Province and headed inland beginning in 1835.

Voortrekker Monument Mammoth granite memorial near Pretoria dedicated in 1936, marking the hundredth anniversary of the Great Trek.

Voortrekkers Afrikaans youth organization similar to the Boy Scouts.

vriend Literally, "friend," a designation for members of the Broederbond. Plural: *vriende.*

Vrye Weekblad *Free Weekly,* dissident newspaper that made its reputation by exposing the death squads of the Civil Cooperation Bureau.

Vryheidsfront Freedom Front, Constand Viljoen's conservative umbrella organization that participated in the 1994 election.

Witwatersrand, University of the The preeminent English-language university in South Africa, in Johannesburg. Called Wits for short.

Witwolve White Wolves, a shadowy, right-wing death squad.

woordeboek Dictionary.

Woord en Daad *Word and Deed,* a *verligte* Calvinist magazine.

Xhosa Second-largest tribe (around four million) in South Africa centered around Transkei and Ciskei.

Ystergarde Iron Guard, the paramilitary force connected to the AWB headed by Eugene Terreblanche.

Zulu The largest tribe (over seven million) in South Africa, centered around and north of the city of Durban in Natal. Also, their language.

PEOPLE INTERVIEWED

Louw Alberts Physicist; convenor of Rustenburg Conference.
Irma Bezuidenhout A foreign service officer. Daughter of Louw and Julie.
Louw and Julie Bezuidenhout Pretoria retail merchant and his wife.
Belinda Blaine Director of the Operation Hunger food program in the northeastern Transvaal region.
Steve and Joeleen Booyens A dentist and former 32nd Battalion soldier, and his wife, a lawyer.
Lourens Booysens A grade-school principal in Elspark, near Johannesburg.
Carel Boshoff A religion professor at the University of Pretoria. He is an ex-chairman of the Broederbond and a *volkstaat* advocate. His wife, Anna Boshoff, is the daughter of former prime minister Hendrik Verwoerd.
Jack and Myrtle Botes Chairman, National Regional Development Council of South Africa, and his wife. He is a National Party stalwart, a former city manager of Pietersburg, Transvaal.
Danie Botha Transvaal National Party organizer.
Elaine Botha Professor of Calvinist philosophy at Potchefstroom University and a signatory of the Koinonia Declaration in 1977.
J. J. D. (Koos) Botha Conservative Party member of Parliament who in 1991 bombed a school to prevent its use by children of ANC members returning from exile.
Piet and Vivienne Botha Rock musician and his wife. He is the son of former Foreign Minister (now Minister of Mineral and Energy Affairs) Roelof (Pik) Botha.
Elizabeth Bradley Executive chairman of Wesco Investments Ltd. and Vice Chairman, Toyota South Africa Ltd.
Elsabe Brink Historian and member of Johannesburg City Council. Daughter of Elsa Joubert and Klaus Steytler.
Isaac Burger President of the Apostolic Faith Mission Church.
Hilda Burnett Democratic Party member of the George (Western Cape) City Council and the retired principal of a women's military college.
Luli Callinicos History professor at the University of the Witwatersrand.
Piet Cillie A journalism professor at Stellenbosch University and a retired chairman of the publishing and media company Nasionale Pers.
Willie Cilliers A minister in the Dutch Reformed Church in Africa, the African "sister" church of the Dutch Reformed Church.
General Johan Coetzee Principal of Graaf Reinett Police Academy. A retired commissioner of the South African Police and former head of the South African Police Security Branch.
Henno Cronje The executive director of the Federation of Afrikaans Culture Organizations (FAK).
Eddie Dames A student at Stellenbosch University.
Achmat Davids A linguist and social worker who lives in Cape Town.

Johannes Degenaar   Retired Stellenbosch University professor of political philosophy.

Marianne de Jong   Literature professor at UNISA and a noted feminist.

Willem (Wimpie) de Klerk   A communications professor at Rand Afrikaans University; the former editor of *Die Transvaler* and of *Rapport*, he is F. W. de Klerk's older brother.

Pieter de Lange   Chairman of the Broederbond 1983–93 and retired professor of education.

Hans du Plessis   A linguist and the director of the Afrikaans Language and Culture Association (ATKV) writing school of Potchefstroom University.

Louwrens du Plessis   Law professor at Stellenbosch University who signed the Koinonia Declaration in 1977. An ANC member.

Hanneke du Preez   Publisher, Regional Research and Reporting Corporation.

Max du Preez   Editor of the dissident weekly newspaper *Vrye Weekblad*.

André du Toit   History professor at the University of Cape Town.

Theuns Eloff   Executive director of the Consultative Business Movement and a business lobbyist. He is a former minister in the Dutch Reformed Church and was a signatory of the Koinonia Declaration in 1977.

Schalk Engelbrecht   General manager of the education group Human Sciences Research Council (HSRC).

Theunis Englebrecht   Writer, music critic, and alternative rock musician ("Randy Rambo").

Annie Gagiano   Professor of English at Stellenbosch University and an ANC member.

Jan Gagiano   Professor of political science at Stellenbosch University. Husband of Annie Gagiano.

Hermann Giliomee   Professor of political studies at the University of Cape Town.

Bobby Godsell   Executive director for industrial relations and public relations with the Anglo American Corporation, a mining conglomerate.

Anton Goosen   Alternative rock musician and lyricist.

Danie Goosen   Professor of religious studies at UNISA.

Jeanne Goosen   Novelist, playwright, and journalist who won the 1991 Central News Agency prize for the novel *We Are Not All Like That*.

Jan Grobbelaar   Mayor of Phalaborwa (northeastern Transvaal), and the owner of J. & F. Engineering, sheet-metal fabricators.

Albert Grundlingh   History professor at UNISA.

Hans Heese   History professor at the University of the Western Cape and a genealogist.

Johan Heyns   Religion professor at the University of Pretoria and a former moderator of the Dutch Reformed Church. He was a prominent Broederbonder. (Assassinated, 1994.)

John Horak   The former morning group manager for the SAAN (South African Association of Newspapers) group who simultaneously spied for the South African Police on English newspapers. He defected to the ANC in 1992.

Pierre Hugo   Professor of political science at UNISA.

Willie Jonker   A theology professor at Stellenbosch University who confessed the "sin" of apartheid at the Rustenburg Conference in 1990.

Elsa Joubert   Novelist and travel writer; the author of *The Long Journey of Poppie Nongena*, published in 1978.

Ansie Kamffer   Agent for countercultural musicians and an ANC member.

Simon Kekane   Professor of politics at Vista University in Mamelodi.

Willem Kleynhans   Political scientist who specializes in party politics, and an early anti-apartheid gadfly.

Manie Kriel   Real estate agent and a National Party member of the Phalaborwa (northeastern Transvaal) City Council.

Cynthia Kros   History professor at the University of the Witwatersrand.

Esther Lategan   The national director of the National Institute for Crime Prevention and Rehabilitation of Offenders (NICRO) and a former Democratic Party candidate for Parliament from Stellenbosch.

Jan Lombard   Former governor of the South Africa Reserve Bank.

André du P. Louw   Professor of political theory at UNISA.

Willie Lubbe   Founder and head of the breakaway archconservative Afrikaanse Protestante Kerk (APK).

Ben and Sebastiana Marais   Theologian and retired professor at Pretoria University who was an early anti-apartheid advocate, and his wife.

H. C. (Bok) Marais   Vice president of the Human Sciences Research Council (HSRC).

Fritz and Germien Meyer   Conservative Party organizer in Phalaborwa (northeastern Transvaal) and his wife.

Piet Muller   A newspaper and magazine columnist and editor for *Rapport* newspaper and *Insig* magazine who was one of the first Afrikaners to make contact with the ANC in Lusaka, Zambia.

Marietjie Myburg   Editorial writer for the *Daily Dispatch* in East London, Eastern Cape.

Henning Myburgh   A mediation worker in Bloemfontein for the Institute for a Democratic Alternative for South Africa (IDASA).

Beyers Naudé   A Dutch Reformed Church in Afrika minister and anti-apartheid activist.

Pieter and Gerda Nel   A Dutch Reformed Church minister in the farming town of Bethal, east of Johannesburg, and his wife.

Annemarie Nutt   Chairwoman of Kontak, an interracial women's group.

Gerrit Olivier   Professor of Afrikaans at the University of the Witwatersrand and the former publisher of Taurus Books.

P. J. T. (Terts) Oosthuizen   A lawyer at the state-owned electric company ESCOM, and a retired South African Defense Force general who led ground forces into Angola.

Harald Pakendorf   Independent political consultant and former editor of *Die Vaderland*.

Jacques Pauw   Investigative journalist known for his exposés on government death squads.

Ina Perlman   Executive director of Operation Hunger.

Stephanie Pickover   TV screenwriter.

Louis Pienaar   A minister in the Afrikaanse Protestante Kerk (APK).

Zach de Beer Postma   Philosophy professor at UNISA.

Pieter Potgieter   Politics professor at Potchefstroom University, Broederbonder, and signatory of Koinonia Declaration in 1977.

Hendrik Pretorius   A founder minister of the Reformed Communities of Equals in Christ church and a gay rights activist.

Louwrens Pretorius   Sociology professor at UNISA.

Rena Pretorius   Professor of Afrikaans at the University of Pretoria and a member of the Publications Appeal Board (state censorship authority).

Henry and Loffie Rauch   A tobacco and cotton farmer in Springbok Flats (near Naboomspruit, Northern Transvaal) and his son.

Johann Rissik   Operation Hunger regional director for the northeastern Transvaal.

Willem and Cecilia Saayman   Theology professor at UNISA and his wife. He is the chairman of the ANC Pretoria central branch.

Mimi and Lisa Saayman   Volunteers in a rape crisis center in Cape Town and the daughters of Willem and Cecilia Saayman.

Eric Schoeman   Real estate agent in Vanderbijlpark, south of Johannesburg.

Marius Schoon   A Program Management Specialist at the South Africa Development Bank and member of ANC. He is a former uMkhonto we Sizwe (MK), or Spear of the Nation, organizer.

John Schram   Canadian diplomat.

Harrie Siertsema   Restaurant owner in Graskop, Northern Transvaal.

F. van Zyl Slabbert   An independent politician and a cofounder of the Institute for a Democratic Alternative for South Africa (IDASA).

Ben Steenkamp   Farmer and gas station owner in Naboomspruit, Northern Transvaal.

PEOPLE INTERVIEWED

Naas Steenkamp   Director of corporate affairs for Gencor, a mining and industrial conglomerate.

Johann and Annette Steynberg   An executive of the Palabora Mining Company, Ltd., a mining company in Phalaborwa (northeastern Transvaal), and his wife. He is a CP Party member of the Phalaborwa City Council.

Klaus Steytler   Writer, and husband of Elsa Joubert.

Dries and Leana Struwig   Retired police interrogator and his wife.

Hans Strydom   Author, journalist, and expert on the Broederbond.

Karl Sullwald   Owner of Sullwald Contractors and a Conservative Party funder in Phalaborwa (northeastern Transvaal).

Sampie Terreblanche   Economics professor at Stellenbosch University and a Broederbond dissident.

Frances Theron   Tour guide at Phalaborwa Mining Company in Phalaborwa (northeastern Transvaal).

Peta Thorneycroft   Journalist for the *Star*, a Johannesburg daily.

Elna Trautmann   Operation Hunger regional director for the Cape Province and a former member of SWAPO.

Martin Trümpelmann   Education professor at Rand Afrikaans University and an ex-Broederbonder.

Jan van Arkel   Theology professor at UNISA.

Servaas van der Berg   Economics professor at Stellenbosch University.

Ina van der Linde   Journalist with the weekly newspaper *Vrye Weekblad*.

H. W. van der Merwe   Retired director of the Center for Intergroup Studies in Cape Town and a retired professor of sociology.

Piet van der Merwe   Chairman of the Commission for Administration (the civil service administration).

Johan van der Vyver   Law professor at the University of the Witwatersrand and the former dean of the law school at Potchefstroom University.

Tjaart van der Walt   Chairman of the Human Sciences Research Council (HSRC) and a former rector (president) of Potchefstroom University.

Dries van Heerden   Freelance journalist working for Afrikaans newspapers.

Manie van Heerden   Founding member of the Conservative Party and a political activist who is also the proprietor of the Shirt Bar.

Kobus van Loggerenberg   A mediation worker with the Institute for a Democratic Alternative for South Africa (IDASA) in Bloemfontein.

Attie and Carol van Niekerk   Author and theology professor at the University of the North (near Pietersburg) and his wife.

Frans and Susan van Rensburg   Retired professor of Afrikaans at Rand Afrikaans University and his wife.

Spore and Yvonne van Rensburg   Former National Party member of Parliament and his wife.

Jan and Joupie van Rooyen   Retired Dutch Reformed Church minister who is an anti-apartheid advocate, and his wife.

Kobus van Rooyen   Chairman of the Media Council, an industry watchdog organization, and a former president of the Publications Appeal Board (state censorship authority).

Andreas van Wyk   Rector (president) of Stellenbosch University.

Attie van Wyk   Concert impresario and musician.

Griet Verhoef   Professor of American history at Rand Afrikaans University.

Braam Viljoen   Farmer and mediation worker with the Institute for a Democratic Alternative for South Africa (IDASA) in Pretoria.

Ton Vosloo   Chairman of the publishing and media (M-Net cable TV) company Nasionale Pers.

Marichen Waldner   Journalist with the newspaper *Rapport*, an Afrikaans weekly.

Piet Warren   Cattle farmer in Gravelotte (Northern Transvaal).

BIBLIOGRAPHY

Adam, Heribert, and Hermann Giliomee. *Ethnic Power Mobilized: Can South Africa Change?* New Haven, Conn.: Yale University Press, 1979.

Adam, Heribert, and Kogila Moodley. *The Opening of the Apartheid Mind: Options for the New South Africa*. Berkeley: University of California Press, 1993.

Akenson, Donald H. *God's Peoples: Covenant and Land in South Africa, Israel, and Ulster*. Ithaca, N.Y.: Cornell University Press, 1992.

Alberts, Louw, and Frank Chikane. *The Road to Rustenburg: The Church Looking Forward to a New South Africa*. Cape Town: Struik Christian Books, 1991.

Arendt, Hannah. *Eichmann in Jerusalem: A Report on the Banality of Evil*. New York: Viking, 1964.

Art Design Architecture 10: Johannesburg Special Edition. Vlaeburg, S.A.: 1992.

Benson, Mary. *Nelson Mandela: The Man and the Movement*. New York: W. W. Norton, 1994.

———. *A Far Cry: The Making of a South African*. New York: Viking Penguin, 1989.

Berger, Iris. *Threads of Solidarity: Women in South African History 1900–1980*. Bloomington: Indiana University Press, 1992.

Berger, Peter L., and Bobby Godsell. *A Future South Africa: Visions, Strategies, and Realities*. Boulder, Colo.: Westview Press, 1988.

Bloomberg, Charles. *Christian-Nationalism and the Rise of the Afrikaner Broederbond in South Africa 1918–48*. Bloomington: Indiana University Press, 1989.

Boonzaier, Emile, and John Sharp. *South African Keywords: The Uses and Abuses of Political Concepts*. Cape Town: David Philip, 1988.

Borstelmann, Thomas. *Apartheid's Reluctant Uncle: The United States and Southern Africa in the Early Cold War*. New York: Oxford University Press, 1993.

Brantlinger, Patrick. *Rule of Darkness: British Literature and Imperialism*. Ithaca, N.Y.: Cornell University Press, 1988.

Breytenbach, Breyten. *End Papers: Essays, Letters, Articles of Faith, Workbook Notes*. New York: McGraw-Hill, 1987.

———. *Return to Paradise*. New York: Harcourt Brace, 1993.

———. *The True Confessions of an Albino Terrorist*. New York: Farrar Straus Giroux, 1983.

Bundy, Colin. *The Rise and Fall of the South African Peasantry*. 2nd ed. Cape Town: David Philip, 1988.

Butler, Jeffrey, Richard Elphick, and David Welsh, eds. *Democratic Liberalism in South Africa: Its History and Prospect*. Middletown, Conn.: Wesleyan University Press, 1987.

Carter, Gwendolen M. *Which Way Is South Africa Going?* Bloomington: Indiana University Press, 1980.

BIBLIOGRAPHY

Cobbett, William, and Robin Cohen, eds. *Popular Struggles in South Africa*. Trenton, N.J.: Africa World Press, 1988.

Cock, Jacklyn, and Laurie Nathan, eds. *War and Society: The Militarisation of South Africa*. Cape Town: David Philip, 1989.

Coetzee, J. M. *Doubling the Point: Essays and Interviews*. Ed. David Atwell. Cambridge, Mass.: Harvard University Press, 1992.

———. *White Writing: On the Culture of Letters in South Africa*. Sandton, S.A.: Radix Press, 1988.

Conrad, Joseph. *Heart of Darkness*. London: Penguin, 1989.

Crocker, Chester A. *High Noon in Southern Africa: Making Peace in a Rough Neighborhood*. New York: W. W. Norton, 1992.

Davies, Rob, Dan O'Meara, and Sipho Dlamini. *The Struggle for South Africa: A Reference Guide*. Vols. 1 and 2. London: Zed Press, 1988.

Davis, Stephen M. *Apartheid's Rebels: Inside South Africa's Hidden War*. New Haven, Conn.: Yale University Press, 1987.

De Gruchy, John W. *The Church Struggle in South Africa*. Grand Rapids, Mich.: William B. Eerdmanns, 1986.

De Gruchy, John W., and Charles Villa-Vicencio, eds. *Apartheid Is a Heresy*. Cape Town: David Philip, 1983.

De Klerk, W. A. *The Puritans in Africa: A Story of Afrikanerdom*. London: Rex Collings, 1975.

De Klerk, Willem. *F. W. De Klerk: The Man in His Time*. Johannesburg: Jonathan Ball, 1991.

———. *The Second (R)evolution: Afrikanerdom and the Crisis of Identity*. Johannesburg: Jonathan Ball, 1984.

De Lange, J. P., et al. *Provision of Education in the RSA: Report of the Main Committee of the HSRC Investigation into Education*. Pretoria: HSRC, 1981.

De Villiers, Marq. *White Tribe Dreaming: Apartheid's Bitter Roots as Witnessed by Eight Generations of an Afrikaner Family*. New York: Penguin, 1988.

Dreyer, Peter. *Martyrs and Fanatics: South Africa and Human Destiny*. New York: Simon and Schuster, 1980.

Du Preez, J. M. *Africana Afrikaner: Master Symbols in South African School Textbooks*. Alberton, S.A.: Librarius Felicitas, 1983.

Du Toit, André, and Hermann Giliomee. *Afrikaner Political Thought: Analysis and Documents*. Vol. 1, 1780–1850. Cape Town: David Philip, 1983.

Du Toit, André, and N. Chabanyi Manganyi, eds. *Political Violence and the Struggle in South Africa*. Basingstoke, Hants., U.K.: Macmillan, 1990.

Ellis, Stephen, and Tsepo Sechaba. *Comrades Against Apartheid: The ANC and the South African Communist Party in Exile*. Bloomington: Indiana University Press, 1992.

Esterhuyse, William, and Pierre du Toit. *The Myth Makers: The Elusive Bargain for South Africa's Future*. Halfway House, S.A.: Southern Book Publishers, 1990.

Finnigan, William. *Crossing the Line: A Year in the Land of Apartheid*. New York: Harper & Row, 1986.

Fredrickson, George M. *White Supremacy: A Comparative Study in American and South African History*. New York: Oxford University Press, 1981.

Gastrow, Shelagh. *Who's Who in South African Politics*. 3rd rev. ed. London: Hans Zell, 1990.

Giliomee, Hermann, and Jannie Gagiano. *The Elusive Search for Peace: South Africa, Israel and Northern Ireland*. Cape Town: Oxford University Press, 1990.

Giliomee, Hermann, and Lawrence Schlemmer, *From Apartheid to Nation-Building*. Cape Town: Oxford University Press, 1989.

Godsell, R. M., and P. J. du P. Le Roux. *Growth, Equity and Participation: Report of the Work Committee on Economics and Labour, HSRC Investigation into Intergroup Relations*. Pretoria: HSRC, 1986.

Goodwin, June. *Cry Amandla! South African Women and the Question of Power*. New York: Africana, 1984.

Greenberg, Stanley. *Race and State in Capitalist Development*. New Haven, Conn.: Yale University Press, 1980.

Grundy, Kenneth W. *The Militarization of South African Politics*. Bloomington: Indiana University Press, 1986.

Hachten, William, and Anthony Giffard. *Total Onslaught: The South African Press Under Attack*. No copyright page.

Harrison, David. *The White Tribe of Africa: South Africa in Perspective*. Halfway House, S.A.: Southern Book Publishers, 1987.

Hexham, Irving. *The Irony of Apartheid: The Struggle for National Independence of Afrikaner Calvinism Against British Imperialism*. New York: Edwin Mellen Press, 1981.

Hope, Marjorie, and James Young. *The South African Churches in a Revolutionary Situation*. Maryknoll, N.Y.: Orbis Books, 1981.

Horowitz, Donald. *Democratic South Africa? Constitutional Engineering in a Divided Society*. Berkeley: University of California Press, 1991.

James, Wilmot, ed. *The State of Apartheid*. Boulder, Colo.: Lynne Rienner, 1987.

Jaster, Robert Scott, and Shirley Kew Jaster. *South Africa's Other Whites: Voices for Change*. New York: St. Martin's Press, 1993.

Johns, Sheridan, and R. Hunt Davis, eds. *Mandela, Tambo, and the ANC: Struggle Against Apartheid 1948–1990*. Oxford: Oxford University Press, 1991.

Johnson, R. W. *How Long Will South Africa Survive?* London: Macmillan, 1977.

Johnson, Shaun, ed. *South Africa: No Turning Back*. Bloomington: Indiana University Press, 1989.

Joubert, Elsa. *The Long Journey of Poppie Nongena*. Johannesburg: Jonathan Ball, 1980.

Kane-Berman, John. *Soweto: Black Revolt, White Reaction*. Johannesburg: Ravan Press, 1978.

Kanfer, Stefan. *The Last Empire: De Beers, Diamonds, and the World*. New York: Farrar Straus Giroux, 1993.

Kenney, Henry. *Power, Pride and Prejudice: The Years of Afrikaner Nationalist Rule in South Africa*. Johannesburg: Jonathan Ball, 1991.

Leach, Graham. *The Afrikaners: Their Last Great Trek*. London: Macmillan, 1989.

Lelyveld, Joseph. *Move Your Shadow: South Africa, Black and White*. New York: Times Books, 1985.

Lijphart, Arend. *Power Sharing in South Africa*. Berkeley: Institute of International Studies, University of California, 1985.

Lodge, Tom. *Black Politics in South Africa Since 1945*. Johannesburg: Ravan Press, 1983.

Louw, Raymond, ed. *Four Days in Lusaka: Whites in a Changing Society*. South Africa: Five Freedoms Forum, 1989.

Malan, Rian. *My Traitor's Heart: A South African Exile Returns to Face His Country, His Tribe, and His Conscience*. New York: Atlantic Monthly Press, 1990.

BIBLIOGRAPHY

Mandela, Nelson. *Long Walk to Freedom: The Autobiography of Nelson Mandela*. Boston: Little Brown, 1994.

Marais, H. C., ed. *South Africa: Perspectives on the Future*. Pretoria: HSRC, 1988.

Marks, Shula, and Stanley Trapido, eds. *The Politics of Race, Class and Nationalism in Twentieth-Century South Africa*. London: Longman, 1987.

Marx, Anthony W. *Lessons of Struggle: South African Internal Opposition, 1960–1990*. New York: Oxford University Press, 1992.

Mayson, Cedric. *A Certain Sound: The Struggle for Liberation in Southern Africa*. London: Epworth, 1984.

McKendrick, Brian, and Wilma Hoffmann, eds. *People and Violence in South Africa*. Cape Town: Oxford University Press, 1990.

Minter, William. *King Solomon's Mines Revisited: Western Interests and the Burdened History of Southern Africa*. New York: Basic Books, 1986.

Moodie, Dunbar T. *The Rise of Afrikanerdom*. Berkeley: University of California Press, 1975.

Moss, Glenn, and Ingrid Obery, eds. *South African Review 6: From 'Red Friday' to Codesa*. Johannesburg: Ravan Press, 1992.

Mostert, W. P., and J. M. Lötter, eds. *South Africa's Demographic Future*. Pretoria: HSRC, 1990.

Mufson, Steven. *Fighting Years: Black Resistance and the Struggle for a New South Africa*. Boston: Beacon Press, 1990.

Neuhaus, Richard John. *Dispensations and the Future of South Africa as South Africans See It*. Grand Rapids, Mich.: William B. Eerdmanns, 1986.

O'Meara, Dan. *Volkskapitalisme: Class, Capital and Ideology in the Development of Afrikaner Nationalism 1934–1948*. Cambridge: Cambridge University Press, 1983.

Pakenham, Thomas. *The Boer War*. London: Weidenfeld & Nicholson, 1979.

Pauw, Jacques. *In the Heart of the Whore: The Story of Apartheid's Death Squads*. Halfway House, S.A.: Southern Book Publishers, 1991.

Phelan, John M. *Apartheid Media: Disinformation and Dissent in South Africa*. Westport, Conn.: Lawrence Hill, 1987.

Pityana, N. Barney, et al. *Bounds of Possibility: The Legacy of Steve Biko and Black Consciousness*. Cape Town: David Philip, 1991.

Political Commission of the Study Project on Christianity in Apartheid Society (SPRO-CAS). *South Africa's Political Alternatives*. Johannesburg: Ravan Press, 1973.

Price, Robert M. *The Apartheid State in Crisis: Political Transformation in South Africa 1975–1990*. New York: Oxford University Press, 1991.

Price, Robert, and Carl Rosberg, eds. *The Apartheid Regime: Political Power and Racial Domination*. Berkeley: University of California Press, 1980.

Ramphele, Mamphela, and Chris McDowell, eds. *Restoring the Land: Environment and Change in Post-Apartheid South Africa*. London: Panos Institute, 1991.

Ramusi, Molapatene Collins. *Soweto, My Love: A Testimony to Black Life in South Africa*. New York: Henry Holt, 1989.

Ranchod, B., et al. *Law and Justice in South Africa. Report of the Work Committee on Juridical Aspects, HSRC Investigation into Intergroup Relations*. Pretoria: HSRC, 1986.

Ryan, Colleen. *Beyers Naudé: Pilgrimage of Faith*. Grand Rapids, Mich.: William B. Eerdmans, 1990.

Serfontein, J. H. P. *Apartheid Change and the NG Kerk*. Emmarentia, S.A.: Taurus Books, 1982.

BIBLIOGRAPHY

————. *Brotherhood of Power: An Exposé of the Secret Afrikaner Broederbond*. Bloomington: Indiana University Press, 1978.

Slabbert, F. Van Zyl. *The Last White Parliament*. Johannesburg: Jonathan Ball, 1985.

South African Institute of Race Relations. *Race Relations Survey*. Johannesburg: South African Institute of Race Relations 1971–1994 (Annual editions).

Sparks, Allister. *Tomorrow Is Another Country: The Inside Story of South Africa's Negotiated Revolution*. New York: Hill & Wang, 1995.

————. *The Mind of South Africa*. New York: Knopf, 1990.

Swilling, Mark, ed. *Views on the South African State*. Pretoria: HSRC, 1990.

Thompson, Leonard. *The Political Mythology of Apartheid*. New Haven, Conn.: Yale Unversity Press, 1985.

Trump, Martin, ed. *Rendering Things Visible: Essays on South African Literary Culture*. Johannesburg: Ravan Press, 1990.

Van Zyl, C. *The De Lange Report: Ten Years On. An Investigation into the Extent of the Implementation of Recommendations of the 1981 HSRC Investigation into Education*. Pretoria: HSRC, 1991.

Van der Merwe, Hendrik W. *Pursuing Justice and Peace in South Africa*. London: Routledge, 1989.

Van der Merwe, H. W., and R. Schrire. *Race and Ethnicity*. Cape Town: David Philip, 1980.

Van Onselen, Charles. *Studies in the Social and Economic History of the Witwatersrand 1886–1914. Vol. 1: New Babylon*. Johannesburg: Ravan Press, 1982.

Van Wyk, At. *The Birth of a New Afrikaner*. Cape Town: Human and Rousseau, 1991.

Villa-Vicencio, Charles, and John de Gruchy, eds. *Resistance and Hope: South African Essays in Honour of Beyers Naudé*. Cape Town: David Philip, 1985.

Wassenaar, A. D. *Assault on Private Enterprise: The Freeway to Communism*. Cape Town: Tafelberg, 1977.

Wilkins, Ivor, and Hans Strydom. *The Super-Afrikaners: Inside the Afrikaner Broederbond*. Johannesburg: Jonathan Ball, 1978.

Wilson, Monica, and Leonard Thompson, eds. *The Oxford History of South Africa*. Oxford: Oxford University Press, 1971.

Woods, Donald. *Biko*. New York: Vintage, 1979.

INDEX

INDEX

413

ABOUT THE AUTHORS

JUNE GOODWIN is a writer of fiction, nonfiction, and poetry. As a reporter for *The Christian Science Monitor* in Africa from 1976 to 1979, she covered South Africa. She also worked for Reuters News Agency in London and New York and filed reports for National Public Radio when she was in Africa. Her previous book on South Africa is *Cry Amandla! South African Women and the Question of Power*.

BEN SCHIFF is a professor of international politics at Oberlin College. He has written two previous books: *International Nuclear Technology Transfer: Dilemmas of Dissemination and Control* and *Refugees unto the Third Generation: U.N. Aid to Palestinians*.

Ben and June spent eight months in South Africa in 1992, where they interviewed more than 125 Afrikaners for this book. They are married, have a daughter, and live in Oberlin, Ohio. Their e-mail address is fschiff@oberlin.edu.